SPEAKING OUT ON HUMAN RIGHTS

Speaking Out
on Human Rights

Debating Canada's
Human Rights System

PEARL ELIADIS

McGill-Queen's University Press
Montreal & Kingston · London · Ithaca

© McGill-Queen's University Press 2014

ISBN 978-0-7735-4304-1 (cloth)
ISBN 978-0-7735-4305-8 (paper)
ISBN 978-0-7735-9183-7 (ePDF)
ISBN 978-0-7735-9184-4 (ePUB)

Legal deposit second quarter 2014
Bibliothèque nationale du Québec

Printed in Canada on acid-free paper that is 100% ancient forest free
(100% post-consumer recycled), processed chlorine free

McGill-Queen's University Press acknowledges the support of the Canada
Council for the Arts for our publishing program. We also acknowledge the
financial support of the Government of Canada through the Canada Book
Fund for our publishing activities.

Library and Archives Canada Cataloguing in Publication

Eliadis, F. Pearl, author
    Speaking out on human rights: debating Canada's human rights system/
Pearl Eliadis.

Includes bibliographical references and index.
Issued in print and electronic formats.
ISBN 978-0-7735-4304-1 (bound). – ISBN 978-0-7735-4305-8 (pbk.). –
ISBN 978-0-7735-9183-7 (ePDF). – ISBN 978-0-7735-9184-4 (ePUB)

1. Human rights – Canada. 2. Canadian Human Rights Commission. I. Title.

JC599.C3E45 2014   323.0971   C2013-907936-X
                                            C2013-907937-8

This book was typeset by Interscript in 10.5/13 Sabon.

To my family

The proceeds from the royalties of this book will be donated to two leading Canadian human rights organizations that I have had the privilege of working with. The first is Equitas – International Centre for Human Rights Education, a non-profit organization that works to advance equality, social justice, and respect for human dignity in Canada and around the world using transformative human rights education programs. The second is the equality effect, a Canadian organization that uses human rights law to protect girls and women from sexual violence, allowing them to get an education and fulfill their economic potential.

Contents

Acknowledgments

Many people offered a helping hand in the development of this book. First and foremost, nearly sixty individuals agreed to be interviewed and offered their time and insights for this project. My sincere thanks go to Raj Anand, David Arnot, Khurrum Awan, Jane Bailey, David Baker, Kim Bernhardt, Margot Blight, A. Alan Borovoy, Pierre Bosset, Paul Champ, Dominique Clément, Irwin Cotler, Gaétan Cousineau, Krista Daley, Shelagh Day, Audrey Dean, Philippe Dufresne, Mary Eberts, Bernie Farber, Leilani Farha, Pascale Fournier, Mark Freiman, Michael Gottheil, Barbara Hall, Alia Hogben, Martha Jackman, Jameel Jaffer, Patricia Knipe, Kathy Laird, Lucie Lamarche, François Larsen, Darren Lund, Jennifer Lynch, Roderick Macdonald, Charlach Mackintosh, Heather MacNaughton, Ravi Malhotra, David Maltas, Gordon A. McKinnon, John Miller, Naseem Mithoowani, Richard Moon, Fo Niemi, Ken Norman, John Pace, Margaret Parsons, Michèle Rivet, Fiona Sampson, Dianna Scarth, Muneeza Sheikh, Colleen Sheppard, Mary Woo Sims, Béatrice Vizkelety, Richard Warman, and Byron Williams.[1] The informed voices of the interviewees trace a richer and more textured portrait of human rights institutions and their work in Canada than I ever would have been able to achieve alone. I am very grateful to all of them for their time and trust. (Certain people offered comments but asked not to be named. Since these individuals spoke on condition of anonymity, their remarks are not attributed. I have noted these instances in the text or notes.)

Although I did not know it at the time, the interviews with Rémy Beauregard and Keith Norton, both of whom were colleagues and mentors, would be among their last. Rémy Beauregard and I worked closely together for six years at the Ontario Human Rights Commission, after which we continued to collaborate in international projects. Rémy was appointed president of the Canadian organization Rights and Democracy in 2008. We met for the last time in late 2009. He died on 8 January 2010 in circumstances that continue to be a source of great sadness for all who knew him. Keith Norton was chief commissioner at the Ontario Human Rights Commission. We also worked closely together and remained friends after I left the commission. He died on 31 January 2010 after a sudden illness. Both men spent their careers serving the public with integrity, determination, and clarity of vision. With their deaths, Canada lost two outstanding public servants and advocates for a progressive and generous vision of human rights.

I owe a particular debt to Ken Norman and Mary Eberts. In our conversations and shared projects, I have benefited from their scholarship, friendship, and guidance.

Max Yalden provided extensive and thoughtful comments on the manuscript. I am enormously grateful for his keen eye, tremendous experience, and clear insights.

Thanks also to Leslie Seidle, who assisted me with polling data on Canadian values and has been a wonderful sounding board for me on a wide variety of issues related to diversity, rights, and pluralism in Canada.

Alan Fleischman, an archivist and librarian with an expertise in human rights documentation, generously introduced me to a unique collection of archival material at the University of Ottawa.

Students Melissa Gaul, Jonathan Katz, Bonnie King, and Erica Martin provided research support. Catherine London and Enid Dixon assisted with editing early drafts of the book.

Melanie Benard, a former student and my research assistant on the project, undertook editing, adding citations, and fact checking, showing great perseverance, professionalism, and commitment. I am very grateful for her cheerful tenacity.

I am very grateful to Ryan Van Huijstee, the managing editor of McGill-Queen's University Press, for the interest and support that the Press has shown for the project. The staff members at the Press all deserve thanks. Jonathan Crago was wonderful to work with; his insights, suggestions, and patience brought the structure and objectives of the book into sharper focus. Joan McGilvray copyedited the manuscript and brought her usual rigour and considerable editing experience to the final manuscript. Her talent for seeing both detail and high-level issues, often at the same time, helped to improve the book at many levels. I am very indebted to her for her humour, tact, and good judgement. Elena Goranescu, production manager, showed great patience, and

David Drummond, who designed the cover, is one of my favourite graphic artists in Canada.

I also thank the anonymous readers for their constructive comments and recommendations that encouraged me to develop major sections of the book in new directions. I owe many of the students in my Civil Liberties class at McGill University's Faculty of Law a special thank-you. Whenever I feel discouraged about what appears to be declining respect for human rights or growing intolerance in Canada, they remind me of something important: there is an extraordinary, empathetic, and engaged generation coming up. This generation will, I think, be much better than mine was at shaping a society where people care as much about each other and the world we live in as they care about themselves.

To Rob, my husband and most constant reader, my thanks for his support and patience in this project as in so many others.

In closing, as is usual in such projects, I assume responsibility for any errors.

About This Book

Speaking Out on Human Rights is about Canada's human rights system and its institutions – commissions, tribunals, and other parts of Canada's public human rights infrastructure. There is already a good deal of debate and scholarship about human rights in Canada, and about human rights in general, as well as the role of the Canadian Charter of Rights and Freedoms (the Charter),[1] and the courts. There are also many books about Canada's human rights system, its evolution, and its role, but most of them are academic or written for human rights practitioners, or, if written for the general public, are responsible for the pervasive and persistent myths that this book seeks to address. To borrow a phrase from an early reader, this book aims to engage a general audience in a more sober consideration of issues that it may only have considered previously in the overheated rhetoric that has characterized so much of the debate in recent years. It addresses not only legal aspects of human rights commissions and tribunals but also the broader role these institutions play in Canada and what has become a very public debate about the legitimacy of that role.

I have written this book primarily through the lens of law. This is partly due to my own legal training but mainly because the issues considered here – from how the system works to what it does and why it does so – are ultimately understood and resolved in the legal realm. The Charter, statutory protections, international norms, and case law create the legal framework in which the system functions.

Admittedly, the legal focus and the goal of appealing to a general readership coexist a bit uneasily. Readers do not need specialized knowledge or technical familiarity with legal issues or the literature. At the same time, distinguishing between rhetoric and reality in some of the more heated debates often requires a level of detail and analysis that only a lawyer could truly love. The book's format attempts to resolve this tension: legal references are placed in notes, which can be omitted by those less interested in legal threads of discussion and analysis.[2] I do not pretend that the references are comprehensive, although I have attempted to cover the most important sources of law. I focus on those works and references that I encountered along the way with the benefit of suggestions from the many interviewees who agreed to lend their expertise to the task.

The book touches on a wide range of subjects that are relevant to human rights systems, ranging from administrative law to the Charter, and from international human rights to the role of the media. It also considers the social and political choices involved in establishing and using human rights systems as policy instruments to mediate and manage multiple forms of rights disputes and to promote a culture of human rights.

Events are captured up to 31 March 2013, although I have added updates where necessary.[3]

Preface

In the early 1990s, a client in Montreal called me about an incident in a shopping centre managed by his company. A bystander had complained about a woman who was breastfeeding and the shopping centre's security guard had asked the woman to cover up or leave. She had left, but the shopping centre manager was worried about a human rights complaint and about rumours of a mass "feed-in" at the shopping centre, organized by pro-breastfeeding advocacy groups. I phoned Quebec's Human Rights Commission.[1] The staff seemed straightforward and solution-oriented: they explained the procedures and the next steps needed to deal with the issue. The matter was resolved with an apology and an agreement that the shopping centre's managers and staff would receive human rights training.

This incident stayed in my mind over the years. When I was recruited by the Ontario Human Rights Commission in 1995, I saw it as an opportunity to learn more about human rights commissions from the inside. At the time, I was the volunteer head of a Montreal-based human rights NGO and, like many in the human rights community, had mixed views about human rights commissions. But I thought it was worth a try.

After a raft of interviews, tests, and evaluations, I was invited to a final meeting. The commission's executive director, Rémy Beauregard, and its chief commissioner, Rosemary Brown, were both present. To prepare, I had reviewed the commission's legislation and case law. Many of the legal issues I read about were standard fare for this kind of administrative agency but reading the press clippings opened my eyes to the Ontario Commission's negative public image. When Chief Commissioner Brown asked me about my impressions, I hesitated and said: "I think there is a lot of work to do." I thought this was a careful understatement, but anyone who has been caught in the headlights of Rosemary Brown's disapproving stare will know what I mean when I say that she was not pleased.

Despite this, or maybe because of it, I began working at the commission in August of 1995 as director of policy and education, on the heels of the June election of a Progressive Conservative Party government under Mike Harris. From the inside, some of the problems I had read about became much easier to understand. It was a troubled organization. There were internal factions among the staff, as well as a deep-seated resistance to change. Every altercation and difference of opinion risked escalating into a human rights complaint or grievance. Several individuals managed to rise above the workplace environment and shine but, overall, widespread and poor or non-existent performance management made long-festering problems appear intractable. Some staff members saw their work – and the mandate of the entire organization – through the lens of their particular identities or communities.

Still, Rémy Beauregard was an experienced and respected public servant. He had implemented bilingualism at Ontario's Office for Francophone Affairs and knew something about managing difficult change. He also knew that he was working in the shadow of others, such as Raj Anand. Anand had been named chief commissioner in 1987 with what he referred to as a "change mandate" from the government to modernize and improve the commission's effectiveness.[2] Early in his term, Anand had attempted a restructuring that involved both firings and hirings. There were media leaks about who was being let go and who was being brought in, as well as accusations of racism and discrimination. These were followed by a protest resignation by a senior official. There were accusations that Anand, who is of South Asian origin, had favoured white managers. The government appointed former deputy minister George Thomson and two senior public servants to conduct a review of the commission's hiring processes. Their final report revealed flaws in the hiring process but no evidence of discrimination.[3] Anand decided to resign from the commission in 1989, prompted, as he recalled in our interview, by the fact that the government had "hung him out to dry."[4] Beauregard, contemplating another attempt to "professionalize" the Ontario Human Rights Commission five years later, was acutely aware of the pitfalls of trying to reform an internally volatile and politically vulnerable organization.[5]

The commission's internal landscape shifted when, in 1996, the Harris government appointed Keith Norton to replace Rosemary Brown as

chief commissioner. Nothing in the Harris government's previous partisan appointments suggested that this appointment offered much to hope
for. However Norton, as an experienced lawyer and educator, had a
range of skills that made him a tremendous candidate for the job: human
rights know-how, legal qualifications, management experience, the ability to navigate both the public and private sectors, and a background in
politics. He had chaired the Canadian Human Rights Tribunal since
1992 and believed strongly in both the role and the rule of law. Norton
was also a former member of Bill Davis's Cabinet and had deep roots
in the Progressive Conservative Party of Ontario. As a gay man, he had
encountered intolerant views in the reform wing of the party and said
that he could not bring himself to run for office with what he called
"that lot."[6] On an individual and personal level, however, Norton had
good relations with many in the party, including Mike Harris, who gave
a eulogy at Norton's funeral in 2010.

Norton proved to be an extremely successful chief commissioner. He
was professional and personable. As a former Cabinet minister, he was
sensitive to the political side of his work and was careful with the public
purse. He also had uncanny instincts for knowing the right time to push
an issue. Dianna Scarth of the Manitoba Human Rights Commission
laughingly recalled, "When Keith Norton sneezed, it made the news."[7]

Norton's arrival gave new impetus to Beauregard's efforts at reform.
Together, they launched a number of successful, albeit predictably tumul-
tuous, changes. Departments were restructured. New strategies were
adopted to improve effectiveness, including an effort to mimic private
sector productivity by introducing the results-based "business plans" that
were all the rage in the public sector. The commission offered its entire
staff professional development and training. Beauregard insisted that
departments handling complaints, policy, and legal issues work together
to develop more integrated approaches.

In terms of its public work, the commission issued research papers
and more than a dozen policies on a broad range of topics in Ontario's
Human Rights Code.[8] Its Policy and Guidelines on Disability and the
Duty to Accommodate set demanding standards for reasonable accommodation, using a social model that refocused complaints on what can
be done to remove barriers to participation rather than on the medical
diagnosis of the complainant.[9] The publication won Ontario's Amethyst
award for excellence in public policy in 2002 and has since been cited in
the courts.[10] Public policy statements on everything from breast-feeding

to racial profiling and the accessibility of public transit were among the milestones that characterize the commission's most successful work.[11] Its work on aging and discrimination prompted the government of Ontario to eliminate mandatory retirement. When Keith Norton died in 2010, these accomplishments were what people remembered and what the media recorded, largely because they had changed many people's lives for the better.[12]

Nevertheless, the Ontario Human Rights Commission never really gained the trust or confidence of the public. Lawyers and activists wanted more control over cases and less gatekeeping by commissions. And despite internal tinkering, some expensive new technology, and a successful early-mediation system, the commission could not allay widespread concerns about bias, backlogs, and bottlenecks. Activists and lawyers who met with the senior management team during my time there in the late 1990s dismissed the internal tinkering and initiatives as distractions from the real issues. By this time, it was clear that Ontario's Human Rights Commission was embattled. Designed in the 1960s to provide a regulatory response to overt discrimination in a "pre-rights" environment, it was struggling, with limited success, to handle the demands of a very different social and legal context.

I left the commission in 2001 to work in the federal public service. I also had the opportunity to participate in international United Nations (UN) missions aimed at providing technical assistance to national human rights institutions (NHRIS) around the world (NHRI is the term used by the UN to refer to human rights commissions and similar government institutions).[13]

Over the next decade, I had the privilege of working with several countries to build or reinforce NHRIS and other types of national institutions in Ethiopia, Iraq, Rwanda, Sudan, Tajikistan, and Timor Leste. Over time, several trends and themes became apparent. At first, governments are generally enthusiastic about accepting financial and technical assistance, and about the benefits of being seen to have a NHRI. The level of initial enthusiasm tends to drop precipitously when it becomes clear that these institutions appear determined to *do* something – and that that "something" often involves investigating complaints against the government or calling attention to embarrassing or unpopular topics.

Governments sometimes respond by looking for ways to curb their now-inconvenient human rights institutions. While NHRIS are supposed to operate at arm's length from government and political interference, there are subtle ways to make human rights institutions and their staff more pliable and less effective. Institutional performance inevitably starts to suffer once such strategies begin to take effect. The all-too-familiar chorus of concerns about delays, bureaucracy, institutional inertia, and incompetence starts to spread and gain momentum. Governments sit back and let the institutions take the heat from human rights groups, stakeholders, the media, and, eventually, the public. NHRIs find themselves isolated and under threat. They have trouble attracting the best and the brightest, creating a vicious circle of difficulty in recruiting good people and institutional underperformance. The result, more often than not, is weakened institutions with little ability to make a real difference.[14]

Two examples provide vivid illustrations of this downward spiral. In Rwanda, respected human rights activist Gasana Ndoba was replaced as head of the National Human Rights Commission of Rwanda by a partisan appointee. A representative of an international human rights NGO told me in 2003 that this alone had transformed the country's commission from a popular (if somewhat disorganized) institution of choice for people who sought justice into what he called a bureaucratic "waste of space." In Timor Leste, the embattled Office of the Provedoria (Protector) for Human Rights and Justice was paralyzed after episodes of public unrest and violence. The government did little to protect the organization or its staff and in 2008, the provedor himself (the equivalent of the chief commissioner) took to sleeping in his office because it was too dangerous for him to go home. The organization was hesitant and uncertain about its role and had very little ability to do much more than make recommendations that were ignored by the government, which had failed to give the organization any enforcement powers. It was clear that any decision to move forward on important human rights issues would further endanger the provedor and the staff.

In 2008 after a series of missions, I was struck by how many of the issues I had seen abroad were relevant in Canada, albeit in different ways and with very different consequences. Most commissions and tribunals in Canada fall short of international human rights legal standards regarding institutional independence, impartiality, and competence. Commissions lack an adequately broad legal mandate to speak out on the full range of human rights issues on the promotional (educational) side of their mandates, and what powers they do have, they rarely use beyond equality rights. Central agencies of government do not always pay sufficient attention to providing administrative support to human rights systems. The curse of patronage appointments, coupled with insufficiently rigorous legal criteria regarding qualifications for appointments and dismissals, as well as non-existent criteria for the renewal of terms of appointment, plague most human rights institutions in Canada.

As well, Canadian human rights laws lack uniformity in terms of the rights they protect and how they are protected. Access to human rights decision-makers like tribunals varies wildly from jurisdiction to jurisdiction, with Ontario providing easy access, while in Quebec, such access is severely restricted. Delays and backlogs have always been a real problem everywhere. Meanwhile, the number of human rights grounds has grown so that there has been an increase in the time, cost, and complexity of human rights litigation. While commissions and tribunals have worked hard to keep up with rapidly changing demands in the context of new social and legal realities, the public's understanding of what these institutions do, what they were set up to do, and what they are capable of doing remains mired in another era or severely tarnished by criticism.

I was also struck by the extent to which human rights systems had become lightning rods for high expectations and strongly voiced frustrations. Many people who took the heady promises of the Charter and the International Bill of Rights[15] to heart have not been satisfied with the way human rights systems work. Commissions themselves are partly responsible for this state of affairs, but legislatures are also at fault as they establish human rights systems and control the breadth of their mandates and their legal guarantees of independence. Legislatures determine how and to which authority human rights systems are accountable, as well as the legal criteria for official appointments, renewals, and dismissals. The executive branch also bears some responsibility, because it controls many of the operational levers of financing and administration. All of this exposes human rights systems to uncertainty and capricious decisions.

While it is important to keep asking whether human rights commissions and other parts of the system can do a better job, and to be unflinching in this assessment, it seems to me that the negative rhetoric about human rights systems in Canada is misplaced and worrisome. It focuses on discussions of elements of the human rights system that are deeply (and sometimes deliberately) misunderstood. Such discussions have distracted policy makers from considering areas where human rights systems do need to evolve and improve. Irwin Cotler, former minister of

Justice, said that: "We need more basic information about the role of human rights commissions; we need a better understanding of their origins and development, of why and how they developed here in Canada, and how they operate, and data about complaints. We need a comprehensive appreciation of what the facts are and what the legal framework is, and we don't have this."[16]

Starting in 2008, I began speaking with academics and practitioners to gain a broader perspective on what was happening in these areas and what it meant. A few informal conversations expanded to almost sixty interviews over four years, mostly through word of mouth and introductions to people who had an expertise in human rights systems. All the interviews were with people who have been at the forefront of the human rights movement – leaders in human rights commissions or tribunals, leaders in civil society, and senior members of the Bar. The majority have years and even decades of experience working directly in or with human rights commissions and tribunals. Each interviewee contributed a wealth of knowledge and a unique perspective on human rights systems in Canada and the law and politics of human rights. It was clear throughout the interview process that not everyone agreed about human rights systems, their accomplishments, or even whether they should exist in their current forms. Nonetheless, each interviewee was committed to a constructive and progressive vision of human rights, consistent with our constitution and our international human rights obligations. Byron Williams, a respected human rights advocate, set the tone for this perspective on human rights systems. Williams heads the Public Interest Law Centre, a public interest litigation group in Manitoba. He cited his organization's recent positive experiences with the Manitoba Human Rights Commission and noted evidence of positive change and alternatives to the current climate of distrust of human rights commissions: "Instead of defending commissions as they are, we need to defend the importance of commissions in our society and think about their evolution."[17]

That strikes me as exactly right.

Canada's human rights system is a legitimate and important interlocutor in the evolving debate and discourse about what human rights are and who should protect and promote them. If Rosemary Brown were here today to ask me again about my thoughts on human rights commissions in Canada, I would still say that there is a lot of work to do to build a better, more coherent, and more effective generation of human rights protections in Canada. There is also work to do to provide a vantage point from which we can assess the system's effectiveness. We need to be mindful of both the accomplishments and mistakes of the past to develop a keener, more informed appreciation for what should come next.

Abbreviations

ACLC	African Canadian Legal Clinic
BOI	Board of Inquiry
CASHRA	Canadian Association of Statutory Human Rights Agencies
CBC	Canadian Broadcasting Corporation
CBSC	Canadian Broadcast Standards Council
CCOHR	Continuing Committee of Officials on Human Rights
CERA	Centre for Equality Rights in Accommodation
CHRA	Canadian Human Rights Act
CHRC	Canadian Human Rights Commission
CHRF	Charter of Human Rights and Freedoms (Quebec)
CHRP	Community Historical Recognition Program
CIC	Canadian Islamic Congress
CJC	Canadian Jewish Congress
CN	Canadian National Railway
CRARR	Center for Research-Action on Race Relations
CRPD	UN Convention on the Rights of Persons with Disabilities
GIC	Governor in Council
HRLSC	Human Rights Legal Support Centre
HRTO	Human Rights Tribunals of Ontario
ICC	International Coordinating Committee of National Institutions for the Promotion and Protection of Human Rights
ICCPR	International Covenant on Civil and Political Rights
ICESCR	International Covenant on Economic, Social and Cultural Rights
LEB	Labour and Employment Board
LGC	Lieutenant Governor in Council

LGBT	lesbian, gay, bisexual, or transgendered
MAG	Ministry of the Attorney General
MLA	Member of the Legislative Assembly
MP	Member of Parliament
NGO	non-governmental organization
NHRA	Nunavut Human Rights Act
NHRI	National Human Rights Institutions
OAG	Office of the Auditor General
OHRC	Ontario Human Rights Commission
OSCE	Organization for Security and Co-operation in Europe
RAPLIQ	Regroupement activistes pour l'inclusion Québec
RDA	Racial Discrimination Act
SLAPP	Strategic Lawsuits against Public Participation
UN	United Nations
UPR	Universal Periodic Review
UQAM	Université du Québec à Montréal
YHRC	Yukon Human Rights Commission

SPEAKING OUT ON HUMAN RIGHTS

Introduction

Whereas recognition of the inherent dignity and of the equal and inalienable rights of all members of the human family is the foundation of freedom, justice and peace in the world

1948, Universal Declaration of Human Rights

Equality, freedom, and human dignity are important ideas: the connection between them is what gives human rights such a powerful and compelling claim on our collective conscience. It also explains why all three are contained in the ringing opening words of the Universal Declaration of Human Rights cited above. Individually, each idea has its drawbacks. Freedom means little if it "liberates" one person but oppresses another. Equality can be static or even oppressive if its cost is loss of freedom. We may all intuitively understand the fundamental significance of human dignity, but as a legal concept, it has proved elusive and abstract.[1] The amalgam of the three ideas is what gives form and content to human rights, as well as providing a powerful vocabulary of both inspiration and complaint.[2]

EQUALITY RIGHTS

Among the three ideas, equality is the most contested. Equality can imply a utopian – some would say dystopian – idea of tedious and imposed sameness. When used in the human rights context, equality does not mean this at all. The Canadian Charter of Rights and Freedoms (the Charter) provides that equality is about the protection and benefit of law and freedom from discrimination:

15.(1) Every individual is equal before and under the law and has the right to the equal protection and equal benefit of the law without discrimination and, in particular, without discrimination based on race, national or ethnic origin, colour, religion, sex, age or mental or physical disability.

Equality is a right on its own, but it is also an overarching principle that affects how other human rights are applied and understood. The International Covenant on Civil and Political Rights (ICCPR), to which Canada has been a party for more than three decades, obliges states "to respect and to ensure to all individuals within its territory and subject to its jurisdiction the rights recognized in the present Covenant, without distinction of any kind, such as race, colour, sex, language, religion, political or other opinion, national or social origin, property, birth or other status." It also guarantees equality before the law and states that persons are entitled, without discrimination, to the equal protection of the law. "In this respect, the law shall prohibit any discrimination and guarantee to all persons equal and effective protection against discrimination[.]"[3]

In its legal sense, equality forms a constitutional bulwark against discrimination. The idea of protecting people against discrimination seems straightforward enough. So does providing "equal protection and benefit of the law." Scratch below the surface, though, and there are competing theories about what anti-discrimination and equality rights really mean. Do they mean treating everyone the same? Or guaranteeing access to the same basic rights, such as adequate food, education, and shelter? Or ensuring that people have a level playing field and equality of opportunity? And what about helping people to participate and interact in society on fair and equitable terms? Equality rights operate on a continuum, ranging from seemingly simple requirements not to treat people differently, to more inclusive requirements that operate to ensure that that people get "equal benefit of the law." At their roots, different conceptions of equality are grounded in divergent views about the role of government and our responsibilities to each other.

Equality rights are protected by at least three layers of legal guarantees. The first and most remote from our daily experience is international human rights law, the second is the Charter, and the third layer – the focus of this book – is human rights legislation, which is enforced by a national network of human rights commissions, tribunals, and other public agencies that, together, comprise Canada's human rights system.

Partly because of these longstanding protections, Canadians think of themselves as champions of human rights, leading the way both internationally and at home. Some, however, might see this view as a triumph of self-regard over reality. Entire swathes of the Canadian population have not only experienced discrimination but have been effectively prevented from benefiting from the application of the rule of law. The events giving rise to inequality may predate human rights language and laws but, for many people, the legacy of inequality lingers. A few examples will suffice, most if not all of which will be familiar to many Canadians.

Equality has been elusive for Aboriginal peoples – many have lost their children, their lands, their languages, and their cultures. Until 2011, they were prevented by Canadian federal law from filing human rights complaints in relation to the Indian Act.[4] Aboriginal women have been the targets of relentless and shocking violence for many years, a tragedy that has only recently begun to attract widespread national and international attention.[5] Children are also among those affected by this historical and institutional neglect and abuse. Aboriginal organizations have been complaining in vain for years that funding levels for child and family services are inequitable and discriminatory.[6] Forty percent of Aboriginal children in Canada live in poverty, two and a half times the rate for non-Aboriginal children.[7]

The United States may have had a longer and more widespread history of slavery but, as most Canadians know, there were slaves in Canada for more than two centuries. From the tragic story of Marie-Josèphe *dite* Angelique, who was tortured and executed for allegedly setting the fire that burned down much of Montreal in 1734,[8] to the treatment of Black Loyalists in Nova Scotia in the late eighteenth century and beyond, and to de facto segregation policies, discrimination against Black communities has been persistent.[9] Nova Scotia, home to one of the oldest Black communities in Canada, was the backdrop for the 1946 case of Viola Desmond, a Black woman dragged from the Whites-only area of a theatre for refusing to sit in the balcony, the area reserved for Blacks, and then prosecuted.[10] She took the fight to have her conviction overturned to the Nova Scotia Court of Appeal but lost.[11] The Desmond case is one of many that have been carefully documented by scholar Constance Backhouse[12] and are only now beginning to enter the broader public consciousness in Canada. In the Civil Liberties class I teach at McGill, most law students said they had heard of the American civil rights activist Rosa Parks but few had heard of Desmond, even though she is credited by Backhouse as being the first Black woman in Canada to use the courts to challenge racism.

Margaret Parsons, head of the Toronto-based African Canadian Legal Clinic, sees the scars of racism in many Black communities in Canada today: "I will never know where my family came from. I will never know what language we spoke. We were severed from our families, our culture and our history. We had to start all over again with rites and rituals. Cultural reparations – museums, educational reparations – these are the things that will make a difference for us. But today, wherever you go in the world, [Black communities] have the highest rates of crime [and] the lowest rates of education. When we came out of slavery we had nothing."[13]

Racism and discrimination were also facts of life for many Asian immigrants to Canada.[14] In the early 2000s, Chinese Canadians sought legal redress for one of these human rights violations, the so-called "Chinese head tax,"[15] a fixed fee imposed on every Chinese immigrant by the Canadian government, starting in 1885. The head tax existed for almost four decades and claimed almost $23 million from the Chinese Canadian Community. A class action lawsuit was filed in Ontario to seek the return of the discriminatory head taxes paid between 1885 and 1923, with compound interest. The plaintiffs lost their case in 2002 before the Ontario Court of Appeal,[16] but the lawsuit brought this little-known historical chapter to the attention of millions of Canadians.[17] In 2006 the Harper government apologized to the Chinese Canadian community. In 2008, The Government of Canada established the five-year Community Historical Recognition Program to acknowledge wartime discriminatory measures and immigration restrictions. The CHRP made $13.5 million available for projects in several communities, about $5 million of which was earmarked for the Chinese community.[18] Although the program received considerable positive feedback when it was introduced, in 2013 the government announced that it was clawing back $500,000 of the $5 million.[19]

Japanese Canadians were targeted as enemy aliens in the Second World War (under the same legislation that had been used against the Ukrainians in the First World War[20]). Many were stripped of their property and civil rights. In 1988 Japanese Canadians reached a settlement with the Government of Canada, leading to the Japanese Canadian Redress Agreement, an initiative of the Mulroney Government. The agreement sought to make amends for government actions against Japanese Canadians, including their internment, relocation within Canada, expulsion or deportation, and deprivation of property.[21]

Canada has a long and sad history of anti-Semitism. Well-known examples include the McGill university quotas in the 1920s, the "no

Jews" signs on Ontario beaches in the 1930s, the 1933 Christie Pits riot, and the common use of restrictive covenants to prevent Jews and others from acquiring land. The covenants were challenged before the courts in the 1940s and beyond, but with only partial success.[22] The Second World War witnessed Canada's shameful official policy of refusing to admit Jews fleeing the Holocaust, a policy documented in the seminal work of historians Irving Abella and Harold Troper, *None Is Too Many*.[23] Every year, B'nai Brith's sobering audits of anti-Semitic incidents in Canada and around the world serve as a reminder that we have not rid ourselves of this scourge.

Early twentieth-century eugenics legislation in Canada authorized the institutionalization and sterilization of people perceived as disabled or "feeble-minded," six years before the Nazi's 1934 eugenics laws were created.[24] The Canadian laws were not fully repealed until the 1970s and lawsuits lingered into the 1990s.[25] David Baker, a leading disability rights activist and the former head of ARCH Disability Law Centre, recalled that, "discussions in the 1980s were about the fact that disability was not even seen as a human rights issue."[26]

THE PRESENT CONTEXT FOR HUMAN RIGHTS IN CANADA

Human rights systems in Canada were not only a response to the shortcomings of the past but a way forward into the future, breathing life into the interconnected ideals of equality, liberty, and human dignity. Human rights laws were the product of a non-partisan political consensus and were introduced by political parties of all stripes. The 1960 Canadian Bill of Rights was enacted by a federal Progressive Conservative government. The Liberal Party introduced the federal multiculturalism policy in 1971. The Charter was entrenched in 1982 under a Liberal government. In 1988 the Canadian Multiculturalism Act[27] gave programmatic content and legislative support to multiculturalism under a Progressive Conservative government.

There is a broad consensus in Canada when it comes to multiculturalism (albeit somewhat less when it comes to its Quebec variant, interculturalism), tolerance, and a commitment to human rights.[28] Between 2010 and 2012, Focus Canada surveys showed that more than 70 percent of respondents considered the Canadian Charter of Rights and Freedoms to be an important symbol of Canadian national identity. Only health care received a higher rating.[29]

This commitment has recently come under threat. In 2006, Ray Pennings and Michael Van Pelt published an article that described the model of government developed after Pierre Trudeau's election as prime minister as operating on a "pan-Canadian consensus" based on, among other things, tolerance and what they describe as an "aggressive human rights polity." The authors argue that that pan-Canadian consensus has now unravelled, replaced by a "new consensus" that does not include multiculturalism, tolerance, or human rights.[30] The *Toronto Star*'s Thomas Walkom memorably dubbed it the "new, grim consensus."[31]

The Pennings-Van Pelt thesis may be exaggerated, but efforts to engineer the demise of the pan-Canadian consensus are not difficult to discern, starting with the federal government's systematic marginalization of human rights and the Charter. In 2006, the federal government terminated the Court Challenges Program (CCP), which had funded Charter-based litigation that successfully challenged discriminatory laws and practices.[32] Longstanding and effective organizations such as the Canadian HIV/AIDS Legal Network have been denied government grants because their funding applications suggested the "weakness" that they might engage in advocacy or, worse, defence of the human rights of people living with HIV/AIDS.[33] The reputation of the once-respected Montreal-based Rights and Democracy agency was left in tatters after what some commentators describe as a hostile takeover in 2010 followed by a challenge to grants made to three human rights organizations alleged to be anti-Israel. The agency limped along for two years until it was eliminated by the Harper government in April 2012.

The Supreme Court of Canada chastised the government twice in the Omar Khadr case[34] in relation to one of the most powerful and universally recognized prohibitions in human rights law, the prohibition of torture. The federal government's lengthy delay in finally repatriating Khadr was nothing short of disgraceful. In 2011, the Supreme Court of Canada again rebuked the federal government, this time for what the Court described as its "arbitrary" decision to refuse permission for the continued operation of a safe drug injection site in Vancouver, BC. Overwhelming evidence showed that the program had been successful in reducing health risks and crime and that the federal decision endangered the lives of drug users in the area and placed residents at risk.[35]

In December 2012, Department of Justice lawyer Edgar Schmidt filed a lawsuit alleging that the department has been failing in its duty to adequately inform Parliament when proposed new legislation risks violating the Charter.[36] Schmidt's lawsuit was startling because it is rare to see a federal public servant criticize his or her employer. His allegations are, however, supported by several legislative bills that appear to disregard Charter rights. Schmidt's allegations have not been proven in court, but they help to explain the baffling lack of interest in, let alone compliance with, elementary human rights norms.

The federal government's omnibus Bill C-10, the Safe Streets and Communities Act, is an example of this attitude.[37] Based on a law and order agenda emphasizing the belief that criminals receive inadequate sentences, it has made mandatory minimum sentences a popular way to gain political points. In taking this position, Conservatives have demonstrated how greatly they are "in thrall" to the US-inspired policy of removing discretion in sentencing from judges.[38] The reality in the United States, however, is that mandatory minimum sentencing frameworks have not only failed to serve the traditional goals of punishment, including proportionality between crime and punishment, but have also failed to reduce crime.[39] The constitutionality of mandatory minimum sentencing has also been cast into doubt. In a 2012 Canadian case that preceded Bill C-10, Justice Anne Molloy refused to apply a mandatory sentence for possession of a firearm that would have sent a twenty-seven-year-old man with no criminal record to a federal penitentiary for three years. The Ontario judge called the sentence cruel and unusual punishment and a violation of section 12 of the Canadian Charter.[40] Experts predict there will be similar responses to the new and increased mandatory minimum sentences in Bill C-10, especially as it applies to Canada's fastest-growing prison populations – women with mental disabilities and Aboriginal persons. Bill C-10 runs contrary to Canada's traditions of fairness, compassion, and equality.[41] There are indications that the Conservatives will have to move away from this policy as evidence of its practical failure, violation of constitutional principles, and huge public cost become better known and understood.

Bill C-31 – Protecting Canada's Immigration System Act – places more importance on protecting systems than on protecting people. In 2012, it created a new class of "designated foreign nationals" who can be detained without due process for what is essentially a mandatory, warrantless, automatic, and unreviewable period of six months following the obligatory initial review after the person is detained.[42] These new provisions raise serious concerns about Bill C-31's compliance with the legal rights in the Charter.

National security and policing organizations are among our most important custodians of public safety and human rights, yet most of them do not report publicly on their compliance with human rights on anything like a systematic basis. Moreover, they are not obliged to do so.[43] In the current environment, in which information-gathering and surveillance of ordinary citizens is increasingly in the news, the lack of public accountability for human rights is or should be a cause for concern.

These are but a few illustrations of what appears to be a pattern of Charter overrides, whereby Justice officials – as suggested by Schmidt's 2012 lawsuit – are instructed to ignore the Charter if there is even a slight chance that a challenge to the legislation might fail in court.[44] The utter lack of interest in the empirical basis for many new laws and policies led one researcher to quip that there has been a shift from evidence-based policy-making to decision-based evidence-making.[45]

Canada's reputation at the international level has suffered. While Canada may have been seen as more laggard than leader in some areas of international foreign policy, in the past it played an important role in human rights, from peacekeeping to its contribution to the establishment of the International Criminal Court.[46] In 2009, Kenneth Roth, head of Human Rights Watch, told a Montreal audience that Canada's international foreign policy record had declined in stature.[47] In 2010 Canada's standing in the Global Integrity Report index dropped from eleventh place to nineteenth out of nearly one hundred countries evaluated since 2007. The drop was largely due to lower ratings for accountability and conflict of interest factors.[48] In 2011, Amnesty International released a report urging Canada to get "back on track."[49] A year later, Amnesty took Canadian officials to task for failing to adequately implement Canada's international human rights obligations.[50]

The human rights backlash has had a direct impact on human rights systems. Stephen Harper is on record as having called human rights commissions a form of "totalitarianism."[51] Controls on discriminatory hate speech – controls that the Supreme Court of Canada has twice upheld as constitutional – were called "dangerous" and "illiberal" by Jason Kenney, who was minister of Citizenship, Immigration and Multiculturalism at the time he made his remarks.[52] In 2012, the federal government did not bother to step in and protect its own legislation, section 13 of the Canadian Human Rights Act (CHRA), when it came under attack.[53]

CRITICISMS OF HUMAN RIGHTS SYSTEMS

This book is not about these developments, about whether there has been a decline in the quality of Canada's democratic governance, or even about whether respect for human rights has eroded. It is about the effect these factors have had on human rights systems as a result of the increasingly inhospitable political and policy environment in which such systems operate. Independent watchdogs and oversight agencies like human rights commissions and tribunals need to be able to function effectively and independently. Respect for the rule of law and the Charter, and the political will to sustain the institutions that protect them are basic elements of any functioning, sustainable democracy. In an environment in which these basic elements are increasingly in short supply, human rights systems are considerably more vulnerable. A study from the 1990s describes the "reputational deficit" of human rights commissions, pointing to their diminished credibility and trust among the public.[54] Things have arguably gone downhill since then. The British Columbia Human Rights Commission was abolished in 2003. The Alberta, Canadian, and Ontario Human Rights Commissions received harsh criticism for their handling of hate speech cases a few years after that, as did the British Columbia Human Rights Tribunal. The Saskatchewan Human Rights Tribunal was abolished in 2011. The Quebec human rights system has eroded to the point that it is excessively difficult to get a case heard by the tribunal in that province. Various politicians and commentators across the country muse periodically and publicly about slashing the mandate of human rights systems or perhaps doing away with commissions or tribunals altogether.

Indeed, criticizing human rights commissions has become an equal-opportunity activity for journalists, activists, and lawyers from across the political spectrum. They accuse commissions of failing to create a sufficiently robust culture of human rights. They say that commissions have not done enough, gone far enough, or moved fast enough. Martha Jackman, an equality rights scholar and a law professor at the University of Ottawa, stated that commissions have been "no friend of human rights." In fact, she argued, commissions stand in the way of advancing the rights of people who are poor.[55] Jackman's views were echoed by many interviewees who work in other areas of human rights law.

On the other hand, rights critics and management-side lawyers argue that commissions go too far, do too much, and promote a seemingly endless catalogue of claims. Respondents also raise concerns about abuse of process, the unfairness of claimants receiving state-funded support, and the impact, stigma, and expense of human rights cases. People on both sides of the spectrum complain about delays and institutional performance. "I don't trust human rights commissions," said Mark Freiman, a senior Ontario litigator describing the Ontario Commission prior to the 2008 reforms: "In order to have a functioning commission, you need the best people. The [Ontario Human Rights] Commission was seen to be a dumping ground for incompetent investigators."[56]

Until the mid-2000s, such discussions took place mostly within the insular world of lawyers and activists. With the exception of the occasional one-off incident or outrage about a particular decision, no one seemed much interested in human rights commissions or equality rights. Those who did care were (mostly) academics or practitioners working for equality-seeking groups. As one journalist said, "I worked at the CBC and, as journalists, we never went to commissions for stories or for [information about human rights cases] because, at the time, they kept such a low profile. Most media did not even know that commissions exist."[57]

Hate Speech Cases

All of that changed in 2007, following a spike in media attention that resulted from two incidents. The first was the conservative online magazine *Western Standard*'s re-publication of one of the Danish "Mohammed-as-bomber" cartoons.[58] Its former publisher, Ezra Levant, also posted material arguing for free speech and against commissions.[59] There were anonymous racist, even genocidal, comments about Muslims on the *Western Standard* web site. Human rights complaints were filed but were withdrawn shortly afterwards. The newspaper apologized.[60]

The second incident involved three complaints filed against Rogers Inc. and its editor after they refused to publish a rebuttal to a string of allegedly anti-Muslim articles in *Maclean's* magazine, a Rogers property. Three Osgoode Hall law students, Khurrum Awan, Naseem Mithoowani, and Muneeza Sheikh, argued that *Maclean's* had published more than twenty articles they felt "went well beyond simply being offensive and became dangerous."[61] On 4 December 2007, they held a press conference to announce the filing of human rights complaints, focusing mainly on an article written by Mark Steyn.[62] (Steyn himself was not a respondent in any of the complaints.) The students were the complainants in the Ontario complaint, which was based on the Ontario Human Rights Code, but they asked the Canadian Islamic Congress and its president to act as the complainants at the federal level and in BC.

Thousands of human rights complaints are filed by Canadians every year, but these were the first that had been brought by Muslims, individually and as a group, against mainstream media on a national scale. Journalists and editors may be accustomed to getting angry calls from people threatening to sue, but mainstream journalists in Canada had not had this kind of complaint before. One complaint would have attracted a lot of attention but three made for a toxic combination of race, religion, and post-9/11 identity politics and triggered a perfect media storm.[63] Most journalists and writers saw the hate speech complaints as a form of censorship or even malicious prosecution. An avalanche of articles and editorials appeared in the press in a concerted and coordinated effort to repeal the human rights laws that regulate hate speech.

Maclean's vigorously denied the accusations of discriminatory speech. Supported by most of the media, it led a crusade to bar human rights commissions from dealing with speech at all. Columnists like Lorne Gunter,[64] George Jonas,[65] and Jonathan Kay[66] started using their regular columns to attack commissions more generally.

Alan Borovoy, who has publicly and steadfastly opposed restrictions on hate speech but is otherwise a strong supporter of commissions, said that he tried a "two-track approach" to the debate. On the one hand, he opposed what he called the censorship inherent in hate speech restrictions. On the other, he sought to support the work of commissions as a whole.[67] He was assiduously quoted on the first and generally ignored on the second.

No one reading the press between 2007 and 2010 could have failed to be amazed by the rapid evolution of the rhetoric. Outrage against the bureaucracy of human rights commissions was not new, but the *Maclean's* hate speech complaints blended free speech, the Muslim menace, and national security threats to create a toxic brew that brought the simmering stew of rage-against-the-government-machine to a full boil. Critics accused commissions of using illicit investigation techniques in hate speech cases. Criminal charges and privacy complaints were laid against commission staff, garnering widespread attention in, among other publications, *Maclean's*.[68] The subsequent decisions of the RCMP and the Privacy Commission to dismiss the charges and privacy complaints as baseless received comparatively scant attention.[69]

Human rights commissions were considered to be guilty by association, portrayed as the harbingers – if not the architects – of social decline. They were called "kangaroo courts," star chambers, and "thought police."[70] They were compared to Nazi and North Korean regimes.[71] They were said to boast "100 percent conviction rates."[72] They were described as affronts to free speech, democracy, and, for good measure, compared unfavourably to extraterrestrials.[73] Such accusations spread quickly through the Internet and the sheer force of repetition allowed them to gather considerable and authoritative weight.[74] Once in cyberspace, the rhetoric against human rights commissions exerted enough gravitational pull to draw sympathetic allies into its orbit, including anti-immigration pundits, extremist right-wing groups, religious activists, and the apoplectic right in general.

Politicians and political parties also noticed that they received more bouquets than brickbats for criticizing human rights commissions.[75] As noted earlier, Tory Member of Parliament Jason Kenney decried the "dangerous" and "illiberal tactics" employed by "activists" in the name of tolerance.[76] While serving as a Liberal Member of Parliament, Keith Martin put forward a motion to repeal the federal prohibition on using telecommunication systems to communicate hate, section 13 of the CHRA. His web site at the time recycled the myths that commissions have "100 percent conviction rates" and that "commission's lawyers" investigate cases to the detriment of respondents.[77] Neither statement is or was true. Martin was called "brave" by the *Globe and Mail* for his motion before Parliament.[78] Given the public attacks on human rights commissions, it was difficult to see how Martin's stance could reasonably have been considered brave.

In 2011 Tory Member of Parliament Brian Storseth tabled a private member's bill, Bill C-304, to repeal section 13 of the CHRA. It received Royal Assent on 26 June 2013, eliminating the moderate and rarely used human rights remedy at the federal level and leaving only a heavy-handed criminal response that results in a criminal sentence for those found guilty.[79]

At the provincial level, Progressive Conservatives in Ontario under Tim Hudack have declared their plans to either "fix" or abolish the province's human rights tribunal.

After Saskatchewan eliminated its human rights tribunal in 2011, the human rights commission dismissed about a third of its staff in an attempt to orient its activities away from complaints management and towards more mediation. The move was controversial, eliciting concerns from unions, academics, and human rights groups.[80]

During Alberta's provincial elections in 2012, the Wildrose Party proposed eliminating both the Alberta Human Rights Commission and the Tribunal and creating a new human rights division of the Alberta provincial court system.[81]

The result of all this has been a distorted and one-sided perception of commissions. Philippe Dufresne, general counsel at the Canadian Human Rights Commission, described his experience: "When I started out, the main criticism was about access to tribunals and delays. It was a complainant-oriented critique. Now, we see concerns about the scope of the [Canadian Human Rights] Act and these concerns are coming from the side of the respondents. We are not hearing the complainants' perspectives at all."[82]

Richard Moon, a law professor and the dean of Windsor Law School, was an active participant in the hate speech debates. In a 2009 report for the Canadian Human Rights Commission, Moon made several recommendations about the commission's jurisdiction over hate speech. Among other things, he recommended that section 13 of the Canadian Human Rights Act be repealed.[83] While writing his report, Moon became increasingly aware of what he described as the unfair, outrageous, and personally malicious things being said about the Canadian Human Rights Commission and its staff.[84] By recommending the repeal of section 13 of the CHRA, Moon said that he had hoped to earn enough credibility to take on the critics. He was invited to speak before an Ontario legislative committee reviewing Ontario's Human Rights Commission and Tribunal and saw this as an opportunity to challenge the freely circulating inaccuracies about human rights commissions. In his opening statement, Moon pointed out the differences between hate speech laws across the country (i.e., between the federal and the provincial systems). He also highlighted the unfair criticism against human rights systems and observed, "there are, unfortunately, a lot of people who are not interested in a meaningful debate."[85] He later wrote, "I want to set out some of the claims made about the [Canadian Human Rights Commission] and describe how they are misleading or just plain false. Second, I want to consider how the deceptive and invented claims of commentators such as Ezra Levant and Mark Steyn have entered mainstream discourse and come to affect public attitudes."[86]

The problem, Moon said, was not only the ridiculous claims about commissions, that the claims were fuelling an anti-rights movement, or even that a thriving racist Internet sub-culture was feeding off the claims. It was that the "deceptive and invented" claims had seeped into the mainstream discourse, legitimized by politicians, editorials, and commentary in the print media and by radio and television programs, blogs, and web sites. Moon argued that the conscious amplification of falsehoods about commissions fostered a public perception that commissions are no longer working for the rights or in the interests of Canadians.[87] According to him, "the most vociferous and indeed the most media-amplified critics of the [Canadian Human Rights Commission] are not interested in this debate. It is easier and perhaps more effective to exaggerate the case, invent injustices, and engage in personal attacks."[88]

Jennifer Lynch, former chief commissioner of the Canadian Human Rights Commission, was a frequent target of the personal attacks, both in the media and in shadow blogs. In 2009, she publicly appealed for support to the Canadian Bar Association (CBA).[89] In response, the CBA issued the following statement: "Critics have decried human rights proceedings as 'kangaroo courts' which provide only 'drive-through justice' and advocated that human rights tribunals and commissions should no longer be permitted to operate. We reject attacks of this kind and reiterate forcefully our support for the continued importance of the work undertaken by these human rights bodies to foster human rights in Canada."[90]

While there were a few such supportive responses, there was studied silence from most human rights advocates. Some said they did not feel compelled to support human rights commissions that had been unhelpful in advancing their own causes. Others were simply unaware of the debate and its implications. Paul Champ, an Ottawa-based human rights lawyer, said, "many of us did not realize what was happening – we just did not take the [right-wing bloggers] very seriously."[91] Journalism professor John Miller, also a target of the right-wing blogosphere, observed that some in the mainstream media were actively promoting the view that free speech was under threat, suggesting that that there were no countervailing or other meaningful human rights issues, including equality rights, at stake.[92] With the exception of a few op eds, human rights commissions were also relatively quiet.

Haroon Siddiqui of the *Toronto Star* was among the few senior editorial writers who tried to take a more balanced viewpoint. He asserted that "free speech cannot be an excuse to hate" and observed that media outlets that had professional and financial interests in squashing hate speech laws were unlikely to show much ability to preserve neutrality in the debate.[93] Rick Salutin and Doug Saunders also offered thoughtful commentary that did not play to the "end-is-nigh-and-so-are-the-barbarians" rhetoric. [94] Others who opposed hate speech laws, like Lysiane Gagnon, managed to take a stand without labelling people as terrorists, sock puppets, or sexual deviants.

On 9 April 2008, five months after the complaint was filed, the Ontario Human Rights Commission (OHRC) dismissed the case against Rogers and *Maclean's* on a preliminary basis for lack of jurisdiction. The relevant prohibition on discriminatory notices, signs, and symbols in Ontario's Human Rights Code does not extend to published opinion and statements. However, in a public statement on its web site, the OHRC also criticized media coverage that promotes "societal intolerance towards Muslim, Arab, and South Asian Canadians."[95] The federal complaint was also dismissed on a preliminary basis.

In British Columbia, the matter went to the human rights tribunal. Much was made of the fact the BC Tribunal had dared to hear the matter, but the reason it had done so was simple: there was no "first decider" to screen the case to determine whether the case should have gone forward because the province had abolished its human rights commission. The very people in the media who had called for the elimination of human rights commissions (including Mark Steyn) then professed themselves to be shocked and appalled that this complaint had made it to a tribunal. Ignorance of the basic legal situation, which was on the public record, was unfortunate, to say the least.[96]

Maclean's itself had some responsibility for the fact that the case went forward to the BC Tribunal to be heard on its merits, as Rogers had not filed a preliminary motion to strike the claim.[97] After the hearing, the BC Tribunal eventually dismissed the case. [98]

According to Margaret Parsons, one of the odd outcomes of the *Maclean's* hate speech debate was that, while the free-speech banner fluttered over the hate speech debates, the public campaign against human rights commissions had actually had the effect of chilling speech: "Many of us fought hard for that section – section 13 [of the Canadian Human Rights Act]. The attacks on section 13 are a huge step backwards in terms of human rights in this country. We are very troubled by this attack on the fundamental right to be free of hate speech. There has definitely been a chilling effect as a result of blog and media attacks on those who oppose hate speech in our community. People are afraid to speak out."[99] The African Canadian Legal Clinic was an intervener before the Supreme Court of Canada in the landmark *Whatcott* case, which affirmed the constitutionality of limits on hate speech. It is noteworthy that in *Whatcott* the Court held that hate speech has a discriminatory impact on the targeted group's ability to respond to the substantive ideas under debate and places a serious barrier to full participation in our democracy.[100]

About half the people interviewed for this book said that they were aware of the effect that personal attacks and insults had had on people.

They were of the view that the invective had probably deterred many who might otherwise have spoken out. The *National Post* suggested that supporters of unpopular hate speech restrictions should just suck it up: "harsh criticism" may be unpleasant, according to an editorial, but it should be seen as inevitable in the rough-and-tumble arena of public debate.[101] Perhaps. But, as noted earlier, the media has a vested interest in its own position. More important, the consequences of speaking up in such an overheated environment became more serious than garden-variety gawking at a media storm or run-of-the-mill rants against government bureaucracies.

Accusations and counter-accusations flew, provoking blog wars and complaints to law societies. Libel cases were filed by, from, and against complainants, respondents, and bloggers. It all got very personal. While commenting on a hearing that had taken place before the Canadian Human Rights Tribunal in a hate speech case, Ezra Levant, a vocal anti-commission activist, falsely accused Canadian Human Rights Commission lawyer Giaconda Vigna of improper behaviour. Vigna sued Levant and won a $25,000 judgment for defamation. Justice R. Smith of the Ontario Superior Court found that Levant had shown reckless indifference for the truth.[102] Vigna had become a target of Levant's public campaign to "denormalize" human rights commissions and Levant's comments were found to be "malicious" in that sense.[103]

Activists such as Richard Warman, Darren Lund, and the three Osgoode students in the *Maclean's* hate speech cases were all complainants in hate speech cases and all found themselves at the receiving end of cyberhate and threats. Both Lund and Warman had to take security measures at their workplaces and their homes.[104] Beyond the invective and name-calling, the former heads of Alberta's Human Rights Commission and British Columbia's Human Rights Tribunal received threats of violence during the hate speech debates.[105] Giaconda Vigna also received threats, according to evidence provided to an Ontario court.[106]

Richard Warman, a public servant and activist who is prominently associated with combating hate speech and over the last decade has filed many complaints under section 13 of the CHRA, has been living with death threats for years.[107] Other activists and organizations, notably Sabina Citron and B'nai Brith, have also filed hate speech complaints in the past. B'nai Brith continues its engagement with the issue, although with reservations about human rights commissions.[108] The Montreal-based anti-racism group CRARR has also used human rights commissions to combat hate.[109] But Warman became identified with the perceived deficiencies and excesses of commissions. "Warman was a hero, a real hero," said Mark Freiman, "but in a sense, he became the human face of all that is [seen to be] wrong with the system."[110] Warman became the target of defamatory verbal assaults. In 2008, he successfully sued blogger William Grosvenor before the Ontario Superior Court of Justice for online posts that the court held to be sufficiently vicious, menacing, and calculated that they qualified not only as defamatory but as an assault in law.[111] In 2009, during a Parliamentary hearing of the Subcommittee on International Human Rights regarding the Canadian Human Rights Commission, a witness called by the Conservatives suggested that Richard Warman should be "publicly hanged."[112] The remark was never censured or withdrawn.

Some politicians and members of the media with whom I have informally discussed these issues have scoffed at threats, even death threats, as trifling or unworthy of serious attention. There is no small irony in these individuals going to the barricades for free speech – for words – while in the same breath trivializing threats against human beings in the name of human rights.[113]

Lawyer and human rights expert Mary Eberts believes these developments have had an impact that extends well beyond hate speech: "We assumed that the structure of the civil rights movement would hold over the years – it hasn't. These people have dragged the skirmish line back to the point where human rights activists can't open their mouths, and the public accepts this as a legitimate outcome."[114] Hostility has engulfed people who are vulnerable or who turn to human rights commissions for help. People with disabilities are seen as freeloaders.[115] People with mental illnesses are portrayed as violent, criminal, or homeless.[116] Members of the extreme right, including neo-Nazi groups, have taken advantage of the human rights backlash to claim that they are themselves the victims of racism and political correctness.[117] Transgendered people have been depicted as freaks or pedophiles-in-waiting who do not deserve rights.[118]

The *Sturm und Drang* has also had the unfortunate consequence of making it harder to push for progressive reforms in areas where changes are actually needed. The free speech fracas has, however, given us a good deal to think about and has created a public space for debate about the human rights system that did not exist before. It has put human rights commissions and other parts of the human rights system on the public's radar screen and raised important questions about human rights policy in Canada. It has re-opened a debate about what human rights commissions were originally intended to do, what they are supposed to be doing, and whether they are actually doing it.

THE "HUMAN RIGHTS" IN HUMAN RIGHTS SYSTEMS

Canada's human rights system has played, and continues to play, a unique and important role in the evolution of human rights. Human rights commissions and tribunals have been important, albeit contested, interlocutors in the broader discourse about human rights, the type of society we want, and how we should go about securing it in Canada. Shelagh Day is president of the *Canadian Human Rights Reporter*, a non-profit journal and legal service that has tracked human rights case law since 1980, "long before any of the major legal journals even recognized that human rights decisions from the administrative system were part of human rights law." Day argues, "much of what is good in the Charter in the context of equality cases comes from human rights commissions. This is a huge contribution from the human rights world."[119] She highlighted the following rulings from "pillar cases" from the Supreme Court of Canada, all of which began in human rights commissions.

- Unionized workers have human rights: collective agreements cannot be used to circumvent or contract out of human rights protections.[120]
- Insurance companies cannot turn people down because of discriminatory factors.[121]
- Women have the right to be free from sexual harassment. Employers cannot avoid corporate liability for sexual harassment in the workplace.[122]
- Women cannot be shut out of jobs because of discriminatory rules and practices that have nothing to do with their ability to do the work.[123]
- People of faith deserve fair treatment at work, and employers must respect religious beliefs and observances by offering reasonable accommodations.[124]
- Children who have dyslexia have a right to special education for the simple reason that all children have the right to receive public education in accordance with the law.[125]

These and many other cases have helped thousands of people by promoting fairer workplaces and more accessible schools and services.

Pierre Bosset is a professor at the Université du Québec à Montréal and a former research director at Quebec's Human Rights Commission. He emphasizes the important role that the commission played in increasing awareness of gay and lesbian rights, racial profiling, and the rights of religious minorities. According to Bosset, "These were areas that changed not only the way organizations worked but also changed the public debate about human rights and its role in society."[126]

Human rights systems have also been instrumental in advancing progressive interpretations of equality law that connect human rights to fundamental rights and freedoms, reconciling conflicts between them and overcoming entrenched social values and practices that create real obstacles for people in their daily lives. The following examples are from cases where human rights commissions have taken a leading role in advocating a more progressive approach before the courts and in public policy:

- People have the right to be free of the effects of public vilification and detestation that hate speech engenders. Hate speech is a form of discrimination.[127]
- Gays and lesbians enjoy equal rights under the Canadian Charter.[128]
- Black drivers have the right to drive taxis and cannot be excluded from the taxi industry.[129]
- Separated and divorced older women have the right to the same public financial assistance as their married counterparts.[130]
- People with intellectual disabilities in Manitoba have the right to community-based living options instead of only institutionalization.[131]
- Everyone has the right to be free from racial profiling, a practice that violates not only equality rights but also basic civil liberties.[132]

According to Mary Eberts, such cases are important because they "pulled discrimination out of the chaos of their facts and called it by its name."[133] Through these and many other cases, the human rights system in Canada has contributed to a shared Canadian identity that is tolerant and supportive of diversity and inclusion. It forms part of the bedrock of jurisprudence that underpins constitutional equality rights guarantees. Having spent years working closely with human rights institutions, I am aware that these positive views of commissions are not popular. As Paul Champ has observed, the criticism of commissions and the fallout of the hate speech debates were "very unfortunate developments. The attacks shifted from human rights commissions to equality rights and to human rights more generally. And this reaches into a certain subsector of society that wants to get rid of legislation that promotes substantive equality altogether."[134]

These attacks should not go unanswered. Human rights institutions have come under threat partly because the attacks on them rely for their effectiveness on pervasive myths and distortions about their legal features and how they work. This book seeks to examine the reality behind these myths, while refocusing the policy debate on equality and the rule of law, as well as principles of independence, impartiality, and competence.

Good governance in human rights institutions matters. Human rights commissions and tribunals have helped to promote fairness in our workplaces, improve the quality and types of services that we can access, and enhanced the accessibility of our educational systems. They have helped to ensure that healthcare is available to everyone and that people can get into decent housing. They are worthy of our sustained attention and support. These themes inform and shape the book's contents.

CHAPTER TOPICS

Chapter 1, "Introducing Human Rights Systems," starts with a sketch of the global context, providing an overview of human rights commissions and similar institutions around the world. It goes on to examine the structure and functions of Canadian human rights systems and explains their focus on equality rights. It provides working definitions of terms used throughout the book, such as "human rights systems," "discrimination," "gatekeeping," "access to justice," "human rights culture," and the "full range of human rights." I also describe key features of human rights systems, with an emphasis on accountability and institutional independence. I then return to the international context and look at a little-known aspect of human rights systems, namely their contribution to and role in the international human rights system.

Chapter 2, "Commissions Then and Now," charts the evolution of human rights commissions and tribunals as ideas, institutions, and vehicles of public policy over the past forty years, starting with early legislative responses intended to counter laissez-faire attitudes in the private sector and judicial unwillingness to address discrimination. I discuss the history of the human rights system from two perspectives: the social movements that prodded legislatures to enact human rights laws and the school of thought known as legal functionalism. Together, these two generated the impetus that led to the first waves of commissions in the 1960s and 1970s. I then track the steps that commissions took over the next two decades to address growing pressures resulting from an increasing catalogue of human rights and the demands imposed by constitutional standards of equality and administrative law principles of procedural fairness and natural justice. I also chronicle the corresponding increase in public dissatisfaction with first-generation systems, leading to the emergence of the next generation of "direct access" systems.

Chapter 3, "Do We Still Need Them?" responds to critics who say that human rights systems have had their day and are no longer useful. It provides data about the current demand for human rights systems, looking at the level of demand as expressed through the number of human rights complaints filed and as a function of the changing contours and content of rights. I assess what "counts" as a right in the calculus of law and critically examine allegations that commissions engage in rights inflation or have been reduced to dealing with watered-down, petty claims that lack a serious legal basis. I also deal with the accusation that commissions are antithetical to modern freedoms and are antidemocratic. Finally, I address the reappearance of laissez-faire ideologies and the idea that market forces should control responses to discrimination.

Chapter 4, "Are They Fair?," discusses the standards that should be used to answer this question, including Charter law, international law, and administrative law principles. I tackle issues that have been prominent in the public debates about human rights systems, including their relationship to the broader justice system and the important differences between human rights systems and criminal law. Chapter 4 considers issues that have been prominent in the media, such as truth, intent, hearsay, contempt of court, and the threat of double jeopardy and multiple proceedings. I also discuss the critique that commissions and tribunals unfairly favour complainants. Picking up the threads from chapter 1 regarding structural elements of human rights commissions and tribunals, namely their funding, independence, impartiality, and competence, I revisit international and administrative law standards to see what these norms have to say about the fairness of human rights institutions in Canada.

Chapter 5, "Signal Cases, Rights Conflicts, and Building a Human Rights Culture," spotlights areas that have attracted public attention in relation to rights conflicts and considers the origins of these cases, while asking whether and to what extent human rights systems should use equality rights to engage with other rights and fundamental freedoms. The first section, "When Rights and Freedoms Divide," examines the characterization of equality rights and other rights and freedoms as inherently oppositional. I offer an alternative perspective, namely that human rights institutions in Canada have always dealt with a complex mix of rights, freedoms, and social values through an equality lens and that this integrated approach is both functional and well established. The second section, "Poisoning the Well," examines specific case studies dealing with competing or seemingly incommensurable rights, such as fundamental freedoms and minority rights. It looks at the role of human rights systems in addressing these difficult types of disputes as part of our legal system.

Chapter 6, "The Way Forward," asks how human rights systems could be restructured to more effectively respond to today's realities and tomorrow's challenges. Gathering observations from the previous chapters, it offers ten ideas for change.

Calling something a human right confers a powerful mantle of legitimacy on the claim. Canadian commissions and tribunals have had a central role in mediating such claims for years. Understanding how the Canadian human rights system works provides insights not only into the system itself but also into the question of whether Canada will continue on its path as a pluralistic, progressive, and open society, and the role, if any, that human rights systems should have in the future. All of these aspects have implications that extend well beyond human rights systems themselves and invite inquiry into the diverse and multicultural experiment that is Canada.

1

Introducing Human Rights Systems

Every individual is equal before and under the law and has the right to the equal protection and equal benefit of the law without discrimination and, in particular, without discrimination based on race, national or ethnic origin, colour, religion, sex, age or mental or physical disability.

Section 15, Canadian Charter of Rights and Freedoms

All persons are equal before the law and are entitled without any discrimination to the equal protection of the law. In this respect, the law shall prohibit any discrimination and guarantee to all persons equal and effective protection against discrimination on any ground such as race, colour, sex, language, religion, political or other opinion, national or social origin, property, birth or other status.

Article 26, International Covenant on Civil and Political Rights

Canada's human rights system is the set of institutional components that work together to form our public human rights infrastructure. Commissions and tribunals are key components of the system and they share what administrative law lawyer Ron Ellis calls a "statutory rights enterprise." He explains: "When governments implement policy through a rights statute, the statute creates the rights, privileges, and corresponding obligations needed to effectuate that policy, and it also structures the delivery system – the organizations and mechanisms required to deliver and administer the policy. The totality of those institutional arrangements and structures can be conveniently referred to as a 'statutory rights enterprise.'"[1]

I use "human rights system" to refer to the collection of institutions with the specific statutory rights enterprise of protecting and promoting human rights, recognizing that this goal is more aspiration than reality. Canada actually has fourteen distinct systems. They may share important historical, legal, and structural features but they also have important and substantive differences that affect people's rights and the ability to access those rights. Each system operates in a silo and has its own idiosyncratic features, functions, and foibles.

Despite these variations, the collection of institutions that make up Canada's human rights system is bound by international norms and constitutional principles such as the rule of law, minority rights and equality before the law. These principles require that we work towards a system that operates in a coherent and reasonably consistent way across the country. That is not the case right now. As it stands, the Canadian human rights system offers highly divergent levels of human rights protections, access to justice, and remedies. As I argue in this book, institutional independence, impartiality, and competence are also central principles in the human rights system, but not all of our human rights institutions reflect these principles.

Canada's human rights system includes the federal jurisdiction as well as the ten provinces and three territories. There are three types of institutions – the two most common are human rights commissions and human rights tribunals (the latter is a generic term that I used to refer to boards of inquiry, adjudication panels, or employment boards, terms that are used in different jurisdictions). There is also a publicly funded human rights legal support centre in Ontario that is available only to complainants.

Other institutions, such as courts, labour relations boards, and ombudsperson institutions, can and do address human rights in their work and form part of the broader justice system.[2] However, human rights institutions such as commissions and tribunals are unique in that their primary responsibility is human rights. That responsibility is conferred by law.

Human rights commissions are the most recognized and oldest part of the human rights system. Twelve out of the fourteen jurisdictions in Canada – British Columbia and Nunavut are the exceptions – have human rights commissions. Commissions are regulatory agencies of government with the responsibility to both promote and protect human rights. Such commissions have a social mission to build a culture of human rights by undertaking education, policy development, and providing advice and assistance to governments, as well as liaising with other commissions and/or the international community. Except in Ontario, which operates on a new model, Canadian commissions are "first deciders," meaning that they screen human rights complaints to eliminate those that obviously do not fit within their mandate.[3] The commissions send the remaining complaints, provided there is sufficient evidence, to specialized tribunals. Accusations that commissions are "kangaroo courts" and the like miss the central point that commissions do not undertake adjudication. It is true that they make screening decisions on a preliminary basis, but they do not hold hearings or decide on cases. That function is reserved for human rights tribunals.

Human rights tribunals, the second element in the human rights system, are specialized decision-makers. Unlike commissions, they do not initiate complaints or work with stakeholders to develop public policy. Tribunal decisions are based on existing law: they do not engage in law reform, advocate for the ratification of international human rights instruments, or comment on the human rights record of governments, except in the context of their own decisions. Tribunals cannot exercise discretion over which issues they do or do not consider. Their mandate, with a few exceptions, is to exercise a judicial function of adjudicating the human rights complaints that they receive. They are not part of the judicial branch of government but, like human rights commissions, are part of the executive branch from a constitutional perspective and are subject to and circumscribed by their statutory rights enterprise. They are judicial, however, in the sense that most of their work is adjudicative, they form part of the broader justice system, and their decisions are binding in law.

At the same time, human rights tribunals are intentionally, properly, and markedly different from courts in the level of formality of proceedings, the application of rules of evidence, and several other features that I discuss in chapter 4. None of these differences diminishes or trivializes tribunals as legitimate adjudicative decision-makers. The test of their legitimacy lies in the way in which they meet the legal requirements of independence, impartiality, and institutional competence.[4]

There are thirteen human rights tribunals in Canada. Only Saskatchewan lacks a tribunal: its human rights commission sends complaints directly to the Court of Queen's Bench.

There is a tiresome tendency among commentators to conflate and confuse commissions and tribunals. A commission's decision to send a complaint forward to a tribunal is often described as a decision on the case, rather than being recognized as a preliminary screening decision that is a necessary precursor to the tribunal hearing. More commonly, tribunal decisions are attributed to human rights commissions, causing no end of confusion when members of the media call to ask human rights commissions to "explain their decision," something that happened with some regularity when I was at the Ontario Human Rights Commission.

The distinction between commissions and tribunals is important. Not only do commissions and tribunals do different things, but the way in which legal standards apply to them differs as well. The particular standards that apply to tribunals as they operate in Canada are considered at length in Ron Ellis's important book *Unjust by Design*.[5] Although Ellis deals with the administrative law system in general, much of his analytical discussion about the difference between what he calls judicial tribunals and regulatory bodies (such as commissions), especially the standards that apply to tribunals, is adopted here in the particular and specialized context of the human rights system. The higher standards of independence that Ellis urges for tribunals are not yet fully established by Canadian law or Canadian courts. However, the important nature of human rights and human rights adjudication is such that we should expect a very high standard of independence for tribunals. Human rights commissions, on the other hand are subject to a more "variable" standard of procedural fairness, given their different role.[6] International standards for independence, impartiality, and competence exist for both commissions and tribunals, but the legislative and operational environment in which human rights systems operate in Canada today means that they are not met by either institution. These issues are taken up at greater length in chapter 4.

Human rights commissions and specialized tribunals in Canada have evolved together, so that the work of one complements and reinforces the work of the other. This is not the case in most other countries, where commissions and similar institutions are often the only component of the human rights system. The institutional complementarity between commissions and tribunals in Canada is legal, historical, and functional. The loss of one or the other gives rise to a vacuum that can prove difficult to fill, as seen in jurisdictions that have experimented in this direction.

The section that follows sketches a global portrait of human rights systems, beginning with the international context and international standards, and compares the different institutional models that exist to Canadian institutions.

I then describe the Canadian human rights system in more detail, starting with its constitutional and administrative law framework and going on to describe its main functions and features, starting with the promotion and protection of rights. I offer a brief explanation of the differences between first and second-generation systems in Canada. I also discuss the extent to which the Canadian human rights system complies with the constitutional guarantee of the equal protection of the law. My analysis is predicated on the strong assumption that there should be a reasonable degree of coherence in and consistency of decision-making across Canada and that people should have comparable access to justice, a neutral decision-maker, and remedies. Mostly, they don't, for reasons that can be laid at the feet of governments. I also discuss the accountability of Canada's human rights system and its relationship to independence, neutrality, and competence.

The last section returns to the international context and looks at the particular role that human rights commissions play, or should play, in the UN human rights system.

HUMAN RIGHTS SYSTEMS: A GLOBAL PORTRAIT

Human rights systems around the world exist in many forms and different legal configurations. Most contain the institution that Canadians know as human rights commissions. At the international level, commissions form part of a larger family of similar institutions called "national human rights institutions," or NHRIS. Most NHRIS, however, are very different from human rights commissions in Canada, because they work in parallel with the justice system, rather than within it. Very few human rights institutions in other countries can receive, screen, and bring human rights complaints before the courts or to a specific specialized tribunal, let alone act as institutional conduits to a hearing or represent parties before the tribunal. In Great Britain, for example, the Equality and Human Rights Commission describes itself as a "nondepartmental public body" that promotes and monitors human rights, undertakes inquiries, and publishes a large number of studies and reports. It does not, however, receive, manage, and litigate human rights complaints. Rather, it provides a range of resources to help complainants find legal representation and file complaints before a wide range of unions, tribunals, councils, and courts.

NHRIS have two main characteristics. First, they are established by law – i.e., by statute or under a country's constitution – to meet the state's obligations to protect and promote human rights. Second, to qualify as an NHRI, the institution must both protect and promote rights. Non-governmental organisations are not NHRIS because, while they may meet the second criterion, they do not meet the first. Human rights tribunals may meet the first criterion but not the second. As mentioned earlier, their role is limited to adjudication and they do not take up proactive functions such as initiating complaints, developing substantive human rights policy, or providing public education that aims to promote a new or progressive interpretation of human rights – all of which are normal activities for NHRIS.

The international standards used to determine whether an institution qualifies as a NHRI are the Principles Relating to the Status of National Institutions (Paris Principles).[7] The Paris Principles are administered by the International Coordinating Committee of National Human Rights Institutions (ICC), which was established in 1993 to coordinate the activities of NHRIS worldwide.[8] The ICC Sub-Committee on Accreditation reviews and analyzes applications for NHRI accreditation under the Paris Principles.[9] Fully compliant institutions are graded "A."[10] Since its first review in 1999, the Canadian Human Rights Commission has been accredited by the ICC as an "A" status institution.[11]

NHRIS exist in a bewildering variety of forms and structures, ranging from research centres to commissions, and from ombudsperson institutions to public protectors and public advocates. According to a 2009 United Nation survey, 58 percent of NHRIS worldwide are structured as commissions. Commissions are particularly popular in North America and in Commonwealth countries, including in Canada.[12]

Human rights commissions in Commonwealth countries such as Australia, Britain, Ireland, and New Zealand resemble those in Canada, at least structurally. They usually have a relatively large staff headed by appointed members, namely a chief commissioner and commissioners. Commissioners are usually appointed to represent a broad range of constituencies, including minority and equality-seeking groups but also business, the non-profit sector, and sometimes government. Commissions tend to focus on human rights rather than on other issues such as government inefficiency, corruption, or red tape. Most NHRIS in the Commonwealth and in the developed north are restricted to dealing with equality rights and discrimination issues.

The next largest category (30 percent) of NHRIS is the ombudsperson institution, based on the classic Swedish model, which is more like the Canadian one in terms of its connection with a judicial tribunal. The Swedish Equality Ombudsman ensures compliance with anti-discrimination legislation by registering and investigating complaints, and can represent victims free of charge. Ombudsperson institutions tend to have smaller offices, are less legalistic in focus, and target government abuses and maladministration. They are especially popular in Central and Eastern European countries.

Other countries (12 percent) have "hybrid" NHRIS that combine features of both commissions and ombudsperson agencies or are research centres or institutes with limited mandates.[13]

According to the same 2009 UN survey, about 85 percent of NHRIS worldwide can address the full range of human rights in their work and are not restricted to equality rights as is the case in the Canadian system. These other rights include, but are not limited to, civil and political rights (the right to be free from arbitrary arrest, for example), social and economic rights (the right to housing and education, for example), women's rights, children's rights, disability rights, indigenous rights, and the rights of racial minorities – in other words, the full spectrum of human rights protected by national and/or international law. NHRIS that have a broad mandate can investigate or accept complaints about anything from torture to the death penalty, from freedom of the press to arbitrary arrest and religious freedoms, and from indigenous rights to housing rights, regardless of whether the underlying issue contains an element of discriminatory treatment.

The remaining 15 percent of institutions are limited to dealing with specific types of rights, usually those linked to discrimination. Canada falls into this group, along with countries such as Britain, New Zealand, Sweden, and Australia.[14] The Canadian human rights system can only accept complaints related to allegations of discrimination. For example, if a person is treated unfairly or aggressively by a police officer, the issue will normally be dealt with by courts and police disciplinary bodies, not the human rights system. However, if the person alleges that the arrest or detention was the result of racial profiling, a commission could accept the complaint even if the incident also touches on legal rights such as the right to due process during an arrest or detention.

According to the same UN survey, 90 percent of human rights institutions worldwide can accept individual complaints.[15] In addition, while 85 percent of NHRIS can transmit complaints to other competent authorities, it is unclear whether such referrals are to bodies that can render binding legal decisions. My experience has been that, unlike the situation in Canada, few if any such referrals are in the form of legal proceedings that are sent to and heard by tribunals or courts, and where the NHRI then acts as an interested party that has standing before the tribunal or court. In most cases, NHRIS in other countries simply transmit complaints to other government departments or agencies, not to judicial tribunals.[16]

Another feature that distinguishes NHRIS worldwide from Canada is their authority over non-state actors such as businesses and NGOS. Internationally, about three-quarters of NHRIS can handle complaints against individuals, businesses, or nonprofits.[17] Among participating states of the Organization for Security and Co-operation in Europe (OSCE), only about a third can accept complaints against the private sector.[18] This appears to be the result, at least in part, of the pervasive influence of "classic" ombudsperson institutions on central and Eastern European institutions. Although ombudsperson institutions vary considerably in their structures and mandates, they were originally designed to control state behaviour and prevent government malfeasance, rather than having a central mandate to protect human rights, hence the focus on government behaviour.

These types of institutions have "protection gaps" because they cannot help victims who claim to have been discriminated against by the private and non-profit sectors. States that have NHRIS of this type cannot protect people from "any form" of discrimination, as required by international human rights law, but are limited to addressing discrimination committed by public authorities.[19] Some countries fill the protection gap by creating new institutions to field such complaints, recognizing that discrimination does not occur only in the public sector. In 2011, for example, 46 percent of the NHRIS in the OSCE region reported that they had created new institutions to deal with complaints against the private sector or to handle specialized types of human rights issues, like women's rights or child rights.[20] Other states have given additional powers to their existing institutions, allowing them to receive discrimination claims from both public and private sectors, although this new authority is generally restricted to equality rights and does not extend to the full range of human rights.

As noted earlier, in order to qualify as an NHRI under the ICC rules, institutions must comply with the Paris Principles.[21] Although the Principles are not legally binding, they make it possible to provide benchmarks based on a number of indicators, including the breadth of the commission's mandate and its legal and operational independence.

The Paris Principles have their limits: they are somewhat opaque and they are not comprehensive.[22] The ICC has had a tendency to assess institutions based on formal guarantees of independence rather than actual independence, and therefore actual effectiveness. In fairness, there has been an attempt in recent years to look at effectiveness "on the ground." A final drawback is that technically the Principles apply only to "national" institutions and not to sub-national commissions such as provincial or state commissions. This restriction creates a problem for federations like Canada where the provincial institutions are not subordinate to the federal one.[23]

Despite their flaws and limits, the Principles are useful benchmarks because they identify structural and legal elements that help to determine the effectiveness and, ultimately, the legitimacy of NHRIS. NHRIS should have the power and authority to:

- both protect and promote human rights. NHRIS may also be authorized to hear and consider complaints and petitions.
- undertake activities either on request or in their own right, and to address the full range of human rights;
- take up, advise, speak out on, and report on any human rights situation, law, or government practice;
- support education initiatives and encourage public awareness about human rights issues; and
- consult and liaise with other human rights bodies.

These functional requirements, in addition to the structural requirements of independence that are discussed later, are central to the social mission of building a human rights culture. Few commissions in Canada have a legal mandate that meets all these requirements. Two provinces or territories – British Columbia and Nunavut – do not comply with the Paris Principles at all because they have no commission.

CANADA'S HUMAN RIGHTS SYSTEM

Many people think of human rights in terms of sweeping declarations and epic courtroom confrontations, but most rights claims in Canada arise in everyday settings and involve employment, housing, education, and services. The main forum for resolving rights claims is the human rights system: human rights commissions and tribunals deal with roughly 7,000 claims every year. These claims must be based on equality rights, although as discussed elsewhere, human rights complaints in Canada often involve other rights and freedoms as well.

Neither the federal nor provincial level of government is given exclusive authority over equality rights or human rights claims in the Constitution Act, 1867.[24] For example, a case about school services for children with disabilities would go to a provincial human rights commission because provincial governments have jurisdiction over education. However, a challenge to the equality of services delivered to Aboriginal children on a reserve would go to the federal commission because Aboriginal matters are federal.

The Constitution Act, 1867 and the Charter are also silent on who has institutional authority over human rights commissions and tribunals.[25] Commissions and tribunals are "creatures of statute," meaning that their legal authority is conferred by legislation and they possess only the powers, features, and functions that the law gives them as part of their statutory rights enterprise. This feature is important in light of public controversy over the legality of human rights systems, their accountability, and their supposed penchant for exceeding their legal remit and wandering into unauthorized areas of activity. While human rights *systems* in Canada do not have constitutional status (there are several countries where the national human rights commission is established and protected under the country's constitution), the Supreme Court has ruled that human rights *laws* are "quasi-constitutional." This ruling means that human rights laws have special authority in relation to ordinary laws: they are fundamental laws that prevail over other legislation, unless otherwise specified.[26]

Key Features

The human rights system in Canada protects and promotes mainly those human rights that focus on discrimination, the central focus of equality law, although there is no definition of discrimination in most human rights laws in Canada.[27] Generally speaking, discrimination involves treating someone differently or unfairly based on a characteristic that is protected by law, such as race, sex, or disability. Refusing to build a ramp in a restaurant for people who are wheelchair users is clearly discriminatory. So is refusing to allow Sikh boys to attend school or play soccer because they wear religious symbols such as kirpans or turbans.

"Positive" discrimination and affirmative action involve special or temporary measures used to promote inclusion and reinforce equality. They are are not violations of human rights laws. Parental leave, pay equity programs, and hiring targets for minorities are good examples. Employment equity programs, which establish targets to improve the representation of certain under-represented groups in key areas such as the public sector, are another example of positive discrimination.

In Canada, there is a deep consensus about the right to be free from discrimination but, as the introductory section pointed out, equality rights are sometimes seen as more controversial. Equality rights are deeply grounded in and informed by protection against discrimination.[28] Section 15 of the Charter guarantees equality rights and ensures that everyone receives equal benefit and protection from the law. Equality also cuts across and shapes other rights and freedoms. This aspect of equality is consistent with non-discrimination, because rights should be available on a fair and equitable basis.[29] This idea is important in order to understand another role of human rights systems, which is to find ways to mediate different and potentially conflicting areas of rights, a topic taken up in more detail in chapter 5.

Finally, equality rights are not subordinate or inferior categories of human rights when compared to, for instance, freedom of speech or the right to vote, although other rights and fundamental freedoms can alter the shape and contours of equality rights. Human rights are interrelated and interdependent and very few can be meaningfully articulated or practically implemented, let alone enforced, in isolation. Canadian courts have rejected the idea that there is a hierarchy of importance among human rights,[30] a position that has profound implications for the work of human rights systems across Canada.

Promoting and Protecting Rights

Commissions are the original and best-known elements of Canadian human rights systems. They protect and promote human rights, dual functions that are required by the Paris Principles. Although the words "protection" and "promotion" are not used in Canadian statutes, the two groups of activities they describe are central to what human rights commissions do.

"Protection" includes receiving, investigating, settling, and mediating complaints. In addition, commissions also do other types of protection-oriented work that is not centred on parties to a dispute but involves a larger range of actors and interests. These other activities may include approving special programs, overseeing or developing employment equity plans, pay equity, or initiating complaints. Commissions in Canada have been engaged in protection work longer than most countries, at least in terms of their ability to receive and investigate complaints of discrimination and to bring such complaints to a hearing.[31]

Tribunals also protect rights but their primary purpose is adjudicating complaints, not developing or crafting public policy.[32] They receive complaints either directly from claimants (as is the case in British Columbia, Ontario, and Nunavut) or through human rights commissions (in the rest of the country, except in Saskatchewan, where there is no tribunal). Specialized tribunals offer important advantages in that their adjudicators have expertise in the subject matter. Because they deal with a narrow area of law, they can accumulate a substantial body of decisions related to a particular subject relatively quickly, which makes deciding cases easier and faster. As Ron Ellis observes, "because of the narrow focus and large volume of cases, [the advantages of the specialized judicial tribunal] can be harvested on a much shorter time lines than in the courts."[33] Tribunals are also usually less formal, less expensive, and more accessible.

For commissions that receive complaints, the investigation process is the source of much criticism and misunderstanding. Figure 1 provides a summary diagram (each system has its own set of rules) describing the general process as it applies in the Atlantic provinces, Quebec, Manitoba, Saskatchewan, Alberta, British Columbia, the Northwest Territories, the federal system, and Yukon. There is no investigation process for complaints in British Columbia, Ontario, and Nunavut.

Commissions stay strictly neutral toward the complainant and the respondent during the process of investigating complaints, including screening the complaint, interviewing witnesses, obtaining documents and physical evidence, and mediation. This neutrality is very important because there is a popular perception that commissions represent complainants at the investigation stage. They do not.

The investigation process is not public.[34] Both claimants and respondents are invited to put forward evidence. Both the claimant and the respondent are interviewed by investigators to allow the parties to present their side of the story. Investigators occupy specialized positions in commissions and have training in subjects such as evidence, human rights law, constitutional law, interviewing, and document management. The investigator is not obliged to disclose the evidence of either party or the identity of witnesses and commissions and their staff cannot comment publicly on ongoing investigations. This confidentiality, while a source of concern to critics, is there for the protection of all parties: at this stage allegations have not yet been investigated, let alone proven.

Once the investigation has been completed, a report is written up and sent to the commissioners, who meet, usually in presence of senior staff,

Figure 1.1
The complaint and investigation process

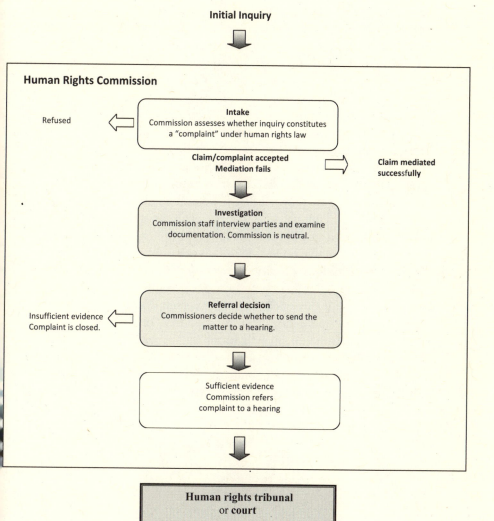

Initial Inquiry

Human Rights Commission

Refused ← **Intake**
Commission assesses whether inquiry constitutes a "complaint" under human rights law

Claim/complaint accepted
Mediation fails → Claim mediated successfully

Investigation
Commission staff interview parties and examine documentation. Commission is neutral.

Insufficient evidence
Complaint is closed. ← **Referral decision**
Commissioners decide whether to send the matter to a hearing.

Sufficient evidence
Commission refers complaint to a hearing

Human rights tribunal
or **court**

to decide whether cases should be screened out, referred to a tribunal, or sent back for further investigation. Only if the complaint goes to a tribunal does the process become open and public. At that point, all parties are entitled to learn the details of the evidence and the identity of witnesses. If the investigation reveals insufficient evidence to justify a hearing, or if there are preliminary grounds for screening out a case, the commission will dismiss the case, which generally puts an end to the claim. Allegations that commissions have "secret processes" or are "star chambers" that produce arbitrary rulings are based on the erroneous assumption that the confidential investigation process undertaken by commissions is part of the same process as the public hearing before tribunals. Confidentiality applies to investigations, but not to the public hearing before a tribunal.

The tribunal is the master of its own procedures and is not, as some critics would suggest, a "rubber stamp" for a commission.[35] If a matter is referred to a tribunal, the commission (if there is one) generally takes over presentation of the case, at which point it does lose its neutrality, becoming a party before a tribunal, either representing its own position in the public interest or representing the complainant.

Unlike tribunals, commissions have a promotional (or educational) mandate that extends far beyond complaints and disputes. "Promotion" refers to broad, proactive powers to undertake public education, develop policy, review legislation, provide advice to government, speak out publicly about human rights issues, and cooperate with other human rights institutions. Much of the work that commissions do integrates elements of both protection and promotion: for example, publishing reports on human rights situations or investigations and monitoring human rights situations combine both protection and promotion activities. They are part of building a culture of human rights. Human rights statutes use different language to express this goal, but, regardless of the wording, the idea itself is functional and transformative, extending beyond processing individual complaints to include strategic and systemic work. Building a rights culture is part of a broad social mission that transcends disputes between the parties.[36] Regulatory agencies have a broader social and legal mission than tribunals.[37]

Building a Human Rights Culture

The idea of building a "human rights culture" is controversial and means different things to different people. Some see it as the basis for ensuring that all members of society enjoy dignity and equal rights, which the Universal Declaration of Human Rights identifies as the foundations of freedom, justice, and peace. Others worry that it undermines equality by promoting special interests.[38] According to Gaétan Cousineau, who was president of Quebec's Human Rights Commission until 2013, "This is our main challenge ... People see human rights as [being] for special interests or for special groups. But the only way to make human rights relevant to the general population is to communicate the message that human rights are for everyone, and that the shared task of building a culture of human rights is not limited to special interests or minorities."[39] At the same time, Cousineau acknowledged that specific issues require specific measures: for example, assuring the rights of Aboriginal peoples, women, minorities, and people with disabilities requires a different, more inclusive approach. Human rights commissions must pay special attention to the effects of discrimination on people whose situations or history requires more tailored responses.

Building a culture of human rights allows commissions to act proactively and strategically, moving beyond human rights complaints. This aspect of their work is illustrated by what happened when the Ontario Human Rights Commission decided to issue a public statement in the *Maclean's* hate-speech complaint.

When the complaint was first filed with the Ontario Human Rights Commission, it was obvious that it was unlikely to go very far. Unlike the CHRA and British Columbia's law,[40] Ontario's Human Rights Code does not permit complaints on the grounds of hate speech or incitement to discriminate except in the narrow area of notices, signs, or symbols used in ads or signs.[41] The Ontario human rights system has no jurisdiction over hate speech or speech inciting discrimination.[42]

Predictably, the Ontario Commission ended up dismissing the matter. Less predictably, in April 2008 it issued the following statement:

> The Ontario Human Rights Commission has decided not to proceed with complaints filed against *Maclean's* magazine related to its publication of an article [by Mark Steyn entitled] "The Future belongs to Islam." ... Th[is] decision means that the claims will not be referred to a hearing before the Human Rights Tribunal of Ontario ... [T]he Ontario *Human Rights Code* does not give the Commission the jurisdiction to deal with the content of magazine articles *through its complaint process.*
>
> Even though the Commission is not proceeding with these complaints, *it still has a broader role in addressing the tension and conflict that such writings cause in the community and the impact that they have on the groups that are being singled out.*
>
> While freedom of expression must be recognized as a cornerstone of a functioning democracy, the Commission strongly condemns the

Islamophobic portrayal of Muslims, Arabs, South Asians and indeed any racialized community in the media, such as the *Maclean's* article ..., as being inconsistent with the values enshrined in human rights codes. Media has a responsibility to engage in fair and unbiased journalism.[43]

There were protests about the propriety of this statement and the effect it would have on free speech, including allegations of smears and "drive-through justice."[44] The commission's stance was simultaneously novel and unsurprising. It was novel because commissions rarely issue lengthy public explanations for preliminary dismissals of cases after screening. It was unsurprising because the commission has a responsibility to build a culture of human rights, a responsibility expressed in the Code as the legal duty to advance human rights and inquire into situations that create social tensions and conflict.[45] The scope of this duty extends beyond the commission's jurisdiction to accept complaints.[46] The Ontario Human Rights Commission does not have legal authority to prohibit speech inciting violence or discrimination, but it has a separate and wider responsibility to speak out publicly on human rights issues; its statement was a reflection of that wider legal responsibility on the protection side of its mandate.

Nonetheless, it was unprecedented in Canada for a human rights commission to speak out against a mainstream publication like *Maclean's*, let alone to criticize a writer in this way. Critics claimed that the commission was doing indirectly what it could not do directly through the complaint, "jurisdiction be damned."[47] The commission's statement was condemned as a form of cheap litigation that benefited undeserving complainants who were using the platform of human rights commissions to attack writers such as Mark Steyn as if they were the "new perpetrators" of discrimination and "traditional bigots."[48] Litigator Mark Freiman said, "this alienates people from the system. The screening of cases needs to be handled better and discretion exercised more appropriately."[49]

Ontario's chief commissioner, Barbara Hall, conceded that the combination of the commission's dismissal of the complaint and the exercise of its authority to speak out on contentious issues might have generated confusion:

Perhaps we were not as effective as we could have been in putting the two together. It may have confused people. However, our mandate is to deal with issues that cause tension and conflict, so our statement was in relation to that. Controversy was created by the way we dealt with this, but another [controversy] may have been created if we'd done it another way. ...

I continue to be asked about the issue of the media all the time. The media must be an important player in the work we do. Lots of times the media is a positive player and can help to show the world to itself, but where it contributes to discrimination, we will raise the issues as they arise.[50]

The Ontario Commission could not legally accept a complaint about hate speech, but the CHRA had the power to do so under section 13. The Canadian Human Rights Commission also has the broader power to inquire into or speak out publicly on matters that extend beyond its jurisdiction over complaints.[51] For example, in the 1990s, the federal commission criticised Canada's slow progress in dealing with Aboriginal issues, even though many of the issues arising on reserves would have been outside the commission's jurisdiction to receive complaints at the time.[52] Many commissions have a wider authority to comment on or report on human rights matters generally, beyond the narrow purview of equality rights.

Building a human rights culture requires commissions to collaborate with organizations and communities. The Ontario Human Rights Commission took on such a role in responding to the Asian angler incidents that took place in Lake Simcoe and Kawartha between 2007 and 2009. The "peculiar crime wave" was memorably described by the *Globe*'s Joe Friesen: "Over the past two years, Asian fisherman from the Toronto area have been getting shoved into Ontario's lakes and rivers with alarming frequency. Some call it 'nipper tipping,' blending an anti-Japanese epithet with the rural hilarity of cow tipping."[53] While the first incidents may have appeared to be little more than drunken stupidity, some of the incidents escalated to serious violence and injury. According to Barbara Hall, there was "a lot of racial stereotyping going on, with accusations that Asians were fishing illegally. But the police found no evidence of this at all." Insults, vandalism of fishing boats and equipment, and physical assaults led members of the Chinese Canadian community to call for criminal prosecutions under hate crime laws. When Hall read about the incidents in the *Toronto Star,* she wondered why so little was being done:

[The commission] set up a hotline with the community agency, the Metro Toronto Chinese and South East Asian Legal Clinic, which was central in bringing this matter to the attention of the broader community. We met with many of the players in several different communities to condemn the attacks and to put into place the infrastructure to change public attitudes. We partnered with police and municipal officials and even with tourism officials to make sure that this was dealt with. We were pleased to see that a couple of organizations created anti-racism groups and the Ministry of Education developed teaching materials. The police were real leaders in this work.[54]

Hall was adamant that, while the commission did not "own" these issues, it did have a role in bringing together the police, the judicial system, and others to find community-based solutions. Criminal prosecutions alone were not adequate to resolve the underlying issue of discrimination.[55] A human rights-based approach allowed the commission to engage with a wide variety of groups and use public education and awareness tools to address discriminatory attitudes.

In 2006, Ontario enacted Bill 107, which removed the Ontario Human Rights Commission's "gatekeeping" role. The job of receiving and screening complaints, as well as undertaking mediation, is now the sole responsibility of the Human Rights Tribunal of Ontario.[56] Bridging the gap between public policy and the administration of justice, the new law strengthened the commission's role in promoting human rights and building a human rights culture. The Ontario Human Rights Commission "is now responsible for developing public policy, as well as addressing tension and conflict in the province in order to bring people and communities together to help resolve differences. This new mandate bestows the unique capacity to address multi-faceted social issues with a broad range of processes."[57] The current legal framework places these responsibilities at the centre of the commission's work. According to an independent 2012 report, this aspect of the commission's work has been a success thus far.[58]

The Right to Equal Protection of the Law

Given the centrality of equality rights to human rights institutions in the Canadian system, as well as in our constitutional framework and in international law, one might expect that Canada's system would protect equality before the law, offering the same level of protection to all Canadians. While there are broad areas of similarity across Canadian human rights laws, there are also important differences.

HUMAN RIGHTS GROUNDS

Human rights laws protect against discrimination by prohibiting unfair treatment of people based on specific attributes or personal characteristics that are called human rights "grounds." These grounds include age, disability, ethnicity, race and colour, sexual orientation, and sex. They account for most human rights claims filed in Canada.

There is also a lesser-known group of grounds that include family status, gender identity and gender expression, social condition, social assistance, language rights, and political beliefs. Depending on where one lives in Canada, one may or may not have protection based on some or most of these grounds. (An overview of the grounds in human rights systems across Canada is set out in tabular form in Appendix 3.)

Family Status: Having a family is part of the human condition. The freedom to choose to become a parent is "so vital that it should not be constrained by the fear of discriminatory consequences. As a society, Canada should recognize this fundamental freedom and support that choice wherever possible."[59] Childcare is part of being a parent and therefore has a close connection to family status.[60] For example, working parents must constantly juggle childcare and workplace demands.

Many families also need to care for elderly or ill relatives, but not all jurisdictions in Canada protect these other family relationships. Ontario's Human Rights Code restricts family status to parent-child relationships, while the CHRA and laws in Alberta, the Northwest Territories, and Nunavut protect a wider range of family relationships. In Alberta, for instance, "family status" is defined as the status of being related to another person by blood, marriage, or adoption.[61] Family status has no protection at all in New Brunswick. Section 10 of the Quebec Charter protects "civil status," which refers to a person's civic identity, including family relations (such as siblings, being a parent) and transgendered status.[62]

The result is that people across the country have quite different rights and responsibilities when it comes to balancing work and family, while employers also have quite different obligations to their employees. Even where there is a right to be free from discrimination based on family status, the case law is not yet settled. Some cases uphold the rights of parents to seek flexible arrangements or "accommodation" at work. Such decisions make these rights a legal obligation and not merely an option for employers who choose to be "nice," as one national newspaper has suggested.[63] Recent developments in the case law are discussed at greater length in chapter 3, but the point here is that the protection varies considerably, ranging from no protection at all, to protection because of a parent-child relationship, to a wider network of family relationships.

Gender Identity and Gender Expression: Severe forms of discrimination against transgender (trans) people, combined with better understanding of their rights, has led some jurisdictions to provide explicit protection based on gender identity or gender expression. Given the relatively small proportion of trans people in the population, such cases represent a small portion of the work of commissions. Still, what the cases lack in numbers they more than compensate for in severity. Trans people report devastating forms of discrimination that range from social exclusion to physical attacks.[64] Despite this, only Manitoba, Nova Scotia, Ontario, Prince Edward Island, and the Northwest Territories offer explicit protection for gender expression or identity.[65] An amendment to the CHRA was before the Senate at the time of writing.[66]

Much has been made of the argument that specific protection for trans people is unnecessary because existing laws can serve the same function, based on the general ground of "sex." That argument was used in Ontario in 2000, for example, when the commission issued a policy stating that trans people could use the human rights ground of sex in appropriate cases when filing a discrimination complaint.[67] I was at the commission at the time – the policy was needed because there was no explicit statutory protection in the Code. As the Supreme Court of Canada has noted, the special nature and purpose of a human rights code and the accepted rules of statutory construction are flexible enough to "give it an interpretation which will advance its broad purposes."[68] However, making use of the ground of sex in this way was a workaround and was not ideal. It failed to address the more particular and specific forms of discrimination that trans people experience. When the law is not specific, people can be subjected to years of litigation while the meaning and scope of their human rights protections are being clarified by tribunals and the courts.

The Ontario government amended the Human Rights Code in 2012, adding the new human rights grounds of "gender identity" and "gender expression."[69] The rights of trans people, as well as their decision to express or identify with a different gender than their assigned birth identity, should be respected. However, because this is not the reality, specific protections are needed. The pejorative and demeaning characterization of the resulting human rights protections as "bathroom bills" and the like, suggesting that trans people will start attacking other users of public facilities or will use them to prey on children, underscores the very stereotypes that human rights legislation is designed to address and shows why these protections are needed.

Social Condition and Social Assistance: Article 2 of the International Covenant on Civil and Political Rights (ICCPR) calls on states to protect people from discrimination on the grounds of "social origin, property, birth or other status."[70] The International Covenant on Economic, Social and Cultural Rights (ICESCR) also guarantees a right to social security, which provides for a right to a minimum level of public assistance in the event that a person is unemployed, rendered unable to work, or otherwise requires financial assistance from the state. While the two grounds are different, they share an important feature, namely that they protect against discrimination related to aspects of a person's social status linked to poverty or to other aspects of socioeconomic status, including receiving public assistance.

The Supreme Court of Canada has not recognized social condition or poverty as an equality ground under section 15 of the Canadian Charter.[71] At least one appellate court has decided that discriminating against someone "in receipt of social assistance" can underpin a Charter equality claim.[72] In general, the courts have been relatively reluctant to develop the right to social assistance and/or to social condition, in part because section 15 of the Charter is said to be restricted to "a personal characteristic that is immutable or changeable only at unacceptable cost to personal identity."[73] Courts are reluctant to recognize economic and social rights.[74]

In this respect, human rights laws are ahead of the Charter and the courts. Every Canadian jurisdiction except the CHRC offers some form of protection on one or more grounds related to social condition, social origin, or source of income, although the range and coverage vary widely. In Quebec, for instance, "social condition" covers virtually any aspect of a person's social origin or status. It can include being in receipt of social assistance but can also extend to poverty, education level, or homelessness. The Quebec Charter imposes no restrictions on the context in which people can raise discrimination claims. The practical impact is that Quebecers are not limited to the areas of employment, housing, and the like when filing complaints. Complaints can be raised in any context, including situations where the individuals have no pre-existing legal connection or relationship.

One striking recent example of such a complaint is the 2013 decision rendered in favour of Francine Beaumont on the grounds of social condition. Beaumont was sixty-three and suffered from a degenerative bone condition. She was unable to work and received social assistance. To supplement her income, Beaumont panhandled and solicited patrons outside a Quebec liquor store (the state-run stores are called the SAQ) in Ahuntsic, a neighbourhood in northern Montreal. Upset by Beaumont's presence outside his favourite liquor store, Robert Deslisle wrote a vitriolic email to the SAQ's customer service staff. Describing Beaumont as fat and stupid, Deslisle reportedly made several suggestions to the SAQ about how to get rid of such people, including "burning ... with a flame-thrower or napalm," "collecting all these walking microbes in a garbage truck and incinerating them," or "a bullet to the back of the head." The SAQ staff, alarmed by the violent tone of the email and concerned for Beaumont's safety, gave Beaumont a copy of the email after police refused to intervene. Beaumont filed a human rights complaint on the ground of social condition and won her case. The Quebec Human Rights Tribunal awarded her $7,500 in moral damages (a category used to describe general damages in Quebec) and $500 in exemplary damages.[75]

"Social condition" is also protected in New Brunswick and the Northwest Territories, where it refers to a person who is a member of a socially identifiable group that suffers from social or economic disadvantage because of source of income or level of education.

Manitoba amended its human rights statute in 2012 to include "social disadvantage" as a discriminatory ground. "Social disadvantage means "diminished social standing or social regard due to (a) homelessness or inadequate housing, (b) low levels of education, (c) chronic low income, or (d) chronic unemployment or underemployment."[76]

"Social origin" is protected in Newfoundland and Labrador.

"Source of income" is protected in every jurisdiction in Canada except at the federal level, in New Brunswick, and in the Northwest Territories. In Ontario a person "in receipt of social assistance" receives human rights protection, albeit only for housing complaints. For example, a person who claims that he is refused an apartment because he is on welfare can file a complaint in Ontario. Being refused entry to a club or other membership-based organization is not, however, grounds for a complaint in Ontario, although it would be in Quebec. Ms Beaumont had a legitimate case in Quebec and in several of the jurisdictions mentioned above, but would not have been able to file a complaint in Ontario or at the federal level.

Language Rights are part of the broader category of human rights in international law and are specifically protected as civil and political rights in the ICCPR. In Canada, language rights are unique rights with their own status and legal history. Section 16 of the Charter states that English and French are the official languages of Canada. Sections 16 to 23 of the Charter establish the special status of these two official languages. In the federal sphere, the Official Languages Act designates a language ombudsperson, the commissioner of official languages, to ensure respect for official languages and to support the development of minority linguistic communities.[77] In New Brunswick, and to some extent in Ontario, language rights have their own separate legal base.[78] Quebec, for its part, protects the French language under the Charter of the French Language, better known as Bill 101.[79]

Aboriginal languages receive special status in several parts of Canada, especially the Territories. Other languages are not given special status but section 27 of the Charter says that the Charter "shall be interpreted in a manner consistent with the preservation and enhancement of the multicultural heritage of Canadians."

It is not my intention to review the state of language laws in Canada but rather to highlight the fact that language rights receive little protection in Canada from the perspective of human rights legislation. Only two jurisdictions in Canada protect language rights in their human rights statutes. Quebec's charter protects language rights, but the Quebec government periodically plans additional restrictions on the rights of English-speaking Quebecers, generating debate about whether English-language minority communities have any significant language rights.[80]

Yukon protects people on the grounds of linguistic background or origin but other provinces and territories do not deal specifically with language rights beyond the protections guaranteed to Aboriginal peoples.

Political Beliefs and/or Association: Freedom of conscience, thought, belief, and opinion are cornerstones of our democratic system and are protected by section 2(b) of the Canadian Charter. Freedom of association is also guaranteed in the Charter at section 2(d). Eight out of fourteen human rights laws in Canada prohibit discrimination based on political beliefs, views, or association.[81] Although it seems straightforward that

one's political beliefs or opinions should not be a valid basis for discrimination, six jurisdictions do not offer this protection as a human
rights ground, namely Alberta, British Columbia, Canada, Nunavut,
Ontario, and Saskatchewan.[82] These protections, like protections of
religious beliefs, are an example of how human rights systems protect
fundamental freedoms and integrate this category of rights into the legal
equality framework. They are also examples of rights that are not immutable personal characteristics, although it is true that political beliefs,
views, and religious faith are closely involved with an individual's personal identity and cannot be changed easily.

Hate Speech and Free Expression: Although few complaints are filed in
Canada on the ground of hate speech and discriminatory speech, this
issue has attracted enormous public attention. The Canadian Charter
protects free expression. Article 19 of the ICCPR upholds the right to
freedom of expression and opinion without interference.

As with all other rights, free expression is not an unlimited right.
Article 20 of the ICCPR provides that "Any advocacy of national, racial
or religious hatred that constitutes incitement to discrimination, hostility or violence shall be prohibited by law." The focus is on advocacy of
hatred in terms of its effects, not the advocacy itself. The prohibition
occurs if the speech incites violence, hostility, or discrimination. It is not
uncommon to hear the argument that incitement to violence is the only
valid justification for limiting hate speech, but this view is manifestly
inconsistent with Article 20, which explicitly includes incitement to discrimination and hostility as well.

At the federal level, section 13 of the CHRA, still in force at the time
of writing, prohibits using the Internet or telecommunications for communications that are "likely to expose people to hatred."[83] Alberta,
British Columbia, Saskatchewan, and the Northwest Territories prohibit
hate speech in publications and statements, although there are important
differences in the language and scope of their prohibitions. Alberta prohibits all statements and publications that expose a person or class of
persons to hatred and that indicate discrimination or an intention to
discriminate.[84] Manitoba prohibits statements that advocate discrimination, but only in respect of activities to which the code applies.

Quebec's Charter does not prohibit hate speech but it does offer safeguards for dignity, honour, and reputation by using libel and defamation
law. The leading case in this area in Quebec is the *Bou Malhab* case
against radio host André Arthur.[85] Over the air, Arthur said: "Why is it

that there are so many incompetent people and that the language of work is Creole or Arabic in a city that's French and English? ... I'm not very good at speaking 'nigger' ... [T]axis have really become the Third World of public transportation in Montreal ... Taxi drivers in Montreal are really arrogant, especially the Arabs. They're often rude, you can't be sure at all that they're competent and their cars don't look well maintained."[86]

Mr Malhab, an Arab taxi driver, sought to institute a class action on behalf of Arab and Creole-speaking Montreal taxi drivers. The member or members of the group who bring an action must show that they have suffered personal injury and in practice this means proving damage to reputation. In this case, the majority of the Supreme Court of Canada held that there could be no compensation because there had been no personal injury to the claimants. The Court did not rule out the possibility of a class action of this nature based on racist comments. However, in the context of a very large group of people with very different characteristics, the court held that no reasonable person would have believed that the comments had damaged the reputations of more than one thousand taxi drivers, and the suit failed.

In Ontario, Manitoba, the Atlantic Provinces, Yukon, and Nunavut, there is no protection against inciting hatred or discrimination except in the narrow category of "notices, signs and symbols." These prohibitions are designed to prevent incitements through discriminatory advertisements and the like, but beyond that, they do not address incitements to hatred or hostility.

These are only a few examples of the uneven protection available in Canada. Canadians do not enjoy equality before the law. Differences in rights protections are – or should be – a concern in a country where human rights have primacy and where equal protection under the law is a fundamental right. Consistency and coherence of decision-making are important markers of fairness and are difficult to achieve when so many jurisdictions have such different protections. Disparities in access to justice across the country are equally stark.

ACCESS TO JUSTICE AND FIRST AND SECOND GENERATION HUMAN RIGHTS SYSTEMS

The term "access to justice" can mean many things, from the formality of legal proceedings to the cost of lawyers or from the time it takes to resolve a case to the availability of alternative dispute resolution mechanisms.

This section discusses one facet of access to justice, the ability to place a case before a neutral decision-maker such as a tribunal. Access to an administrative decision-maker "may make the difference between justice and injustice being done. The rule of law is no less significant in an administrative hearing room or decision-making process than [in] a courtroom[.]"[87]

To understand how the Canadian human rights system attempts to address access to justice in the human rights context, it is important to distinguish between first and second-generation human rights systems. Although these terms are not officially part of the human rights lexicon, they serve as useful shorthand for the issues addressed in this chapter and in the book more generally. First-generation systems were the first kind of human rights system in Canada. The original idea was that an institution, a commission, would be the "first decider" on human rights complaints, acting as a "gatekeeper." Eleven out of fourteen jurisdictions in Canada are first-generation: the federal system, the Atlantic Provinces (New Brunswick, Newfoundland and Labrador, Nova Scotia, Prince Edward Island) the Prairie Provinces (Alberta, Manitoba, Saskatchewan), Quebec, the Northwest Territories, and Yukon. In order to ensure that commissions were not deciding cases they had themselves investigated, considerations of fairness and about bias led most jurisdictions to create separate and specialized tribunals. All first-generation systems except Saskatchewan's have two components: a human rights commission and a tribunal.[88] As noted before, Saskatchewan has a commission, which refers cases to a court.

First-generation systems do not render decisions on complaints, except for screening to decide whether they should go on to a tribunal for a full hearing.[89] The distinction between commissions and tribunals is sometimes blurred by the fact that some commissions call their referral decisions "final." They may be final as far as commissions are concerned, but the final decision on the case takes place elsewhere. Commissions make a substantive or determinative assessment on the merits of the case only in terms of deciding if the complaint falls outside the statutory remit of the commission.[90]

All commissions in first-generation systems receive and investigate complaints, acting as gatekeepers for the tribunal (or, again, in the case of Saskatchewan, the court). They attempt to settle cases, usually through mediation. Of the four largest systems in Canada (the federal, British Columbia, Ontario, and Quebec systems), only the federal system still has a commission that acts as the sole gatekeeper for its tribunal. Quebec is a first-generation system, but it allows people to bypass the commission entirely and file complaints directly with the courts, although, since this route is expensive, it is rarely used. Ontario's Commission no longer serves a screening function and British Columbia no longer has a commission.

Over the years, first-generation systems have come in for growing criticism. Human rights activists, lawyers, and community advocates have argued that these systems failed to provide access to justice because too many cases were screened out by commissions. Claims rarely reached a tribunal or took so long to do so that justice was denied. As one prominent human rights lawyer argued, first-generation systems failed to provide access to justice because a litigant with a strong case faced a great many barriers in getting access to a decision-maker: "We just wanted commissions to get out of the way and let us do our jobs."[91] Respondents were unhappy with the cost of long, drawn-out investigations, not to mention the frustration experienced by all parties when the whole process had to begin again from scratch at a tribunal.

Canadian organizations and advocates took their grievances about the lack of access to justice in first-generation human rights systems to the United Nations. In November 1998, the United Nations Committee on Economic, Social and Cultural Rights, in its third periodic review of Canada, recommended that "all human rights claims not settled through mediation [be] promptly determined before a competent Human Rights Tribunal, with the provision of legal aid to vulnerable groups."[92] The UN Human Rights Committee, which oversees the ICCPR, made similar comments, and repeated them in 2006 in its observations on Canada:

> The Committee regrets that its previously expressed concern relating to the inadequacy of remedies for violations of articles 2, 3 and 26 of the Covenant remains unaddressed. It is concerned that human rights commissions still have the power to refuse referral of a human rights complaint for adjudication and that legal aid for access to courts may not be available.
>
> *The State party should ensure that the relevant human rights legislation is amended at federal, provincial and territorial levels and its legal system enhanced, so that all victims of discrimination have full and effective access to a competent tribunal and to an effective remedy.*[93] [Emphasis in original.]

Scholars, practitioners, and activists commented publicly on these developments, which were instrumental for Bill 107 in Ontario, which created direct access in Canada's largest human rights system.[94] Claimants now make application directly to the tribunal and there is no prior investigation. Tribunals screen, mediate, and decide on complaints.

British Columbia and Nunavut moved to second-generation systems five years earlier, but neither has a commission.

The principal reason for divergent levels of access to justice is structural and depends on the differences between first-generation and second-generation systems. Quebec and Ontario illustrate the stark disparities between different levels of access to justice. On paper, Quebec (a first-generation system) has a progressive human rights statute. However, only a small number of cases filed with the Quebec Commission, about 5 percent, ever make it past the screening process to go on to the Quebec Human Rights Tribunal.[95]

Ontario's second-generation system allows all applicants direct access to its tribunal and about 80 percent of cases make it past the tribunal's preliminary screening stages.[96] Ontario thus offers an extremely high level of access to justice in terms of access to a neutral decision-maker, while Quebec is among the least accessible human rights jurisdictions in the country. A complainant is at least fifteen times more likely to get to a tribunal in Ontario (after preliminary screening) than in Quebec.

REMEDIES

The Supreme Court of Canada has said, "[h]uman rights remedies must be accessible in order to be effective."[97] In other words, it is all very well to have rights, but if a person cannot seek justice by asking that discriminatory behaviour be stopped, or by asking for compensation, then rights mean very little. The ability to access remedies is another basic part of access to justice.

Human rights systems aim to compensate victims and eradicate discrimination.[98] What qualifies as compensation varies considerably in Canada. Some jurisdictions only permit claimants to recoup pecuniary damages, meaning direct or tangible damages. Nova Scotia limits damages to "any injury."

Most other jurisdictions permit some form of non-pecuniary damages. The language used to describe this category varies widely and includes kinds of damage such as moral damages, damages for loss of dignity, or for pain and suffering. Amounts can vary significantly. For example, the CHRA caps damages for pain and suffering at $20,000. In Ontario, there is no longer any cap on awards, and a 2012 Ontario report recommended that the Ontario Human Rights Tribunal significantly increase its awards of damages in this category.[99]

Even though "compensation" is the objective most closely associated with human rights complaints, the second objective, namely protecting the public interest by eradicating discrimination, should not be forgotten. Half the systems in Canada (federal, Manitoba, Northwest Territories, Nunavut, Quebec, Saskatchewan, and Yukon) fulfill this objective by providing for an exceptional form of damages called exemplary, special, or punitive damages. While it is arguable that these types of damages are a form of compensation, they also have a public interest dimension in underscoring the significance of human rights and signalling the consequences of especially egregious behaviour, which is usually but not always the behaviour of respondents.[100] The CHRA refers to this as "special compensation." Manitoba, the Northwest Territories, Nunavut, Quebec, and Saskatchewan allow punitive damage awards against the respondent. Yukon permits exemplary damages against *complainants* in the event that a complaint is found to be frivolous, vexatious, or is based on false information, thereby causing injury to the respondent's reputation.[101] For example, if a complainant has a personal conflict with someone and files a human rights complaint as a form of vengeance, knowing that the allegations are untrue but with the objective of embarrassing and humiliating the respondent, in the Yukon human rights system a respondent would have the right to seek damages.

Another category is systemic remedies aimed at eradicating discrimination.[102] These necessarily go beyond individual complaints and have remedial repercussions not only for the complainant but also for people who are in the same or similar circumstances. They are directly aimed at eradicating discrimination but do not necessarily have a compensatory dimension.

For example, racial minorities and women have filed human rights complaints over their inability to get firefighting jobs due to height and weight requirements. Such requirements were standard for many years because they served as proxies to ensure that firefighters had the requisite physical capacity. However, closer inspection revealed that not all these criteria are genuine job requirements. Human rights orders to change these requirements have meant that people of shorter stature and women have been eligible to compete for these positions, and a more open recruitment process has allowed employers to determine whether applicants are capable of doing the job. Such orders have a long history of being upheld by the courts: they modify or eliminate discriminatory rules, systems, and practices and make a difference not only for claimants but also for other people in the same situation.[103]

While systemic remedies are standard in human rights systems, they are not as broadly formulated in the courts, which tend to be more closely focused on remedies for the plaintiff. Systemic orders may have been restricted by a Supreme Court case in 2012 called *Moore*.[104] *Moore* dealt with a British Columbia school board's decision to eliminate remedial learning supports for children with severe learning disabilities. The tribunal had not only granted financial compensation to the child's parents but had provided systemic orders against other parties. The first of these ordered the British Columbia government to allocate funding based on actual incidence levels of severe learning disabilities. It also ordered that the province establish mechanisms to ensure that accommodations for students were appropriate and meet legislative and policy goals. In addition, school districts were required to have a range of services to meet the needs of students with severe learning disabilities. The second order was against the school district and its delivery mechanisms and was aimed at ensuring that the services met stated legislative and policy goals.[105] In its ruling the Court sought to establish a unified approach to human rights remedies for both individual and systemic discrimination. It held that, although individual remedies can have a broad impact, complainants must be at the centre of all remedial orders. It ordered that systemic evidence should not be used to widen courts' remedies beyond the initial claims.[106] The Supreme Court's ruling in *Moore* did not uphold the systemic orders.

It would be unfortunate if "compensation" were so narrowly construed that litigants were forced to repeatedly initiate cases on the same grounds in order to change discriminatory rules or systems. It is possible that the Court was sending a message about the care needed in framing complaints at the outset and about framing remedies in a way that is relevant to the complainant's case. It is also possible that the presence of regulatory agencies such as human rights commissions as parties to the case at the outset of cases would have facilitated framing the remedies in a way that addressed the broader arguments in the public interest. However, this was not possible in British Columbia because there is no commission.

I believe the court was mistaken in applying the narrower approach used by courts to human rights tribunals. Most human rights laws in Canada permit tribunals to make a wide range of remedial orders, including special programs and plans, employment equity programs, ordering steps that have an "ameliorative effect" on the discriminatory practice, and orders to do or to refrain from doing "anything" linked to the human rights violation.[107] Like many other regulatory agencies, human rights commissions have historically taken a broad range of interests into consideration and sought to develop solutions that balance benefits and costs for many parties.[108] In the rush to centre remedies on claimants, and to force tribunals to do the same, the Court appears to have placed less emphasis on eradicating discrimination and more on a formal and highly structured approach to remedies that ignores the broader remedial authority contained in many human rights laws.

A good example of a broader remedial approach is a 2005 incident involving racial profiling case of a young Black man in Ottawa. Chad Aiken was pulled over by police in 2005 on the grounds that the car's occupants were not wearing seatbelts. They had, however, been wearing seatbelts and the encounter quickly became hostile and confrontational. Quick thinking by Aiken's girlfriend meant that the exchange was recorded.

Aiken: Can I get your badge number sir?
Police: No, you can't.
Aiken: Why can't...
Police: 666 is my badge number...
Aiken: Why can't I get your badge number? And your name is...
Police: 666! Constable Hollett.
Aiken: You're not gonna give me your badge number at all?
[Pause]
Police: You got two seconds to get in the [police] car.[109]

Aiken alleges he was then taken into custody and assaulted. As of the date of writing, the police force claims that it has been unable to identify the officer. A human rights complaint was filed. Aiken was represented by the African Canadian Legal Clinic (ACLC). After several years, the matter went to a hearing at the Human Rights Tribunal of Ontario. In 2013, the matter was settled between the Ontario Human Rights Commission and the Ottawa police. One of the settlement terms was a two-year study, one of the largest ever undertaken in Canada, to track the race of people pulled over in traffic stops. Two things are noteworthy about the settlement. The first is that Aiken himself did not agree to it: according to an interview with his lawyer from the ACLC, Aiken wanted a broader settlement that addressed random pedestrian stops as well as vehicle stops. At the time of writing, Aiken was planning to continue his case before the tribunal.[110] In the end, the settlement with the commission had nothing to do with the complainant and therefore it was not compensatory. The commission was exercising its responsibility to work in the public interest to eradicate discrimination and build a culture of human rights using a broad approach to solutions addressing the interests of many parties, not all of whom were involved in Aiken's specific situation. The second noteworthy aspect of the case was that a prospective two-year monitoring study is not the type of forward-looking remedy that a court would normally order, or over which it would retain jurisdiction. But it is the type of systemic order that is integral to the functions of human rights systems and their work in building a human rights culture.

It is not clear what the *Moore* case will mean for cases like Aiken's and for systemic orders in the future, or whether there are now differences between other jurisdictions and British Columbia where the *Moore* case occurred.[111] Legal observers will be keeping a careful eye on systemic remedies as a result of the *Moore* case.

Accountability and Independence

There is a public perception that human rights systems, and commissions in particular, are unaccountable in law and unaccountable to the public more generally. This perception was widely propagated during the hate-speech debates. Former Liberal M P Keith Martin recycled many of the inaccuracies about the Canadian Human Rights Commission that were in circulation at the time, including the curious claim that "commissions" are unaccountable to Parliament.[112] (The CHRC is the only commission in Canada accountable to Parliament because it is, of course, the only federal human rights commission in Canada.) Martin's comments attracted a good deal of support and media attention, in part because they resonated with the feeling among some of the public that human rights commissions are not only antithetical to fundamental freedoms but are also unaccountable and therefore undemocratic.

Human rights systems in Canada are subject to at least three interconnected layers of accountability: judicial oversight by the courts, reporting requirements under human rights laws, and controls exercised by the executive branch of government through the public service hierarchy and public administration rules and practices. All three layers of account-ability operate within the framework of their own statutes, the Charter, and administrative law.[113]

As noted earlier, human rights commissions and tribunals are consti-tutionally part of the executive arm of government, not the judiciary. As such, they are subject to administrative law, a well-developed set of legal principles that govern all agencies, boards, and commissions. There are hundreds of these in Canada, including labour relations bodies, employ-ment standards agencies, refugee determination boards, rental tribunals, and a host of others. These types of institutions are not "junior, imitation or quasi-courts. They are instrumentalities of government policy that are, nonetheless, required to act fairly."[114] Although they form part of the executive branch from a legal perspective, their human rights activi-ties must be carried out independently. The fact that they are not courts does not make tribunals illegal, rogue, or arbitrary dispensers of justice.

Human rights systems are accountable to the executive branch or to the legislature through legal requirements that they file annual reports accounting for their expenditures and describing their activities. The administrative heads of commissions are normally accountable to a minister or deputy minister in their host ministries. In Canada, Quebec, and Yukon, where commissions have more structural independence, chief commissioners are accountable to Parliament, the National Assembly, and the legislature, respectively. In addition, the public service imposes administrative controls through budget processes, business planning, performance measures, audits, and other rules that apply to the entire public service. These controls ensure, or are supposed to ensure, fiscal probity, good internal governance, and compliance with public service standards.

It may seem contradictory that commissions and tribunals are sup-posed to operate at arm's length and independently from government on the one hand and yet demonstrate accountability on the other. However, independence refers to decision-making on complaints and substantive human rights work generally. Institutions must be free from bias, reason-able apprehensions of bias, internal collusion, and external manipula-tion. Independence in this sense does not mean that human rights systems can do whatever they want, but rather that they must be free from politi-cal or improper interference in their human rights work. Independence does not diminish accountability and it does not mean that commissions or tribunals are exempt from the application of the Charter. The Supreme

Court of Canada has observed that independence from government is not the same thing as lack of accountability under the Charter: "the Commission ... cannot ... escape Charter scrutiny merely because it is not part of government or controlled by government."[115]

The balance between accountability and independence can be tricky. Human rights systems are routinely required to handle cases where their paymaster, the government, is a respondent to complaints. Commissions frequently take policy positions aimed at changing legislation and government practices. They make public statements that may be unpopular with those in power. It is critical that all parties are secure in the knowledge that there will be no interference or collusion in the process of handling complaints or in policy development. Business, union, and stakeholder interests hold greater or lesser sway over government policy, depending on which party is in power, and they can make their influence felt in many ways. Independence is of the utmost importance in protecting the ability to speak out on contentious issues without undue prior restraint or interference. At the risk of stating the obvious, decisions on human rights complaints, about which policy decisions, and about which issues to speak up about should not depend on who is in power.

The question of broader accountability to the public for human rights commissions is complex. Human rights commissions are public policy actors in their own right: they have legal responsibilities to achieve particular goals and to further a culture of human rights. As discussed in chapter 2, human rights commissions have their roots in social movements and it is not surprising that civil society organizations such as human rights NGOs sometimes assume that commissions should share views similar to their own. Respondent organizations such as businesses, schools, and retail services naturally have a different view. The reality is that various constituencies and organizations use commissions to achieve their own disparate – if not diametrically opposed – goals. Commissions must move carefully among these various interests, stakeholders, and advocates, fulfilling their legal mandate while managing a delicate relationship with the government authorities that control their funding, make appointments, and decide which members will or will not be renewed in their positions.

Navigating these disparate interests is complex, but it reinforces rather than detracts from the public accountability of human rights systems as instruments of both law and policy. People sometimes overlook these facts amidst accusations that commissions are an affront to democracy and that – a personal favourite – they should be "tamed" or reined in.[116]

CANADA AND THE INTERNATIONAL
HUMAN RIGHTS SYSTEM

When Canada ratifies human rights treaties, the rights they contain do not automatically take effect within Canada. For a variety of reasons that are beyond the scope of this book, Canada's constitutional structure requires that Canada implement international commitments before they have any legal effect within Canada. Usually, this is done by enacting laws, although in some instances Canada has taken the position that policy initiatives will suffice. The Charter and human rights laws are examples of how national law is used to implement international human rights obligations. Even without legislation, the Supreme Court has said that international commitments have "a critical influence on the interpretation of the scope of the rights included in the *Charter*."[117] In 1987, Chief Justice Brian Dickson said that the interpretation of the Charter conforms to the spirit of the "contemporary international human rights movement."[118] International human rights law exerts an important influence over the Charter.[119]

There are also other, practical, reasons for caring about international law, according to Max Yalden, former chief commissioner of the Canadian Human Rights Commission.

In the first place, much of our Canadian human rights law and practice finds its origins in international declarations and covenants, to which Canadians have contributed substantially. A further reason is simply that sound international standards and effective machinery for observing and checking on their implementation can only improve the chances for human rights on the domestic scene as well.

Moreover, the whole process of global rule-making, including the establishment of international human rights norms and monitoring bodies ... represent[s] the world community's best effort to establish a form of international legitimacy for standards that would be tantamount to legal requirements in the domestic context.[120]

While human rights commissions derive their authority from their own laws, international law is an important source of inspiration and guidance and the "outside-in" effect of international norms has an impact on the work of human rights commissions. International law helps provide content, context, and meaning to human rights standards that might otherwise be unspecified or disputed. In the 1990s, for example, the

Ontario Human Rights Commission began systematically using international human rights standards as a basis for its interpretation of the Ontario Human Rights Code as it developed its own policies and guidelines.[121]

International law affects not only the way law is interpreted at home but also how human rights commissions interact with the international human rights system. More recently, international instruments have called on states to designate what are called independent "mechanisms" or institutions to protect and promote rights. Human rights commissions are natural candidates to take up these functions and responsibilities.[122]

The Paris Principles require NHRIS to promote the ratification of international human rights instruments, thereby encouraging countries to undertake important commitments to fulfill human rights obligations. For countries that have already ratified human rights instruments such as the ICCPR, the UN authorizes NHRIS to submit reports to the corresponding UN treaty bodies or committees. UN procedures usually allow human rights commissions to attend meetings in their own right when delegations from their countries are presenting reports. Since 2007, ICC-accredited NHRIS with an "A" status (i.e., institutions that are fully compliant with the Paris Principles) have been entitled to make oral statements, submit documents, and have separate seating in all sessions of the UN Human Rights Council.[123] NHRIS can also participate in other international fora, treaty bodies, and mechanisms to provide alternative or complementary information to the reports submitted by their countries.[124]

Such activities should not detract from commissions' mandated human rights work at home, but instead pave the way for commissions to learn from developments in other countries and to communicate their views independently to the international community about what is happening in their own country.

CONCLUSION

Human rights systems in Canada are part of an international family of institutions that have the legal responsibility to promote and protect human rights. The type of structure with which we are most familiar in Canada is the human rights commission, which is also the most prevalent form of human rights institution worldwide. Canadian human rights systems offer superior protection compared to many international institutions for several reasons. First, they have a strong and long-standing institutional base as part of the Canadian public human rights infra-structure and, second, commissions can refer cases directly to tribunals and courts, resulting in binding orders. In practice, this means that claimants can obtain legal, enforceable remedies. Canadian human rights systems are either first or second-generation systems. In first-generation systems, commissions play a gatekeeping function in addi-tion to their role of building a rights culture. With the exception of Saskatchewan, all first-generation human rights systems in Canada have both a commission and a tribunal.

Although human rights systems in Canada are broadly similar, they offer uneven protection to Canadians in terms of rights, the way in which rights can be accessed, and the remedies that are available. The diversity of Canadian human rights systems from the institutional, legal, and functional perspectives is not entirely negative: Canada boasts a rich diversity of institutions that create a dynamic social laboratory capable of providing important information about how well each system is working. It also permits us to discover how different rights are evolving and to assess which types of systems are most effective in protecting and promoting human rights. Some differences allow for flexibility in policy approaches and in responses that are sensitive to regional and local reali-ties. On the other hand, this diversity means that people in Canada are not all equal before the law: they do not enjoy the same rights, the same degree of access to a neutral decision-maker, or the same types of reme-dies for human rights violations.

Human rights systems provide independent oversight and must be at arm's length from government. At the same time, they must be account-able for their performance and for compliance with government stan-dards with regard to the administrative aspects of their work. Contrary to popular impression, human rights systems are in fact accountable through the mechanisms noted earlier (e.g., reporting requirements, public service administrative controls) and are further subject to judicial oversight, principles of administrative law, and, of course, the Charter. While accountability is central to the legitimacy and effectiveness of any public institution, human rights institutions require specific types of independence in order to do their work with a degree of neutrality and with minimal political interference or influence. However, under both administrative law and international standards, Canadian human rights commissions and tribunals only partially meet standards of indepen-dence, impartiality, and competence. These issues will be discussed fur-ther in chapter 4.

Finally, human rights institutions have an important but poorly understood role to play at the international level. They now have far more opportunities to interact with the international human rights system. These new procedures permit greater levels of formal and structured intervention than were available when human rights systems first emerged in Canada more than half a century ago. They also permit national human rights institutions to provide input into the Universal Periodic Review Process of the United Nations.

The next chapter examines more closely the development of equality law and human rights systems as instruments of law and policy. It considers the way in which their evolution has affected our understanding of how human rights commissions and tribunals function, and the public understanding of their roles and responsibilities.

2

Human Rights Systems Then and Now

We would not have the Charter we have now had it not been for the grass-roots and social movements that created a culture of human rights and that made it all possible.

Mary Eberts[1]

This chapter looks at the development of human rights systems as the product of social movements and as vehicles of public policy. Contemporary human rights systems are fashioned from different strands of civil, political, economic, and social rights, and are bound together by equality law into a single regulatory framework. The evolution of human rights laws spans seven decades, from the early anti-discrimination prohibitions in the 1930s and 1940s to the fair practices laws in the 1950s, the first consolidated human rights laws in the 1960s and 1970s, and the emergence of second-generation human rights systems in the 2000s.

There are already many excellent histories of human rights systems in Canada, and this chapter does not try to summarize or synthesize them.[2] Rather, I consider different perspectives that show how our understanding of discrimination and equality has evolved, focusing on three forces that have been particularly influential: social movements, the legal school of thought called functionalism, and the confluence and mutual reinforcement of international developments after the Second World War that resulted in domestic pressures to comply with international human rights norms. All these developments were linked to the broader moral reordering ushered in by a wider recognition of human rights, which has extended and continues to extend well beyond Canada. Before embarking on that discussion it is helpful to glance back and look at the circumstances that prepared the ground for these developments.

LOOKING BACK

Canada's human rights systems evolved for a simple reason: before they existed, there was no effective recourse against discrimination and the courts were unwilling or unable to create one. In a post-Charter Canada, it may be difficult to imagine a world where people who experienced discrimination had no way of seeking redress. Roderick A. Macdonald, F.R. Scott Professor of Constitutional and Public Law at McGill University's Faculty of Law and one of Canada's most distinguished scholars, draws a portrait of Canada's legal landscape before the 1950s for his students, pointing out that there was no general protection against discrimination. "When I teach my law students, I bring them back to a different period. It was a period when law was understood and applied quite differently. [They must] cast their minds back and imagine a different society and a different legal environment than the one that we have today."[3]

Macdonald highlights two well-known cases. In 1939, in *Christie v. York*, the Supreme Court of Canada upheld a tavern owner's refusal to serve a Black man, Fred Christie, a beer after a hockey game.[4] The Court held that freedom of contract prevailed and that merchants were entitled to do business with whomever they choose. This was not the only time such discrimination had occurred – Blacks had been refused service in theatres and hotels in other cases.[5] The idea of laissez-faire generally prevailed and allowed such practices to continue. According to Macdonald, laissez-faire means that "you do not use notions of equality to overturn agreements that are freely negotiated, you do not use the courts to palliate inequities, and you do not engage in parallel exercises of justice to redistribute wealth or social goods."[6]

Another well-known example involves the practice of using restrictive covenants to prohibit the sale of land to anyone other than White gentiles.[7] In 1945, a case called *Re Drummond Wren* defied the judicial conservatism of cases like *Christie v. York* and attempted to establish human rights as part of Canada's underlying principles of public policy. Drummond Wren, a White man, successfully challenged a discriminatory restriction that prohibited transferring his land to "Jews and persons of objectionable nationality."[8]

Although *Drummond Wren* was celebrated, it was a somewhat qualified victory. The parties had sought to apply the 1944 Racial Discrimination Act (RDA), an early anti-racism law in Canada.[9] The RDA, however, prohibited only the publication or display of discriminatory notices, signs, and symbols. It did not prohibit racist restrictions contained in deeds of property, and could not easily be used to resolve property disputes. In his ruling Justice Mackay acknowledged that the RDA expressed what he described as the public policy against discrimination that he was uphold-ing in striking down the covenant. *Drummond Wren* was a short-lived victory: only six years later the Supreme Court of Canada declined to apply it in another case involving a restrictive covenant on a sale of land.[10] Despite its failure to take root, Macdonald calls the *Drummond Wren* decision "remarkable and courageous for its time."[11]

Drummond Wren became the exception that proved the laissez-faire rule. Attempts to use the courts to prohibit discrimination were failing because there was no broader culture of human rights, let alone an acceptance of "notions of equality" that could overcome accepted prac-tices. As a result, there was no pressure on legislatures to enact protec-tions. The rule of laissez-faire predominated until it was upended by two developments. One was social movements, including the civil rights movement. The second was a legal school of thought called functional-ism that helped legislatures see regulatory agencies as public policy tools. Together, these two developments fostered an environment that was more hospitable to progressive laws and favoured the development of a regulatory response by legislators that made rights real in practice.

Social Movements for Human Rights

Human rights owe a good deal to the activism of social movements such as grassroots organizations, the civil rights movement, and organized labour. Dominique Clément, a sociologist who studies the evolution of human rights and human rights systems in Canada, argues that human rights are not simply legal tools lying around waiting to be picked up and used.[12] Rather, rights are developed and shaped by hard work and community efforts. Social movements and the people and groups behind them were at the heart of the early human rights movement in Canada.[13]

A few civil liberties associations had begun to appear in the 1930s, some of which had been formed following the Gouzenko affair in 1946. Igor Gouzenko was a Soviet cipher clerk who defected to Canada in 1945 and provided the Canadian government with information about Soviet-managed espionage in Canada. His information prompted the federal government to use the War Measures Act to suspend the usual rights and freedoms, and several suspected spies were arrested, detained, and denied legal rights such as access to counsel.[14] The Gouzenko affair prompted the formation of several groups to protest the government's abuse of individual rights, which brought the issue of civil liberties to public attention.

Between the 1930s and the 1960s, workers' committees and trade unions pressed to integrate equality rights into the labour movement. The Jewish Labour Committee (JLC) was among the most important of these groups in Canada. According to Alan Borovoy, the JLC was originally established in the United States and moved north to alert Canadians to the dangers of Nazism. After the Second World War, the JLC turned its attention to mobilizing the labour movement against racism.

Borovoy identifies labour activist and organizer Kalmen Kaplansky as having played a crucial role: "I wish [Kalmen Kaplansky] had had more credit for what he did. Kaplansky came to Canada in about 1929 and got active in the labour movement, becoming the first director of the Canadian Jewish Labour Committee, an offshoot of the US group ... Morris Lewis, father of David, was the secretary of the Jewish Labour Committee at that time ... Kaplansky came up with the idea of a network of labour movements across Canada ... and he was the driving force behind the creation of the Toronto Joint Labour Committee to Combat Racial Intolerance in 1947."[15]

Clément observes that Kaplansky, like many people working in similar groups at that time, was not working from a broad conception of human rights – many of the concepts, norms, and legal frameworks that we use today had not yet emerged. But he was aware of the need for a wider constituency and advocacy base than the Jewish community alone could provide, recognizing that single-group advocacy would be less effective than a wider coalition.

The JLC sought partners and allies in the Black community. The head of the African Canadian Legal Clinic, Margaret Parsons, highlighted the relationship between the Black and Jewish communities at that time: "African-Americans were very powerfully supporting Jewish communities and families. They were often the only ones who gave us a chance. The same was true in Canada. My mother cleaned houses for Jewish families. They were the only ones who would hire us."[16]

Ontario had introduced the RDA in 1944 (just before the *Drummond Wren* case). It prohibited newspapers and radio stations from publishing or displaying notices, signs, symbols, emblems, or other representations indicating racial discrimination, a term that was understood to cover both race and creed.[17] In 1947, the Saskatchewan Bill of Rights Act went even further, not only prohibiting discrimination but protecting civil liberties such as free speech, legal rights, voting rights, and the right to peaceful assembly.[18]

Neither the RDA nor the Saskatchewan Bill of Rights was very successful: for one thing, they relied on criminal prosecution, a heavy-handed and ultimately ineffective way to protect human rights, let alone promote them as part of a broad public policy. Although Saskatchewan's Bill of Rights prohibited discrimination, Ken Norman, a professor of law at the University of Saskatchewan, observed that he was not aware of any successful discrimination claims under that legislation.[19] Complainants were left on their own to attempt to seek justice before the courts.

In the 1950s and 1960s, labour groups worked with the civil rights movement and focused on a narrow range of social and economic areas related to employment, housing, and services customarily available to the public. The movement at that time was dominated by men; women were notably absent in the work of early civil liberties groups in Canada.[20] Discussing his research on civil liberties organizations in the 1950s and 1960s in Canada, Clément observed:

> I was very surprised – it was about racial and ethnic minorities – but not much else. Women's rights were ignored. Even the work of the *women's* committees in early rights movements was not focused on women's rights! The civil liberties movement was a very male movement, one dominated by the Jewish community taking a leadership role in the 1950s and 1960s. [It] focused on certain forms of anti-discrimination, but nothing on discrimination against women ... People like Vivien Mahood, and later on Mary Eberts, Rosie Abella, and others, would have a very important role, but overall, at the time, it was very male.[21]

The challenge was to broaden the reach of laws prohibiting discrimination and, most importantly, to create something more effective than criminal prohibitions to deal with discrimination – something that would help to change people's minds and hearts. Ken Norman recalled his first encounter with this idea when he was a law student:

> I am a kid from a small town in Saskatchewan. When I was a law student, there was another kid from a small town, Walter Tarnopolsky. He was my teacher in law school. He had the idea of Human Rights Commissions, the idea of the iron hand in the velvet

glove. "The trouble with rights on paper," he would say, "is that they are not rights in action." Tarnopolsky criticized Tommy Douglas's 1947 [Saskatchewan] Bill of Rights. It was only enforceable by a form of criminal prosecution – no one could bring a complaint ... so you were left with private prosecution. It was not access to justice.[22]

Without a civil or administrative law process to allow people to bring complaints, a quasi-criminal process or the criminal law system was the only recourse. Moreover, criminal law has its own objectives, which include punishment, deterrence, and retribution. An alternative was needed that would create a regulatory process that did not involve criminal prosecution but would make it possible to bring a complaint and seek justice. The idea that a regulatory commission could serve this function, not only by receiving complaints but by promoting a broader culture of human rights through education and awareness, was a new approach. It combined the ideas of furthering civil liberties, combating discrimination, and creating the right to equality in key areas: employment, housing, and public services. And it was completely different from criminal law and would improve access to justice. This regulatory approach would ultimately be implemented by legislatures, helped by a nudge from a legal concept called functionalism.

Functionalism

The standard histories of human rights laws in Canada usually go back to the 1940s. There had, however, been isolated legislative efforts to create such laws in the 1930s. A prohibition against discrimination based on race, ethnicity, and religion appeared in a 1932 Ontario statute regulating risk assessments for automobile insurance.[23] In 1933 in British Columbia, discrimination was prohibited in unemployment and relief works.[24] A year later, Manitoba enacted a group libel law, pre-dating by more than four decades the anti-discrimination provisions in contemporary human rights laws against hate speech.[25]

Fair practices laws arrived in the 1950s and targeted employment discrimination in the private sector, the public sector, and in trade unions. Small employers and nonprofit organizations were exempt.[26] The Supreme Court of Canada described these laws as "designed to eliminate discriminatory treatment of a person on grounds [that are] irrelevant to the substantive considerations involved [based on] criteria that were offensive and violative of equality before the law."[27]

In the late 1950s, members of a labour committee had gone to see the premier of Ontario, Leslie Frost, to encourage fair practices legislation prohibiting discrimination in housing. Frost reportedly responded that the province was not ready.[28] In 1961, Alan Borovoy organized a large deputation that included labour, municipal, and church groups, and Frost conceded that the time might have come. Borovoy had prepared a brief on the proposed legislation and, ultimately, the legislation passed. According to Borovoy, "This was a huge victory for the community at the time."[29]

Anti-discrimination protection emerged slowly, but protections were fragmented. Over time specific protections eventually coalesced into a more holistic concept of human rights,[30] an iterative evolution that is shared by many other branches of law.[31] The shift from fragmentary rights to a concept of human rights is often described as having occurred in the mid-to-late 1940s with the birth of the United Nations and the 1948 Universal Declaration of Human Rights. However the impetus for the kind of institution that would protect and promote those rights came in part from another idea, that of functionalism. Rod Macdonald credits functionalism with creating the framework for a different way of thinking about laws and the institutions needed to implement laws. Citing the writings of Karl Llewellyn and Felix Cohen in the 1920s and 1930s, as well as the influential legal materials of the 1950s by Henry Hart and Albert Sacks from Harvard, Macdonald describes this aspect of the work of legal realists in terms of the practical utility of law rather than its theory.[32] Llewellyn is famously associated with the idea that rights on paper are worse than useless; the real test is the measure of what institutions and judges do about disputes.[33] By encouraging people to look at what institutions actually do with law and how they apply it, this new framework helped people realize "just what might be possible using law in a democratic society."[34]

The idea of implementing human rights laws by using commissions – public agencies with a regulatory responsibility for protecting and promoting human rights and fostering a culture of rights – offered a different approach from the earlier, criminal-oriented statutes. It also allowed an end run around the faint-hearted judiciary of the mid-twentieth century, putting the power and possibility of law in the hands of the executive branch by using a regulatory agency.

In New York, a commission to combat discrimination had been created at the state level through the 1945 Ives-Quinn Law against Discrimination, the first state legislation to prohibit discrimination in employment.[35] Modeled in part on President Roosevelt's 1941 Fair Employment Practices Commission, the Ives-Quinn law created the New York State Commission against Discrimination, which had specific jurisdiction over the private sector. The commission's business was to investigate complaints and attempt reasonable settlements or resolutions, preferably without litigation.

The bipartisan Ives-Quinn law was supported by Black, Jewish, Catholic, and immigrant communities. It was attacked by those who felt that human rights laws should not be used in an idealistic attempt to control employers or infringe on freedoms, in particular laissez-faire approaches and freedom of commerce.[36]

In Canada, Alan Borovoy and F.R. Scott were among the activists who pushed for institutions that would "do something" about human rights and human rights disputes. They saw commissions as a way of moving from criminal prosecution to investigating cases in an administrative context and to actively promoting rights in the public and private sectors, targeting businesses and services as well as government.[37] Efforts to create a commission in Ontario encountered opposition similar to that in New York and Ken Norman recalled strong attacks on the proposed creation of the Ontario Human Rights Commission.

> Ontario was taking a lot of flak at the time for the same sort of "kangaroo court" arguments that you hear from Mark Steyn and Ezra Levant and others. Guys like Ian Hunter could go the distance with today's anti-rights activists. Hunter thought that commissions were Mephistopheles, if not the devil. I ended up writing a series of articles talking about why administrative tribunals should be set up and why they are a good thing. I explained the need for human rights commissions as an administrative response to a need. A lot of what is being said now [about human rights commissions] was also being said back then in the context of developments in Ontario.[38]

Ultimately, opposition was overcome in Ontario in 1961, as it had been in New York almost two decades earlier. The disparate strands of anti-discrimination provisions and fair practices laws were consolidated into a single statute, the Ontario Human Rights Code, within a regulatory framework that also applied to the private sector.[39] A year later, Nova Scotia followed suit. Between 1963 and 1970, Alberta, New Brunswick, Prince Edward Island, British Columbia, Newfoundland, and Manitoba enacted their own human rights legislation.

Quebec enacted its Charter of Human Rights and Freedoms in 1975.[40] Its procedures, at least on paper, offer access to justice by providing two options for complainants to file human rights complaints: directly in the courts or with the human rights commission. In developing its own Charter, Quebec benefitted from experiences in other jurisdictions over more than a decade, while also drawing on international human rights law to enhance the protection of economic and social rights as well as protections for civil and political rights as an integral part of the human rights framework.

Saskatchewan embarked on a similar initiative a few years later. Ken Norman was teaching law at the University of Saskatchewan when he was appointed chairman of the Saskatchewan Human Rights Commission (SHRC) in June of 1978:

> At that point, the commission had no substantive law of its own to administer. It only had carriage of complaints under fair employment and accommodation practices statutes. I spent the next several months working on a comprehensive human rights code draft, drawing from Ontario, BC, Quebec, and the US Civil Rights Act. In the latter regard, I proposed a regulatory role for the commission with regard to "affirmative action." And, drawing from Quebec, I proposed incorporating the fundamental freedoms of the Saskatchewan Bill of Rights into the Code ... Thanks to a new electoral mandate, the NDP government saw fit to introduce my draft absent my proposal to add sexual orientation into the Legislative Assembly in May of 1979. And, with almost no debate the Code was enacted and I became the first chief commissioner of the SHRC.[41]

Norman observed that the bill "sailed through the Legislative Assembly," avoiding most of the fierce criticism that had marked the debate in Ontario.[42]

Three factors were instrumental to the success of a functional approach leading to a regulatory response. First, as noted earlier, Canadian courts had shown themselves to be unwilling or unable to develop the law in the area of human rights, which encouraged social movements to push legislators to step in and enact progressive laws that applied to the private as well as the public sectors. Second, it was recognized that an independent and specialized human rights system could use regulatory powers and could draw on decision-makers with expertise in human rights. As well, a commission, as a public agency, would bear the costs of investigating claims.[43]

"You need an administrative agency that has these programmatic objectives conferred by law. A commission can take the big idea of human rights and translate it into [an] operational reality," Norman argued. That "big idea" was expressed in the UN's 1948 Universal Declaration of Human Rights (UDHR).[44] "Through education, rule-making, and policy development, one could do things that only an administrative agency with a broad program for promoting and protecting rights could do, using tools that only an administrative agency can achieve. These are not things a judge can do."[45]

Another impetus for the emergence of a human rights system was international human rights law. The UDHR[46] was an inspiration for Canadian human rights legislation and indeed the preambles of most human rights laws contain language that mirrors the UDHR. Its powerful language served to anchor Canada's first wave of consolidated human rights statutes in the broad norms of international human rights law and in an inclusive vision that continues to underpin human rights statutes today.[47]

In 1976, Canada acceded to the International Covenant on Civil and Political Rights (ICCPR).[48] This accession coincided roughly with the enactment of the Canadian Human Rights Act (CHRA),[49] which was described at the time as a "mechanism" for implementing the ICCPR and its first Optional Protocol, as well as the International Covenant on Economic, Social, and Cultural Rights (ICESCR).[50] Canada's accession to these international instruments was the subject of the first federal-provincial ministerial conference on human rights in 1975, chaired by then-secretary of state, the Honourable Hugh Faulkner. The final communiqué of the conference noted:

Canada took a major step towards ratifying the three UN instruments on human rights. Agreement was reached whereby the federal and provincial governments will act in concert in the implementation of the instruments. The ministers met to consider the UN international human rights covenants, the Canadian program, and to support the first UN decade for action to combat racism and racial discrimination, and the new federal human rights bill ... Agreement was reached between the federal and provincial governments on procedures and mechanisms for implementing the international covenants and the international protocol ... The minister of justice, the Honourable Ron Basford, introduced the discussion of Bill C-72, the Canadian Human Rights Act, that was given first reading in Parliament last July.[51]

Human rights systems were now equipped not only with powers to compel compliance but with a softer set of tools that included the authority to engage in education, policy, research, and public awareness. Together, these diverse policy instruments were intended to both protect rights and promote a rights culture. The first generation of human rights systems had arrived.

FIRST-GENERATION SYSTEMS

The idea behind first-generation human rights systems was simple: people should be able to file complaints with few formalities and without entry barriers such as filing fees or needing a lawyer.[52] Beyond handling complaints, human rights commissions would work at several levels to help build a culture of human rights. The prohibition against discrimination was supplemented by measures to encourage a more inclusive society: "Inclusive equality embraces a vision in which cycles of exclusion are broken as a result of the transformative processes of institutional and social change. Such processes occur at many levels, including the individual, institutional and societal."[53]

The early days of the Ontario Human Rights Commission reflected the idealism and hope of this early period. Kim Bernhardt was a human rights officer at the Ontario commission at that time and recalled with fondness and pride the important role that the commission played in its early days, reminiscing about the charismatic leadership and passion of people like Dan Hill, the first director of the Ontario Commission:

Dan Hill was a visionary leader in the Black community at the time, and was a big supporter of the Human Rights Commission. He was originally American and was very conscious of the civil rights movement; maybe that was a factor in his activism. Dan Hill and Alan Borovoy did amazing things together. I recall the work done in "testing," early on, when people would go out into the community to look at apartments and test the availability of housing for minorities, and into the practices of employment agencies that were reportedly screening people out based on their racial background. People were very committed [to their jobs].[54]

Alan Borovoy also recalled the excitement of the time and the close partnership between the Ontario Commission and civil liberties organizations. He said that he worked in an informal tag team with the commission, raising the public profile of discrimination issues, naming and shaming, and opening the door for the commission to come in and develop a regulatory response.

> Organizations in the community worked together with the Ontario Human Rights Commission. We were in close communication all the time. This was the way that we would work together: when we [the Labour Committee for Human Rights] heard about things that were going on in the community, when we would get wind of things that were happening, [Dan Hill] would phone me and I would find out what was going on ... I would raise hell. I would call other people, call the media. Dan would then come in and conciliate the matter. It was a system that worked.[55]

The early days of Saskatchewan's system were also positive. The Saskatchewan Human Rights Code[56] gave the province's commission the regulatory authority to address discrimination across several sectors and the Saskatchewan Human Rights Commission was recognized early on as a national leader in human rights protections.[57]

In British Columbia, the 1969 Human Rights Act established a Human Rights Commission.[58] In 1973, the NDP government replaced the Act, which was viewed as relatively weak and ineffective, with the Human Rights Code.[59] The Code was very progressive: it made it illegal to discriminate without "reasonable cause" and it expanded the commission's staff to include a full-time team of investigators. The Code also required the investigation of all human rights complaints. According to Dominique Clément, BC's Human Rights Commission became known for its solid investigative work. The commission's investigators were generally considered to be competent and knowledgeable. They managed complaints and served as a social "safety valve" for people, providing a place to express grievances where complainants felt their concerns would be addressed. The BC Commission's structure and processes were "innovative and successful." "But," Clement said, "the [Social Credit Party] just hated it – they could not stand the fact that there was an independent human rights body out there."[60]

Clément cited a 1976 incident involving a group of women in Langley, BC, who wanted to go curling in the evenings. The women were refused access to the club because only men got to curl at night and they decided to file a human rights complaint. As it happened, the mayor of Langley was also the president of the Social Credit Party. A call was made to the minister of Labour, who then called the director of the BC Human Rights Commission, Kathleen Ruff. According to Clément, Ruff was instructed to stop investigating the case – "or else." Ruff stood her ground and the case went forward. Although the commission may have won that battle, it ultimately lost the war: Ruff left the commission in 1979 and the government shut down the commission in 1984.[61] In 1984, the Code and the commission were replaced by a weaker statute and a small Human Rights Council.[62]

Evaluating the Commissions

By the late 1970s, the Ontario system was experiencing signs of strain as well, although for different reasons. In a 1977 report, the Ontario Human Rights Commission cited concerns about its lack of independence from government, inadequate protections in the Human Rights Code, and increasing numbers of human rights complaints.[63] The commission expressed concern about delays, inadequate legal powers, and backlogs.

The growing emphasis on case management and on compiling statistics, as well as on the size of the caseload, began to occupy considerable time and resources. There were questions about whether these things were compromising the commission's ability to deliver on its main job of eliminating discrimination. In her 1984 letter of resignation from the Ontario Human Rights Commission, Kim Bernhardt stated that the commission had become more concerned with the number of cases it handled than with actual occurrences of discrimination.[64] Similar concerns persisted for the next two decades in Ontario and across the country. Commission employees, especially those who had come from a minority community background, were becoming disenchanted with the bureaucracy and the focus on public service performance metrics.

The trajectory of the Canadian Human Rights Commission (CHRC) illustrates similar tensions.[65] At the federal level, the CHRC was audited at least three times by the Office of the Auditor General of Canada (OAG). The first audit was in 1985, seven years after the commission had opened its doors.[66] This was one of the OAG's new "value for money" audits (audits that go beyond a simple review of how funds are spent to carry out a qualitative assessment of whether the funds spent offered good value for money).

The OAG began its audit report with the usual observations about the CHRC's structure. At the time the CHRC had three main branches: Claims and Compliance, Public Programs, and Research and Policy. The commission's budget was $9.2 million, half of which was devoted to processing human rights claims. The OAG honed in on case processing: "Our audit focused on the processing of claims from individuals, the major program activity of the Commission."[67] In taking this path the OAG was employing what evaluators sometimes refer to as a deliberate strategy: a conscious choice to focus on one area to the exclusion of others.[68] The choice of claims processing was perfectly defensible: complaints are the most visible and public area of any commission's activities, as well as the most familiar point of contact with the institution for many people. More important, delays *were* a problem at the Canadian commission, as they were elsewhere in the country. With an annual intake of about 330 cases per year at that time, there was a two-year backlog.

The CHRC was asked to develop standards for its own performance. It informed the OAG that six months would be a reasonable timeframe for processing a case. However, the OAG's audit revealed that the CHRC's average processing time for selected "older" cases – from filing to disposition – was four times longer, twenty-four months. The commission's intake and investigation phases alone were taking as long as litigation before the courts.

The OAG recommended that the CHRC reduce the backlog and achieve the six-month standard by (1) improving its strategic focus through a disciplined planning process and (2) making use of management tools such as operations manuals. These recommendations were based on three assumptions: first, that the CHRC's case work was "auditable"; second, that the focus on case management, to the exclusion of other mandate areas, was a valid choice; and third, that the six-month target was realistic, provided that the recommended management tools were implemented. Each of these assumptions proved to be problematic.

First, it was far from clear in 1985 that any human rights commission in Canada was systematically capturing case information data in a way that permitted the development of accurate trends or forecasts, let alone meaningful and realistic timeframes. Complaints management is a complex process. Without good data that documented experience over several years, it was difficult to tell if the selected case-handling standards were feasible or could serve as performance measures. The combination of complexity, limited experience in assessing what acceptable and realistic delays should be, and inadequate data suggested that complaints management in human rights systems was an emergent area and not yet auditable, at least not at the federal level.[69]

Second, while the OAG's characterization of complaints management as the CHRC's "major program of activity" was defensible as an area of focus, the OAG did not follow up with an audit of the other major areas of activity under the CHRA, which would have included promotional activities related to public education and policy work. With the benefit of hindsight, we now know that protection activities (mainly complaints management) and promotion (education, awareness, advice, and policy) are equally important functions for human rights commissions.[70] At that time, however, the standard of a twin, balanced mandate for human rights institutions (a standard that would emerge from the Paris Principles in the early 1990s) and of evaluating commissions in terms of an integrated approach to both major functions was not yet established.[71] Finally, the OAG assumed that improvements in bureaucratic processes would result in improvements in case management, particularly with respect to delays.

None of these assumptions held up. In 1988, the OAG issued its *Follow-Up of Recommendations in Previous Reports*.[72] As its name suggests, this report evaluated the CHRC's progress since 1985. The report begins rather optimistically, underscoring the commission's progress in identifying the nature and underlying causes of delays in investigations. The OAG commended the CHRC for having developed a "comprehensive operating manual" that included roles and responsibilities for all parties as well as policies and procedures, standards of performance and work, and a "quality assurance program." It also commended the CHRC for having identified ways of addressing its dual mandate of enforcement and education through its new planning process, which had been implemented in 1986. Unfortunately, the OAG report did not examine or discuss any of the "identified ways" of addressing the CHRC's dual mandate. There had been no improvements in the CHRC's delays and backlogs and the CHRC had "yet to determine" which of the identified causes of delays it could actually address. Still, the OAG professed satisfaction with the CHRC's progress because the commission had "acted positively on [the OAG's] 1985 recommendations and ... initiated corrective action on all issues."[73]

At this juncture, the CHRC appeared to realize that its backlogs were not going to improve any time soon, although statistics showed that the commission was actually closing more cases than it had at the time of the 1985 audit. According to the 1988 report, the CHRC had informed the OAG that "the number of outstanding complaints will not be decreased in the near future."[74] This was a sensible response. Not only did the statistics suggest that the number of complaints was rising, but several developments were underway that would alter the content and complexity of human rights work in important and profound ways.

New Understandings of Discrimination Law

The first of these developments was a change in the way that discrimination law is understood and litigated. These changes are clearly delineated in research by Colleen Sheppard that focuses on equality and discrimination law. Sheppard is not the first to have examined discrimination and equality, the way they are connected, and the overarching idea of inclusion. However, her work groups the different factors together, which helps to clarify what these developments signify for human rights systems.

First, discrimination is not always an exceptional, one-off incident. It can also be the product of embedded rules or ways of doing things. Second, discrimination should not be focused on intention but rather on effects. In fact, requiring that intention be present in a legal determination of discrimination can actually serve to perpetuate discrimination. For example, if a property manager routinely refuses to rent available apartments to Blacks, South Asians, or Aboriginal people, a complainant does not have to demonstrate what the manager was thinking or intending. All that needs to be shown is that the complainant was refused the apartment and that another person of a different racial or ethnic group was later allowed to rent the apartment. Unless the property manager can demonstrate a non-discriminatory reason for refusing to rent (the first applicant had two large dogs, for example, in a no-pets apartment complex) the complainant would likely win the case. The courts, not human rights systems, have repeatedly affirmed the importance of focusing on discriminatory effects. If a complainant also had to prove state of mind, very few cases would ever succeed. The ongoing public perception that intent should be relevant to making a discrimination claim appears to be the result of the erroneous belief that discrimination law is part of the criminal justice system, where intent *does* matter.

A related point is that formal equality (i.e., requiring that all persons be treated the same way) is rarely useful in identifying or describing discrimination. Treating someone with a disability the same way as someone who does not have that disability is not a very helpful way to support social inclusion. A more substantive approach to discrimination looks at the impact of systems and rules and recognizes that people sometimes have to be treated differently in order to be treated equally.

Finally, for the purposes of human rights complaints, it is not always adequate to refer to a single ground of discrimination. In some cases human rights complaints are framed by distilling people down to a single identity. Indeed, a particular personal characteristic like race or disability may be the sole or unique factor involved. In other cases, however, we can see the compounded effects of different and diverse grounds.[75] Compounded or intersecting effects of different grounds of discrimination can create different consequences for people who experience human rights violations. "Intersectionality" is one of the terms used to express the idea that people not only have multiple identities but also that different kinds of discrimination can reinforce each other. Human rights law has had to deal with this type of complexity as part of the struggle to protect rights.

All these elements, working together, have helped to fashion a more complex and nuanced understanding of discrimination and equality over the years. They have also made human rights litigation more focused on social inclusion and more closely connected to building a culture of human rights.

The Canadian Charter of Rights and Freedom

A second major development was the introduction of the Canadian Charter of Rights and Freedoms in 1982 and its equality rights guarantee in 1985.[76] The Charter breached the previously insurmountable walls of Parliamentary supremacy and profoundly changed the face of human rights law and practice in Canada.

The connection between human rights commissions and constitutional rights may not seem immediately obvious. The Charter covers a wider range of rights than those dealt with in anti-discrimination laws, which are generally limited to equality rights claims. The Charter only applies to government action, while human rights laws apply to both the private and public sectors. However, with the arrival of the Charter, the statutory and quasi-constitutional prohibition against discrimination came to rest on the more stable moorings of the constitutional right to equality in the Charter.

The Charter considerably raised the cost and stakes of human rights litigation in Canada. What were previously seen as merely administrative disputes could now be transformed into full-blown constitutional cases. Human rights commissions began to rely on Charter principles and jurisprudence in their legal and policy work; human rights tribunals began citing Charter jurisprudence in their decisions.

The "kangaroo court" criticism suggests that human rights institutions are not subject to the Charter. Initially, there were doubts about whether human rights tribunals, as administrative tribunals, could be considered "courts of competent jurisdiction" under the Charter and thus be able to legitimately apply it in their rulings. Starting in 1986 the Supreme Court of Canada made a number of rulings on the issue.[77] In 1989 the Court confirmed that *all* exercises of statuatory discretion are subject to the Charter,[78] including discretionary decisions rendered by administrative tribunals. A trilogy of cases in 1990 and 1991 established that specialized tribunals with the expertise and authority to decide questions of law are actually in the *best* position to hear issues related to the constitutionality of their own laws.[79]

Although administrative tribunals and the standards that apply to them are discussed in more detail in chapter 4, it is worth noting the significance of these rulings here. In their daily lives, far more people interact with administrative tribunals than with the courts. Administrative tribunals include agencies that deal with landlord-tenant disputes, labour relations, refugee and immigrant status, workers' compensation, tax assessment appeals, and a host of other areas. They are less formal and costly than the courts. As noted in chapter 1, decision makers such as tribunal members are specialists and tribunals aim to promote fair, impartial, and more rapid decisions. As well, litigants are less likely to need representation by counsel than if they were in courts where only lawyers can represent litigants. It would have been odd indeed to prevent human rights tribunals from applying the Charter, given the Charter's status as the constitutional bedrock for the very rights that human rights systems seek to protect and in a legal context that far more people are likely to interact with than the courts.

In a 2010 case – *R. v. Conway* – the Supreme Court of Canada reinforced this line of thought. The Court decided that administrative tribunals (in *Conway*, the administrative tribunal was the Ontario Review Board, a tribunal that oversees the treatment, assessment, detention, and discharge of people who have been found not criminally responsible by reason of mental disorder) have the right to determine whether a Charter violation has occurred and to fashion legal remedies in appropriate cases.[80] It is worth taking a closer look at the decision, because it speaks to concerns that administrative decision-makers such as human rights tribunals are providing inferior or substandard justice because they are not courts. The Court ruled that we do not have one Charter for the courts and another for administrative tribunals. Administrative tribunals that apply the law also have the authority to apply the Charter to issues that arise in the proper exercise of their own statutory or legal functions. In short, the court affirmed that administrative tribunals must act consistently with the Charter and its values: "Moreover, the jurisprudential evolution affirms the practical advantages and the constitutional basis for allowing Canadians to assert their *Charter* rights in the most accessible forum available, without the need for bifurcated proceedings between superior courts and administrative tribunals. Any scheme favouring bifurcation is, in fact, inconsistent with the well-established principle that an administrative tribunal is to decide all matters, including constitutional questions, whose essential factual character falls within the tribunal's specialized statutory jurisdiction."[81]

This is not to say that there are no problems with the way in which administrative tribunals function in Canada. There are problems related to lack of independence and impartiality that are linked to deficient statutory provisions and to susceptibility to influence from the executive branch. These issues are discussed at greater length in chapter 4.

Maintaining Human Rights Advances

The third development was the realization that many of the victories and landmark decisions that originated with commissions and tribunals have not always stood the test of time, in part because individual complaints do not necessarily give rise to longstanding or system-wide changes. Tribunals do not use the principle of *stare decisis*, which would oblige them to follow previous decisions or precedents. Since administrative tribunals are not courts, this makes sense. However, human rights lawyer Mary Eberts observed that "the half-life of many human rights achievements has proved to be shorter than we thought, and we learned that we have to be vigilant. Many of the advances we thought had been definitively achieved seemed to be evaporating. This obviously had an impact on human rights commissions as well, since some of these cases had to be litigated all over again."[82]

Eberts cited the "spouse in the house" rule as an example. The rule was designed to cut back the level of social assistance paid to a person who decided to co-habit with someone else. In this case the person would be deemed to be in a spousal relationship, and the reduction in benefits was justified by the assumption that other sources of income were now available to the household. Single people who lived with someone else, even for a short time ("try-on relationships") found that their benefits were reduced. These rules had a particular impact on single women. In response to community pressure, the government abolished the rule in 1987. After that, only "enduring" relationships could trigger a reduction of family benefits. Almost a decade later, the spouse in the house rule re-emerged under the regime of the Harris government as part of its overall effort to tighten eligibility for a wide range of social benefits in Ontario.[83] In October 1995, the rule to establish economic interdependence as soon as there was evidence of cohabitation was reintroduced. The result was that single parents, especially single mothers in Ontario, were deemed to be spouses much more quickly and lost their family benefits as "sole support parents." The rule had to be challenged again. It was declared discriminatory and unconstitutional in the landmark 2002 case of *Falkiner v. Ontario*.[84]

Another example was Ontario's Employment Equity Commission, which had been established in 1992 with much fanfare by Bob Rae's NDP government. Lack of equity in employment for entire groups of people – people with disabilities, say, or racialized minorities – is not something that can be addressed only or even mainly through individual complaints. It can be dealt with more effectively through an approach that can address structural conditions of disadvantage in employment, such as those experienced by women, Aboriginal peoples, people with disabilities, and racialized minorities. One of the Harris government's first acts upon assuming power in 1995 was to abolish the Employment Equity Commission and fire the employment equity commissioner, Juanita Westmoreland-Traoré.

I was at the Ontario Human Rights Commission at the time. The staff were watching the communications coming from the government very closely, and they were far from reassuring. The government pledged that employment equity would not fall by the wayside and that the Ontario Human Rights Commission would handle these matters in the future.

This reassurance was something of a sleight of hand. As noted earlier, employment equity is not a system based on individual human rights complaints but rather on long-term and systematic monitoring and auditing of employers with the aim of achieving a fairer and more balanced workforce. Although the public now expected the Ontario Human Rights Commission to deal with employment equity work, such activities were something the commission had neither the legal mandate nor the resources to undertake. The only mechanism at the commission's disposal was the individual complaints system and, perhaps, in a pinch, an attempt to fashion a systemic remedy by pooling individual complaints against a single employer and then seeking a remedy that would eliminate discriminatory rules and practices. However, at the time the Ontario Commission's "systemic unit" lacked the capacity and skills for this work.

The gulf between individual and systemic complaints, and the resulting need to litigate and relitigate the same issues, is also illustrated by cases challenging the accessibility of retail services offered by institutions such as banks, cinemas, and restaurants. Shelagh Day was involved in a case in the 1980s that challenged the Odeon theatres' seating and services for wheelchair users.[85] Disability activist Michael Huck in Saskatchewan spearheaded the case and brought it to the Saskatchewan Commission. According to Day, "It was an extraordinary thing to be involved in this case, using the law to deal with the barriers that had been set up. [Huck] was an activist, and he had to live through the case going all the way to the Saskatchewan Court of Appeal. The process lasted for several years and it took a considerable personal toll." Day said it would have been impossible to sustain the years of litigation without a commission to carry the case forward and force what was at that time a recalcitrant theatre chain to better accommodate patrons with disabilities.[86] However, a decade later and two provinces away, Ontario's Commission was still working with Odeon to make its theatres accessible.

Hate speech restrictions are another example of how human rights gains can be pared back. As noted earlier in this chapter, prohibitions on hate speech were among the earliest forms of legislative attempts to prohibit extreme forms of group libel in the 1930s. In the 1970s, the first version of the CHRA prohibited the use of telephone systems to communicate hate messages under section 13.[87] Extremist and anti-Semitic groups challenged the law early on, but the Supreme Court upheld it by a narrow margin in the 1990 *Taylor* case.[88] Consistent with its mandate and its past practice, the Canadian Civil Liberties Association, in much the same tradition as the American Civil Liberties Union and similar groups, also opposed the legislation.

However, the circle of those unhappy with hate speech laws broadened to include not only civil liberties groups but also an eclectic assortment of evangelical and conservative religious groups, right wing activists, free speech absolutists, and white supremacists. In 2009, a decision by the Canadian Human Rights Tribunal suggested that such groups were making headway. In *Warman v. Lemire* the tribunal refused to apply the CHRA on the grounds that it violated constitutional free speech protections. The tribunal decided that the CHRA had been rendered newly vulnerable by a 1998 amendment that created a penalty of up to $10,000 for hate speech. The penalty clause was seen as a punitive sanction and said to be incompatible with the objectives of human rights legislation. The tribunal refused to apply either section 13 or the penalty clause.[89] The tribunal did not have the authority to actually strike down the law as unconstitutional (only courts have that power), but the refusal to apply the provisions elicited considerable glee among those unhappy with the idea of regulating hate speech. In 2009 and 2010, court decisions in Alberta (*Boissoin*) and Saskatchewan (*Whatcott*) added grist to the mill by overturning tribunal decisions that had upheld hate speech complaints.[90] By this time, the attacks against human rights commissions were at their apex.

The pendulum began to swing back in 2012. The Federal Court of Canada reversed the tribunal's decision in *Lemire,* arguing that the unconstitutionality of the penalty clause did not necessarily entail the unconstitutionality of section 13 of the CHRA.[91] The upshot was that the Canadian Human Rights Tribunal had committed an error by declaring section 13 to be unconstitutional as well.

At about the same time, the Saskatchewan case of *Whatcott,* a case involving hate propaganda against gays and lesbians, was making its way to the Supreme Court of Canada. *Whatcott* was an important case because it considered provincial restrictions on hate speech in Saskatchewan's human rights law and the discriminatory effects of hate. The case thus had significance not only for Saskatchewan but also for other jurisdictions that placed limits on hate speech and gave human rights systems the power to regulate it. It was quickly recognized as the key case on hate speech and human rights commissions in Canada, and a number of associations representing minority racial and religious groups, who understood all too well the dangers of hate propaganda, sought leave to intervene before the Supreme Court of Canada.[92] B'nai

Brith and the African Canadian Legal Clinic intervened to support the legislation, as did several human rights commissions as well as religious groups and the Canadian Bar Association, to name a few. In 2013, the Supreme Court of Canada finally and unanimously recognized hate propaganda as a form of discrimination and upheld the role of human rights commissions in regulating such speech.[93] It was, however, too late for section 13 of the CHRA, as the Conservative-dominated government ignored the 2012 and 2013 rulings by the Federal Court in *Lemire* and the Supreme Court of Canada in *Whatcott* and went on to pass a law repealing section 13 of the CHRA anyway.[94]

Challenges and Changes to First-Generation Systems

All of these developments, from the introduction of the Charter, to new approaches to discrimination and equality law, to rights rollbacks, made the legal environment for human rights systems considerably less predictable and more complex. The early 1990s ushered in yet another set of challenges, namely a recession and fiscal restraints for most of the public service. While spending for human rights systems on the whole had increased across Canada in the 1980s, in the 1990s budgets were frozen and in many instances actually fell.[95] In Ontario, this trend continued into the next decade. In the fiscal year 1993–94, the Ontario Human Rights Commission's budget was $13.3 million.[96] By 2000–01, it had dropped to $11.1 million.[97] By 2008–09 (the last year in which the commission was funded to fulfill its gatekeeping role), its budget was $13.6 million, roughly the same as it had been in 1993 without adjusting for the value of the dollar.[98]

There was an uneasy sense that commissions were responding to the challenging fiscal environment and mounting caseload pressures by turning complaints away too early in the process or by taking shortcuts that reduced the quality of their investigations. Commissions' relations with civil society organizations (the term used to collectively describe NGOs, lawyer's associations, community service groups, and community clinics) were becoming increasingly strained. Reports at the federal level as well as in Ontario, British Columbia, and Alberta reiterated these themes.[99] According to Byron Williams, head of Manitoba's Public Interest Law Centre:

[Our] relationship [with Manitoba's Human Rights Commission] has had its peaks and valleys, and the valleys were in the 1990s. In the mid-1990s, our office was turning away from the commission and turning to the courts for a few reasons. First was delay. We would say, "[the commission is] where good cases go to die." We were also unimpressed with the intellectual rigour of investigations and of the deliberations before the [Human Rights] Board. In the 1990s, we filed several significant complaints. We probably carried only five or six of them through to completion during this period.[100]

In 1992, an important study of the Ontario human rights system was published that attempted to tackle all the hydra's heads – bottlenecks, backlogs, bias – and the deteriorating relationship with civil society organizations. *Achieving Equality: A Report on Human Rights Reform* became known as the Cornish Report after its chair, Mary Cornish. Commissioned by the Ontario government, the report proposed major reforms to the province's human rights system.[101] One of its proposals was to increase access to a decision-maker by recommending a *right* to a hearing by a tribunal, to be known as an Equality Rights Tribunal.[102] It gave a prescient nod to the increasing power of labour relations boards to make decisions on human rights: the Cornish Report proposed that labour arbitrators should also have the authority to decide human rights issues where an element of the grievance is an alleged violation of human rights in the employment context. This proposal was important because some decision-makers had argued that human rights commissions and tribunals had jurisdiction over human rights matters to the exclusion of labour relations boards.

The Cornish Report envisaged a new role for the Ontario Human Rights Commission, which would lose its gatekeeping function. Claims would be filed directly with the tribunal. Much more emphasis would be placed on a "storefront" presence for the commission to ensure easy access to information and services. A strengthened tribunal would undertake mediation and, of course, carry out adjudication. A separate community-based, publicly funded service would offer legal aid.

When the Cornish Report came out in 1992, Ontario's NDP government was struggling with a recession and a budget crisis and the costs of making the changes were seen as prohibitive. In 1995, the Conservative Harris government shelved the report and it disappeared from public servants' conversations except as "that expensive idea."[103]

With no major reforms forthcoming and no prospect of new money, the Ontario Human Rights Commission began looking inside its own processes for other ways to manage the caseload and budget pressures. It focused on what was then section 34 of Ontario's Human Rights Code as a way to screen cases out of the human rights system. The general purpose of section 34 was to ensure that the commission did not expend resources dealing with cases that were too old, frivolous, or outside its jurisdiction. As it read before the reform of the Ontario system in 2006, section 34 also permitted the commission to turn away cases that could and should have been dealt with elsewhere. The commission began using section 34 more aggressively, for example by referring cases to labour relations boards, thus diverting them from the human rights system. Given the large number of complaints the commission received from unionized workplaces, or that might have been dealt with in other settings, this strategy brought results. Out of the more than 2,500 complaints filed in 1995–96, the commission referred only thirty-seven cases on to a full hearing.[104]

While the more aggressive use of section 34 of the Code was legally defensible, it marked a significant shift in the way the commission handled cases. The change in policy had been made without public consultation and was communicated in only a perfunctory way. Activists were angry and accused the commission of dumping meritorious cases early in the process in order to manage the caseload.

In 1997 the commission attempted to push for limited legislative reforms that would allow certain types of complaints to circumvent investigation and go directly to the tribunal for a hearing. However, the ministry did not accept these internal recommendations.[105]

Meanwhile, at the Canadian Human Rights Commission, the number of cases was continuing to rise: incoming cases increased by 250% between 1985 and 1995 while the federal commission's budget grew by about 80%.[106] When the OAG visited the CHRC for another audit in 1998, it again trained its sights on complaints processing, skipping over the other aspects of the CHRC's mandate, arguing that this approach was necessary because "the audit of its claims management process required more time and resources than anticipated."[107]

The OAG's key findings were: "Although major efforts have been made to improve the handling of complaints, it still takes a long time for a complaint to be reviewed – an average of about two years for the Commission and about a year for the Tribunal. In 1997, almost one half of the commission's 900 open cases were still being investigated one year after the signing of the complaint."[108] The OAG did not assess the quality of the CHRC's work in the cases that had been processed. When the commission complained about this oversight, the OAG was dismissive: it said that it was unable to examine the quality of the commission's investigations because it would "be costly, time-consuming and imprac-tical."[109] The OAG is not known to be a stranger to costly and time-consuming audits. However, the assessment of impracticality is probably closer to the mark. In all likelihood, the OAG would have had little idea how to go about assessing the quality of a human rights investigation at that time, even if it had wanted to take this on.

The audit revealed that the CHRC had made efforts to improve its data management after the 1985 and 1988 reports, and changes to inter-nal procedures had resulted in better overall management processes. However, these efforts had not reduced either the delays or the backlog. A broader analysis of the CHRC's mandate and of the rapidly evolving legal and social context in which it was operating would have revealed that something more serious was involved than internal management processes. In addition to the legal developments mentioned earlier, and the pressure that they placed on human rights systems, there was also the "new narrative" of Canada's growing ethnic diversity. Recent immi-grants were placing growing importance on aspects of Canada's consti-tutional identity such as rights and the rule of law.[110] Stakeholders from these communities were asserting their place and using human rights systems more actively, joining with other activists, community organiza-tions, and civil society organizations more broadly. Together, these indi-viduals, advocates, and groups became important interlocutors in the assessment of how well human rights systems were functioning, offering a vibrant new source of information for audit organizations.[111]

Evaluation experts have noted that the presence and greater political engagement of stakeholder groups has resulted in a shift in the distribu-tion of power in performance audits.[112] By adding stakeholders, with their diverse perspectives, to the equation, auditors were engaging with a new group of players and this had implications for the dynamics of how audits were undertaken, as well as the results of those audits.

In its 1998 audit of the CHRC, the OAG actively sought wide input from these new players, which included many of the people who had been pushing for human rights reform in Ontario since the Cornish Report. The main areas of stakeholder concern identified in the 1998 OAG audit included:

- Cursory investigations and case dismissals without full investiga-tions;
- Delays in case processing, which undermine fairness;

- Commissioners dismissing or not pursuing claims when conciliation fails; and
- Commissioners not providing sufficient information on the reasons for their decisions.[113]

The OAG was now confronted with a difficult situation. Its prescriptions for dealing with delays had been duly carried out, but in terms of the original objective – reducing delays – the results were disappointing. The OAG therefore changed course and proposed a full legislative review. The OAG suggested that a direct access model be considered:

> Some stakeholders suggested that the parties be allowed to take their cases directly to the Tribunal or the Federal Court for a hearing on the merits of their case. This could decrease the time and cost of resolving complaints, particularly when complainants and respondents have significant resources and expertise.
>
> The role of the Tribunal would need to be reconsidered if complaints were brought directly to the Court. To protect the public interest, the Commission could have a statutory right to be an intervener in all cases. ...
>
> We agree that a fundamental review by Parliament is needed. The various issues we have identified are for the most part interrelated and cannot be easily addressed individually.[114]

In response, the government of the day set up the Canadian Human Rights Act Review Panel, with the mandate to review the federal human rights system. The panel's report came out in 2000 and included 165 recommendations.[115] Easily among the most detailed and carefully crafted study of any human rights system in Canada to date, it made specific proposals to deal with nearly all of the major controversies and criticisms encountered by human rights systems, based on reference to prior reports and a wide range of consultations across Canada. It also made several substantive and farsighted suggestions regarding the federal commission's jurisdiction over issues such as Aboriginal rights, in particular, the repeal of section 67 of the CHRA, which prohibited Aboriginal people from filing certain types of human rights complaints. The report also recommended introducing gender identity as a ground for discrimination under the CHRA. It would be more than a decade before Parliament acted on these last recommendations.

If the recommendation regarding direct access to the Canadian Human Rights Tribunal had been put into effect, the Canadian Human Rights Commission would have lost its gatekeeping role. However, the commission would still have had significant functions under this proposal and would have continued to have a major role in the human rights system. To address concerns about perceived bias, the panel recommended that a publicly funded legal clinic undertake the role of providing assistance to claimants. The recommendations seemed to reflect a widespread consensus among stakeholders about the need to modernize the human rights system and ensure that it had the capacity and legitimacy to do its work properly.

The federal government did not implement any of the panel's proposals at the time the report was released. The CHRC continued to work within its own framework, endeavouring to find non-legislative strategies to conserve its resources and work more effectively. In 2003, it initiated an internal policy aimed at limiting its advocacy role by representing only select complainants before the Canadian Human Rights Tribunal. In practical terms, this non-legislative policy change meant that, even if the commission was satisfied that a complaint should go forward for a hearing, certain complainants would have to pursue their cases alone. They would therefore be forced to assume their own legal costs. The practical result was that the commission would attend the hearing only if a case raised a new point of law or other issues of strategic importance. There was no clear legislative basis for this new strategy but nothing prevented it either: in fairness, the CHRA is rather murky on the point. However, the Supreme Court decided in 2011 that the legitimacy of this policy is at best doubtful.[116]

Although the Canadian Human Rights Act Review Panel's wide-ranging recommendations were not implemented at the time, its report gave voice to community and advocacy concerns, especially regarding the gatekeeping role and related issues of delays and access to justice. Other reports in other jurisdictions would make similar points.[117] Many activists and lawyers felt that commissions had become estranged from the social movements that had helped to create them and that the formative idea of functionalism seemed to have lost its vigour in practice. Growing dissatisfaction with human rights systems may have provided the impetus for progressive reformers to push for legislative change but it also provided grist for political mills and especially for governments seeking to rid themselves of these controversial and often inconvenient institutions. Commissions were becoming more vulnerable to calls for reform, not all of which would come from pro-human rights voices.

THE SECOND GENERATION

British Columbia

In 2003, for the second time in two decades, the British Columbia government replaced its human rights system, creating a new system with a diminished legal framework. The first consequence was the abolition of its human rights commission, amidst criticism of it as ineffective and allegations of internal bickering and dysfunction.[118] Shelagh Day said that the first casualty of this restructuring was Chief Commissioner Mary Woo Sims. Sims had been out of town attending a conference shortly before the announcement that the commission would be abolished and learned of her dismissal through a response to a question posed in the House. "Mary Woo Sims may be the only person who was ever fired during Question Period."[119]

The events that gave rise to the new regime were set in motion in 2001. Sims received a call from a deputy minister telling her that the minister was going to be making an announcement in the House: several agencies, boards, and commissions would be under review. "As part of that review," she recalled, "I was told that my Order-in-Council appointment was going to be revoked. They knew I was going to be out of town [when the announcement was made publicly]. I was so shocked that I did not know how to respond. I don't know of anyone else who had ever been dealt with in quite this way." Confirming Day's version of the events, Sims said, "It was, in fact, during Question Period, and it was a set-up question."[120] Sims' mandate ended abruptly in 2001, a year before its scheduled termination. The incident raised concerns about premature removals from office and their impact on the integrity of administrative systems and on fairness to administrative decision-makers, especially since the new legislation did not come into force until March 2003.

Details about the reform were provided in Bill 64.[121] A new direct access system would enable people to file claims directly with the human rights tribunal. During second reading of the Bill in 2002, the attorney general explained: "[W]e are moving from an approach based on multiple agencies with confusingly intersecting mandates to an approach with one statutory agency. ... Complaints will no longer be lost in the dark void of endless and inconclusive investigations. Instead, victims of discrimination will have direct access to a tribunal that can resolve their complaints[.] ... The tribunal will emphasize mediation and the early resolution of disputes rather than adjudication ... and it will adjudicate the complaints that require adjudication."[122]

The BC Human Rights Tribunal is now the only independent statutory public institution in the province's human rights system. It has exclusive jurisdiction to hear human rights complaints.[123] Public education and related promotional responsibilities are divided between the government and the BC Human Rights Coalition, a charitable community-based organization. The coalition runs a human rights clinic in partnership with the Community Legal Assistance Society, offering legal services to claimants.[124] The loss of a commission and the absence of a public institution to support claimants raises concerns about privatizing human rights complaints and about the decline of the public interest dimension of human rights litigation.[125] Unrepresented claimants, especially those who are vulnerable or have mental disabilities, are particularly disadvantaged when they appear before the tribunal.[126]

There is no longer anything in the BC system that qualifies as a human rights institution under the Paris Principles. The International Coordinating Committee of National Human Rights Institutions (ICC) has never accredited a tribunal as a national human rights institution (NHRI). A tribunal cannot do all the things that a commission can do and should do within the meaning of the Paris Principles.[127] The Principles require that independent NHRIS *both* protect and promote rights.[128] BC lacks a publicly funded *independent and statutory* body that proactively promotes human rights. The tribunal cannot carry out the full inventory of commissions' functions, such as proactive and progressive research, policy development, consultations, publications, taking public positions on current and controversial issues (outside decision-making functions), providing human rights advice to governments, and interacting with international human rights mechanisms. NGOs can fulfill some of these functions, but they are not statutory bodies established as part of government. The government can end contracts with NGOs at any time without the public process required to amend a statute and get rid of a human rights institution. Finally, although the BC government has assumed the commission's education mandate, it obviously is not independent of itself.

Human rights tribunals, like all administrative tribunals, engage in some educational and promotional activities, but as judicial decision-makers they must remain neutral and stay close to their central functions of holding hearings and rendering decisions. Accordingly, tribunals promote awareness about their procedures, publish annual reports, and report on their own decisions. Beyond that, "it is widely understood [to be] necessary to maintain some separation between adjudication and education and advocacy."[129]

BC's human rights system remains vulnerable. In 2008, the BC Human Rights Tribunal rendered a decision in the high-profile *SELI* case, which found that there had been discrimination in the treatment of temporary professional workers from South America.[130] The BC government had negotiated an international venture agreement with several parties to build the Canada Line rapid transit tunnel for the 2010 Vancouver Olympics. The Construction and Specialized Workers' Union Local 1611 had filed a complaint against SELI Canada Inc. on behalf of foreign workers from Central and South America, alleging discrimination in wages and pay conditions: South American workers hired for the project received lower wages and had inferior working conditions as compared to their European counterparts. Both groups of workers had come to Vancouver to build the tunnel. They had comparable skills and qualifications, and were on temporary work visas.[131] The respondents argued that the terms and conditions had been negotiated and agreed to in advance by the international partners and were consistent with international compensation practices. Their argument was essentially that laissez-faire should prevail because the discrimination had been negotiated into an international venture agreement. In its decision, the tribunal analyzed the working conditions of the Latin American workers as compared to the European workers on the same project and decided in favour of the complainants.[132]

Given the significant costs involved and the international dimensions of the case, the tribunal decision in favour of the workers generated considerable controversy. According to Shelagh Day, the *SELI* decision was unpopular with business groups and led to speculation that the BC government would dismantle the tribunal.[133] The government floated the idea of moving all employment-related claims, including human rights claims, to a "super tribunal," regardless of whether the matter involved employment standards, occupational health and safety, or human rights. This would have stripped the BC Human Rights Tribunal of most of its caseload.

A special report commissioned by the British Columbia Law Institute in October 2010 rejected the idea of scrapping the tribunal. The report noted that government should undertake such a drastic change only *after* a full consultation process. The institute also found that: "[T]he tribunal does an excellent job [of] making the process accessible to parties who are not knowledgeable about legal processes as well as accommodating the particular needs of parties, including [those with] significant mental health issues. A number of participants commented that unrepresented human rights complainants can be very demanding but that the [tribunal] handles these individuals appropriately and sensitively."[134] To date, the BC government has not taken any steps to follow up on the idea of dismantling the tribunal, but the incident illustrates the fragility of human rights systems and their political vulnerability.

The SELI case was finally settled between the parties in 2013, with the forty Latin American workers receiving tens of thousands of dollars in payments, ending five years of legal wrangling that followed the tribunal's 2008 decision.

Ontario

As discussed in chapter 1 and earlier in this chapter, alarms had been sounding across Canada since at least the 1990s about the impact of gatekeeping on access to justice. When Canadian activists took their grievances to the United Nations, they argued that diminished access to justice meant that Canada was in violation of its international treaty obligations under the ICCPR,[135] among other legal instruments.[136]

The Cornish model had continued to have enormous resonance in the broader human rights community, and it resurfaced in 2006 to furnish the conceptual scaffolding for Ontario's major human rights system reform, Bill 107.[137] The primary sections of the bill came into force in 2008. Keith Norton was the chief commissioner in Ontario at the time and did not support the reform: "I thought the [first-generation] model was okay and the gatekeeping system did not need to be abolished. People need access to justice, and vulnerable people need advocates. I'm not sure the new system can meet these needs. I blame Michael Bryant and a small group of disgruntled lawyers who drove the process and misled public servants about the extent of consensus on the ground."[138] The long and acrimonious public debate over the reforms in Ontario almost tore the human rights community apart. Michael Bryant, who was attorney general at the time, was quoted as having said: "This is the first time that the province has attempted to reform the human-rights system in more than 40 years. Now I know why."[139]

François Larsen, a public servant who had been a manager in both the Quebec and Ontario human rights systems, had been in Ontario during the Bill 107 debates. Larsen said that his opposition to Bill 107 was not just about the commission keeping its traditional territory or maintaining the status quo: "Gatekeeping allowed the commission to keep its finger on the pulse through complaints and to understand what was actually happening on the ground," he said. "The day-to-day flow of complaints and inquiries was the lifeblood of the system. It allowed the commission to better understand trends and respond to them. Without the ability to screen complaints, it is more difficult to do the work effectively."[140]

These views were not shared by others who later worked in the new system. Michael Gottheil, former head of the Human Rights Tribunal of Ontario, acknowledged the divisions within the human rights community, but he also argued that there was a real need for change.[141]

Results from Changes in BC and Ontario

The concerns expressed by Shelagh Day and others about the privatization of human rights in BC are moderated in Ontario. The drafters of Bill 107 consciously avoided the harsher aspects of BC's reform.[142] Ontario's current legislation goes a long way toward protecting the right to a hearing, an essential element of the Cornish model fifteen years earlier. According to Michael Gottheil, "no other jurisdiction in Canada gives you the right to a hearing under the legislation."[143] BC's new system allows many more complaints to be dismissed on a preliminary basis without any form of hearing.[144] Practically speaking, this means that a complainant is much more likely to have some sort of a hearing in Ontario, even at the screening stage, whereas in BC, preliminary decisions that result in the dismissal of cases are more likely to take place with no hearing at all.

Litigators with experience under Ontario's previous system appear to be more satisfied with the current model. Paul Champ said, "we get to the tribunal much more quickly; I know people talk about privatisation and so on, but the Ontario system is much better for clients and the long waits are gone."[145] Michael Gottheil and Heather MacNaughton said that the Ontario and BC Tribunals have both succeeded in addressing delays and securing access to justice (i.e., an increased likelihood that complainants will get to present their case to a decision-maker.) Statistics show that the second-generation systems in Ontario and BC deal with cases much more quickly than first-generation systems. Comparisons can be somewhat tricky since first-generation systems entail three distinct timeframes: the time before the commission (the period from the date of filing to the date the case was resolved, closed, or sent to the tribunal by the commission), the time in transit from the commission to the tribunal, and the time before the tribunal. When the average age of complaints was calculated in Ontario under the previous system, the best performance by the Ontario Commission in terms of the first period was nine months to a year.[146] However, many of the cases in this group of complaints would have been settled, withdrawn, or abandoned much faster than that, as such claims would not have been subject to the long process of investigation. If one examined only claims that were investigated, the time involved for the first period – the time before the commission – was consistently much higher. Before Bill 107, the average time for investigated claims from the date of filing to the date they were sent to the tribunal was 28.8 months.[147] According to the 2012 *Report of the Ontario Human Rights Review* (the Pinto Report), the entire process, encompassing all three timeframes, took almost five years to complete: "[U]nder the previous human rights system, the average timeline measured from the filing of a complaint was as follows: It took just over 2-1/2 years for the Commission to refer a case to the Tribunal. It took around 4 years to get to a hearing at the Tribunal; and it took 4.7 years to get to a Tribunal decision on the merits of the case."[148] Under Ontario's second-generation system, the entire process lasts on average 12.7 months, almost four times faster.[149]

This comparison may be somewhat unfair to first-generation systems. By focusing on the cases that go to a tribunal, one is necessarily weeding out those cases that are withdrawn, abandoned, and settled by a commission in a much shorter timeframe. If one includes these cases, and assuming that their average age is in the range of one year, second-generation systems are still at least twice as fast.

In BC, the numbers are similar. Heather MacNaughton indicated that the timeline under the new system was in the six-month range during her stewardship.[150] Annual reports in BC do not provide a consistent tracking of the average age of cases. However, even assuming that the average age has increased and now roughly equates with Ontario's, this represents an improvement in speed compared to the first-generation system in BC. (In the *Blencoe* case the Supreme Court of Canada noted that it took about three years for a case in BC to get to a tribunal.)

Ontario's reforms have also meant that more people are likely to look to the human rights system to resolve problems because the system is now seen to be more effective and accessible. According to Michael Gottheil, from the beginning, Ontario's direct access model has been "tracking higher incoming complaints" and resolving them more quickly than the Ontario Commission ever did.[151] Gottheil acknowledged that the combination of a huge case intake and weak screening criteria has placed the tribunal under considerable pressure. He said the tribunal streams cases that have no reasonable prospect of success through an early "hearing" conducted via telephone conference.[152] In short, the ability to have access to a neutral decision-maker is greater in the Ontario system. Under the BC system, as noted earlier, the tribunal is authorized by law to dismiss far more claims on a preliminary basis without a hearing.

Many aspects of the Ontario reform thus appear to have been positive. The structure of the Ontario system has several other features that are superior to the British Columbia reform. For instance, it has retained a commission as part of its human rights system. While the commission has a more limited protection role, it can initiate and undertake inquiries, a role that is substantial enough to allow it to pass muster as a human rights institution by the Paris Principles. Under Ontario's reformed Human Rights Code, the commission also has a stronger policy role, buttressed by an express requirement that the tribunal must consider commission policies in its deliberations – although it is not obliged to accept them. Finally, applicants[153] can now seek legal assistance at the publicly funded Human Rights Legal Support Centre, which is the newest and third part of Ontario's human rights system.[154] BC does not have an equivalent institution.

Given the connection between adequate funding and institutional performance, it is instructive to look at the relative costs of first- and second-generation systems. Ontario has invested in a system with three institutions instead of two. Not surprisingly, the new system is more expensive than its predecessor.

According to its 2011–12 annual report, the cost of the British Columbia Human Rights Tribunal is roughly the same as that of the Ontario Tribunal in the second-generation system, adjusting for the lower number of complaints in BC. The single component in British Columbia's system is less expensive than the three components in Ontario's. However, the BC costs do not include the cost of the outside

Table 2.1
Budget of Ontario's human rights system

	2003/04[1]	2004/05	2005/06	2006/07	2007/08	2008/09[2]	2009/10[3]	2010/11	2011/12
OHRC	12.2	12.5	12.9	13.4	13.9	13.7	5.9	5.5	5.6
HRTO	0.87	0.99	1.0	0.93	9. 4	9.9	11.1	9.1	9.1
HRLSC	N/A	N/A	N/A	N/A	N/A	4.6	5.3	5.3	5.3
Total	13.0	13.4	13.9	14.3	14.9	28.2	22.3	19.9	20.1

Notes

Based on Printed Estimates in $M

1 - 2003/04 - The OHRC and the HRTO were transferred from the Ministry of Citizenship to MAG

2 - 2008/09 - The HRLSC budget reflects 9 the months of operation (established as of June 30, 2008)

2 - 2009/10- The HRTO budget included additional funding to address s. 53(3) and (5) transitional cases

OHRC   Ontario Human Rights Commission
HRTO   Human Rights Tribunals of Ontario
HRLSC   Human Rights Legal Support Centre

Source: Andrew Pinto, *Report of the Ontario Human Rights Review 2012* (Toronto: Queen's Printer for Ontario, 2012) at 176.

legal clinic services and the fixed costs and program expenses of public education for human rights within the BC government.

Permitting direct access to a tribunal in both BC and Ontario has addressed concerns about bias and the multiple hats worn by commissions in their promotional role and in both investigating complaints and supporting claimants before the tribunal. In Ontario, this latter role was transferred to the Human Rights Legal Support Centre (HRLSC). In BC, as noted earlier, it is filled by a community-based legal clinic.

Ontario's new HRLSC is restricted to providing support to applicants and has become the main point of contact and the "face of human rights" in Ontario.[155] Previously, the commission provided representation and legal support in all or almost all of the cases it referred to the tribunal, albeit only after the referral decision was made. In contrast, 70 percent of applicants under the second-generation system are self-represented,[156] although applicants can seek legal advice at any time in the process. Another important difference, at least from the applicant's perspective, is that the HRLSC does not create a bottleneck in terms of access to the tribunal.

However, that does not mean that there are no bottlenecks. Both Raj Anand and Kathy Laird, the chair and executive director of the HRLSC respectively, acknowledged that the centre faced difficulties in handling calls and inquiries.[157] By November 2011, the HRLSC had a 79 percent answer rate, but average wait times remained high at eight minutes.[158]

The HRLSC introduced creative strategies to manage the demand at the front-end of Ontario's new system. For instance, a cooperative program in a pro bono legal services organization asks lawyers to offer their services for free while learning about how the human rights system works.[159]

Kathy Laird reported that out of the 11,000 inquiries the HRLSC received in its first two years of operation, approximately 1,500 individuals received in-depth legal services from a centre lawyer, ranging from legal assessments, legal research, and application preparation to representation at mediation or at a hearing. The centre provided what Laird called "full representation" at the tribunal to almost 500 clients. By 2011–12, the HRLSC was receiving about 25,000 inquiries a year.[160] Unlike the first-generation system, claims do not have to go to intake or investigation. The centre turns many claims away, even those within its jurisdiction, something the previous commission did not have the power to do. The tribunal's 2012–13 statistics indicated that almost 80 percent of claimants who appear before it are unrepresented.[161]

Some critics in the legal community feel that not enough lawyers are available for complainants. In response, Gottheil argued that: "Enhancing access to justice is not only about many people having more lawyers. Just lawyering people up is not a solution ... Some will argue that the tribunal should look like a court, with passive judges. This is not accessible justice. We use an active adjudicative model, which is important, especially when you have unrepresented complainants ... [It] is extremely important that the parties feel that they were really heard."[162]

The 2012 Pinto Report had a different perspective in terms of the importance of "lawyering people up." It said that the HRLSC represents only 12 percent of applicants before the tribunal. The report considered this "low rate to be unacceptable and inconsistent with the equilibrium envisaged by the Code reforms which require the Centre to at least partly address the power imbalance inherent in the direct access system where parties are primarily responsible for advancing their own case."[163]

David Baker, an experienced litigator in both the first- and second-generation Ontario systems, said that the new devil is in the procedural details. He argued that interim motions and applications (for example, seeking preliminary dismissal of complaints, interim orders, or requests to defer a case) are threatening to take the place of delays as the biggest problem in the new system: "Anyone can be motioned to death in the tribunal system now. The only question is when."[164]

The role of the Ontario Human Rights Commission is still a work-in-progress. Like several of the interviewees in Ontario, Baker felt that people were still "waiting to see" how the commission was going to move into its new role, and how it would handle its much-vaunted systemic initiatives and public inquiries. Gottheil said he was unsure about the new mandate: "I support the commission, but I do worry that it is leaning more towards becoming a research body."[165] Chief Commissioner Barbara Hall rejected the notion that the Ontario Commission would "just be about glossy publications and brochures. We are planning on doing more education and creating more partnerships to address systemic issues. We want to broaden the groups with whom we are working on these issues. We are very excited about the response to making mental health one of our priorities. This is an issue that has major social implications and it is 'out there' as a social issue, as we have seen with initiatives like Michael Kirby's work on the Mental Health Commission of Canada."[166]

Hall said that the Ontario Commission is also monitoring cases at the tribunal and in the courts, and is proactively looking for situations in which it can or should intervene. "Ultimately, we are interested in impact and in achieving change, and we will use all the tools that we have." Prior to the Bill 107 reforms, the Ontario Commission had no meaningful capacity to address or initiate complaints on a strategic or systemic basis even though the legal basis was present for it to do so. Building this capacity over time will be a significant challenge and, according to the Pinto Report, the commission has not yet reached its full potential. Stakeholders reflected the concern that the commission is too removed from the fray. The Pinto Report stated: "I find that the Commission has made major strides in fulfilling its revised mandate and that cooperative strategies to build in human rights compliance have been important to its success. However, the consensus of stakeholders was that the Commission has withdrawn from certain parts of its mandate and has therefore not quite achieved the right balance. In order to fulfill its *complete* mandate, the Commission must: (1) engage in more strategic litigation at the Tribunal; (2) be more accessible to the public; and (3) reconnect with the private employment sector."[167]

Despite these shortcomings, direct access has led to several improvements, including improved access to justice, but only in the sense of access to a decision-maker. Delays are down, but access to justice for disadvantaged claimants is a more serious issue in BC. Ontario has fewer of the negative features, while retaining many positive ones.

In summary, second-generation systems have the following positive features:

- Improved access to human rights adjudication for claimants;
- Rapid entry into adjudication, which speeds up the overall complaints process;
- Increased transparency, as the claims process takes place before a tribunal that has rules governing disclosure of evidence and procedure;
- Better control for parties to a complaint because they can direct their own litigation; and
- Elimination of perceived conflicts of interest. (In first-generation systems, commissions are seen to act as advocates for complainants, but they are also required to act "neutrally" in the public interest).

On the negative side of the equation, direct access models:

- Do not comply with the Paris Principles, unless they still have a commission, as is the case in Ontario.
- Contribute to the privatization of human rights adjudication by eliminating or minimizing the role of advocates for the public interest (again, unless commissions are preserved to fulfil this function).
- Create barriers for complainants with mental disabilities or who have difficulty engaging with a complex legal system, unless support is provided.
- Lack a publicly funded institution that offers information to respondents, bearing in mind that the Ontario HRLSC is limited to supporting complainants and cannot provide information to respondents.[168]
- Cut commissions off from the daily flow of complaints and inquiries. Commissions may therefore become more focused on abstract or theoretical issues and less sensitive to current issues. One way of addressing these concerns is for commissions to invest in strategic litigation, as the Pinto Report suggested for Ontario's Commission.
- Are expensive. Tribunals and legal support centres employ expensive human resources such as registrars, assessors, case managers, lawyers, and full-time decision-makers.

The comparison between Ontario and British Columbia reveals that direct access – in and of itself – is not necessarily the only key to success for second-generation human rights systems. What is also vital is a commitment to access to justice, support for claimants, and the existence of a commission to both protect and promote human rights. The potentially negative impact of tribunal-only systems without these other features is illustrated by Nunavut.

Nunavut

In 2003, Nunavut created its second-generation, direct access human rights system, without a commission or a public support structure for complainants.[169] By March 2012, Nunavut's Human Rights Tribunal had received only sixty-four complaints and only two of those had gone to a hearing.[170] Amidst allegations of dysfunction, the government asked Shelagh Day and Gwen Brodsky to review Nunavut's human rights system. In their report, tabled in June 2012, Day and Brodsky recommend that Nunavut establish a human rights commission as part of a legislative review process:[171]

This Report identifies a serious structural problem that must be fixed for the [Nunavut Human Rights Act (NHRA)] to function effectively. Specifically, certain essential functions are missing from Nunavut's human rights system.

Stakeholders consulted during this review identified a number of functions not provided for in the current NHRA, but which, given the experience of the last six years, they now consider essential to making the NHRA effective for the people of the Nunavut. Each of these functions is significant, but for the most part they ... cannot or should not be carried out by the Nunavut Human Rights Tribunal. The core responsibility of a Tribunal is adjudication, and it is widely understood as necessary to maintain some separation between adjudication and education and advocacy.

As recounted to us, the experience of the Nunavut Human Rights Tribunal, and those interacting with it over the last six years, has made it evident that Nunavut needs the functions that are usually carried out by a Human Rights Commission. These functions, though they would be performed by a separate body, would facilitate and strengthen the work of the Tribunal.

[...]

The Tribunal was not given a mandate to:

• provide broad human rights education to the residents of Nunavut;

- provide pro-active education to respondents about compliance with the NHRA;
- provide pro-active education to those who need the *Act*'s protections;
- undertake studies, research, or inquiries;
- develop guidelines or policies;
- proactively address concerns about systemic discrimination;
- provide assistance and advice to applicants regarding framing their notifications, evidence, documents, precedents, or witnesses;
- advocate for applicants before the Tribunal (or in court in the event of judicial review or appeal proceedings).[172]

Saskatchewan

Saskatchewan has taken an entirely different route from any other jurisdiction in Canada. In 2010, the Saskatchewan government introduced Bill 160, which went in precisely the opposite direction from BC and Ontario.[173] Instead of abolishing the province's commission, it abolished the tribunal. Bill 160 came into force in 2011. Following this, the commission underwent major internal restructuring. Borrowing from Manitoba's model, which has invested in a successful mediation system, the Saskatchewan Commission's resources are being focused on settling complaints, although it continues to perform a gatekeeping function by investigating and screening complaints. Complaints that make it through the commission gatekeeping system are now sent directly to the Saskatchewan Court of Queen's Bench instead of being sent to a tribunal.

While critics of Bill 160 agreed that Saskatchewan's Human Rights Tribunal had not been efficient, they noted the lack of public consultation prior to the reforms. There had been no attempt to address the problems by providing adequate resources for the tribunal, or by ensuring adequate statutory criteria to ensure the competency, qualifications, and merit of tribunal members.[174] According to Ken Norman, there were other criticism as well: "Bill 160 scraps the Human Rights Tribunal along with its informal rules of evidence in favour of the Court of Queen's Bench governed by the Queen's Bench Rules of Court. To be clear, lawyers and no one else get to play in this court ... under these voluminous rules.[175]

David Arnot, Saskatchewan's chief commissioner and a former judge, was in favour of abolishing the tribunal from the start. A well-regarded jurist, Arnot posted the following statement on the commission's website in 2010: "Tribunals originally became part of the human rights process in Canada in order to make the process simpler and to speed up decision making. In the last decade, however, human rights law, practice, and issues have become increasingly complex. The Commission now believes it is time to address those complexities by having judges decide cases."[176] Interestingly, Arnot's arguments for abolishing Saskatchewan's tribunal (speed and simplicity) were the same reasons used to justify the elimination and trimming of the BC and Ontario Commissions in favour of direct access systems. Arnot also emphasized the importance of a new, commission-directed mediation process that would accelerate case management. The legislation also speeds up decision-making by making the commission both first and last decider, at least for preliminary dismissals. The office of the chief commissioner becomes a decision-maker of last resort for complaints dismissed at the commission level.

Abolishing the tribunal appears to have been an astute move in terms of public relations. Vocal commission-critics were satisfied that the government had decided to jettison an element of the human rights system, thus deflecting attention from the commission. However, the decision to jettison the tribunal means that Saskatchewan has lost access to the advantages of an administrative decision-maker: subject-matter expertise, the ability to accumulate a substantial body of decisions in relatively short order, and accessibility. Concerns about judicial independence, also voiced by Arnot, are fair concerns.[177] Such concerns can and should have been addressed by structural guarantees of independence, neutrality, and competence for the tribunal instead of getting rid of it. These issues are discussed at greater length in chapter 4.

The developments in BC and Saskatchewan, coupled with the vociferous attacks on human rights commissions in the context of the hate speech debates, have prompted some writers to inquire about the connection between these changes and a broader conservative strategy of "denormalizing" human rights commissions and dismantling human rights protections.

What is it with the attack on rights agencies by conservative governments across Canada? Where does this lack of respect for rights defenders come from?

A clear pattern of attacking these agencies is emerging in Canada as conservative governments, large C or small, have been elected. It began in 2001 with the election of the Gordon Campbell government in British Columbia. One of his early acts was to dismantle the BC Human Rights Commission in favour of direct access to a tribunal.

Recently, the Harper government announced it is dismantling the International Centre for Rights and Democracy in Montreal, an agency that was established by the Brian Mulroney government. Saskatchewan's Human Rights Commission is on life support now with the dismantling last year of the Saskatchewan Human Rights Tribunal, and the layoff or retirement of half its staff this year.[178]

It is too early to tell whether Saskatchewan's new model will be faster or more efficient than its predecessor. The test will not be only the success of the mediation system, which, based on Manitoba's results, has great promise. Rather, it lies in the concentration of discretion in the office of the chief commissioner, who retains ultimate discretion as to whether or not to refer a matter to the court. The "first decider" thus becomes the "final decider" with very little access to appeals.

Quebec

Quebec has had a modified first-generation system for its entire existence. Complainants have more access to adjudication, at least on paper, than anywhere in Canada. The reality, however, is vastly different from the theory. There are two reasons for this. The first has to do with narrowed access to the Quebec Human Rights Tribunal, and the second deals with the tendency in Quebec to encourage human rights cases to be heard by other types of administrative tribunals outside the human rights system.

On the first point, complainants can file complaints with the commission, or they can seek redress directly before the courts in civil suits. Only the first route is generally used because of costs. Prior to 1997, there was a third route. Where the commission had declined to take charge of a case, the claimant could still proceed to the Quebec Human Rights Tribunal through a process called substitution.[179] In 1997, access to the third route was essentially cut off by the Quebec Court of Appeal in a controversial decision in *Menard v. Rivet*.[180] The court decided that, notwithstanding what seems to be clear wording in the Quebec Charter, parties cannot go before the tribunal without the support of the commission except in the very rare circumstances where the commission finds evidence of discrimination but nonetheless decides in its discretion not to proceed to the tribunal. There are some cases where the commission has decided to let cases go forward, but very few.

The second reason is that the courts have permitted human rights complaints to be diverted away from the human rights system into other administrative systems, notably labour relations boards, which have a strong tradition of deference to labour arbitrators and even a presumption of arbitral exclusivity.[181] While the Supreme Court of Canada has decided that there is no hard and fast rule about whether cases should go to labour arbitrators or human rights commissions,[182] the cumulative and practical impact of this trend has been that unionized emplyees have little or no access to the human rights commission in Quebec. According to Montreal activist Fo Niemi, the result has been "disastrous," leaving people with little in the way of remedies and no access to justice.[183]

The statistics support his claim. Between 2005–06 and 2011–12, the tribunal received on average only about 38 cases a year from the commission.[184] As discussed in chapter 1, the referral rate to the tribunal of between 5 and 10 percent in Quebec during that period compares unfavourably with the 80 percent of cases in the second-generation system in Ontario that have made it past the preliminary screening stage since 2008. The difference has significant implications for access to justice. For the former head of the tribunal, Michèle Rivet, access to justice is a paramount consideration. Rivet thought it would be a "monumental error" to abolish the commission in Quebec, but she expressed serious concern about the Quebec's Human Rights System: "The Tribunal was created in 1990 to accelerate things and to create a more open process. How can it do this if there are so few cases coming forward? As president of the Tribunal, I am responsible for its proper functioning as part of the Quebec judiciary. I have to defend the Tribunal's existence, but there is a public expense involved in maintaining a Tribunal, and few cases coming through. But one has to be honest and say what is happening. The Commission must deal with its cases more effectively."[185]

Many of the issues regarding delays and bottlenecks that were so problematic in Ontario's first-generation system are still front and centre in Quebec, even if they are less frequently discussed publically. "The delays, backlogs and inertia at the Quebec Commission are very serious," said Niemi, who runs one of the major anti-racism organizations in Montreal. Like most activists in Quebec, and unlike activists in many other provinces, Niemi strongly supports the commission, even its gatekeeping function, but said that the current model and the current level of productivity are not acceptable.[186]

CONCLUSION

With the support of social movements, legislatures across Canada enacted human rights laws, giving rise to first-generation systems with a strong regulatory framework. The Canadian Charter of Rights and Freedoms, as well as Canada's obligations under international human rights treaties, have deepened the connection between Canadian human rights systems and international human rights law.

Criticism of first-generation human rights systems by progressive advocates has focused on effectiveness, speed, access to justice, and the separation of investigative and adjudicative functions. Criticisms from the political right have also been about better performance and effectiveness, but have gone further and alleged that human rights institutions have strayed from their appointed mandates and become involved in some areas, including economic rights, regulation of the private sector, and hate speech, that they were never intended to address.

An overview of some of the milestones for human rights systems shows how mistaken the latter criticisms are. The work of civil liberties groups in Canada was directed toward ensuring access to a blend of economic and social rights (rights to housing, education, and services, as well as civil rights and fundamental freedoms (political rights, religious rights and certain legal rights, for example). All of these rights are bound together and mediated by the principle that all rights should be available to all members of society equally, without discrimination. The role of equality law, as framed in the Charter, is also a centerpiece of civil and political rights.[187] Framing discrimination in terms of its effects and not its intention was the necessary consequence of a shift away from criminal law and has resulted in systems that are capable of addressing discrimination in its many forms, regardless of which category of rights is engaged.

Second-generation human rights systems emerged largely as a response to the concerns of progressive human rights advocates. They differ from first-generation systems mainly in providing direct access to decision-making bodies, which has demonstrably addressed concerns about access to justice and delays. The combined experiences of Ontario, British Columbia, and Nunavut suggest that an important factor in the success, credibility, and impact of second-generation systems is the retention of a commission as part of the public human rights infrastructure.

Human rights systems remain vulnerable institutions. Governments and sometimes even the courts have not always been prepared to respect their autonomy and independence. The threat or reality of elimination, peremptory firings, rights rollbacks, and administrative interference are part of the history of human rights systems in Canada. Their vulnerability is not only a function of the inadequacies of commissions or tribunals themselves but also of changing demands on the systems.

Despite the shortcomings, false starts, and uphill struggles described in this chapter, human rights systems have played an important role in developing human rights law and in improving lives. Human rights systems have been the legislative response to judicial "inactivism" and to widespread and blatant forms of discrimination. There has been enormous progress in Canada in terms of respect for human rights and the stability of the institutions that support them. These successes, however, raise fair questions about the ongoing relevance of human rights institutions and the extent to which the reasons for creating them still exist. Chapter 3 explores these issues.

3

Do We Still Need Them?

"Are we done now? Is this equality?"
Kim Bernhardt, 14 September 2009

Chapters 1 and 2 outlined the main functions and features of human rights systems and described why they were put in place. Human rights laws and human rights systems were a reaction to the failure of the judiciary in an earlier era to recognize the need for effective remedies and develop the common law to provide them. But aren't things different today? Some in the media certainly would have us think so – a *National Post* commentary cheerfully reported in 2013 that, "racism, sexism and homophobia have become rare in Canadian public life."[1]

It is true that overt discrimination is less prevalent, or at least less acceptable, but it has not disappeared. Progress in attitudes in Canadian society should not be used to support the illusion that discrimination has disappeared or that people no longer need protection. As Fiona Sampson, a commissioner with the Ontario Human Rights Commission pointed out: "the critics of human rights commissions have a good point when they say that the role of commissions has changed. However, where they are off base is to say that women have achieved equality or there is no more racism. Just look at the annual reports of commissions and the news headlines. Even if advances have been made, it would be a mistake to shut down human rights commissions because that would leave people without a remedy."[2]

Looking at commissions' annual reports and at news headlines (as distinct from media commentary about cherry-picked cases), it is impossible to conclude that discrimination is a thing of the past. The critics who have put commissions and tribunals on "trial by anecdote" have not actually looked at what is behind the thousands of cases that go to tribunals every year in Canada.[3] Lawyer Kim Bernhardt acknowledged that "issues are not always as open, sharp or ... severe as they may have been in the past, but ... you have to know that racism, sexism, and homophobia are still present."[4] Alan Borovoy, who has been watching the human rights field develop for several decades, said that the problems may be more subtle and less obvious today, "but they are still there."[5]

This chapter examines the evidence for the assertion that human rights systems are redundant or outdated from five perspectives. The first deals with whether there continues to be an ongoing demand for human rights systems and discusses some of the reasons for renewed or new demands. The second deals with changes in the way rights are described, understood, and litigated. The third takes on the charge that human rights systems are engaged in rights inflation and that they deal with petty, silly, and frivolous claims. The fourth considers the accusation that human rights systems are undemocratic. Finally, I look at the renewed calls for laissez-faire approaches to regulating discrimination, which call for the elimination of human rights systems, the restriction of their application to the public sector, or the use of market-based incentives.

DECREASING DEMAND?

If it is true that discrimination is disappearing, then the numbers of human rights complaints should be on the wane as well. The statistics suggest otherwise. Roughly seven thousand human rights complaints are filed in Canada every year.[6] The numbers may vary in a given year depending on the economy and the jurisdiction, but the overall trend, at least since the 1980s, is not one of diminishing demand.

Two studies that examined trends in the 1980s and 1990s analyzed the annual number of claims and the size of caseloads at human rights commissions over a combined seventeen year period. The first study showed that between 1980 and 1997 caseloads increased anywhere from 50 to 400 percent, except in Quebec where they dropped by 25 percent.[7] The second shows that between 1989–90 and 1995–96, the number of claims received/accepted by six human rights commissions in Canada increased by about 68 percent.[8]

In addition, if one compares the average number of claims in the four largest jurisdictions in Canada (British Columbia, Canada, Ontario, and Quebec) between 1989–92 and 2009–12, there was an increase of almost 50 percent over that period.

Table 3.1
Average cases filed per year in four major jurisdictions

Jurisdiction	Average number of cases filed per year		% change
	1989–1992	2009–2012	
British Columbia (BC Human Rights Council and Tribunal)[1]	576	1,126	95
Federal (CHRC)[2]	935	1,635	73
Ontario (OHRC/HRTO)	2,166[3]	3,155[4]	45
Quebec (CDPDJ)	1,259[5]	1,330[6]	6
Total	4,936	7,246	47

1 British Columbia Human Rights Council, Annual Reports, 1989–1992; British Columbia Human Rights Tribunal, Annual Reports from 2009–10, 2010–11 and 2011–12, online: BCHRT <http://www.bchrt.bc.ca/annual_reports/index.htm>.

2 Canadian Human Rights Commission, *Annual Report: 1992* (Ottawa: Minister of Supply and Services, 1993) at 104; 2012 *Annual Report* (Ottawa: Minister of Public Works and Government Services, 2013), online: CHRC < http://www.chrc-ccdp.gc.ca/sites/default/files/chrc-annual-report-2012_0.pdf. The figures refer to received complaints.

3 Ontario Human Rights Commission Annual Reports; 1989–90; 1990–91; 1991–92; Human Rights Tribunal of Ontario, Annual Reports from 2008–09, 2009–10 and 2010–11, online: HRTO <http://www.hrto.ca/hrto/?q=en/node/26>.

4 Human Rights Tribunal of Ontario, *Annual Report 2009–2010*; *Fiscal Year 2010-11 – New Applications, Fiscal Year 2011-12 – New Applications* online: HRTO <http://www.hrto.ca/hrto/?q=en/node/152> [HRTO, *Fiscal Year*].

5 Figures provided by the Commission des droits de la personne et droits de la jeunesse.

6 Commission des droits de la personne et des droits de la jeunesse, *Rapport d'activités et de gestion: 2011-2012* (Montreal: CDPDJ, 2011), Table 16 at 44, online: CDPDJ <http://www.cdpdj.qc.cach 3 T.docx>.

Ontario and British Columbia, both now second generation systems, show the most significant increases in the 1989–92 and 2009–12 period. The increases suggest that when people have the chance to file human rights claims directly with a specialized tribunal, without having to go through a gatekeeping commission, they will do so in large numbers. The increases in the federal system are due in part to its new jurisdiction over Aboriginal claims following legislation that took effect in 2011 because of the repeal of section 67 of the Canadian Human Rights Act (CHRA).

Returning to Ontario, it is important to understand the reasons for the increased demand for the tribunal after 2008. The *National Post* said in 2011 that there has been "a 10-fold increase in hearings over the past three years. It is institutionalized bonanza for anyone who carries a grudge against his or her boss or landlord."[9] Had the editorial board of the *National Post* made even a cursory examination of this "10-fold" increase, they would have seen that the three-year period to which they refer was the period in which the commission lost responsibility for receiving human rights complaints and the tribunal gained it. Looking at the increase in the number of complaints received and handled by the tribunal without understanding that it was just a shift of complaints from one institution to another led the *National Post* to the mistaken impression that this increase represented a net increase of claims into the system. The actual figures tell the real story: in the 2007–08 fiscal year, the Ontario Human Rights Commission received 3,492 complaints. It referred 331 cases to the tribunal for a hearing. In 2011, Ontario's Commission received no complaints (Bill 107 was, by this point, fully in force). The tribunal received all of the complaints, 3,167 of them.[10] Failure to understand the context, and apparently to even inquire into it, led to the mistaken impression of a 10-fold increase in the human rights "bureaucracy."

The outlier is Quebec, which has stayed relatively stable in terms of complaints received. However, this statistic reflects the fact that it has become increasingly difficult to get a case heard by the Quebec Tribunal. This problem has had the effect of discouraging potential applicants, especially those from unionized workplaces, whose claims tend to be automatically bounced out of the human rights system. Large numbers of cases either are shunted to other tribunals or never make it to the human rights system at all. Between 2000 and 2005, for example, the tribunal received an average of fewer than forty cases per year. In 2007, the former president of the Quebec Human Rights Tribunal, Michèle Rivet, in partnership with Quebec's bar association, the Barreau du Québec, decided to initiate a research project to investigate what other human rights systems in Canada were doing as a way to address what she viewed as a serious problem of access to justice. The project led to a conference on the issue and the publication of a book about Canadian human rights systems, especially the reforms in Ontario following Bill 107.[11] One of the key observations was that direct access systems were producing superior results in terms of access to justice and delays, as discussed in chapter 2.

Initiating such a project was unusual, given the tribunal's role as a neutral decision-maker. Rivet, however, had presided over the Quebec Tribunal for two decades and was alarmed at the trickle of incoming cases. Rivet said that she went to the minister of Justice to discuss the problems, but there was no appetite for reform. While there has been no push from stakeholders in Quebec on the scale seen in British Columbia or Ontario, activist Fo Niemi said that there is keen interest among activists in improving access to the tribunal.[12]

CHANGES IN DESCRIPTION, UNDERSTANDING, AND LITIGATION INVOLVING RIGHTS

Assessing "demand" for human rights systems requires more than simply counting complaints. No one in the human rights system or elsewhere wants to see demand rise – fewer complaints should signal a more accepting society. But an increase in the number of complaints does not necessarily indicate a more racist or discriminatory society either. The introduction of new human rights grounds and the changing contour and scope of familiar ones are responsible in part for the increases. As awareness of human rights improves, people are more likely to file claims about incidents that would previously have gone unreported. The way in which human rights cases are described, understood, and litigated has changed dramatically over the years. In the sections below, I discuss five examples: disability rights; sex discrimination, harassment, and gender equality; immigrants and temporary workers; family status; and Aboriginal rights.

Disability Rights

As late as the 1980s, disability was seldom seen as a human rights issue in Canada.[13] Today, between one-third and one-half of human rights complaints filed across the country involve disability, and it is one of the most vital and progressive areas of equality rights. The factors underlying these changes are partly demographic, but they are also the result of rapid progress in science, a much better understanding of the limitations imposed by disabilities, and more nuanced social attitudes about the connection between equality, liberty, and human dignity. A vital culture of human rights and strong advocacy by disability communities have helped to diminish the stigma surrounding disability and change perceptions.[14]

There are urgent reasons to treat disability seriously and to find ways to improve a social infrastructure that often excludes people with disabilities, at enormous cost. People with disabilities are less likely to be employed, more likely to be poor, and more likely to receive government assistance than people without a disability.[15] The number of people affected is much greater than might be thought – according to Statistics Canada, 16.5 percent of Canadians reported having a disability in 2006. The federal government estimates that by 2051 one in four Canadians will be sixty-five or older.[16] An aging population is more likely to experience disability. There is also greater awareness of mental disability and mental illness. Although there is no comprehensive national or provincial/territorial database on the prevalence of mental health problems and disorders, it is estimated that about one in five Canadians will experience a mental health issue in their lifetimes.[17] These include mental illness related to depression, addiction disabilities, anxiety, Alzheimer's, and schizophrenia. Relatively few human rights complaints are filed in relation to many of these types of disorders, but this does not mean that there is no problem or that equality has been achieved.

Neurodevelopmental disorders such as autism also pose significant human rights challenges. In the United States, rates of autism have gone from 1 in 2,500 births in 1960 to 1 in 88 today, and parents have become activists and litigants in the fight for resources and services.[18] In Canada, one of the most important battles for resources has involved the effectiveness and availability of intensive behaviour therapies. Litigator Mary Eberts has said that attempts to require the government to provide proven therapies for autistic children were "dealt a death blow" by the 2006 *Wynberg* case.[19] Thirty families brought the case on behalf of thirty-five autistic children after the Ontario government decided to restrict access to an intensive early intervention program to children under age six. The parents argued that it was discriminatory to stop providing therapy after age five. They succeeded at trial but lost on appeal, in part due to the 2004 Supreme Court of Canada decision in *Auton*.[20]

In *Auton*, the parents of several autistic children brought an action similar to that in *Wynberg* against the British Columbia government, arguing that the government had violated the children's equality rights on the grounds of age and disability. A unanimous Supreme Court ruled that the denial of treatment did not infringe the children's equality rights because the relevant health legislation guaranteed only core services and the treatment in question was not considered a "core service." Children with autism could therefore no longer depend on the government to deliver intensive behaviour therapies. Eberts, who was involved in the *Wynberg* case, said that "these were not emergent therapies – they are proven treatments. They are the *only* treatment, something that the

Government of Ontario actually admitted at the time. But here we have our most senior courts behaving like American health insurance companies, denying coverage. It was awful."[21]

One of the themes of this book is the importance of integrating equality rights into legal notions of liberty and human dignity.[22] In the *Auton* case, an advocate who is herself autistic made an argument for the opposite proposition, namely for the importance of integrating dignity and liberty interests into equality rights. Michelle Dawson, the only intervener before the court in *Auton* who was autistic, argued that autism is not a disease and cannot be treated as if it were an illness. Indeed, she argued that inappropriate treatments account for much of the suffering of people with autism:

Autism is not a mental illness. Autistics have suffered terribly for being treated inappropriately and unethically as though mentally ill. It is well known that autistics have, in the past and present, become trapped in the mental health system. Subject to unethical medication, restraint, and incarceration, they have been destroyed, often despite functioning competently prior to being mistreated.

If the prejudices and assumptions present in the conclusions of the courts below are allowed to stand, untreated autistics who do seek to participate in and contribute to Canadian society will continue to face intolerance and discrimination.[23]

Mental health and mental illness are surrounded by stereotype and stigma. There are painful and challenging questions about what "normal" means beyond statistical averages, and about our tendency to view anything that deviates from that image of "normal" as something to be labelled, delineated, and fixed. Many of these issues are increasingly the focus of current work from human rights commissions in Canada. Barbara Hall of the Ontario Commission observed that the high financial and social burdens of mental illness have led governments to search for solutions. One response was the creation of the Mental Health Commission in 2007–08. According to Hall: "this issue has become more front and centre as the likes of Michael Kirby and the Mental Health Commission [of Canada] have become more present. There is a big need out there, but few complaints [have been filed in this area]." During the Ontario Human Rights Commission's public consultations on human rights, mental health, and addictions, many people pleaded that more be done to reduce the stigma of mental illness. Many of us know rationally that discrimination is wrong but often cannot get over deep-seated emotional reactions rooted in fear of difference. Hall said, "the desperation of the families that live with mental illness was clear."[24] These consultations, the largest in the Ontario Commission's history, culminated in the 2012 report *Minds that Matter*.[25]

> There are signs that a shift is underway in how people with mental health issues or addictions are viewed. Mental health has been made a government priority at the provincial and federal levels. The U.N. *Convention on the Rights of Persons with Disabilities* changes the focus on persons with disabilities from recipients of charity to holders of rights. By ratifying this convention, Canada has agreed to take steps to ensure equality and non-discrimination in many aspects of life for all people with disabilities. Across Ontario, there is increasing awareness and acknowledgment of the major barriers that people with mental health issues and addictions face. Individuals and organizations are asking for more education about mental health and for changes to laws and policies to end negative stereotyping and discrimination.[26]

An important factor in the work of commissions has been increased emphasis on inclusion and full participation in society. One aspect of this approach has been the move away from the medical model of disability (which focuses on diagnoses and treatments) towards a social model. This shift focuses on removing barriers to encouraging participation, and on reframing many of the disadvantages that people with disabilities experience as a product of society's negative reactions and failure to adjust policies, infrastructure, and systems to be more inclusive. This shift began almost a half century ago: "In 1965, [the] 'medical model' of disability began to change. That year marked the publication of a seminal article that proposed a completely new approach to thinking about disability. Author Saad Nagi argued that every day people with disabilities encounter barriers to their daily activities that are not caused by their impairments but [rather] by an environment that does not take account of their impairment. ... In other words, Nagi proposed, disability is effectively a social disadvantage that an unsupportive environment imposes on top of an individual's impairment."[27] The focus has shifted from handicaps and diagnoses to equality, universal design, and barrier-removal.[28]

Professor Ravi Malhotra, a human rights and disability rights scholar at the University of Ottawa, said that the question is no longer "why is this person in a wheelchair?" but rather "why is there no ramp?"[29] In 2000 the Supreme Court of Canada recognized the social model of disability in a case that reframed discrimination law in Canada by examining social attitudes toward and perceptions of handicaps.[30] The shift to a society that accepts people with disabilities means more than just accepting difference – it is about the translation of attitudes and perceptions into accessible resources, structures, and facilities.

Even human rights workers within human rights commissions have found this shift difficult. It is easy to decide if someone has a disability based on a clear medical diagnosis but it is conceptually and practically much more difficult to develop a legal framework for discrimination in terms of social responses to disability and removing barriers to participation. As one researcher has noted, "There is no fine dividing line which can be drawn between disability and "normality," and between capability and inability. Such lines as are drawn are necessarily arbitrary. The better view is to record disability and able-bodiedness as being extremes on a broad spectrum or continuum of human behavior and experience. A person may be disabled or nondisabled at different times of life and/or for different purposes or activities."[31]

In 1998, the policy branch of the Ontario Human Rights Commission initiated internal discussions to amend existing policy documents to reflect a social model of disability. Given that disability was one of the most significant grounds of discrimination in human rights complaints in Canada and in Ontario, it did not seem much of a conceptual stretch nor a difficult policy decision to make this issue an internal priority. Nonetheless, many staff members in the Ontario Commission balked at the proposal. During training sessions and during the course of the development of the policy internally, they complained that the change would make their lives more difficult and result in increased workload. Major external consultations were undertaken in 1999, and the results confirmed the practical importance of changing the focus to social responses to disability. The results also indicated that this was clearly the direction that the courts were taking. Nonetheless, it would take several years before this approach was fully accepted and integrated into the commission's work.[32]

The shift to a social model means that the institutional attention of human rights commissions correspondingly shifts to the social infrastructure that creates barriers for people with disabilities. Malhotra said that transportation is "the number one priority." Lack of accessible transportation, including public transit, prevents people from getting to work, getting to school, and living the kinds of lives that able-bodied people take for granted. He noted that Canada lags far behind the United States in this area, largely because Canada did not face the same pressure to accommodate veterans with disabilities after the Vietnam War.[33] It was not until the Supreme Court of Canada's 2007 *Via Rail* decision that people with disabilities in Canada secured anything like a nation-wide right to travel and use public services.[34] The *Via Rail* case involved a complaint by the Council of Canadians with Disabilities to the Canadian Transportation Agency. The issue was the lack of accessibility of the Via Rail Renaissance cars for wheelchair users. The Supreme Court of Canada, in a 5–4 majority, decided that VIA Rail should have made its rail cars accessible to passengers with disabilities, rejecting Via's argument that it would cost too much, absent convincing evidence that it was impossible to adapt the cars short of undue hardship. Incredibly, Via Rail fought the case for more than a decade. The *Via Rail* case, however, has limited application outside its own facts, and progress in the area of transportation and public transit has been uneven and slow. Many aspects of transportation services need to be re-examined and rethought from the ground up, from subways and metro systems to buses and paratransit services, to ensure that persons with disabilities can have access to the goods and services the rest of us take for granted.[35]

Human rights commissions have played an important part in efforts to promote better transit and transportation services across Canada. The Ontario Human Rights Commission began developing discussion papers, holding public consultations, and adopting policy positions on accessibility standards for public transit in 2001.[36] Toronto is far ahead of my home city of Montreal, where only 10 percent of the metro (subway) system is accessible to wheelchair users and others with mobility restrictions. Projections from the Société de transport de Montréal indicate that Montreal's metro system will be fully accessible only in 2085. By comparison, almost half of Toronto's subway system is wheelchair accessible and the entire system will be accessible by 2037. In 2011, the disability rights activist group RAPLIQ (Regroupement activistes pour l'inclusion Québec) filed a systemic human rights complaint against the Société de transport de Montréal after years of negotiations had failed to produce adequate outcomes.[37] The complaint is now before the Quebec Commission and is a good example of the type of systemic issue that can be brought before human rights systems at relatively little cost to advocacy organizations and people with disabilities, and with a view to changing social structures and infrastructure.

Lawyer and disability rights activist David Baker has thought long and hard about how societies can adapt themselves to be more inclusive and universally accessible. He acknowledged that the development of legal standards to accommodate people with disabilities, and the resulting impact on the private sector, might have caused some backlash from employers and service providers. However, he emphasized that failing to accommodate people with disabilities is not only illegal, it is also economically unsound and counterproductive: "Without human rights, all we have is the obligation to compensate – not to accommodate. Where I would engage with some people [who oppose accommodation] is to ask whether it is productive to pension people off if they have sustained a degree of disability. If people with disabilities are not accommodated, they will be out of the workforce. The alternative is starvation or long-term demands on strained social programs. If employers don't like accommodation, how do they feel about paying higher workers' compensation premiums?"[38]

The question of how far human rights systems and the courts will go in addressing systemic complaints raises fundamental issues about the resources, programs, and health services that can be expected and demanded. In the 2012 Supreme Court case *Moore v. British Columbia*,[39] Jeffrey Moore's parents sought intensive remedial instruction for Jeffrey because of his severe form of dyslexia. Without remedial instruction, Jeffrey would have been unable to read or write at a functional level. Following government cutbacks, however, the only available public diagnostic centre had been closed, which had the effect of ending access to public programs for severe learning disabilities. Jeffrey could obtain intensive and effective remedial instruction only through private schools. Jeffrey's father filed a complaint with the BC Human Rights Tribunal on behalf of his son.

Evidence presented before the tribunal indicated that intensive supports are necessary for children with severe learning disabilities and that early intervention is important.[40] In a lengthy decision, tribunal chair Heather MacNaughton ruled that both the ministry and the school district were liable for the costs related to discrimination against Moore, not only for tuition at a private school and for remedial instruction but also for implementing a broad range of remedial measures designed to ensure the availability of early intervention programs. The case went up on review to the Supreme Court of British Columbia, and the reviewing judge decided that there had been no discrimination. The Court of Appeal dismissed the appeal.

On further appeal, the Supreme Court of Canada restored the tribunal's order against the school district. The school district had argued that its financial situation had left it no choice but to terminate the special learning programs and close the diagnostic centre. The Court, however, agreed that the school district had failed to consider alternatives for special needs students, which undermined the district's argument that it had been justified in its decision to close down existing facilities. Justice Abella wrote the Supreme Court's unanimous decision and articulated a powerful argument for state responsibility for educating all children: "[T]he reason all children are entitled to an education is because a healthy democracy and economy require their educated contribution. Adequate special education, therefore, is not a dispensable luxury. For those with severe learning disabilities, it is the ramp that provides access to the statutory commitment to education made to *all* children in British Columbia."[41]

This important case came up through the British Columbia's human rights system, and it is noteworthy that the Ontario, Manitoba, Saskatchewan, Alberta, Quebec, and Canadian human rights commissions intervened before the court in support of Moore's claim, as did disability organizations, the West Coast Women's Legal and Action Fund, and the First Nations Child and Family Caring Society of Canada. The intervener opposing Moore's claim and the principle of equal access to public education was the Canadian Constitution Foundation.

The case illustrates two important points. First, preventing discrimination may require more than simply prohibiting discriminatory actions: it may also require public services to spend money and create programs in order to ensure that people have access to public services. The Supreme Court was careful to state that it was not engaged in the business of creating social programs. However, in finding the school liable for significant tuition fees and related expenses incurred by Jeffrey's father, the court sent a clear message to the education sector that before cutting programs for people with disabilities, officials should look extremely carefully at alternatives. Second, human rights systems have a broad mandate to compensate claimants for discrimination but also to eradicate discrimination. As noted in the section on remedies in chapter 1, eliminating a discriminatory rule or practice is something that goes further than compensating a single individual. Human rights systems are uniquely well suited to provide these types of remedies, although, as the court mentioned in its decision in *Moore*, they must ensure that the claimant remains at the centre of the human rights complaint.

The UN Convention on the Rights of Persons with Disabilities (CRPD) was adopted on 13 December 2006 and ratified by Canada in 2010.[42] It is now part of Canada's international human rights obligations. The CRPD calls on states to establish "independent mechanisms," usually arm's-length institutions like human rights commissions, to promote, protect, and monitor disability rights.[43] However, despite its ratification of the CRPD, Canada has failed at many levels to respond to the most basic needs of people with disabilities. "In employment, is there a difference between no ramp and [a sign saying] Irish Need Not Apply? In a democracy, should the MLA of a voter with disabilities have an inaccessible office? Maybe these examples don't rise to the level of past racial injustices, but make no mistake – this is discrimination of the hurtful, malicious, deliberate, small minded, ignorant kind ... In more than three years since ratification [of the CRPD], Canada has neglected its obligation to implement and monitor the treaty, and currently has no plan to do so. Or even a plan to have a plan."[44]

Human rights commissions are not the only stakeholders, advocates, or policy actors in this area but they are an important part of the ongoing public conversation about what ability, normalcy, difference, and diversity mean to us as a society, and what should be done to deal with these important social issues.

Discrimination, Harassment, and Gender Equality

Women have made remarkable progress in Canada, but the struggle for equality is far from over. This section looks at three important but quite different issues that engage human rights systems, namely the ongoing prevalence of harassment in the workplace, the low rate of representation of women in political life, and equal pay and pay equity.

The Supreme Court of Canada recognized sexual harassment as a form of discrimination only in a 1989 case called *Janzen*. In the case, a male restaurant employee had harassed women by making unwanted sexual advances. He argued that his behaviour was not discriminatory because it was based on the women's attractiveness, not on their sex. The court said: "To argue that the sole factor underlying the discriminatory action was the sexual attractiveness of the appellants and to say that their gender was irrelevant strains credulity. Sexual attractiveness cannot be separated from gender."[45]

Janzen was decided twenty-seven years after the first human rights system emerged in Ontario in 1962. It took a further twenty years to take root in British Columbia, where sexual harassment is still not specifically mentioned as a form of sex discrimination in its human rights law, providing another example of fundamental human rights issues that continue to have to be litigated and relitigated. It was not until a 2012 decision from the BC Court of Appeal in the case of *Friedmann v. MacGarvie* that the seemingly elementary point that sexually harassing a tenant was a form of discrimination was clarified.[46]

Sexual harassment is still overwhelmingly an issue that affects women.[47] During his time as executive director at the Ontario Commission, Rémy Beauregard observed that young employees, pregnant women, women in low-paying jobs, and recent immigrants are especially vulnerable:

> I remember a [young woman] from an Eastern European country who had taken a low-paying job in a Toronto beauty salon. She was sexually harassed by her boss. She had no union. Her English was lousy, and this job was her only "Canadian experience." She was afraid to talk about what was happening. She was humiliated. This girl went through hell and knew she would have a difficult time finding another job without a reference from her only Canadian employer. And there were a hundred [victims] like her.
>
> One of the things that really shocked me was how prevalent cases like this are – cases of out-and-out discrimination – especially in small businesses like this one that hire new immigrants, unskilled workers, or people who just don't know that they have a choice by refusing to put up with bad behaviour.[48]

Workplace discrimination against pregnant women or women who are planning to become pregnant is still a frequent subject of complaints brought to human rights commissions and tribunals. Young women with insufficient insurable hours to qualify for maternity leave and parental benefits are especially vulnerable because they are far more likely to put up with discrimination.[49] Jessica Maciel, a pregnant twenty-year-old single woman, made the news when she was fired on her first day of work. Her Mississauga employers ran two beauty salons and fired Maciel after she informed them that she was expecting a child. She filed a complaint and in 2009 the Human Rights Tribunal of Ontario awarded her $35,000 in damages and lost wages, plus interest.[50] The salon owners were required to implement a systemic remedy: a policy to protect pregnant women from encountering discrimination in the future. According to Maciel's lawyer, the Human Rights Legal Support Centre in Ontario receives about forty calls per week from women facing similar types of blatant and overt discrimination.[51]

Harassment is part of a continuum of violent behaviour against women that starts with verbal and emotional abuse and ends with physical violence. One incident that stands out in my mind is the 1996 murder of Theresa Vince in Chatham, Ontario. Vince, fifty-six, was a long-time human resources professional who worked for Sears. She decided to retire early to get away from her boss, Russell Davis, who had harassed her for years. Davis finally shot and killed Vince before turning the gun on himself. In 1997, a coroner's inquiry was struck to look into Vince's death and heard evidence of Davis's obsession with Vince. One of the lawyers for the family tried to make the inquiry about the Ontario Human Rights Commission and its procedures, even though there was no evidence at all that Vince had tried to contact the commission. There was a good deal of discussion about whether Vince had filed a human rights complaint about sexual harassment or even contacted the Ontario Human Rights Commission about it. Because of the potential role of the commission, I was called as a witness to the coroner's inquiry. I testified that there was no evidence whatsoever that she had contacted the commission at any point. The reality was, and is, that human rights commissions are not the police. In Canada, commissions are not structured to protect people in emergency situations. Even if Vince had called, a complaint would not likely have been effective in preventing her death. Any government agency that receives a call signalling a dangerous situation or a potential crime should call the police immediately, and procedures to that effect were implemented at the commission shortly after these events.

Afterwards, in the waiting area outside the hearing room, I watched while Theresa Vince's relatives and their lawyers formed a circle and came together in an expression of sadness and solidarity. A man who had also been watching the proceedings approached me and quietly identified himself as a close relative. He said, "Theresa was a very independent person – we came from another generation. She would never have filed a human rights complaint." I knew Vince had not tried to contact the commission, but was stunned that it may not even have occurred to her or if it had, that it would not have been considered seriously as an option. I have no idea whether his characterization of Vince's behaviour and thoughts on the matter was accurate. However, his comment stayed with me. People approach situations of harassment and discrimination in different ways, for different reasons. One is generational, as may have been the case here. Another is a concern to preserve privacy and personal autonomy. I mention this because one often reads in the press that human rights commissions are a manifestation of a nanny state that removes personal responsibility and autonomy from people, fostering a culture of complaint. There are people who, by virtue of temperament and experience, see almost everything as a potential human rights complaint. But this type of behaviour, however fractious and confrontational it may be, does not detract from the sad reality that sometimes even the most resilient and independent among us need support and help.

Since then, advocacy by the Vince family and many others has led to the enactment of Bill 168, the Occupational Health and Safety Amendment Act, 2009. The act gives workers the right to refuse work if they believe they are at risk of violence. Employers are also required to take precautions to protect workers from domestic violence if that violence crosses into the workplace.

There are areas of inequality in Canada in which human rights systems are not engaged but should be. One such area is the representation of women in political life. Statistics show that women made up 24.7 percent of the politicians in the House of Commons in November 2013, compared to the global average of 21.8 percent in lower houses.[52] Although Canada is above the international average, it ranked 47th out of 146 nations in 2013, trailing behind the expected front runners such as Finland, Norway, and Denmark, but also behind Lesotho, Rwanda, and South Sudan.

Canada dropped six places in the international ranking by the World Economic Forum's Global Gender Gap Index, to 20th in 2013 from 14th in 2006. (The index ranks countries based on women's economic participation and opportunity, educational attainment, health and survival, and political empowerment.) The Global Gender Gap Index points to Canada's relatively weak performance in the political empowerment category as primarily responsible for Canada's ranking.

We rarely hear about Canadian human rights systems speaking out about improving the representation of women in public life. The situation is quite different in Europe, where women's representation in political and public life is a major public policy issue.[53] Although this issue is not necessarily an appropriate area for human rights complaints, it is an important area in which commissions can be involved with education and advocacy for improved ways to engage women in public life. The British Equality and Human Rights Commission tracks what it calls "power gaps" for a number of human rights grounds (including gender) and monitors progress on the number of women in public and elected office.[54] The commission has been reporting on the number of women MPs in Great Britain and comparing it to other European countries, looking at barriers to gender equality, such as caregiving responsibilities, health, and the standard of living for women in relation to the general population. The commission report *How Fair Is Britain?* found that the percentage of women MPs is higher in many European countries than in the Westminster Parliament and that, although the number of women MPs is rising, "Men remain vastly over-represented, accounting for nearly 4 out of 5 MPs."[55]

Women continue to experience inequality in the area of pay equity (equal pay for equal work). Pay equity is law at the federal level and in several provincial jurisdictions.[56] In practice, however, "equal pay rights have not actually resulted in equal pay."[57] According to the World Economic Forum's 2012 Global Gender Gap Report, Canadian women's average income across the workforce is eighty-one cents for every dollar earned by men. Within the same job categories, the report says the news is worse, with women being paid seventy-three cents for every dollar earned by men.

Pay equity cases are fought tooth and nail by the federal government and drag on for years, if not decades. In 2011, the Public Service Alliance of Canada and the Canadian Human Rights Commission won an epic battle with Canada Post over a pay equity complaint involving some 6,000 women who had been systematically underpaid.[58] The case had been filed with the Canadian commission an unbelievable twenty-eight years earlier. Compensation reportedly totalled about $2.5 billion, including interest. A year later, nurses who worked as medical adjudicators for the Canada Pension Plan Disability Program settled hundreds of gender discrimination complaints in a landmark agreement valued at $150 million.[59] That case had been fought for eight years.

Given the federal government's ongoing, repeated, and staunch opposition to pay equity in cases like these, an independent body such as the

Canadian Human Rights Commission must have authority over equity cases and audits, especially when the most significant transgressors will be the government itself and large federally regulated employers.

In what appears to be a pre-emptive effort to avoid future cases, the federal government enacted the Public Sector Equitable Compensation Act in 2009.[60] Despite the act's hopeful name, this law is actually aimed at removing pay equity as a right, making it subject to the collective bargaining process and removing the full right to bring a pay equity complaint to the Canadian Human Rights Commission. At the time of writing, the act was not yet in force.

Equality disparities continue to affect women's ability to be free from discrimination and harassment, to enter political life, and, finally, to achieve the right to equal pay for equal work. Most jurisdictions in Canada address pay equity through human rights legislation, labour standards laws, specific pay equity legislation, or a combination of all three.[61]

Immigrants and Temporary Workers

Acquiring permanent residence is the process by which a person immigrates to Canada. It usually takes place when a person is selected overseas, after meeting numerous requirements, and then "lands" in Canada, at which point permanent resident status is conferred. Between 1993 and 2013, Canada welcomed about five million permanent residents,[62] most of whom have gone on to become Canadian citizens. Over the last decade, more than 70 percent of new permanent residents have come from Africa, the Middle East, Asia, and the Pacific.[63] These immigrants contribute to the rich tapestry of diverse cultures and languages in Canada, but often face well-documented barriers to employment, housing, and integration, barriers higher and more persistent than those faced by immigrants from Western Europe. Not everyone has the right to enter Canada to live or work, but the basic rights in Canadian society should hold fast for people who *are* here and who interact with Canadian officials and legal systems. Maintaining them is not just important as part of a human rights culture; it is also important to attract and keep workers in the Canadian labour market.

Preventing discrimination against people who are not citizens or permanent residents but are in Canada is not a complicated idea, but it is controversial. It took a Supreme Court ruling in the 1985 *Singh* case to confirm that "everyone" physically present in Canada is entitled to life, liberty, and security of the person under section 7 of the Canadian Charter.[64] Singh's refugee claim had been denied based on an administrative paper review of his file, with no hearing. He challenged the system and won on the grounds that the process violated his rights under section 7 of the Charter, which provides that "Everyone has the right to life, liberty and security of the person and the right not to be deprived thereof except in accordance with the principles of fundamental justice." Critics appeared to be astonished that the word "everyone" in section 7 of the Charter actually meant "everyone." Because of the significance of refugee claims from the perspective of international law and the risks faced by claimants who are refused, the Supreme Court of Canada decided that the refusal to grant an oral hearing was a breach of constitutional rights.[65] As a result, refugees are entitled to present their refugee claims in person at a hearing.

Over the years, and despite *Singh*, there have been multiple instances where people who are not citizens have faced human rights violations. Some of the most famous of these have taken place in the national security context,[66] while others have been in the context of refugee law. In 2012, the federal government reversed a long-standing practice of offering basic healthcare to refugees, and introduced new restrictions on health care and benefits for several categories of refugee claimants. The Interim Federal Health Program in Canada was originally created in 1957 to provide health services to refugees and refugee claimants. The idea was to "bridge" men, women, and children requiring healthcare until such time as they were accepted as refugees or deported. In June 2012, eligibility and coverage for these services, including medical emergencies, was severely restricted under a new Order in Council.[67] The move has caused outrage among healthcare providers across the country and prompted a lawsuit by Canadian Doctors for Refugee Care and the Canadian Association of Refugee Lawyers, along with three individual patients. They have asked the Federal Court to declare that federal government health cuts to refugee claimants are unconstitutional and illegal.

The idea that non-citizens enjoy rights has given rise to concerns about access to rights for diaspora communities and immigrants as well as refugees, not to mention concerns about their opportunities to share in Canada's wealth.[68] Section 15 of the Canadian Charter guarantees equality rights to "every individual," and human rights laws do not generally distinguish between Canadian citizens and non-citizens in terms of who can file a human rights complaint. However, there are distinctions between citizens and noncitizens when it comes to basic social benefits and these distinctions target those who are the most vulnerable. New Canadians experience discrimination at higher levels than the general population and certain groups of immigrants, especially recent arrivals, tend to fare poorly in Canada. Immigrants who have lived in Canada for fewer than five years are more likely to feel they have experienced discrimination compared to immigrants who have lived in Canada for more than five years (26 percent and 18 percent, respectively).[69] Immigration experts and commentators cite a wide variety of factors that may be responsible for these figures, including the length of time it takes to build up professional and social networks and to obtain Canadian working experience and language skills. Researchers say that discrimination is also involved.[70]

None of this is (or should be) news. Newcomers face many barriers, such as lack of recognition of foreign credentials, exclusionary "Canadian experience" requirements, constraints on family reunification, limited paths to citizenship, and uneven access to social security protection and benefits. Employment accounts for about three-quarters of all human rights complaints in Canada (with the exception of Quebec, where the numbers are lower for the aforementioned reasons related to the diversion of cases away from the human rights system). Although most human rights systems in Canada do not identify complainants in terms of their immigration status, several other grounds (including national origin, place of origin, and citizenship) serve as proxies for this category.

Byron Williams is the executive director of the Public Interest Law Centre in Manitoba. His organization has worked to expand access to accreditation for foreign-trained doctors by representing the Association of Foreign Medical Graduates. In 1999, a complaint was filed with the Manitoba Human Rights Commission because medical graduates from countries like South Africa, New Zealand, the United Kingdom, and Australia benefited by receiving conditional licensing more quickly than people with comparable training from other countries. As a result of the complaint, unequal licensing standards were removed by 2003 and conditional licensing was extended to all foreign-trained doctors. "It has been very gratifying to see foreign-trained doctors being able to practice their profession. I still get cards from people thanking me for giving them the chance to practice medicine."[71] Manitoba's human rights commission played a central role in reaching a resolution in the case.

The experiences of temporary workers illustrate the inequalities facing newcomers to Canada and have an increasing role in the work of human rights systems as well as in broader policy conversations about the role of these workers in Canadian society. The number of temporary workers brought in under Canada's Temporary Foreign Workers Program has more than doubled since the 1990s[72] and has brought in waves of people to fill (mostly) low-paying jobs. Migrant workers, seasonal agricultural workers, and live-in caregivers (domestic workers) are temporary workers, although some of them eventually obtain permanent status. They do not benefit from the protections of the International Convention on Migrant Workers[73] because Canada has not ratified this convention. (Like several of the other countries that have not signed, Canada is a net importer of migrant workers.) Many of these workers do not enjoy the equal pay, social benefits, or fair treatment at work that Canadians expect as a matter of course. Migrant workers can find themselves in unhygienic and unhealthy working conditions, with poor pay, greater vulnerability to harassment, and just plain lousy treatment. Domestic workers are also vulnerable because of the isolation of their workplaces and the fact that many live-in, with limited control over their working conditions. Commissions are attempting to deal with the complex interaction of social benefits, immigration status, and the particular vulnerability of temporary workers, immigrants, agricultural and seasonal workers, and new arrivals to Canada. Cases like *Centre Maraîcher Eugène Guinois* illustrate why these issues remain a priority.[74]

The *Centre Maraîcher* case did not take place in the 1940s, the 1960s or even the 1990s but in Quebec in 2000–01. The Centre Maraîcher in Quebec is one of Canada's largest commercial vegetable farms and grows mainly lettuce and carrots. Due to Quebec's short growing season, farming communities in the province have intensive seasonal labour needs. Like many other farms in Quebec, the Centre Maraîcher uses day labourers to prepare the fields and bring in crops. The "Longueuil workers" involved in the case were bused to the farm from the municipality of Longueuil (just south of Montreal). They were predominantly Black permanent residents who had worked in agriculture for a long time. The working conditions of these employees were appalling by any standard. They were segregated from the other workers, banned from using common facilities like bathrooms and eating areas, and relegated to a tiny, filthy cabin with no running water, changing area, or clean meal space. Unlike the building reserved for the "regular" workers, which had running water and toilets, the Longueuil workers' cabin lacked toilets and a usable sink. It was rarely cleaned. The following notice was posted in the cabin:

To all the Longueuil workers

You have your area (cafeteria) for the lunch hour, please respect this agreement and do not go into the area for regular workers. Thank you for keeping your cafeteria clean at all times (Unofficial translation)

The notice was eventually accompanied by graffiti that said: "Blacks are pigs" – graffiti that had been left in place by management for about two years. The day labourers complained of racial taunting and harassment in the workplace.

The workers filed human rights complaints and the matter was sent to the Quebec Human Rights Tribunal. The Centre Maraîcher and its managers were found liable for discrimination and harassment. Justice Rivet, then-president of the tribunal, imposed damages for lost wages and for mental distress ("*dommages moraux*"), as well as punitive damages due to the nature and extent of the discrimination.

This case is interesting for several reasons. Although it bears all the hallmarks of a 1950s segregation case, it received little attention in Quebec, let alone in the rest of Canada. Consider, for a moment, what would have happened to the complainants in the *Centre Maraîcher* case if there had not been a human rights commission or a comparable public institution providing support. Legal services would have been out of their reach: as day labourers they earned less in a week than what an established lawyer in a mid-sized firm charges for a few hours.

Sadly, such cases are not unique, nor are they relics of the past. In 2011, Quebec's Human Rights Commission issued a major report on systemic discrimination against migrant workers.[75] In February 2012, it released an advisory opinion stating that live-in caregivers, seasonal agricultural workers, and other temporary foreign workers, especially low-skilled workers, are subject to systemic discrimination based on ethnic or national origin, race, social condition, language, and, in the case of live-in caregivers, gender.[76] These workers are excluded from or limited in their ability to access key protections, such as those provided under Quebec's Labour Code. The same applies to benefits in the case of industrial accidents or occupational illnesses, as well as legal aid, social assistance, parental leave, and access to language classes. The Canadian-born children of new mothers on temporary work visas may not be entitled to Medicare. Certain temporary programs bind workers to specific employers who may be abusive or pay less than the legal minimum wage.[77]

Canada's fast-changing labour needs are a function of a demographic that relies on immigration to maintain and strengthen its population. Despite the importance of bringing in new people and skills, the ability of capital, corporations, and financial products to move across borders has outstripped our collective capacity or will to manage the movement of human beings and ensure their fair treatment.

Even professionals and skilled tradespeople can find themselves subject to discrimination because of their national origin or citizenship. As described in chapter 2, the British Columbia SELI case involved the building of the Canada Line tunnel for the 2010 Olympic Games in Vancouver. Complaints had been filed as a result of the differential treatment of two groups of foreign temporary workers who had come to Vancouver to build the tunnel. SELI argued that these pay differentials had been negotiated and freely agreed to, and were consistent with international compensation practices.

After months of deliberation, the tribunal's three-member panel, which included Chair Heather MacNaughton, issued its ruling. The tribunal found that race, colour, ancestry, and place of origin were the main reasons for the differences in pay and ordered the respondents to compensate the Latin American workers. Each member of the complainant group was further awarded $10,000 for injuries to their dignity, feelings, and self-respect. The total award against SELI, SNC Lavalin, and SELI-SNC exceeded $2 million. The judgement was challenged and the parties finally settled in 2013.

The SELI case highlights how human rights cases are litigated when the contracting parties are not all based in Canada. Wages and working conditions may differ significantly from country to country. Discrimination resulting from negotiations undertaken at the international level is perceived and treated differently than the local variety. It is clear that a Canadian employer hiring Canadians should not treat people differently based simply on their country of origin. Heather MacNaughton pointed out that twenty years ago such cases would not have been treated as human rights cases at all, but would have been left to market forces to sort out.[78] Despite a controversy in 2013 over the use of temporary workers in the Canadian banking sector, the reliance on temporary workers in Canada is likely to mean that these issues will remain relevant for human rights systems across the country.

Family Status

As discussed in chapter 1, protection on the grounds of family status varies widely across the country. Family status was introduced into the Ontario Human Rights Code in 1982, twenty years after the Code was enacted. In the mid-1990s, "family status" accounted for about 3 percent of human rights complaints in Ontario.[79] By 2011–12, this figure had reached 8.4 percent.[80] In 2012–13, it comprised 11 percent of claims.[81]

Several factors account for these social and legal shifts, including the pressure to achieve equality rights in employment. There is a significant intersection between gender and family status: in 1989, the Supreme Court of Canada stated the obvious when it recognized women's unique role in childbearing and raising families. However, the court went on to make the more controversial point that it would be unfair to impose all the social costs of pregnancy and childbearing on women – for example, the career consequences for women who choose to care for children – when they choose to work outside the home.[82] The 1989 decision set an important precedent because it required that the social burden of raising a family be shared and that women not be disproportionately affected.

Childcare responsibilities are especially onerous in provinces where parents lack universal, publicly subsidized daycare. As well, the aging of the population imposes daunting burdens on working couples who have to manage competing demands on their time from children and aging parents. Finally, the move towards more fluid and inclusive families means that there are more single-parent families, families with same-sex spouses or partners, blended families, families caring for older parents, and so on. This makes it easier for people to define their own families and to access legal protections, as noted earlier in chapter 1.

Employees who seek accommodation to care for family members usually request workplace flexibility, including work scheduling and alternative work arrangements. If employers refuse these requests, "family status" is usually the ground cited in the employees' human rights complaints. The reasoning is straightforward: family members with caregiving responsibilities should be able to participate in the workforce on equitable and fair terms. and inflexible workplaces favour employees who have a spouse at home, can afford hired help, or do not have dependants. This creates a disadvantage for parents, especially single working parents who have care responsibilities for ill or disabled dependents.

Although most employment standards law allows parents to take some form of caregiving leave, such leave is generally reserved for serious cases and is available only for a short period of time. Compassionate leave is also available, but the bureaucratic procedures can be intimidating and cumbersome for both employees and employers. In any event, compassionate leave is not the same thing as obliging employers to adjust workplace schedules, job descriptions, or shifts. It does not address longer-term and chronic needs but is only designed to provide income support in circumstances where a family member is near death.

Recognizing the shared social responsibility for raising a family is fundamental to understanding the role that "family status" plays in human rights law. Human rights commissions in Canada have played an important role in advancing progressive interpretations of family status in the workplace. In 2006, the Canadian commission won an important case against Canadian National Railway (CN). Catherine Hoyt was a CN employee whose husband also worked for the railroad. She had an unpredictable schedule due to her lower level of seniority, and she and her husband needed childcare arrangements for their two-year-old. CN took more than three months to respond to Hoyt's request for more flexibility in her schedule, eventually offering her an unpaid leave of absence. The company argued that Hoyt was not subject to differential treatment since CN did not accommodate other parents with childcare needs. The tribunal found CN to be in breach of its duty to accommodate Hoyt on the basis of family status.[83]

In 2013, the Federal Court of Canada strengthened the connection between family status and childcare obligations, particularly for women in the workplace. In another case, Fiona Ann Johnstone was a customs inspector with the Canadian Border Services Agency. After her children were born, she requested accommodation in the form of a fixed daytime shift, which would allow her to work thirteen-hour shifts over three days. This arrangement would have allowed her access to childcare while remaining a full-time employee. Her employer refused, offering her part-time employment instead. The court held that the loss of her full-time status was discriminatory. The ground of family status included the obligations flowing from a parent-child relationship, which in this case included childcare.[84]

The case law is not unanimous on the extent of the burden on employers, and there has been at least one appellate case imposing a lower burden on employers.[85] Nonetheless, the *Hoyt* and *Johnstone* decisions point to a wider and more progressive interpretation of family status, which imposes commensurate and higher obligations on employers.

According to a publication from the Work Life Law Center in the United States, the number of discrimination cases involving family responsibilities increased by nearly 400 percent between 1989 and 2008.[86] In 2007 and 2011, the US Equal Employment Opportunity Commission provided guidance on how to apply existing laws that forbid discrimination based on gender, pregnancy, or disability in order to protect caregivers of children and aging parents.[87] Canada already has extensive protections for gender, pregnancy, and disability but caregiving and its relationship to family status is a newer frontier.

In other countries, human rights institutions are working towards obtaining fairness for families through the promotional side of their mandate. In 2007, the gender equality ombudsperson in Sweden (now the equal opportunities ombudsperson) carried out a public awareness "Stroller Campaign" to inform parents about the Swedish Parental Leave Act, which came into force in 2006. The Act strengthened protections for parents (especially new parents) who had childcare responsibilities. It prohibits employers from penalizing people on parental leave or parents who need to be home to care for sick children. Protections extend to job applicants as well. The campaign used a model "family-friendly" employer to provide tips and information to other employers about how to accommodate employees with new parenting responsibilities.[88] The work undertaken in Sweden is a practical example of a human rights institution's initiative in a changing and important area of human rights law that has a major effect on working families and working women.

Aboriginal Rights

Following a request by the Indian Affairs Branch of the government, the Canadian Corrections Association undertook a study and published its report *Indians and the Law* in August 1967. During the field work for this report, "the research staff was constantly confronted with, and shocked by, the depressing conditions that so many Indian and Métis people of Canada live with every day of the year." The report observes that "the majority of them lack such basic necessities as running water, electricity, plumbing, telephones, roads and other transportation facilities." Not only in remote locations, but also in cities, this disadvantage was disturbing. The report notes, "In several of our largest cities they have been forced by lack of funds to congregate in slum areas where the conditions of filth and poverty practically defy description." Indian and Métis children, says the report, "are represented in the child care population out of all proportion to the size of the group in the general population."[89]

There are many reminders, past and present, of the legacy of human rights abuses and their impact on Aboriginal peoples. The report cited in the paragraph above was written half a century ago and, although by no means applicable to all Aboriginal communities, its observations still resonate. For many Canadians, the experiences of children who attended residential schools and their parents have only recently come to the fore in any detail, largely as a result of the work of the Indian Residential Schools Truth and Reconciliation Commission. As mentioned in the introduction, Aboriginal women have been the targets of widespread and often lethal violence, and there have been calls for a national inquiry into the phenomenon of missing and murdered Aboriginal women. Between 1997 and 2000, Aboriginal women in Canada were almost seven times more likely to be murdered than non-Aboriginal women.[90]

These issues are integrally and fundamentally Aboriginal issues. Aboriginal peoples are affected for the sole reason that they *are* Aboriginal peoples. At the same time, such issues are also and fundamentally human rights issues, grounded in the quest for dignity, equality, and justice. Aboriginal issues remain Canada's most pressing human rights concerns. Despite this, the institutional silos into which rights are often divided in this country have separated Aboriginal rights from human rights for a long time, in part because Aboriginal law is a distinct branch of law with distinct rights and a unique constitutional foundation. Due to the special constitutional status of Aboriginal peoples, human rights systems in Canada have had a limited impact on their rights. Until 2011, for example, section 67 the CHRA prevented people on First Nations reserves from filing any human rights complaint dealing with an issue under the Indian Act. It provided that: "Nothing in this Act affects any provision of the Indian Act or any provision made under or pursuant to that Act."

Outside the federal area, a few human rights laws identify and protect the specificity of Aboriginal rights. Nova Scotia protects "aboriginal origin" and Alberta protects "native spirituality."[91] Newfoundland and Labrador protects the special arrangements for Inuit and Innu peoples that provide benefits employment, training, and contracting.[92] The law in each of the three territories recognizes Aboriginal rights. For example, the preamble to the Nunavut Human Rights Act provides that "it is just and consistent with Canada's international undertakings to recognize and make special provision for Inuit culture and values that underlie the Inuit way of life."[93]

The stark inequalities experienced in many Aboriginal communities cannot be decoupled from inequalities in education, health, and other public services. Mistrust of government institutions has meant that few issues reached human rights commissions. During my years at the Ontario Human Rights Commission, a few First Nations communities told us that they did not see commissions as capable of addressing the deep and enduring fissures in the relationship between Canada and Aboriginal peoples.[94]

Four recent developments suggest that things are changing. The first is the repeal of section 67 of the Canadian Human Rights Act, discussed earlier. This welcome development took place in 2008, more than thirty years after the section's "temporary" inclusion in 1977.[95] The Canadian Human Rights Commission described section 67 as the only provision in Canadian human rights law that restricted the access of a particular group of persons to the human rights process.[96] Its repeal was a major advancement not only for First Nations peoples but for all Canadians who value the rule of law. The repeal took effect in 2011, after a three-year transition period, and the results have been striking. In 2012, there was a surge in the number of human rights complaints brought by members of First Nations communities, showing a strong willingness to take advantage of the right to file a discrimination complaint against both First Nations governments and the government of Canada. The Canadian Commission's 2012 annual report showed an increase of almost 800 percent in the number of complaints from First Nations people and Aboriginal groups.[97] This is a now a significant area of the federal commission's work, and one that is on the increase for all the right reasons.

Second, in the 2013 *Daniels* case, the Federal Court of Canada decided that the federal government has jurisdiction over Métis and non-status Indians.[98] This decision, if it holds, will have a major impact on the work of the Canadian Human Rights Commission in its role as the main human rights system in the country dealing with Aboriginal claims since non-status Indians and Métis people account for about half the Aboriginal peoples in Canada.

The third development is a case known as *First Nations Child and Family Caring Society of Canada (Caring Society).*[99] Even before section 67 of the Canadian Human Rights Act was repealed, First Nations were using the federal human rights system to highlight and remedy systemic discrimination. (Section 67 prevented complaints only in relation to the Indian Act and the provision of family services and services for children in care is not a decision made under that act.) In 2007, the Caring Society and the Assembly of First Nations filed a human rights claim over inadequate federal funding for Aboriginal children and family services on reserves. According to the evidence presented by the Caring Society, on-reserve children receive 22 percent less funding than off-reserve Aboriginal and non-Aboriginal children. The Caring Society argued that the underfunding constitutes discrimination.

The federal government disputed these figures and tried to get the case thrown out on preliminary, technical grounds, arguing that child services are not human rights issues that come under the jurisdiction of the Canadian Human Rights Commission. Four years after the claim was filed, the tribunal dismissed the matter without hearing the full case. The chair of the tribunal, Shirish P. Chotalia, QC, an appointee of the Harper government, rendered the decision. She accepted the federal government's argument that the federal government does not provide funding for child welfare services for anyone other than First Nations children living on reserve, because services for other Canadians are provided by the provincial government. Therefore, the federal services were found not to be comparable to provincial child welfare services. Without a comparator group, it was further argued, no discrimination could be made out. This variation on the "separate but equal" doctrine meant that an entire section of the Canadian population could receive manifestly inferior services solely based on ancestry or race, without having any remedy in human rights law.

The Caring Society sought judicial review. In April 2012, the Federal Court of Canada issued a stinging rebuke to the tribunal for its mishandling of the complex case and sent the matter back for another hearing by a "differently constituted panel." The decision was upheld by the Federal Court of Appeal a year later.[100] Chotalia, the embattled chair, resigned in November 2012, four years before the end of her mandate.

The tribunal began four weeks of hearings on 25 February 2013. *Caring Society* is a good example of a systemic case: it is more far-reaching and policy-oriented than most individual human rights complaints. Nonetheless, it falls within the Canadian Human Rights Act and speaks to precisely the types of discrimination at a systemic level that human rights systems are or should be designed to deal with.

The fourth important development was Canada's tardy but welcome 2012 decision to support the UN Declaration on the Rights of Indigenous Peoples.[101] The Declaration does not create binding legal obligations but it reinforces Canada's recognition of individual and collective indigenous rights. It emphasizes the importance of Aboriginal peoples' specific cultural, social, and economic circumstances and the relevance of these circumstances to understanding and defending their rights. The persistent rights issues faced by Aboriginal peoples, ranging from violence to inferior social services and living standards, are powerful arguments that human rights commissions should make Aboriginal issues a priority.[102] The Declaration emphasizes the right to promote, develop, and maintain Aboriginal institutions that can address the rights of indigenous peoples. If commissions prove to be unable or unwilling to work collaboratively across the country in taking Aboriginal human rights issues forward, the Declaration foresees the possibility of distinct Aboriginal institutions that will be able to do so.

Many key areas of Aboriginal rights are in a state of uncertainty, and the extent to which human rights systems have the authority to tackle large scale and systemic issues is still unresolved. Despite this, it is clear that this is a growing and rapidly changing area of law

RIGHTS INFLATION?

People use rights language all the time to defend or attack all kinds of behaviour.[103] Seemingly contradictory and irreconcilable claims are made about human rights and about what can (or should) count as a right. At a theoretical level, human rights are understood as the rights that we all have because of our shared humanity.[104] This definition is fluid and open-ended. Since human rights systems are restricted to dealing with the rights contained in their statutes, this book takes a more functional approach, focusing on the catalogue of rights guaranteed in human rights laws and recognizing the close links among these laws, the Charter, and international human rights law.

The catalogue of rights has grown considerably over the years. Civil and political rights (including the rights to life, liberty, and security, fundamental freedoms, equality and non-discrimination rights, mobility rights, and legal rights)[105] and economic, social, and cultural rights (including rights to employment, education, health, adequate food and housing, and minimum standards of social assistance) all form part of the basic human rights lexicon.[106] Thematic rights protect the specific rights of groups, such as women, children, people with disabilities, and refugees.[107] Canada has undertaken to respect, protect, and fulfil the full range of these rights by formally undertaking a large number of international obligations.

The ongoing evolution of rights does not occur because human rights systems decide to create new rights or because these systems need to justify their existence and come up with new things to do. Rather, it reflects the decision of the state to recognize international obligations and to implement them in national law and policy as well as the evolution of our own society and legal structures.

Nonetheless, disagreements about the legitimacy of certain rights may seem to lend credence to the idea that human rights commissions engage in rights inflation. Newer rights are by definition unfamiliar and it can take a long time for these rights to be fully understood and fully accepted. As recently as 2010, the Court of Appeal of Saskatchewan suggested in the *Whatcott* case that we should be more tolerant of hate propaganda directed against gays and lesbians as compared to, say, similar propaganda directed in earlier years against religious or racial minorities.[108] The court observed that social movements advocating for different rights have appeared at different times. Thus recognition of the rights of race and religion appeared first, while gender equality, disability rights, and gay and lesbian rights appeared later. This observation itself is not problematic, nor is the underlying concern to make sure that we have a viable and rational social debate about what counts as a human right and what does not. What was problematic was that the Court of Appeal appeared to attach legal significance to the sequencing of existing rights. While hate speech based on religion or ethnicity was seen as a recognized form of discrimination, hateful speech based on sexual orientation was framed as a matter of ongoing public discussion so that gays and lesbians are less likely to be constitutionally protected. The Court of Appeal did not see Whatcott's publications depicting homosexuals as diseased predators on children as sufficiently discriminatory to require legitimizing the constitutional protection of homosexuals.

It is true that the right of gays and lesbians to be free from discrimination was not contained in the first human rights laws. Nor, for that matter, was there any protection against age discrimination in Canada in the form of mandatory retirement. As noted earlier, family status began to be included in statutes in the 1970s, and, again, it is only recently that the case law has begun making the connection to childcare and other family responsibilities. In short, the desire to freeze human rights laws – or any other category of law – is regressive. It is not reasonable to fail to protect rights simply because they were not on the minds of the advocates for the first laws.

The same reasoning applies to hate speech prohibitions. It should be clear by now that it is not true that hate speech is a recent addition to human rights laws. As has already been noted, in 1934 Manitoba's group libel law prohibited hate speech on the grounds of creed and race.[109] The very first version of the Canadian Human Rights Act prohibited the use of telephones to communicate hate speech.[110] The CHRA coincided with Canada's accession to the International Covenant on Civil and Political Rights (ICCPR), which requires countries to prohibit both expression that infringes the rights and reputations of others as well as advocacy of national, racial, or religious hatred that constitutes incitement to discrimination, hostility, or violence.[111]

A related critique is that the "rights evolution" has been unduly influenced by equality rights. Equality rights are accused of diminishing fundamental freedoms, which some see as an unacceptable outcome.[112] As discussed in chapter 1, human rights laws protect, and sometimes balance, competing fundamental rights and freedoms. At the same time, rights are interconnected and interdependent. It is impossible to develop a coherent understanding of equality rights without thinking about how they interact with other rights, with liberty, and with human dignity. The reverse proposition is true as well. Human rights commissions have been mediating and managing these conflicts and interactions within their areas of jurisdiction for years. This topic is discussed at greater length in chapter 5.

Yes, But Are These Real Rights?

Equality rights are not an inferior or subordinate category of rights. Equality helps to ensure that rights are available to all people without discrimination. The notion that one set of rights can damage another reflects a pre-Charter mentality that places civil and political rights in opposition to other rights and freedoms. This has made it difficult to place civil liberties in an equality framework, or even to understand that equality rights play an important role in making liberty an attainable ideal for everyone, not just for those who are privileged, articulate, and literate. Human rights systems work at the nexus of equality, liberty, and human dignity. For instance, cases involving racial profiling, police brutality, and even national security raise both civil liberty and equality issues.[113]

Racial profiling has become an important area for human rights commissions over the years; the Quebec and Ontario Commissions have both developed research initiatives aimed at profiling.[114] One case that caught the public's attention in Montreal involved Glenroy Valantine Rice, a Black man in his fifties who was grabbed, handcuffed, and violently arrested by Montreal transit officials in 2012. The incident occurred for no discernible reason other than his race and possibly his failure to respond to a request made in French, a language he did not understand. Rice was subsequently detained and fined by transit officials. Quebec's Human Rights Commission investigated the complaint and found that Rice had experienced racial profiling and discrimination. It recommended punitive and moral damages.[115] This is only one of many such cases that have come to the attention of the public in recent years in Quebec.

Not all discrimination cases involve civil liberties. Some involve economic, social, and cultural rights, which are often seen as aspirations rather than as justiciable "real rights." There is something generational about the idea that the "great freedoms" that encompass civil and political rights operate on a higher level and are distinguishable from other rights by their justiciability. Ken Norman remarked, "Look what happened to Franklin Roosevelt's second bill of rights [on economic and social rights]," he said. People who think that economic and social rights are bolshie sorts of socialism are out there, but that generation is slowly but surely leaving."[116] Although some see economic and social rights as unenforceable or nonjusticiable in the courts, many of the areas in which commissions routinely operate – education, housing, employment, and social services – are in part about economic and social rights. Such rights have been the most-litigated human rights in this country for decades.

Social rights, and in particular the right to social assistance and the right not to be discriminated against on the grounds of social condition, are controversial. A common objection is that these rights do not protect immutable characteristics but rather aspects of a person's circumstances or condition that can be changed. It is true that immutable or inherited characteristics, such as race, colour, or sex, tend to be the ones that people associate with human rights protections. But it is not true that human rights are limited to immutable characteristics, even among civil and political rights. People can and do change their opinions, their political views, and their religions, and yet these mutable aspects of our human condition are all protected rights under human rights law because they are so intrinsically bound up with who we are. It should follow that mutable characteristics connected to the most basic human needs, which sometimes result in profound forms of discrimination, should not be excluded from protection, at least not for reasons of mutability alone. For years, human rights commissions have been dealing with complaints related to social assistance, social origin, or social condition. These protections reflect international law and an international consensus about basic human needs and the state's obligations to work towards their fulfillment. The norms in international human rights instruments and in most Canadian human rights statutes acknowledge these fundamental human needs and are reflected in the full range of human rights. The human rights system has been protecting against discrimination in these areas in Canada for decades. It has done so with little fanfare and without the sky falling in.

The objections to these rights are based on the idea that human rights should not be used to create rights such as the "right to welfare."[117] However, the International Covenant on Economic, Social and Cultural Rights (ICESCR), which Canada acceded to more than thirty years ago, specifically obliges states to recognize a right to social security, including social insurance.[118] Appellate courts have held that people who receive public assistance are protected under the Charter's equality rights provision.[119] The rationale for these protections goes to the heart of both equality and human dignity. The right to social security is central to human dignity for people faced with circumstances that deprive them of their capacity to work because of sickness, disability, maternity, employment injury, unemployment, old age, or the death of a family member. It can also protect people in circumstances where access to affordable health care is an issue, or where there is insufficient family support, particularly for children and adult dependents.[120]

Housing provides another illustration of the scope and limitations of anti-discrimination protection in Canada and its connection to social and economic rights. Housing is a fundamental human right in international law and the ICESCR requires every state to provide an adequate level of housing.[121] The great South African jurist Albie Sachs was a member of the South African Constitutional Court that rendered the decision in *Government of South Africa v. Grootboom et al*[122] which held that South Africa had an obligation to provide decent housing for the many poor people who were living in informal and inadequate housing arrangements at the end of apartheid. A generous and expansive interpretation of South Africa's constitution, its recognition of the fundamental obligation to help the poorest and most vulnerable, is a signal achievement. Although South Africa is still a developing country with enormous wealth disparities, it performs better than the majority of sub-Saharan African states when it comes to housing.[123]

In Canada, public recognition of housing rights lags far behind the work being done by its human rights systems. Housing, or a right to housing, is viewed as an aspiration that is best left to legislatures rather than being a genuine and justiciable right. An editorial on homelessness published in the *Globe and Mail* in 2010 declared that only elected legislators, not unelected judges, have the expertise to establish social programs and choose between competing interests. The editorial warned that allowing the courts to deal with housing issues (including the fight against homelessness) could lead to "a myriad of social problems" and to battles for scarce resources.[124]

Decisions about the allocation of scarce resources do belong with legislatures, at least in the first instance. However, it should not be necessary to add that we now have a Charter and human rights laws, and all government decisions are subject to that legal framework. Section 15 of the Charter requires courts to assess the constitutionality of all forms of government action, including social programs. Despite suggestions that courts have run amok by legislating from the bench, a review of Supreme Court decisions shows that claims of judicial activism, in the sense of inappropriate incursions into legislative powers, are highly suspect.[125] If, on the other hand, fears of judicial activism, such as those voiced by the *Globe and Mail*, required courts to ignore the Charter, sit by, and do nothing when legislatures violate human rights, we would quickly revert to a pre-Charter world where legislatures could violate rights with impunity.

Courts have in fact established a wide range of rights that deal directly with the allocation of resources. Examples include the right to insurance proceeds for common-law couples,[126] the right to sign language interpretation in the public health care system,[127] the right to pension benefits for divorced and separated women,[128] and the right to an education for children with severe learning disabilities.[129] Advocates have been fighting for "scarce resources" before the courts for more than a quarter century, ever since section 15 of the Charter took effect in 1985. Undoubtedly, this fight has led to "a myriad of social problems" because legislatures have then had to align Canadian law and policy with the

Charter. Sometimes, this entails a direct confrontation with divisive social issues, as we have seen with abortion, euthanasia, LGBT rights, and a host of others. I would argue that this is the kind of problem we want, in the sense that addressing such issues is not only a defining feature of constitutional litigation involving rights claims but also a necessary part of the ongoing dialogue between the legislature and the judiciary in a country that values the rule of law.

Canadian courts (or editorial boards) may not yet be ready to deal with the legal implications of homelessness, but many aspects of housing rights have been explicitly recognized by human rights commissions and the courts for years. Human rights systems in Canada receive a total of roughly 350 housing-related complaints per year, many of which raise broad systemic issues about human rights and housing. These include practices like the 30 percent minimum-income rule, where a rental agent can refuse to rent an apartment to someone if the rent comprises more than one third of the applicant's income. Discriminatory rental practices create real barriers for people with low incomes and have a disproportionate impact on women, young people, and people in receipt of public assistance.[130] According to research prepared for a 1998 case in Ontario, they are also demonstrably ineffective ways of ensuring that tenants pay their rent.[131]

However, more than a decade after that 1998 case, a 2009 study by the Centre for Equality Rights in Accommodation (CERA) of rental agents' responses to requests for apartments from different groups in the City of Toronto found that many discriminatory housing practices still exist.[132] CERA undertook the research to encourage policymakers to bring discrimination into their discussions about housing and to make the connections between discrimination, homelessness, and housing insecurity. According to Leilani Farha, then head of CERA, the rates of discrimination against people with mental disabilities, single parents, Black single parents, and South Asians were "pretty stark."[133] Figure 3.1 puts the rates in perspective.

As the figure shows, about a quarter of households receiving social assistance, South Asian households, and households headed by Black single parents experienced moderate to severe discrimination when they inquired about apartments. More than a third of people with mental disabilities experienced discrimination.

The alternative to affordable apartments and social housing is homelessness or seriously inadequate housing, which is associated with a host of other social problems. Housing insecurity is a national concern

Figure 3.1
Rates of discrimination in housing (Toronto)

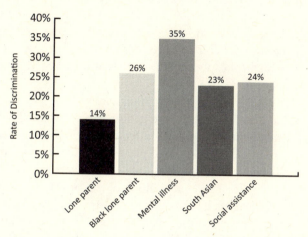

Source: *Sorry, It's Rented* (Toronto: CERA, 2009).

because homelessness and housing affordability exact significant social and economic costs. Problems are exacerbated by lack of leadership and the failure of past strategies to move beyond emergency and short-term solutions.[134] Seeing homelessness and housing insecurity as a human rights issue will not solve the whole problem, but it does put pressure on governments and housing providers to understand that these are fundamental human rights and policy priorities, and need to be treated as such.

Closely connected to the argument that commissions do not deal with "real" rights is the assertion that human rights systems are preoccupied with watered-down, weird, or trivial versions of rights. Smaller-scale inequalities may not seem worthy of attention, let alone litigation. But what may seem small-scale to some may have devastating impacts on others, especially when the cumulative effect is to generate the stereo-types that sustain the principal scaffolding of discrimination:

Micro-aggressions seem petty, in a world where available redress may often seem heavy-handed. ... Formal grievances ... are heavy weapons; using them is often thought to carry high cost. The per-ceived lack of *appropriate* modes of redress therefore helps to perpet-uate micro-aggressions. This is especially true where the aggrieved person does not want to lose privacy or professional image. What can an African American vice-president do, if someone he is negotiating with sneers in private? What can a female plant manager do, if the boss stares directly at her bosom whenever they are alone? Until the person of difference learns how to handle these events effectively, (which takes work), the apparent lack of redress is, at best, frustrating.[135]

Individual differences, prejudice, and group-based differences have generated considerable research on inter-group relations and inequities in North American and European workplaces. [136] The compounded effect of derisive or dismissive comments, acts, and oversights can create a culture of contempt for targeted minorities. As one author put it, "the language of human rights applies not just to the abuse of others on the grand scale; it also relates to the small acts of inhumanity that disfigure the lives of people in the West."[137]

Canadian equality rights scholar Colleen Sheppard discusses the "micro-level context," arguing that the standpoint of those who have less power in society or who have been marginalized should be considered and validated because such individuals are best-placed to comment on their own needs and perspectives: "Persons using wheelchairs know more about wheelchair accessibility into a building than those who need not notice whether they climbed a step or steps in entering a building. Parents of children with disabilities know more about educational services and special needs education than parents whose children do not have mental or physical disabilities."[138] The specificity of human experience is not so minor or particular that it becomes unknowable or trivial. Instead, according to Sheppard, it is the basis for framing discrimination, which "takes us beyond isolated individual stories of betrayal, loss, abuse, and denial by connecting them to patterns of group-based exclusion and harm."[139] "Micro-contexts" and micro-aggressions may seem trivial to those who do not have to live through them, but their effects can be discriminatory. At the same time, the integrity and credibility of human rights systems require that we be able to distinguish between forms of discrimination that merit legal intervention and those that do not. Every human rights system in Canada contains legal provisions designed to screen out trivial and vexatious complaints.

Nonetheless, commissions are sometimes cast as officious bureaucrats trolling back alleys for fringe claimants, creating a self-perpetuating cottage industry of dubious claims. Articles that sensationalize and trivialize complaints about gender identity are reframed as the querulous demands of surgery-seeking transsexuals.[140] Two cases are discussed below that use the same technique. In one, ethnic discrimination against a child is reduced to a spat over bad table manners. Vicious verbal abuse of gay clients in a restaurant is recast as thin-skinned whining about the consequences of free speech, and the firing of a disabled employee's who had developed a debilitating allergy is transformed into the alarming "right" of restaurant employees not to wash their hands.[141]

These strategies are used to great effect to trivialize equality rights by focusing on the context in which they arise, diverting the reader from the actual right being claimed. The resulting spin can indeed make cases look somewhat bizarre. If this approach had been used in the 1960s, the sit-ins and civil rights protests at lunch counters and other retail services in southern Ontario could have been framed as battles to ensure a "right to have lunch" instead of the right to equal treatment for Blacks. The Viola Desmond case could be reframed as "a right to go to the movies" instead of a fundamental civil liberties issue. A closer and more empathetic look at such cases helps to bring the "real" rights in such seemingly strange cases into clearer focus.

The cases attracted considerable media scrutiny around the time of the hate speech debates and became part of the campaign to "denormalize" human rights commissions. The first is Beena Datt's much-publicized 2007 "hand washing" claim against McDonald's in British Columbia. The second is the Quebec case of Luc Cagadoc, a seven-year-old Filipino boy who was allegedly harassed by employees at his school.

Beena Datt, an immigrant from Fiji, worked at McDonald's for twenty-three years. Over time, she developed a painful and debilitating skin allergy to the soap used at her workplace. The medical evidence said that this rendered her hands "unusable." Datt ended up losing her job. She filed a human rights complaint and won her case.[142] Anti-commission activist Ezra Levant seized on the complaint to say that the decision was "crazy," and that employees in the restaurant industry would now be able to claim a right not to wash their hands.[143]

The media comments outraged Patricia Knipe, a journalist working in communications at the Manitoba Human Rights Commission. Knipe recalled reading an excerpt of Ezra Levant's book *Shakedown* in *Maclean's*. "The article got so many things wrong," she said. "I am a journalist and am protective of my profession. I was appalled that *Maclean's* would let people think that this was a real journalist writing about real news."[144] Knipe disputed Levant's characterization of the case as allowing employees serving food not to wash their hands: "In fact when you read the case, it is clear that the tribunal was very cautious about public health and applauded McDonald's for its commitment to public health and hygiene. This element of the story was completely mis-represented. When you read the actual decision, you see the hard choices that both the employee and the employer had to make: What would happen to her employment? What would happen to an employee of twenty-three years?"[145] The crux of the case was that the employer should have made more efforts to find Datt another job and to investi-gate alternatives that would not worsen her condition. The BC Tribunal did not conclude that food should be prepared without hygiene stan-dards. Rather, it took pains to point out that the employee's disability did not prevent her from undertaking other tasks or other jobs, and that there was a possibility that Datt could have been accommodated with-out undue hardship to McDonald's.

Levant also took a personal swipe at Judy Parrack, the BC Human Rights Tribunal member who decided the case, calling her a "former divorce lawyer and left-wing lobbyist."[146] Legal commentators have recognized, however, that the *Datt* case was not quite as presented by Levant,[147] and Parrack's "crazy" analysis was subsequently cited with approval by the British Columbia Supreme Court in a 2011 decision.[148]

Why did the *Datt* case become a target? Why was there no sympathy, let alone empathy, for someone who wanted to work, had a long service record, and had few other employment options? For starters, Datt was a soft target. The likelihood of an unemployed fast-food worker accumu-lating the wherewithal to mount a campaign against an established media commentator like Ezra Levant was pretty much non-existent. As neutral decision-makers, human rights tribunals were not about to leap into the fray either. It was easy to predict that there would be few who would challenge the attacks against British Columbia's Human Rights Tribunal, Parrack, or against Datt herself. Rather than looking at the human rights issue that was squarely before the tribunal, the case was re-cast to suggest that human rights were being used to reduce hygiene standards in the food industry.[149] As Knipe noted, the media are impor-tant because they provide a neutral third party that can bring perspective and legitimacy to the news. However, the media treatment of the *Datt* case failed on both counts.[150]

The next case involved Luc Cagadoc, a seven-year-old Filipino boy who was a student in Quebec's Marguerite-Bourgeoys School Board.[151]

Martine Bertrand, a lunchtime monitor, took exception to Luc's messy eating habits and boisterous behaviour. Luc's school records disapprovingly noted that he "fills his mouth with noodles using his fork and his spoon." According to Luc's mother, Marie Gallardo, it is traditional in Filipino culture to use a fork and spoon instead of a fork and knife. After Luc complained to his mother, Mrs Gallardo tried to speak to the school principal in person and sent the school a registered letter. She was ignored. When she went to the school to speak with the staff, she received a threatening legal letter warning her to abide by the school board's Code of Conduct.

Because of his behaviour at lunch time, Luc was punished and told to sit apart from his friends. He was teased and became more socially isolated. When Luc forgot to wash his hands before lunch, Bertrand asked him whether people in "his country" washed their hands before sitting down to eat. Fed up with the school's lack of response, Gallardo filed a human rights complaint and went to the press. This resulted in national and international media coverage. The school board and the principal lined up behind Bertrand. Luc eventually changed schools.

With the exception of Bertrand's "hand washing" comment, Quebec's Human Rights Commission did not consider the incidents to be discriminatory: Luc had been acting up and the issue of hand-washing alone did not merit a decision to send the case to the tribunal. The commission decided that it was not in the public interest to litigate the matter and declined to take the case to the tribunal. However, using a unique provision in Quebec's Charter of Human Rights and Freedoms – section 84 – which permits claimants to bring a case to the tribunal at their own cost if the commission has refused to bring the case on their behalf,[152] Mrs Gallardo was able to proceed to the tribunal on her own, with the support of Montreal's Filipino community.

The tribunal found that Luc's treatment was partially related to his ethnic origin. Testimony from the school board and its officials pointed to the institution's indifference to Luc's cultural background:

To fully understand the impact of these events on L.C., one must place oneself in the position of a seven-year-old child in a different cultural context than his parents.

As he begins to build his own identity, develop self-esteem and learn which social behaviours are acceptable, along comes an authority figure ... who punishes him for behaviour that he learned directly from his parents and that is part of his personality ...

Although Mrs. Gallardo had alerted [the school officials] about the impact these incidents were having on her son ... [her] concerns were not taken seriously and were treated as exaggerations. ...

[The school officials] may have thought these events were harmless and humorous, but the fact is that L.C. was hurt and his personal integrity and dignity were violated, contrary to articles 4 and 10 of the [Quebec] *Charter*.[153]

The tribunal awarded $12,000 in damages against the school board, the principal, and the lunch monitor (Ms Bertrand). The case was appealed to the Quebec Court of Appeal in 2010. The Center for Research-Action on Race Relations (CRARR), a Montreal NGO, supported the Gallardo family. CRARR's executive director, Fo Niemi, predicted that the case would likely be overturned on technical grounds: the commission had found only some of the evidence indicated discrimination and there was a concern about whether the tribunal was even entitled to take the case based on the entire set of facts. According to Niemi, the media treated the case like a trivial cafeteria squabble that had been blown out of proportion by the human rights system.[154] However, there is another layer to the story. In 2008, Niemi filed an unsuccessful press council complaint about a *La Presse* journalist's report on a *Gallardo* press conference.[155] When Gallardo won her case at the tribunal in 2010, Niemi publicly declared it a victory for the Filipino community. Journalists at *La Presse* were waiting. Columnist Patrick Lagacé wrote a scathing column personally attacking Niemi as a "clown" (coincidentally, this was the term used to describe young Luc) who made unsubstantiated accusations of racism at every turn. Lagacé compared Niemi, who is of Vietnamese origin, to a disoriented soldier after the Vietnam War, diving under tables at the smallest sound.[156]

The response of Yves Boisvert, also of *La Presse*, was more measured and his focus was more on the institution than on individuals. He argued that the elevation of a cafeteria squabble to a human rights dispute called the legitimacy of Quebec's Human Rights Tribunal into question.[157] The case was spun into a petty squabble that inappropriately consumed the resources and attention of a public institution. Boisvert's column generated sufficient concern in the legal community that the head of the Quebec Bar Association issued a public statement expressing support for the tribunal and its work.[158]

On 15 May 2012, the Quebec Court of Appeal rendered a decision confirming Niemi's fears about the technicalities of the case, significantly narrowing access to the tribunal.[159] The Court of Appeal decided that the tribunal can only grant remedies in relation to incidents that the commission had previously found to be discriminatory. The court upheld a $2,000 award against the lunch monitor, but not the larger awards against the school board or the principal. The tribunal, supposedly an independent institution, was whittled down and became an administrative arm that operated downstream from the commission, able to address cases only within the narrow parameters of the facts as understood by the commission, an administrative body that has no authority to hear evidence.

Pierre Bosset, a law professor at the Université du Québec à Montréal, pointed out that media commentary on human rights in Quebec has become increasingly conservative and reactionary. He argued that this affects the way in which people see human rights institutions and understand their work. It also encourages the view that human rights systems engage in frivolous or tendentious cases, thus undermining their legitimacy.[160]

In closing, a closer analysis of the demand for human rights systems in Canada reveals not only that the number of cases has risen steadily over the years but that the contours of existing rights are shifting and evolving in a way that has brought little-used human rights grounds to the fore. Family status as a ground has shifted largely because of the demands of child care and elder care in families where there are two breadwinners who require job flexibility. Aboriginal rights and human rights have become more interconnected, changing the way in which human rights are litigated. In these and the other developments discussed in this chapter, entirely new categories of rights have emerged and rights beneficiaries are now able to claim them. In every legal system there are cases that appear silly or frivolous, and situations where complainants file vexatious or abusive claims. They are generally not difficult to discern. Outrageous complaints that are a real abuse of process and where people have experienced no discrimination are discussed at greater length in chapter 4. The appropriate response to such cases is to develop and use fair and effective procedures to prevent such cases from going forward. It is not to jettison the system entirely.

ARE HUMAN RIGHTS COMMISSIONS UNDEMOCRATIC?

Human rights systems stand accused of becoming "thought police" or officious bureaucrats, bumbling into areas they were not meant to address.[161] In the 1999 interview mentioned in the introduction, Stephen Harper said: "Human rights commissions, as they are evolving, are an attack on our fundamental freedoms and the basic existence of a democratic society. ... [I]t is in fact totalitarianism. I find this is very scary stuff."[162] Although it was not entirely clear which fundamental freedoms were in danger of imminent demise at the time, the refrain has been taken up under the free speech and laissez-faire banner by Tory pundits like Tom Flanagan, conservative activists like John Carpay, and others.

It was also front and centre in Mike Duffy's May 2008 interview of columnist Mark Steyn on CTV. Steyn was introduced as someone who had had a complaint filed against him.

> Mike Duffy: Mark, the speech police say that they need [section 13 of the Canadian Human Rights Act] to protect us from racists and bigots. What do you say to that?
>
> Mark Steyn: ... It is disgraceful, really, that a government tribunal is sitting in judgment over the editorial decisions of private magazines in Canada.
>
> Mike Duffy: You say ... [that] "native populations are aging and fading and being supplanted remorselessly by a young Muslim demographic." Now we have young Muslims saying that this is hate speech! Sounds to me that it's a simple reflection of the facts!!
>
> Mark Steyn: Yes, that is a fact ... that is more appropriate to totalitarian jurisdictions.

The exchange contains multiple errors designed to reinforce the myths about human rights systems and Muslims. The use of the term "police" in the introduction depicts human rights systems as illegitimate or pseudo-criminal courts. Then there is the curious use of the term "native," which apparently encompasses everyone except the remorselessly reproducing "Muslim demographic." The interview also speaks directly to the supposed anti-democratic leanings of human rights systems.

Human rights systems are often anti-majoritarian, but this does not mean that they are anti-democratic. Minority rights are not always represented, let alone protected, by the majority that elects a government. Human rights systems provide checks and balances. They are democratic in the sense that human rights laws are enacted by legislatures and human rights systems. Their accountability is established by law and subject to several layers of judicial and administrative controls.

Human rights systems are also democratic in another way: they offer a more accessible and cost-effective forum for thousands of Canadians who would not otherwise be able to afford legal costs. Contrary to many reports in the media, neither party appearing before a commission needs a lawyer. Except in Quebec, no one requires a lawyer before human rights tribunals either. Accusations that human rights systems are undemocratic really have nothing to do with democracy at all. They arise from the belief that commissions are investigating cases that they have no business dealing with. The Alberta complaint against the *Western Standard* for republishing the Danish Mohammed-as-bomber cartoon was a case in point. Alberta's Human Rights Commission had the jurisdiction to deal with the case and eventually decided to dismiss it. The decision, however, took a very long time (according to some reports, it took three years) and the delay led to a good deal of trouble. Charlach Mackintosh, the former head of Alberta's Commission, acknowledged: "We are not really set up to assess or triage cases that are on the edge of what commissions should look at."[163] This view was echoed by Jennifer Lynch, who was the chief commissioner of the Canadian Commission when the *Maclean's* hate speech complaint was filed.[164]

Concerns about commissions dealing with issues that are "on the edge of what commissions should look at" are not new or inherently problematic, in the sense that people routinely use the law to expand and assert their own interests, and to test for innovative approaches to rights claims. The difficulty with these types of issues is that they essentially raise new points of law or test the boundaries of human rights laws. Commissions themselves have not proved very effective in dealing with these issues in a timely way, even if they usually get the solution right in the end, as they did in the Alberta case. When commissions are asked to deal with broader social issues that are unusual in scope or subject matter, the result is often controversial. In the 1990s, the Ontario Commission investigated claims that came to be known as the "Variety Stores" cases. The complaints had been filed because "soft" pornography magazines like *Penthouse* were readily available on the shelves of many convenience or corner stores in Ontario (and, of course, in Canada more generally). The claimants argued that since the magazines were "goods" offered for sale, they fell within the definition of "goods and services" under Ontario's Human Rights Code and were discriminatory because they displayed casually demeaning messages about women.[165] The respondents, who owned the stores, suddenly found themselves on the receiving end of complaints about a very controversial social policy issue, namely the role of the state in regulating pornography and the connection of this issue to equality rights for women. The commission ultimately dismissed the cases. One of the claims was dismissed following a preliminary motion and in 1996 the commission dismissed the other claims because the evidence against the storeowners and the current state of the law made further inquiry "inappropriate."[166] It was the right answer, but it had taken a long time to get there.

Commissions do not like to dismiss cases early on in the process, even in situations where respondents allege that the complaints are vexatious or frivolous. This reluctance may stem from the fear that valid cases will be dismissed, worry that commissions will be perceived as too pro-respondent, or an institutional culture of caution that fears legal challenges. There is clearly a need for faster dismissals in appropriate cases.

Even when human rights commissions are acting squarely within their legal remit, they are accused of taking on cases that are characterized as a form of social engineering. Litigating to promote a social agenda, which is sometimes described as "lawfare," has recently acquired a whiff of sulphur. Nevertheless, it is as old as North America's civil rights movement and has been used to great effect by organizations such as Amnesty International, the American Civil Liberties Union, and the Canadian Civil Liberties Association to advance rights-based agendas and to sensitize the public.

THE RETURN OF LAISSEZ-FAIRE

Much of the backlash against human rights systems is based on rejection of the human rights culture and of the legal framework of equality rights in particular. Critics argue for alternative or pre-existing legal frameworks, including laissez-faire economic theories, reflecting Rod Macdonald's characterization of laissez-faire in the legal realm before 1950: "you do not use notions of equality to overturn agreements that are freely negotiated, you do not use the courts to palliate inequities, and you do not engage in parallel exercises of justice to redistribute wealth or social goods."[167]

In 2009, conservative policy advisor Tom Flanagan made a small splash when he wrote in the *Globe and Mail* that human rights laws should not apply to the private sector.[168] The idea is not new – in 1945, opponents of New York's Ives-Quinn Law against Discrimination attacked the use of human rights laws as an idealistic attempt to control employers.[169] Mike Duffy's interview of Mark Steyn, quoted above, also has an undercurrent of laissez-faire, expressing outrage about the fact that a tribunal would "sit in judgment" of a "private" magazine.

The resurgence of laissez-faire may be a blip on the screen of a few writers, but it is ahistorical and ignores important legal and social developments, including the idea that human rights are universal and apply to everyone, not just government. It is not, moreover, especially helpful or realistic to envisage the world as a marketplace where the invisible hand regulates human rights as it does pork belly futures. The market has done a particularly bad job when it comes to people with disabilities. According to David Baker, "the market place is not kind to people with disabilities. It has historically kept them in poverty and has not allowed them to use their abilities and their talents."[170]

It is difficult to believe that anyone would want to return to a pre-rights world or move to one where market incentives are the sole or main policy response to discrimination. It is just as hard to believe that a national newspaper would take such views seriously enough to give them space. However, some people apparently do and a major newspaper did. The argument is that discriminating today has become an expensive business. As rational, self-interested actors, members of the private sector will undoubtedly sort out these problems on their own. In this scenario, Viola Desmond goes back to her seat in the Blacks-only balcony of the Nova Scotia theatre until public pressure is mobilized and theatres realize their policies are costing them money.

Peter Hogg is one of Canada's leading constitutional scholars. In his textbook, Hogg says: "The real threat to equality in Canada comes not from legislative and official action but from discrimination by private persons. ... Economic liberties and freedom of contract, which imply a right to deal with whomever one pleases, come into direct conflict with egalitarian values, and in all Canadian jurisdictions, the former have now been subordinated to the latter by the enactment of human rights legislation."[171]

A country that purports to care about individual rights and democracy cannot ignore the private sector. The private sector is where most people in Canada work. It is also the source of most housing and services. Restricting the application of human rights laws to the public sector would eliminate human rights for millions of Canadians, roll back years of progress, and create a licence to discriminate across the country. It would also ignore the history of the civil rights movement and the broad and purposive interpretation that should be brought to bear in human rights law.

CONCLUSION

A functioning democracy involves far more than duly elected legislatures. It includes the active participation of civil society, the press, individual citizens, and social movements. Human rights commissions are part and parcel of this participatory approach to democracy and an important contributor to the social discourse on human rights. A multiplicity of views and institutional perspectives provides a healthy, albeit cacophonous, solution to what would otherwise be a rigid and narrow political space for debate and dialogue. Removing commissions from the broader public debate about human rights would weaken not only our public human rights infrastructure but the fabric of our democratic structures.

As this chapter has shown, sustained demand for human rights systems is evident in the sheer number of human rights complaints filed each year. There is no evidence that increases in claims are due to rights inflation. Indeed, the evidence points the other way. In many cases, the increases in the number of complaints reflects greater social acceptance that discrimination based on characteristics like disability is not acceptable and, in turn, greater willingness by those discriminated against to file human rights complaints. As well, rapidly changing social and economic circumstances are reshaping and re-framing many familiar rights. New rights are emerging because of both Canadian constitutional law and international human rights law. These are legitimate developments, consistent with our democratic structures, and should be both expected and encouraged as part of our deepening understanding of the connection between human rights and the human condition.

Although human rights systems are still needed, there have been numerous pointed criticisms of their work, their practices, and their procedures. In the next chapter I consider these criticisms of human rights systems in connection with their legitimacy and fairness.

4

Are They Fair?

Just because commissions and tribunals don't follow the same rules as the courts does not mean that they are illegitimate.

Alan Borovoy[1]

In recent years, criticisms of human rights systems have become more prevalent and pervasive; the hate speech debates in particular generated a campaign to "denormalize" human rights systems.[2] Such criticisms have left the impression that human rights systems in Canada are "kangaroo courts" and "star chambers," unfair and flawed.[3] Alan Borovoy, a leader in Canada's civil liberties movement, was candid when asked about his views on the kangaroo court epithet: "How do you spell 'horseshit'?" he asked, smiling, "I don't agree with the commissions' role in hate speech, but commissions do important work. Just because [they] don't follow the same rules as courts does not mean that they are illegitimate."[4] The impression of illegitimacy is persistent, however, and depends for its vigour on several ideas that are either inaccurate or misguided.

- Human rights tribunals and boards are pseudo-courts: they use informal proceedings that don't follow "normal" court rules, including evidentiary rules such as hearsay.
- Human rights proceedings are pseudo-criminal proceedings but provide none of the legal protections for respondents.
- Human rights systems expose people to the risk of double jeopardy.
- Someone can be found "guilty" even if they're telling the truth or simply because a claimant is "offended."
- The usual defence of "lack of intent" cannot be used before human rights institutions.

- Human rights systems are "shakedowns" that force innocent respondents to pay.
- Human rights commissions support claimants, which is unfair to respondents.

Such accusations have had two consequences. First, they have exposed commissions and tribunals to criticisms that depend on deeply misguided beliefs about human rights systems and how they work. Second, they have diverted attention away from the real problems that human rights systems are experiencing, thereby shielding human rights institutions and, more importantly, governments from pressures to engage in meaningful reform.

MYTHS AND MISPERCEPTIONS

Shouldn't They Be Like Courts?

The idea that human rights commissions and tribunals dispense a diluted or deficient form of justice appears to stem at least in part from the belief that these institutions should function like courts. Since human rights institutions make decisions about fundamental issues such as rights, in one sense it is reasonable to expect them to look like courts and to follow the rules that we associate with court proceedings. However, they are not courts and there is no need for them to be identical to courts.

In November 2008, I had an exchange with a Nova Scotia–based columnist who is a smart and vocal critic of commissions and tribunals. He thought that tribunals' failure to mimic courts was proof of their shortcomings. When I explained that human rights institutions follow a set of rules based on administrative law and sometimes look a bit like courts but often do not, he was surprised to learn that an administrative justice system exists, let alone that human rights tribunals and commissions are part of it. This exchange taught me something about why so many of the critiques about human rights systems have had so much traction.

As discussed in previous chapters, the administrative justice system includes a huge range of agencies, boards, commissions, and tribunals, many of which are involved with fundamental rights. From refugee rights to housing rights, and from occupational health and safety to labour rights, people are far more likely to encounter the administrative justice system than the regular court system. Given this, Canadians should care deeply about whether these systems are fair and independent.

From a constitutional perspective, human rights institutions are part of the executive branch of government. However, this does not mean that the standards of fairness and independence under which they operate should be diluted or diminished. Commissions are not tribunals and they are not adjudicators, but they are still subject to basic principles of natural justice and procedural fairness. Human rights tribunals *are* adjudicators and do operate differently from courts. Tribunals are less costly and formal, more accessible and, with the exception of Quebec's tribunal, the heads of their tribunals are not judges. But they are subject to the Charter. In 2011, the Supreme Court of Canada said that courts should defer to the decisions of human rights tribunals because of tribunals' specialization and expertise, at least when tribunals are interpreting their own statutes and laws or rules closely connected to them.[5] However, such recommendations have not stopped critics from voicing misgivings.

The controversy over whether administrative systems can and should dispense justice is not new, nor is it restricted to human rights systems. There is a long and acrimonious history of dispute, starting in the late nineteenth century, about the propriety of assigning judicial decision-making responsibilities to entities other than courts.[6] This is partly because of concerns about the rule of law and the potential for the exercise of arbitrary power. However, as discussed in the second section of this chapter, the answer to such concerns lies in guarantees of independence, impartiality, and competence. It does not lie in insisting that judicial functions take place only in courts, in eliminating components of the human rights system, or in shunting 7,000-plus human rights complaints into an overburdened court system.

Evidence, Relevance, and Hearsay

Human rights tribunals take a different approach to the rules of evidence than courts. One example of this is their approach to the hearsay rule. Hearsay evidence is evidence that comes from someone or something other than the original source. It is normally excluded because the truth of a statement is most reliably presented by the person who originally made the statement. The classic example is a witness who overhears someone else's statement, and then recounts it to a court. Courts usually exclude this type of evidence, although there are many well-established, although complex and technical, exceptions to the rule. Strict application of the hearsay rule would place unrepresented litigants, such as those at human rights tribunal hearings, at an unfair disadvantage. (In Ontario, for example, about 70 percent of applicants are unrepresented.) As well, dispensing with the strict form of hearsay enables parties to get to the nub of issues more efficiently. Gordon McKinnon, a senior litigator and administrative law specialist in Manitoba who has appeared before several kinds of administrative decision-makers outside the human rights context, noted, "In most administrative hearings, what you are looking at is hearsay evidence. Workers' compensation decisions will often be based on hearsay evidence, including medical reports and other documentary reports that are admissible at the hearing but are still hearsay. They would not generally be admitted in court without calling in the actual doctor or author who wrote the document. In an administrative hearing, however, the rules are relaxed to permit the evidence without this type of expense and additional time."[7] Requiring fifty witnesses to establish fifty separate statements in connection with one set of facts in an administrative hearing would cripple the system. According to litigator David Baker, very few human rights cases actually turn on hearsay; when they do, tribunals have tools to deal with the evidence in a manner that is fair to both parties.[8] Most administrative tribunals can admit hearsay evidence, but they must still assess its reliability and relevance. The main difference between their approach and that of the courts is that unfair, unreliable, or prejudicial evidence is dealt with in a different way. To return to the earlier example of the BC Tribunal decision in the *Maclean's* hate speech case, the tribunal admitted evidence about certain blog posts submitted by the complainants as proof that Muslims were being exposed to hatred and contempt. These posts would arguably have been inadmissible before a court unless the authors had been found and called to testify. However, the tribunal ended up according the blog posts little or no weight: it was plain from the tribunal's decision that authenticity was an issue: no one had demonstrated who actually wrote or posted them[9] and therefore to have given them any weight would have been unfair and prejudicial to the respondents, Rogers Inc. and Ken MacQueen.

One of the key factors in determining the admissibility of evidence is relevance, and this is true in both courts and tribunals. In the case of *Warman v. Lemire*, many of the deficiencies of human rights tribunals and commissions, including the way they admit evidence, was at issue.[10] Margot Blight was one of the lawyers acting for the Canadian Human Rights Commission in that case. The principles of law in hate speech and some of the subject-matter in *Warman v. Lemire* were similar to those in the 2002 case of *Citron and Toronto Mayor's Committee v. Zündel*, which was brought against Holocaust-denier and anti-Semite Ernst Zündel.[11] However, Blight saw important differences between Marc Lemire's tactics and those of Zündel a decade earlier. Blight described Zündel as having tried unsuccessfully to use the hate speech complaints against him as a platform to express his views on Jews and the Holocaust. Blight thought that Lemire was "more focused on other things, and operates in a different context: the Internet age. [He] decided to fight back by attacking the commission directly, so a lot of what the case was about was the commission itself, and every critique of the commission was dredged up."[12] The respondents in the *Lemire* case persuaded the tribunal to admit evidence about the way in which the Canadian Human Rights Commission investigated hate speech cases. Prior to the hate speech crisis, Blight said, no one had really used this tactic and the tribunal appeared to be unsure how to deal with it.

"There was endless evidence about how bad the commission was supposed to be, and this fed the media stories for days on end. The willingness of the tribunal to let all this evidence in was problematic in terms of its relevance."[13] The way in which the evidence rules were used by the tribunal strongly favoured Lemire. The Federal Court of Canada held later that the tribunal should have discounted the evidence as irrelevant for the simple reason that it had nothing to do with the hate speech complaint and was in fact a critique of the jurisdiction of the Canadian Human Rights Commission in its lawful mandate of investigating hate speech cases. The Federal Court decided that the tribunal had exceeded its jurisdiction by improperly admitting evidence about the commission's statutory role in handling section 13 investigations.[14] Had the tribunal agreed to hear the evidence but then discounted it later as irrelevant, the issue would not have arisen.

The formality of evidentiary rules varies between tribunals in Canada. At one extreme is the Quebec Human Rights Tribunal, which is presided over by a judge of the provincial court and observes stricter rules of evidence. Smaller jurisdictions with tribunals structured as ad hoc panels tend to be less formal. The point here is that authenticity, relevance, reliability, and fairness to the parties are just as important in tribunals but the process for handling them is often different. The same goes for probative value, namely whether a piece of evidence can show a disputed point to be true.

Remedies: Understanding the Objectives
of the Human Rights System

The Supreme Court of Canada decided in the *Blencoe* case that the human rights system is about compensating claimants and eradicating discrimination.[15] However, these two objectives are not necessarily coextensive. A remedy that aims to eradicate discrimination can depart from compensation by imposing sanctions. Sanctions, like penalties, have been the subject of criticism because they are seen as incompatible with what the human rights system was designed to do. One source of this criticism was a very public debate about a penalty clause in section 54(1)(c) of the CHRA in *Warman v. Lemire.*[16] Section 54(1)(c) dealt with orders that a tribunal may make with regard to hate speech that is communicated by telephone or on the internet (section 13). The section authorizes a penalty of up to $10,000. Because of the use of the word "penalty," some have assumed that the clause is criminal, but it isn't. Rather it is (or was) a public interest sanction aimed at eradicating discrimination. It was the only penalty clause of its kind in the Canadian Human Rights Act (CHRA), but it signaled a particular public interest element related to discriminatory behaviour.

Marc Lemire was alleged to be a webmaster for web sites containing racist material and hate speech. The Canadian Human Rights Tribunal found that Lemire had published a post that was "likely to expose homosexuals and Blacks to hatred or contempt."[17] Lemire challenged section 13 of the CHRA. Even though section 13 had been upheld as constitutional in the 1990 *Taylor* case, the penalty clause had been introduced later, in 1998. The tribunal member who decided the case, Athanasios D. Hadjis, decided that prior to 1998, the hate speech prohibition had played only a "minimal role in the imposition of moral, financial or incarcerating sanctions, the primary goal being to act directly for the benefit of those likely to be exposed to the harms caused by hate propaganda."[18] However, after the amendment, it was argued that the penal section could no longer be characterized as "minimal." Hadjis ruled that it was incompatible with the freedom of expression guaranteed by article 2(b) of the Charter and refused to apply both sections 13(1) and 54(1)(c) of the CHRA.

"Compensation" in human rights laws varies significantly from jurisdiction to jurisdiction, as described in chapter 1. Remedies such as punitive and exemplary damages, for example, go beyond compensation and pecuniary damages to punish egregious behaviour and to impose moral or financial sanctions. With respect to punitive damages, the Supreme Court of Canada's 2010 decision of *Vancouver v. Ward*, contained an explanation in the Charter context.

> [56] A final word on exemplary or punitive damages. In *Mackin*, Justice Gonthier speculated that "[i]n theory, a plaintiff could seek compensatory and punitive damages by way of 'appropriate and just' remedy under s. 24(1) of the *Charter*": para. 79. The reality is that public law damages, in serving the objects of vindication and deterrence, may assume a punitive aspect. Nevertheless, it is worth noting a general reluctance in the international community to award purely punitive damages: see *Taunoa*, at paras. 319–21.[19]

According to the Supreme Court of Canada, punitive damages can be awarded as the result of "malicious, oppressive and highhanded" conduct.[20] In a 2011 case, Quebec's Human Rights Tribunal described the role of punitive damages in the human rights context: "The preventive function of punitive damages is fundamental; punitive damages have a dual objective of punishment and deterrence, but cannot exceed what is sufficient to achieve those objectives. ... It is not a question of compensating the plaintiff but of punishing the defendant as the defendant deserves, of discouraging both the defendant and others from acting in that manner in the future and expressing disapproval of such events in all respects."[21] In other words, these financial and moral sanctions are unconnected to compensation.

In *Lemire*, the Canadian Human Rights Tribunal missed most of these nuances. Had it looked across the country, it would have found that most human rights systems include a range of remedies that impose moral and financial sanctions. These remedies do not transform the human rights system into a criminal system of justice.

When the Federal Court of Canada later overturned the tribunal's decision in *Lemire*, it ruled that the tribunal had erred by admitting irrelevant evidence, as noted earlier, and because it had failed to sever section 54(1)(c) from section 13.[22] This technique would have allowed the tribunal to excise unconstitutional provisions from the statute without having to invalidate section 13. Leaving section 13 intact would have allowed the tribunal to comply with the Supreme Court of Canada's decision in the 1990 *Taylor* case (upholding section 13 as constitutional).[23] The Federal Court sent the matter back to the tribunal. The net result was that section 54(1(c) remained inoperative, while section 13 of the CHRA was salvaged. The Federal Court's decision in *Lemire* attracted far less attention from the media than the tribunal decision. The uproar over the penalty cleared the way for Bill C-304, which was passed in 2013 to repeal section 13 and the penalty clause along with it.[24]

The handling of the *Lemire* case has troubling implications for human rights systems that extend well beyond the penalty clause in the CHRA. In its aftermath, in 2008 the Canadian Human Rights Commission released a report proposing the repeal of section 54(1)(c). The commission agreed with the widely held view that the penalty clause does not "fit easily" within the human rights system.[25] The commission may have felt it was sidestepping a difficult legal argument by conceding the illegality of the penalty clause and sacrificing section 54(1)(c) to save section 13. However, its decision exposed human rights laws across Canada to other collateral attacks: all statutes contain provisions that impose what the tribunal had described as moral, financial, and even incarcerating sanctions. None of these provisions "fit easily" within the human rights system either, at least not as it has been articulated and framed in recent years.

In the case of penalties imposed by administrative tribunals, there is a long history of the legitimate use of such provisions, especially in statutory schemes to defend the public interest. Even the fact that some regulatory regimes contain criminal sanctions does not mean that the entire statute is transformed into a criminal law regime. Gordon McKinnon pointed out that: "All the professional discipline bodies I deal with have a component that would contain some sort of a fine. Medical, legal, and nursing disciplinary bodies, for example, would all have some sort of fine or sanction attached to them. So do taxi board companies and liquor licensing boards. This does not make them criminal in nature in this sense; [sanctions] are a standard part of the administrative regulatory scheme."[26] Such provisions go beyond compensating claimants and contain "moral or financial" sanctions. Complaints systems that are based in part on protecting the public interest commonly contain such sanctions.

Criminal sanctions that exist in human rights laws, as noted earlier, include sanctions for violation of orders, obstruction of justice, or reprisals against complainants or witnesses. These provisions are clearly not compensatory. They are not even about remedies at all. They are about ensuring respect for the justice system. Section 60 of the CHRA, for example, creates summary conviction offences (minor crimes that are processed without a jury trial) in the case of obstruction and reprisal.

Prosecution is undertaken in the "regular" court system and is subject to the consent of the attorney general. In such cases enforcement mechanisms and sanctions are used to uphold the rule of law

François Larsen, a director at Quebec's Human Rights Commission, emphasized the importance of enforcement: "There is a naïveté among progressives that I call the 'institutional Kumbaya': 'We are all going to get together and hold hands and be nice to each other. Education will do the trick.' It does not always work that way. Commissions and tribunals need legal powers, and complaints processes are part of this work."[27] Legal powers do not corrupt or taint the whole human rights system, just as sanctions do not transform regulatory systems into criminal regimes. Many countries have human rights institutions that lack the "teeth" of enforcement. These institutions are limited to education, research, and the like.[28] Their recommendations can be, and frequently are, completely ignored.

Most of the public debate around the repeal of s. 13 was based on the argument that the section duplicated criminal hate speech provisions. There are many behaviours that can be and are dealt with either by civil or administrative sanctions, or by criminal law, or both. Libel, negligence, and fraud, for instance, can give rise to both civil suits and criminal prosecutions. Legislators have multiple legal tools to address public policy issues and to deter, punish, or compensate people for proscribed behaviours. Removing the less intrusive and heavy-handed tool – the administrative tool – weakens our legal system's responsiveness and leaves criminal law and jail as a sole response.

Conciliation, Capitulation, or Revenge?

Human rights legislation aims to compensate claimants and eradicate discrimination. Every human rights system has several legal tools available to achieve these objectives. Examples include early settlement or mediation, conciliation, and directed mediation. All of these terms are used at different phases of the complaint process in different human rights systems, but their shared objective is to get people to settle complaints amicably.

Most first-generation human rights statutes in Canada contain a clause that requires that human rights commissions attempt to settle complaints. As the cost and complexity of litigation have grown over the years, there has been increasing reliance on different types of settlement techniques. This trend is not unique to human rights and coincides with a push from the entire judicial system to get cases out of the courts. Alternative dispute resolution emerged as an area of law and practice in the 1980s as a way to reduce the number of cases before the courts, reduce delays, and put an end to last-minute deals made by lawyers who were seemingly more interested in quick settlements than in justice.

No one can, however, be forced to participate in the settlement process, let alone to settle. Nonetheless settlement, particularly mediation, which is the most common technique used in human rights systems in Canada, has been the target of fierce criticism. When I was working in the Ontario system, we heard claims that people had been strong-armed into settling by mediators who brandished the prospect of delays of up to three or four years to incite people to settle. While the delays were not exaggerated, using them in this way was seen as a form of inappropriate pressure to force people into accepting settlements. Settlements were also seen by critics as failing to serve the public interest because mediated agreements are frequently confidential and thus lack transparency: no one other than the parties in confidential settlements is aware of what occurred. As a result, the public interest aspect of the proceedings was said to be lost.[29]

Mediation became so controversial at the Ontario Commission that its entire mediation service was totally scrapped when Bill 107 took effect in 2008.[30] One official, who spoke off the record, told me that transferring the commission's mediation system, with its procedures, staff, and systems, to the tribunal after Bill 107 was never seriously contemplated.

It is still useful to look at a 1998 statistical report on Ontario's mediation work because it offers insights into the way the process was seen during the experimental period in the late 1990s when the Ontario Human Rights Commission introduced early, structured mediation, and because it speaks to many of the criticisms about mediation:

- Respondents showed greater general satisfaction with mediation compared to complainants, suggesting that criticisms about mediation being complainant-friendly are misplaced.
- Respondents were more likely than complainants to say that their concerns had been heard.
- About 75 percent of complainants and respondents strongly agreed that mediation officers were fair and neutral.
- Between 70 and 80 percent of complainants and respondents felt they were equal participants in mediation.

• Both respondents and complainants said they would choose mediation again in future cases, and 92 percent of respondents' representatives reported that they would do so.[31]

Keith Norton remained a supporter of mediation more than a decade after this study: "I've never understood the accusation that the myriad people who have gone through the system and managed to reach a successful resolution of their cases, to their mutual satisfaction, could reasonably describe themselves as having been coerced."[32] About 70 percent of complainants and respondents in the 1998 study said they had not experienced any pressure to settle, although twice as many complainants as respondents felt they had been pressured (22 percent versus 11 percent).[33]

In 2012, the Pinto Report, which examined the Bill 107 system in Ontario also noted high levels of satisfaction with the mediation process in the new direct access system: "Most participants were generally satisfied with mediation. Mediation occurs relatively early in the process and the mediators are helpful in resolving complaints. Tribunal members conduct mediations that are guided by a rights-based orientation and which are informed by the member's adjudicative experience and many mediations result in public interest remedies."[34]

It is noteworthy that the mediation in Ontario's new system occurs as part of the tribunal's internal process, not the commission's. Emphasis is much more on the parties' rights than on their interests. Success at mediation is assisted by the presence of counsel: the Human Rights Tribunal of Ontario has an overall mediation success rate of 65 percent but that number jumps to 85 percent when the Human Rights Legal Support Centre is representing the applicant. This says something about the importance of expertise at the table when settlement discussions are underway.

There are principled objections to mediation and to alternative dispute resolution more generally. One of the classic critiques is provided in Owen Fiss's article "Against Settlement."[35] Fiss argued that settlements aimed at purchasing peace without securing justice are inherently suspect, which may well be true when rights are ignored in favour of expediency. Critics from the right use different language, but they also see settlements as fundamentally unethical. One prominent accusation is of a "shakedown."[36] According to Ezra Levant, human rights claimants demand "large cash payments," and human rights commissions are "a tool for hustlers to shake down their enemies for cash."[37]

While he is correct that financial payments can be involved in settlements, he is completely wrong about how these payments come about, and about their moral legitimacy. As in most legal situations, parties in human rights disputes are invited to resolve or settle their cases without going to court. Complainants often seek financial settlements instead of incurring the risk and burden of a full hearing. Respondents are entitled to refuse to settle or accept a settlement for motives that can be perfectly legitimate. For example, if during mediation it becomes clear that a complainant would likely win her case, then a mediator would advise both parties of this likelihood, as well as the implications this would have for the extent of the damages that the respondent would have to pay. The mediator would invite the parties to consider a settlement offer whereby the respondent would pay the complainant a settlement amount that reasonably reflects the remedy to which the claimant would be entitled, instead of proceeding to a full hearing with all the risks, costs, and reputational damage of litigation. This type of agreement does not carry the extortionate flavour that Levant and others ascribe to it. Every part of Canada's justice system contains formal and informal opportunities for parties to resolve their differences without the damage and cost that litigation inevitably involves. In the criminal justice system, there are plea bargains; in the civil courts, there are mandatory pre-trial mediations. In the human rights context, if the respondent believes that no discrimination has occurred and wishes to prove the point, there is a full right to refuse to settle or even to embark on mediation discussions. The respective rights of all parties have to be considered as well as the broader public interest. Most human rights systems have moved or are moving in this direction.

There are several ways to gauge the success or failure of settlement attempts. None of them is entirely satisfactory in isolation, but together they provide a good set of indicators: rates of resolution (usually expressed as a percentage of settled cases that involve mediation), the parties' overall satisfaction with the process, whether the process is perceived as maintaining a balance of power between the parties, the relationship between the outcome and the parties' rights, and the expertise of the mediator. This latter point is especially important according to Byron Williams, a Manitoba practitioner. The Manitoba Human Rights Commission contracts with high-level mediators for complex and high profile cases and Williams thought such an approach had made a major difference both in the utilization of a commission's mediation services and in the overall success of the system.[38]

Anyone who has been involved in settling human rights cases knows that settlement discussions can be abused by parties – for example, when a party uses discussions to drag out the process or to gain a strategic advantage. Mediators deal with these tactics by setting time limits to push the parties towards resolution and to avoid undue delays. Williams said: "I do not see a problem with the trade-offs inherent in mediation. This has been one of the things that saved us in Manitoba: investigations do not take forever anymore."[39] The Manitoba human rights system's directed mediation process has had a high level of success. The Manitoba commission describes the process in the following terms: "The Board of Commissioners will refer a complaint to Board-Directed Mediation if it determines that there is enough evidence of a contravention of the Human Rights Code to warrant the complaint going to the next stage in the complaint process. This determination is based on the evidence in the Investigation Assessment Report and any submissions from the parties in response to the report."[40] The success of the Manitoba system was an important influence in the 2012 restructuring of the Saskatchewan Human Rights Commission, which has redirected its resources away from litigation and towards mediation.[41]

Without settlement efforts, many cases will inevitably end up at hearings that are often bitterly contested and highly adversarial. Many respondents drag cases out for years, a situation that is in no one's interests. Colleen Sheppard, a former commissioner in Quebec, said: "I'm not sure that I have a clear answer as to what the system should be, but it is far too adversarial the way it is right now … The adversarial nature of cases and long delays mean that even when you win, you lose. There are too few opportunities to resolve issues quickly and amicably."[42]

Mediation provides one of those opportunities, and it has been highly successful in settling complaints, offering a variety of ways to resolve cases. It is generally seen as fair and balanced when the mediator is competent and respected, and both parties genuinely wish to resolve the matter.

The allegation that the entire human rights system is inherently corrupt or extortionate may result from some litigants' use or abuse of settlement discussions as a way to seek a strategic advantage. But the strategic use of settlements is not always an indication of corruption: Mr Levant himself is on record in 2003 as having offered Darren Lund $20,000 to settle a defamation case on behalf of Levant's client Stephen Boissoin after Lund filed a hate speech complaint against Boissoin.[43] The case is discussed in more detail in chapter 5, but it is worth pointing out here that although some offers to settle may well be "shakedowns" and "tools for hustlers to shake down their enemies for cash," there may also be perfectly valid reasons to settle a case.

Outrageous Complaints and Abuse of Process

Respondents have few useful tools at their disposal to protect themselves against frivolous, malicious, or vexatious complaints. During the *Maclean's* hate speech debates, a common critique of human rights systems was that the students had been permitted to file what critics saw as manifestly abusive complaints. As discussed in chapter 3, most human rights statutes allow respondents to seek preliminary dismissal of such cases, but the success rate tends to be relatively low, in part because the evidence in support of preliminary dismissal is usually the same evidence that the respondent would have to use in any event in its defence.[44] Commissions tend to be hesitant to use their dismissal power for fear that complaints may be dropped too early in the process. In first-generation systems, respondents often have to wait for some form of investigation to take place in order to dismiss baseless or malicious complaints.

In the frivolous category, I recall one case in Ontario in 1995 when I was at the commission. A customer had ordered chicken nuggets at a fast food restaurant. He then complained that he got fried chicken instead. The matter escalated when the customer alleged discrimination. The accusation was that the person taking the order had stereotyped the customer by assuming that the customer, who was Black, had ordered fried chicken. Incredibly, the case was investigated. When the branch director presented the file to the commissioners, I recall that Rosemary Brown, who was then the chief commissioner, was incensed. She instructed that such cases should not be investigated in future and expressed outrage at the waste of public funds. There was not much doubt that the complaint had no legal foundation, but the reluctance to simply get rid of such cases on a preliminary basis was deeply entrenched in the commission at the time. More recently, an equally idiotic fast food complaint was dismissed on a preliminary basis but more expeditiously by the Human Rights Tribunal of Ontario. The complainant had filed a complaint anonymously as a radical (male) feminist, claiming that he wanted to make a point about A&W restaurant's "heteronormal" Burger family and that it was discriminatory against LGBT communities. The complaint was given short shrift; the case assessment directive described the matter as frivolous, vexatious, and outrageous. The tribunal chair observed that it was an unacceptable waste of public resources to initiate a complaint for reasons other than the fact that the complainant believes that his rights were violated.[45] The case provides some evidence that tribunals may be more willing to use preliminary dismissal powers.

In the *Maclean's* hate speech case, there is no evidence that the issue was frivolous, nor that the complainants were behaving in an abusive or vexatious matter. In fact, no evidence whatsoever in this regard was considered or accepted by the tribunal in British Columbia or by the commission in Ontario. The case was determined to be out of jurisdiction in Ontario, but not for these reasons.

One possible recourse for respondents who are the subject of vexatious claims is libel and defamation proceedings. These suits must be initiated within a relatively short timeframe and, because human rights proceedings can take years to resolve, limitation periods will usually have expired on the defamation case by the time a human rights complaint is decided. During the long delays, details about the complaint can be widely disseminated if one party decides to use the media to publicize the complaint. This can damage reputations, but the damaged party may be unable to sue within the time allowed: in many jurisdictions in Canada, reprisal against a party or witness is a criminal offence (summary conviction). A defamation suit brought in response to human rights complaints may be considered a reprisal, which creates a strong disincentive to anyone considering filing a defamation case. Very few human rights statutes in Canada clearly articulate the relationship between human rights complaints and defamation proceedings or other lawsuits related to the complainant's behaviour. Yukon's Human Rights Act allows the tribunal to award damages for malicious contravention and for injury to a *respondent's* reputation. Section 76 of the Quebec Charter offers another solution, by stopping the clock for limitation periods on defamation so that the parties' rights are preserved while the human rights complaint is being processed.[46]

Sometimes, lawsuits are indeed filed as a form of retaliation or reprisal. In such circumstances, the complainants are the ones who need protection. These types of suits are called Strategic Lawsuits against Public Participation (SLAPPs), and they are retaliatory lawsuits brought against individuals who have spoken out or taken a position on an issue of personal or public interest. One writer described them this way: "The purpose of SLAPPs is to limit the freedom of expression of the defendants and neutralize their actions by resorting to the courts to intimidate them,

deplete their resources and reduce their means of action."[47]At the time
of writing, Quebec had legislation on the books against SLAPP suits.[48]
I am not aware of other jurisdictions that have followed suit, but the
innovation is interesting and protects public interest litigation.

Criminal Law and the Human Rights System

The conflation of human rights and criminal law is fuelled by the use of
terms like "prosecution," "police," "charges," guilty," and "accused."[49]
The televised interview of Mark Steyn by Mike Duffy, described in chapter 3, referred to Steyn as someone who had had a complaint brought
against him by the "speech police." While few writers use criminal-law
language, they have been widely copied and recycled. Since most people
likely have little knowledge of or interest in human rights commissions
and tribunals, the impressions that they do have may well have been
influenced by language like this, creating an image of a justice system
gone amok. The term "prosecution," for example, is more properly associated with criminal charges brought by law enforcement officials.
Human rights complaints are not criminal prosecutions by the state but
administrative complaints brought by private individuals and organizations.[50] Similarly, "charges" is the term used to describe the process of
formally accusing someone of violating criminal law: it is not appropriate in the context of human rights complaints, which do not correspond
to charges under criminal law. Finally, the term "accused" in the context
of human rights systems is misleading. It is true that people may use
"accused" in a non-technical sense, in much the same way that a busi-
nessperson can be "accused" of breaching a contract, or a child can be
"accused" of negligently throwing a baseball through someone's win-
dow. Neither of these is a criminal accusation, and the person responsible does not receive a criminal sentence or risk jail time because of what
commissions or tribunals do. The use of language that is generally
reserved for the criminal realm helps to foster and feed the misunderstandings about human rights systems.

Commissions and tribunals aim to compensate claimants and to eradicate discrimination, not to criminalize it. The Supreme Court of Canada,
in the *Blencoe* case, said, " The investigation period in the human rights
process is not one where the commission 'prosecutes' the respondent."[51]
This general statement is an accurate description of human rights law
and helps to both explain and define the important differences between

the old quasi-criminal provisions, which were indeed aimed at punishment, and the contemporary system, which is not.

It is true that several human rights statutes in Canada still have criminal or quasi-criminal offences whereby *any* violation of human rights law, including discrimination, can result in either a civil or a criminal proceeding.[52] They are throwbacks to the earlier quasi-criminal laws from the 1940s and 1950s and are rarely if ever used.[53] Nonetheless, to accord with current thought in this field, legislatures should remove these types of hybrid recourses, where they exist.

Intent

Human rights systems have also been criticized for not considering intent as a potential "defence" in human rights claims. Here again, it is the conflation of human rights law with criminal law that provides the force for this argument – which, if legitimate, would be a powerful criticism. Criminal law generally requires proof of the defendant's state of mind or intent. Discrimination claims, however, are not criminal and focus on *effects*, so the role of intent is considerably muted. In a unanimous Supreme Court of Canada decision in 1985, the court stated:" [W]e are dealing here with consequences of conduct rather than with punishment for misbehaviour. In other words, we are considering what are essentially civil remedies. The proof of intent, a necessary requirement in our approach to criminal and punitive legislation, should not be a governing factor in construing human rights legislation aimed at the elimination of discrimination. It is my view that the courts below were in error in finding an intent to discriminate to be a necessary element of proof."[54] The Supreme Court observed that insisting on "intent" as a prerequisite for discrimination has had insidious consequences, noting its influence on the notorious "separate but equal" doctrine in the United States, which helped reinforce the segregation of African-Americans.[55]

In 1987, the court examined the intent issue again in a discrimination case frequently referred to as "Action Travail des Femmes," the name of the complainant organization. This case dealt with hiring and promotion policies by CN that excluded women from blue-collar jobs. The Supreme Court upheld the employment equity program that the Canadian Human Rights Tribunal had imposed on the employer. Although CN's policies may not have been *intended* to discriminate against women, they had the demonstrated *effect* of preventing or discouraging women from getting blue-collar jobs.[56] Cases like this helped change the way that discrimination is understood and litigated.

Three years later, the Supreme Court applied the same reasoning to the act of exposing people to hatred under section 13 of the CHRA in the *Taylor* case: "An intent to discriminate is not a precondition of a finding of discrimination under human rights codes[.] The preoccupation with effects, and not with intent, is readily explicable when one considers that systemic discrimination is much more widespread in our society than is intentional discrimination. To import a subjective intent requirement into human rights provisions, rather than allowing tribunals to focus solely upon effects, would thus defeat one of the primary goals of anti-discrimination statutes."[57]

Requiring proof of objective and verifiable effects in discrimination cases helps protect respondents as well as complainants. In the *Maclean's* hate speech case in British Columbia, section 7(1)(b) of the BC Human Rights Code required objective evidence that Mark Steyn's article, or *Maclean's* refusal to publish a rebuttal to it, exposed others to hatred or contempt. The decision depended on objective evidence, based on the balance of probabilities, and not subjective perceptions.[58] The tribunal permitted evidence from blogs and online comments to be entered into the record as potential evidence but accorded them little weight. As noted earlier, the complainants lost in British Columbia in part because they were unable to objectively demonstrate the effects of the impugned publication in terms of Muslims' exposure to hatred.[59] They were further unable to prove who had written the comments and to demonstrate that the comments were really a response to the articles in question.[60]

Intent does have a limited role in some jurisdictions: section 3 of the Alberta Human Rights Act says:

No person shall publish, issue or display or cause to be published, issued or displayed before the public any statement, publication, notice, sign, symbol, emblem or other representation that

(a) indicates discrimination *or an intention to discriminate* against a person or a class of persons, or
(b) is likely to expose a person or a class of persons to hatred or contempt ... [.][61]

This provision deals with discriminatory speech and requires *either* an intent to discriminate *or* evidence of a publication that indicates discrimination.

The issue of intent came to the fore again in 2013 when the Supreme Court, reaffirming its decision in *Taylor*, explained once again in *Whatcott* why intent is not a requirement for discrimination: "The preventive measures found in human rights legislation reasonably centre on effects, rather than intent. I see no reason to depart from this approach."[62]

INTENT AND CONTEMPT OF COURT

A person who wilfully breaches human rights law and fails to respect a human rights tribunal order can be cited for contempt. If this occurs, the person can end up in prison and it has been argued that this means that human rights complaints can put people in jail. According to Philippe Dufresne, a lawyer at the Canadian Human Rights Commission, such views reflect a "complete lack of understanding of contempt proceedings" in relation to human rights cases.[63] Contempt proceedings are designed to ensure respect for the justice system. They apply to *all* types of cases, whether they arise from a criminal, civil, or administrative system. In order to be cited for contempt related to failure to comply with an order, an individual must wilfully engage in actions prohibited by the order.[64] Under the Federal Court Rules, contempt of court occurs when a person disobeys a court process or order, interferes with the orderly administration of justice, or impairs the court's authority or dignity.[65] The following examples show how contempt, human rights proceedings, hate speech, and the roles of commissions, tribunals, and courts are connected.

In the 1990 *Taylor* case, the Canadian Human Rights Tribunal issued a cease and desist order against John Ross Taylor under section 13 of the CHRA because of hate messages Taylor was still sending by telephone.[66] The cease and desist order was filed in Federal Court, but Taylor and the Western Guard Party ignored it and continued to send their messages. The Federal Court found them in contempt of the order and the Western Guard Party was ordered to pay a $5,000 fine. Taylor, its leader, was sentenced to a year of imprisonment. The sentence was then suspended on the condition that the tribunal's cease and desist order be obeyed. It was not, and the suspension was therefore lifted: the Western Guard Party had to pay the fine and Taylor had to serve his sentence. The Supreme Court saw the term of imprisonment and its connection to the issue of intent as an element in contempt proceedings, distinct from the underlying human rights complaint: "[A] term of imprisonment [for contempt] is only possible where the respondent *intentionally* communicates messages which he or she knows have been found likely to cause the harm described in s. 13(1), and I therefore cannot agree that the possibility of a contempt order issuing against an individual unduly chills the freedom of expression."[67] In other words, it was the intentional failure to comply with the tribunal's order that gave the court the authority to find Taylor in contempt.

Two decades later, in *Warman v. Tremaine,* the communication of hate was no longer taking place through the telephone but through another form of federally regulated telecommunications, the Internet.[68] The Federal Court's description of the facts is set out below. It is worth noting the critical role of intent in the Federal Court's decision regarding contempt of court in relation to wilful disobedience of an order.

Terry Tremaine has deliberately flaunted an order of the Canadian Human Rights Tribunal to cease communicating matters that are likely to expose persons to hatred or contempt on prohibited grounds. He is in contempt of the order of the Tribunal – indeed, he brags about it and admitted it before me. The issue, *however, is whether he is in contempt of this Court. I reluctantly conclude he is not. The only reason he is not is that the Commission failed to bring to his attention the fact that it had registered the Tribunal's order with this Court.*

Mr. Tremaine thinks (or perhaps just wishes) he is better than others because of the colour of his skin. He is a white supremacist. Although his dislike of others based on the colour of their skin knows no bounds, he has particular enmity for blacks and Canada's aboriginal peoples.

He is also a neo-Nazi. He is virulently anti-Jewish. He draws no distinction between Jewishness and Zionism. According to him, Jews are parasites who will take over the world unless they are stopped. The blacks are their stupid lackeys and the First Nations are in league with them. He is fond of Adolf Hitler; who got it right – even though the holocaust is a hoax.

Not content to keep his thoughts to himself, he has used the Internet to place them where they can be found[.][69]

Since the Canadian Human Rights Tribunal is not a court, it has only the powers contained in its own statute and can only request that a person be cited for contempt. The Federal Court was the "court of record" and the court that received the request in the form of an application.[70] The case was ultimately dismissed, because Tremaine was not aware that the tribunal's order had been registered in Federal Court and therefore lacked the requisite intent to be cited for contempt of court. Here, intent mattered.

Double Jeopardy and Forum Shopping

Another concern about human rights systems is that they permit "double jeopardy" and forum shopping because the same or similar complaints can be filed in several Canadian jurisdictions.

The idea of double jeopardy evolved as part of criminal law in order to prevent people from being charged again for a crime for which there had been a prior conviction or acquittal. Double jeopardy is prohibited by the Charter and applies to criminal proceedings.[71] The criticism that human rights systems can subject people to double jeopardy stems from the *Maclean's* hate speech cases: the three human rights complaints were launched in relation to the same or similar set of facts (albeit with different parties to the proceedings) in three human rights systems. They were filed under the administrative provisions dealing with discrimination[72] with the Canadian Human Rights Commission, the Ontario Human Rights Commission, and the British Columbia Human Rights Tribunal. However, because none of the three complaints was criminal in nature, the term and concept of "double jeopardy" did not apply. There were no criminal charges, convictions, or acquittals. Leaving aside the technical issue of double jeopardy, it was entirely appropriate for the three cases to have been brought in three jurisdictions because our constitutional system forces people to claim their rights separately in each jurisdiction where violations are alleged.

The complaints were intended by the law students who drafted them in each jurisdiction to serve as the basis for a national campaign against what the students saw as hateful portraits of Muslims published by *Maclean's*. The facts of the case, namely online and print publication across the country, led to multiple claims arising from a single situation or set of allegations, raising the issue of forum shopping. Forum shopping refers to looking for the best place to bring a complaint in order to get the decision wanted by the complainant. It is a practice that raises concerns about the costs and risks of litigating in multiple jurisdictions. Although cases like the *Maclean's* hate speech case are rare, in some situations the same or similar human rights claims could be filed in several or even all of the fourteen human rights jurisdictions in Canada. This possibility has nothing to do with flaws in human rights commissions' processes, abuse of process, or even with forum shopping. It is the result of the fact that Canada has no single, national human rights commission with the authority to combine cases in multiple jurisdictions into a single proceeding. The division of powers in the Constitution Act, 1867 is such that multiple proceedings in human rights systems are not only possible but a likely outcome if complaints arise in more than one jurisdiction. One way of preventing multiple proceedings and untangling the complexity and expense of having multiple regulators proceed with separate complaints would be to have a national human rights body in lieu of the fourteen systems that currently exist. However, there is currently no obvious authority to impose a national or unified regulatory approach to human rights. [73]

While it may be unfair that respondents have to fight the same or similar human rights complaints in multiple jurisdictions, it is also unfair that complainants have to file and litigate complaints concerning the same set of facts in multiple jurisdictions. There is merit to the idea of having a more coordinated national approach to simplify and reduce the costs of procedures for all of the parties involved when multiple proceedings occur. Although s. 27(1)(c) of the CHRA addresses the issue of potentially conflicting decisions in different jurisdictions, it does not directly deal with forum shopping. The Canadian Human Rights Commission has said that it will work with other jurisdictions to address multiple proceedings, but the status of this collaboration or its outcome is unclear.[74]

Truth

During the hate speech debates, critics argued that human rights proceedings allow people to be found "guilty" merely because they have offended someone, even if the offensive statements are true. In fact, offence and hurt feelings are not relevant to establishing discrimination. It may well be that people who are subject to hate speech are offended, but that is not the legal test for discrimination.

Truth is not irrelevant to human rights proceedings. Claimants must prove their allegations to be true on the balance of probabilities. This standard of proof, which applies to all discrimination cases, is much lower than the criminal standard of "beyond a reasonable doubt." It is the same standard of proof used in civil cases before the courts.

Hate speech raises an additional dimension, because respondents in hate speech cases argue that the truth of the impugned speech merits analysis as part of a free and open debate. Free speech is protected, but this constitutional protection is lost when speech provokes unusually strong and deep-felt emotions of detestation and vilification.[75] Proving that this is the case requires objective evidence of the effects of the speech itself and not its truth. Assertions that entire groups of people are inherently criminal, inferior, diseased, or dangerous simply because of their race, gender, religion, ethnicity, or similar characteristics are evidence *in themselves* that the targeted group is or will likely be exposed to hatred. This standard is derived from the Charter and the Charter standard is what is used to benchmark human rights laws. According to the Supreme Court of Canada in the *Whatcott* case: "Representations vilifying a person or group will seek to abuse, denigrate or delegitimize them, to render them lawless, dangerous, unworthy or unacceptable in the eyes of the audience. Expression exposing vulnerable groups to detestation and vilification goes far beyond merely discrediting, humiliating or offending the victims."[76]

There can be no meaningful inquiry into the "truth" of propositions to the effect that entire groups of people are bestial, degraded, or likely to be pedophiles. These are not "ideas" that can be countered with more speech.[77] John Ross Taylor, the respondent in the seminal 1990 *Taylor* decision, described his anti-Semitic and racist publications as "truth literature." He invited listeners to engage with the "truth" that Jews deserve to be deported en masse to Madagascar.[78] Several years later, a respondent in another case argued that citizens should march gay people to the outskirts of town and "trample them into peat bogs" as the ancient Celts supposedly had.[79] As Richard Moon said: "A truth defence is not required because hate speech is necessarily untrue. Hate speech makes the claim that the members of an identifiable group share a dangerous or undesirable trait – that they are by nature violent or corrupt or dishonest – and must be stopped by violent means if necessary. Our commitment to equality entails a rejection of any view that the members of a racial or other identifiable group are inherently inferior or dangerous."[80]

When it comes to hate propaganda, truth is not a defence even in the criminal context, at least when it comes to publicly inciting hatred under s. 319(1) of the Criminal Code. It is, however, a defence in the case of wilfully promoting hatred when actual incitement (meaning the provocation of unlawful behaviour, or urging others to behave unlawfully) has not occurred.[81]

There is another reason to be careful about insisting on truth as a defence in the human rights context: to do so would render writers and

journalists more vulnerable to hate speech complaints if their assertions turn out to be false. Mark Steyn's notorious article "The Future
Belongs to Islam" predicted a Muslim takeover with the only remaining
question, according to Steyn, being "how bloody the transfer of real
estate will be," while his 28 April 2006 article, "Celebrate Tolerance, or
You're Dead," depicted "contemporary Islam" as prone to bestiality
and pedophilia.[82] These articles danced on the edge of what a national
magazine should have been publishing. However, they were positioned
by *Maclean*'s as part of a widely debated theory about the implications
of immigration and demographic data on Muslims in Western society.
In that respect, Steyn's musings about Muslim depravity were no better
or worse than those of other American and Western European writers
fixated on a radical Islamist "Eurabia."[83]

It turns out that predictions about "Eurabia," "Londonistan," and the
like are based on studies and data that have turned out to be inaccurate
or wildly exaggerated. For example, one widely cited 2004 study by the
National Intelligence Council in the United States proposed demographic scenarios that included a major population increase of Muslims
in Europe by 2025.[84] The study was reportedly based on "consultations" and meetings with "futurists," staff in NGOs, and "academic and
other sources."[85] It failed to mention that, even assuming the highest
possible reproductive rates, the Muslim population would only reach 8
percent. This hardly constitutes a demographic takeover. As *Newsweek*
writer William Underhill observed, the figures were "speculation based
on speculation."[86] Underhill cited Grace Davie of the University of
Exeter, Jytte Klaussen at Boston's Brandeis University, and Carl Haub,
a senior Washington-based demographer, who described the predictions as, respectively, "scaremongering," "a quite deliberate exaggera-
tion," and "absolutely absurd." Books like Eric Kaufmann's *Shall the
Religious Inherit the Earth?* and Doug Saunders' *The Myth of the
Muslim Tide* have demolished arguments about the imminent destruc-
tion of our Western society but have received only moderate attention
in Canada and nothing like the media attention showered on the opposing viewpoint.[87]

The point is not, however, the accuracy or inaccuracy of statistics. The
uncontradicted evidence before the tribunal in the BC *Maclean's* hate
speech case was that Steyn's article contained historical, religious, and
factual inaccuracies.[88] Writers should have the right to be wrong, just as
Steyn and others have the right to be wrong about their demographic
predictions. However, they cannot – or should not – be able to publish

material in order to drum up public support for exposing entire groups of people to speech that casts the victims as inherently inferior or dangerous based on their race, religion, or other personal characteristics that are protected by human rights laws. Such material helps foster hostility and paves the way for discrimination. There is a long, sad history of these tactics and their noxious effects.

The fact that prohibitions on inciting hatred are based on the effects of the speech and not on the speech itself is consistent with Canada's international human rights obligations under the International Covenant on Civil and Political Rights (ICCPR).[89] Article 20 of the ICCPR states that "[a]ny advocacy of national, racial or religious hatred that constitutes incitement to discrimination, hostility or violence shall be prohibited by law." The Covenant only prohibits speech that "constitutes incitement to discrimination, hostility or violence." It is the incitement that is cited in international human rights law, not the speech itself.

Lopsided Justice?

Canada's human rights system accepts complaints and investigates them free of charge. However, this has led to allegations that commissions side with complainants and that respondents are legally and financially disadvantaged. Respondents do not see why human rights systems support complainants. After all, in the criminal regime, it is the accused who is provided with lawyers by the state.

As has been mentioned in several earlier parts of this book, human rights systems are not criminal systems and a finding by a human rights tribunal that someone has committed a discriminatory practice does not result in incarceration. As well, commissions do not represent claimants during the intake, investigation, and mediation processes. Commissions remain neutral while they receive, screen, mediate, and investigate complaints. (Obviously, this observation only applies to first-generation systems. Complaints are not investigated in second-generation systems). Once a complaint is sent for a hearing, though, commissions are no longer neutral. Offering legal assistance to claimants once the matter gets to a tribunal raises different issues because at that stage many commissions represent the complainant or the public interest, which often coincides with a complainant's interests. At this point, the rationale is that supporting complainants who are the victims of human rights violations is consistent with Canada's obligations under international law to respect, protect, and fulfil human rights.

Human rights treaties require states to provide effective legal remedies for victims.[90] People whose jobs, homes, and access to basic services are at stake need guidance and protection from reprisals. According to Shelagh Day, Canada supports victims of discrimination "simply because we, as a society, have made a collective ... and social decision that discrimination is unacceptable."[91] Keith Norton put it another way: "I would argue that it is a fundamental role of the state to protect the most vulnerable. The problem with the way in which human rights commissions are being seen now, at least in some circles, is that the critiques are coming from people who have never met a vulnerable person in their lives."[92]

Both complainants and respondents benefit when the public system pays to provide complainants with legal information. Providing good legal counsel early on helps prevent weak cases from flooding tribunals. Whereas the vast majority of claims in the criminal justice system are brought by the state (through the police), the vast majority of human rights complaints are initiated by individuals and organizations. According to Kathy Laird, an internal study over a ten-month period at the Human Rights Legal Support Centre in Ontario showed that about 85 percent of applicants who won their cases at the Ontario Human Rights Tribunal had received legal services or representation from the centre; only 10 percent of unsuccessful claimants had been represented by the centre.[93] These figures say a great deal about the importance of identifying genuine discrimination cases early on, screening out non-meritorious cases, and moving meritorious cases forward.[94]

Respondents experience considerable stress and anxiety when they receive complaints, and they also require support. As counsel to respondents, Gordon McKinnon is sympathetic to people who receive complaints. "Will the commission be competent and reasonable? People do not know." In most cases, he said: "A lot of my job is to be a support for these people, and they need a lot of personal support. They receive these letters and they are very upset, even if it really is just a formality before the case is dismissed. It is very difficult to make people understand that there is a process to go through, even if the complaint is likely to be dismissed. People take this sort of thing very personally."[95] Under the bluster of critics' attacks on commissions is the insecurity and fear that respondents experience when confronted with legal procedures that are not well understood, as well as the feeling that the process is one-sided. Respondents such as small businesses and non-profit organizations may see themselves as at a disadvantage since they do not receive free legal counsel whereas some complainants do.

According to the 2012 Pinto Report, the "vast majority" of complainants in the pre-2008 system had no legal representation of their own at the stage of mediation and investigation, the period when the commission remained strictly neutral between parties.[96] After the Bill 107 reforms, the statistics show that 82 percent of respondents retain a lawyer when they appear before the tribunal, whereas 27 percent of complainants have their own lawyers. The Human Rights Legal Support Centre represents 11 percent of claimants before the Ontario Tribunal.[97] The rest do not have lawyers at all. In that 11 percent of cases in Ontario in which complainants are represented by state-paid counsel, there is strong evidence that there has been discrimination and therefore, the public interest in eradicating discrimination is present and compelling.

However, it is true that human rights systems should offer information to both respondents and complainants during the earlier stages. In first-generation systems in Canada, commissions provide information and guidance to respondents through web sites and a public call centre. This type of support is no longer available in direct access jurisdictions like British Columbia and it is quite limited in Ontario. Respondents, especially small business owners and non-profits, do not always have the wherewithal to hire counsel, and some form of support and guidance should be provided for respondents. These services can be offered through a special information line and/or Internet services operated by commissions, as recommended in Ontario in the Pinto Report.[98] Alternatively, a government-sponsored specialized advisory service can be set up for respondents in jurisdictions that no longer have commissions, as in British Columbia and Nunavut. If we believe that respondents are part of the solution, then an investment in helping them understand their obligations under human rights law and ensuring that they are reasonably equipped to deal with complaints is not an unreasonable investment. These recommendations are taken up again in chapter 6.

Secrecy

Commission investigations in first generation systems are confidential. They are not hearings, and they are not public processes. Investigation processes can seem impenetrable, even for those who are familiar with human rights commissions. A first set of concerns arises because complainants are encouraged to frame their allegations simply, in a way that clearly identifies the human rights grounds on which their claims are based. Well-written and powerfully articulated complaints can make broad allegations without having to disclose evidence up front. Complaints formulated in this way can be devastating to respondents, who see only the broad accusations but little substance to support the allegations. As well, respondents are rarely informed of the identity of corroborating witnesses at the investigation stage.

David Matas is an international human rights lawyer who has served as counsel for B'nai Brith for many years. In 2003, a conference dealing with suspected risks of Islamist terrorism was held for police and other security personnel in Winnipeg. Information relayed and distributed at the conference allegedly encouraged or advocated profiling of Muslims in policing and other security services. A complaint was filed in 2004 citing B'nai Brith as a sponsor of the conference and alleging that the documents distributed at the event violated section 18 of the Manitoba Human Rights Code, which deals with discriminatory signs and statements.

Matas explained the difficulties encountered when the complaint was filed with the Manitoba Human Rights Commission: "B'nai Brith received a hate speech complaint, and we were faced with a situation where the complainant was actually not the person who was at the meeting where the alleged statements were made. In fact, as far as we know, B'nai Brith was not there either. We got an escalating series of demands from the commission, and the commission threatened to raid our offices." He shook his head and added: "it was one of those cases where there was nothing there. The whole thing seemed heavy-handed. It consumed a lot of staff time and was a huge fishing expedition."[99]

The Manitoba Commission's executive director, Dianna Scarth, countered that the Manitoba legislation expressly permits third-party complaints, but she emphasized that the complainant and the details of the allegations must be identified. According to Scarth, the commission's powers are set out in the Manitoba Code and they include the ability to search and seize evidence at the premises of either party if a party fails to comply with a request. (All first-generation systems in Canada have similar powers.) When a party inquires about the nature of the commission's powers, as occurred in this case, the written response from the commission explaining those powers could have resulted in the perceived threat of a "raid."[100] Such divergent accounts of the same investigation are not uncommon and reveal just how complex and adversarial the investigation process can be. The complaint did not succeed, but for non-profit organizations with limited budgets and personnel, human rights complaints like the one described by B'nai Brith can be overwhelming.

The lack of disclosure to the other party at the investigation stage contributes to the perception that there is a shroud of secrecy around the process. Commissions commonly shield witnesses in order to prevent reprisals, an important consideration given the long duration of some investigations. Preventing reprisals is especially important in the context of ongoing relationships, for example where witnesses or even the complainant may still work for the respondent employer. Reprisals can take many forms, from firing a witness, to evicting a tenant who is supporting a claimant in a housing case, to harassment and further discrimination.

In first-generation systems, this situation is compounded by the fact that the tools available to eliminate complaints early in the process (e.g., if the claim is vexatious, trivial, or in bad faith) are sometimes of limited use. As discussed earlier, commissions are frequently reluctant to dismiss cases on a preliminary basis and even if proceedings are taken to address reprisals, they often take far too long.

Direct access systems have eliminated most of these concerns. Parties get to sidestep the entire investigation process (along with its confidentiality issues) and go straight to a hearing. Direct access minimizes the length of time that the identity of witnesses is kept confidential, which has the additional benefit of minimizing opportunities for reprisal. Moreover, parties before a tribunal can bring interim motions to protect their rights before the tribunal.

DELAYS

Delays have always been the bane of first-generation human rights systems. Commissions all over the country have experienced a familiar pattern of efforts to "fix" their backlogs. Commissions' annual reports dutifully document high caseloads and propose possible causes and solutions, typically followed by a regime of dedicated efforts to attack the caseload through more investigation and screening resources, which usually results in a short-lived victory. The whole cycle then repeats itself in a few years.

Ontario's pre-reform system was a case in point. In 1994–95, the Ontario Human Rights Commission's caseload was about 2,400 cases. Aggressive triage or advance screening diverted cases out of the human rights system, notably into the labour relations process. This significantly lightened the commission's caseload but not its backlog of cases. Between 1996 and 1998, the commission, with special funds from the government, introduced an expensive new IT system. It also enhanced its use of early mediation and these efforts produced high settlement rates. Teams of investigators were appointed to attack the backlogs. In 1999, the commission's caseload was 2,386. In 2001, it was down to 1,781 complaints. By 2005, the backlog was up to 2,733.[101]

It has been argued in the criminal context that significant delays can amount to a loss of personal liberty and security of the person under the Charter but attempts to make parallels between criminal proceedings and human rights proceedings have not been successful. In the *Blencoe* decision, the Supreme Court of Canada ruled that a two-year delay in the human rights system did not violate constitutional rights.[102] To date there has been no definitive determination about what type of delay would be considered so long as to be unconstitutional, and there have been some very lengthy cases.

In 2011, a settlement was finally reached in what was probably one of the longest-running human rights cases in Ontario's history. *McKinnon v. Ontario Ministry of Correctional Services* was settled in August 2011 after twenty-three years. The original complaint had been filed in 1988, alleging workplace discrimination based on Aboriginal ancestry. The first board of inquiry decision in 1998 found the workplace to be "poisoned by discriminatory conduct." A decade later, the ministry still had not adequately addressed the discrimination issues. In 2011, the ministry finally agreed to measures that would ensure compliance with human rights law, including the development of systemic initiatives in partnership with the Ontario Human Rights Commission.[103] As previously discussed, delays for fully investigated cases in Ontario's first-generation system were in the range of almost five years between filing and the tribunal decision. The *McKinnon* case obviously took much longer, but this was in part because of forward-looking systemic orders that required oversight by the board of inquiry.

The Supreme Court of Canada has held that delays alone do not warrant judicial intervention. As a practical matter, this means that a significant delay is not in and of itself sufficiently unfair to justify a request by a respondent to stay human rights proceedings as an abuse of process. Rather, the right to a fair hearing must be affected. For example, where delays cause harm to parties because of the death or incapacity of witnesses, the loss of physical evidence, or other factors that affect the right to a fair hearing, the courts may intervene.[104] Even if the right to a fair hearing is unaffected, courts may still intervene but the proceedings must be "unfair to the point that they are contrary to the interests of justice." Cases that meet this standard depend on evidence that delays are inordinate and unreasonable. However, delay in and of itself will not be determinative: according to the Supreme Court of Canada the commission or tribunal would have to be responsible for long, unexplained, and unjustified delays that result in unfairness that is both unacceptable and oppressive.[105]

Delays that do not meet this standard can still wreak havoc and impose considerable stress on both the parties involved and the public purse. Direct access systems perform considerably better in this regard than first-generation systems. According to Heather MacNaughton and Michael Gottheil, former chairs of the BC and Ontario Tribunals respectively, the elimination of gatekeeping has improved matters considerably. According to MacNaughton, the second generation BC system boasted an average timeframe, from filing the complaint to the case being finalized and closed, of six months to a year. This is a definite improvement over the three-year delay in the previous system just to get to the tribunal, not including the time at the tribunal itself.[106] Similar successes have been achieved in Ontario, where about a year is the norm, as compared to almost five years for fully investigated cases under the first-generation system.[107] These improvements have had a material impact on access to justice and the reduction of delays.

INDEPENDENCE, IMPARTIALITY, AND COMPETENCE

Even if the myths about Canada's human rights system are not well founded, it does not follow that all is well. The central importance of the principles of the rule of law and equality before the law was discussed in chapter 1. Lack of consistency in human rights grounds, access to justice, and remedies all point to deficiencies in the human rights system and its respect for both of those principles. This section deals with different aspects of the rule of law and equality before the law from the perspective of independence, impartiality, and competence.[108]

Human rights systems, like all administrative law systems, are part of the executive branch. This creates a tension between the rule of law, on the one hand, and the fact that executive control or influence can reduce independence, compromise impartiality, and diminish the competence of appointees, on the other, leading to bias, conflict of interest, or the appearance of both. In 1985, the Supreme Court of Canada identified conditions for the independence for tribunals: security of tenure, financial security, and the degree of administrative control over a tribunal. All of these conditions bear directly on the "exercise of [a tribunal's] judicial function."[109] They also affect the coherence and consistency of decision-making, which are connected to the rule of law and equality before the law.

International human rights law imposes additional standards, namely that everyone is equal before courts *and* tribunals in the determination of rights and obligations in "a suit of law," and that everyone has the right to a "competent, independent and impartial" tribunal.[110] Canadian administrative law does not set as high a bar for administrative tribunals. No comparable guarantee of procedural justice and judicial independence for tribunals has been established by the courts or in the Charter. The result is that tribunals in Canada enjoy a lower degree of independence than courts.[111]

Statutory criteria for merit-based appointments and for fair and unbiased removals are also indicators of a tribunal's independence. Both commissions and tribunals require financial independence, and operational independence in substantive human rights decision-making is essential.

By all these standards, Canada's human rights system as it is currently structured is deficient. Ad hoc appointments, excessive proximity to governments or between tribunals and commissions, and flimsy or non-existent qualifications compromise the credibility of at least half of the tribunals and commissions in Canada.[112] Only two jurisdictions, Quebec and Canada, have procedural protections for parties who appear before administrative decision-makers such as human rights tribunals.[113] In comparison with the international standards, the best that can be said of Canada's administrative law standard is that it confers a "sort-of-quasi-right to institutional independence."[114]

The key Canadian Supreme Court decision on the applicable standard in the human rights context is the decision in *Bell Canada*.[115] In it, the Court pointed out that tribunals have a certain range of functions, the parameters and legitimacy of which depend on the tribunal's home statute, which in that case was the Canadian Human Rights Act. The Court did indicate that there is a common law principle of a high degree of independence for tribunals, such as the federal tribunal, that fall more closely on the judicial end of the spectrum.[116] Earlier decisions from the Supreme Court of Canada, notably *Ocean Port*, sent a different signal, namely that administrative tribunals do not enjoy judicial independence.[117] Legal writers have suggested that this means that independence can be moderated or even eliminated by statutory language should the government so choose.[118] However, the Supreme Court of Canada has also said that independence reflects or embodies a constitutional principle of judicial independence, which is assessed by considering the status or relationship of the tribunal to other entities, especially the executive branch of government.[119] I believe that administrative law lawyer Ron Ellis is absolutely right when he argues in his book *Unjust by Design* that judicial independence should apply to administrative tribunals.[120] This more stringent standard is especially compelling in the area of human rights adjudication, given the constitutional nature of the rights being adjudicated.

Breadth of Mandate (Human Rights Commissions)

Human rights commissions are not tribunals, but they still require independence in order to do their work. This includes institutional freedom to take up any human rights issue. At the international level, the Paris Principles establish independence as a fundamental requirement for national human rights institutions (NHRIS): "A national institution shall be given as broad a mandate as possible, which shall be clearly set forth in a constitutional or legislative text, specifying its composition and its sphere of competence."[121]

Governments have a responsibility to ensure that commissions can address the full range of human rights. NHRIS must be independent when it comes to the freedom to speak out, provide advice to government, and issue opinions, recommendations, proposals, and reports. They can only do so if they are able to freely consider any question falling within their competence and to hear any person or obtain any information necessary for assessing situations within their competence. They are further entitled to address public opinion directly or through the press in order to publicize their opinions and recommendations.

One of the most obvious ways to restrict the independence of commissions is to limit their legal powers. Governments can simply enact legislation that restricts what human rights commissions can do, or amend laws to roll back rights. This is what happened at the federal level when the government passed legislation in 2013 removing the Canadian Human Rights Commission's ability to handle discrimination complaints based on hate speech, despite the fact that two successive Supreme Courts had declared such powers to be legitimate in Canadian law and consistent with Canada's international human rights obligations.

In Canada, commissions are generally restricted to discrimination issues, but this applies to the protection side of their work, namely handling complaints. Canadian commissions can only receive human rights complaints that are related to discrimination claims and can still meet the standard of the Paris Principles if they have the ability to address the full range of human rights on the promotional side of their work (for example, speaking out on a wide range of human rights issues). However, only about half of the commissions in Canada are allowed by their statutes to speak out about or report on human rights beyond discrimination issues. Even those that can do so – the federal, Quebec, Ontario, Nova Scotia, and Saskatchewan Commissions, for example – are limited in one way or another (see Appendix 3 for the mandate and functions in each jurisdiction).

Reporting Requirements

All but three Canadian commissions report to ministers and provide their annual reports to ministers instead of being accountable to legislatures and thus to elected officials and the broader public. In Alberta, New Brunswick, Nova Scotia, and Yukon, legislative provisions allow the executive (acting through the mechanism of a governor in council or equivalent official at the provincial and territorial levels) to appoint staff, approve internal by-laws, make regulations regarding internal governance, or all three. Manitoba also has a reporting relationship to a minister, but at least its law states that the commission is independent. Reporting to legislatures enhances transparency and direct public accountability, an issue that was discussed in chapter 1. This does not mean that ministries or departments have no responsibility for human rights legislation. At the federal level, for instance, the commission reports to Parliament, but the minister of Justice still has statutory responsibility for the Canadian Human Rights Act although this does not translate into operational influence.

Reporting to a minister can be limited to annual reporting or it can be more extensive. In Alberta, former Chief Commissioner Charlach Mackintosh said, "one of my main jobs was keeping the minister informed. I met with the deputy and the minister every week at 7 AM. I gave them briefings – there were to be no surprises. We had a memorandum of understanding with the ministry."[122] It is noteworthy that this was not a reciprocal exercise.

The dance of keeping "the minister informed" while trying to maintain independence has always been delicate, especially in Alberta, where even commission staff and bylaws are under the control of the minister.[123] Mackintosh, who is now retired, was a respected, capable, and strategically astute public servant who managed to keep the peace with his political bosses. Still, bonne-ententisme is no substitute for an independent reporting relationship that is circumscribed by legal criteria, in Alberta or elsewhere.

As for tribunals, the Canadian, Ontario, Quebec, BC, and Nunavut Tribunals have a high degree of independence set out in their laws. (Following the 2011 reforms in Saskatchewan, the Court of Queen's Bench receives all cases from the Saskatchewan Human Rights Commission.) Elsewhere in Canada, however, tribunals lack comparable independence. Although there have been efforts to address basic issues such as keeping tribunals and commissions institutionally separate, the legal reality is still problematic. In Alberta and Prince Edward Island, the tribunal members are actually drawn from among the commissioners. In Nova Scotia, the commission appoints tribunal members. In Manitoba and New Brunswick, the appointment of tribunal members is not informed by statutory criteria in their respective human rights laws, but at least in Manitoba they cannot be commissioners.

A shift to more public accountability in legislation would diminish the direct influence that the executive authority can exercise over the human rights system. One of the most important of these sources of influence is appointments, renewals, and removals.

Appointments, Renewals, and Removals

Uneven or non-existent statutory requirements for professional qualifications and experience diminish the credibility of appointments of commission and tribunal members, and cast doubt on the appearance of independence, impartiality, and competence. The credibility of both the appointee and the system itself suffer when appointees are or appear to be beholden to those who appointed them. This contributes to the reality or appearance of patronage or to the selection of people who are ideologically acceptable to the government of the day.[124]

Independence demands that there be appropriate criteria that include aptitude, experience, and qualifications. Only about half of Canadian human rights laws provide for such criteria for both commissioners and tribunal members.

Expertise in both human rights law and in adjudication are important for tribunal members for obvious reasons. A positive example is Ontario, where section 32(3) of the Human Rights Code requires that candidates for the tribunal have two qualifications over and above "experience, knowledge or training," namely aptitude for impartial adjudication and aptitude for applying alternative adjudicative practices and procedures that may be set out in the tribunal rules.

Human rights statutes in Alberta, Manitoba, Nova Scotia, Prince Edward Island, and Yukon do not have any requirements or qualifications for tribunal members in their respective human rights statutes. The New Brunswick system does not have a human rights tribunal but uses the provincial Labour and Employment Board. British Columbia's Human Rights Code requires a "merit-based" process but provides no details as to what this means. Again, these are areas of disparity among human rights statutes that point to the need for a uniform approach and more rigour. Those statutes that do set out criteria for appointments of commissioners or tribunal members specify little beyond "merit," which is undefined and vague.

The next issue is who does the appointing. Commissioners and tribunal members in Canada are generally appointed by the lieutenant governor or governor in council. This places some degree of distance between the executive branch and the tribunal, but it is formalistic: for all intents and purposes the decision belongs to the executive and usually to a minister. However, there are jurisdictions where even that formalistic protection of independence disappears, when tribunal members are named by the commission itself (in Alberta, Nova Scotia, and Prince Edward Island).[125] This issue is discussed in more detail later in this chapter.

Independence is further compromised when senior staff–level appointments are made by the government, rather than through the public service, which at least includes some guarantee of merit-based and competitive hiring. Nova Scotia's commission director, the operational head of the agency, is an order in council appointment and no criteria or qualifications for the position are set out in the Nova Scotia Human Rights Act. Quebec's process is better: the president of the commission is appointed by a two-thirds vote in the National Assembly. In Yukon, the chief adjudicator is named by the legislature and in the Northwest Territories the adjudication panel members are named by the commissioner of the territory on recommendation of the Legislative Assembly.

The third issue is transparency. Legal requirements for formalized input from the public or stakeholders are virtually nonexistent throughout Canada. In Quebec, the government sometimes seeks the input of the Quebec Bar Association and community organizations, but this is not a legal requirement and the practice varies from government to government.

The fourth issue is the connection between independence and the ability of the head of the institution to manage its members. No jurisdiction in Canada requires the prior approval of the incumbent chair or president for the appointment of commissioners, with the result that loyalties will often lie elsewhere rather than in the office of the head of the commission.

Fifth is the connection between appointments, independence, and patronage. No human rights law in Canada explicitly provides for at-pleasure appointments or uses that terminology. Several, however, fail to specify particular terms of office or grounds for dismissal, which amounts to the same thing, unless removals are specified as being for cause. Those that do have more specific requirements (the Saskatchewan Commission, the Canadian and Nunavut Human Rights Tribunals, as well as Newfoundland and Labrador, Northwest Territories, Ontario, and Quebec, for example) do not require an open and formal competitive process, except for Ontario Tribunal members.

A well-known report on federal administrative tribunals and agencies released in 1990 said that the résumés of appointees to the Canadian Human Rights Tribunal in 1986 had demonstrated that the appointees lacked qualifications and had limited awareness of the job they were about to undertake.[126] The CHRA now provides that tribunal members must have "experience, expertise and interest in, and sensitivity to, human rights," which is an improvement, but there is no transparent process for assessing the actual quality of candidates and for determining whether or not those qualifications are, in fact, being met or measured.

Even those statutes that do provide for a specific term may not actually offer much protection in reality.[127] The length of terms in Canada tends to be too short, in the range of three years, and this also affects independence. It usually takes two years for members to learn the mandate, the jurisprudence, and the administrative history and practice of the institution.[128] Ron Ellis's analysis of the importance of adequate terms of service (he focuses on the labour relations context where the terms tend to be longer) makes the point: "In the federal jurisdiction, there has been a long-standing cap of ten years, and experience has shown that the traditionally rigid enforcement of that cap ensures the annual mid-career exodus of the federal tribunals' most useful members."[129]

Keith Norton headed both a human rights tribunal and a human rights commission. He was critical of what he viewed as a tendency towards partisan appointments at the level of part-time commissioners and he doubted whether most Canadian jurisdictions can claim credible and transparent appointment processes.[130] Conversely, good processes and good people can make an enormous difference. Manitoba's Byron Williams said, "I would say that our relationship has changed materially for the better for a couple of reasons: the Manitoba Human Rights Commission has changed its processes and has added some gifted people; the commission has made some tremendous hires in recent years, including people who have clerked at the Supreme Court of Canada ... There have been excellent appointments to the Board of Commissioners, people who are committed to human rights and who are committed to progress."[131]

One consequence of poor or politicised appointments is that short terms of office become the only mechanism available to limit the damage and remove members who are not competent. The argument for longer terms of office can only be addressed when the criteria for appointments are improved through greater rigour and transparency in the application process, the publication of functions and job requirements, and recognition of the need for clear core competencies.[132] All of this would enhance the integrity of and public confidence in human rights institutions and improve the consistency and quality of decision-making.

Then there is the question of renewals or reappointments. Most human rights laws permit renewals, but few jurisdictions offer adequate protection from arbitrary removals or connect renewals to a transparent process for assessing the performance of the incumbent. The 2010 decision not to renew Heather McNaughton as chair of the British Columbia Human Rights Tribunal occurred at the last moment, despite her strong adjudicative record and demonstrated administrative skill. Shelagh Day observed that while "it is not helpful to speculate about motivations, there is a poor history in this province [BC] ... and there have been efforts in the past to make human rights institutions more deferential. So when they don't give proper notice to a chair, they clearly are not considering and respecting the position or the lives of the people who are actually holding these jobs; this is disrespect for the institution and this is clearly a problem."[133] MacNaughton had been chair of the tribunal since 2000 and the decision not to renew her term was perhaps to be expected. Nevertheless, observers pointed out that the government left her dangling until just days before the end of her term, leaving her to wonder whether a decision on any given case might affect her reappointment.

Then there is the issue of removals, as occurred when the government decided to get rid of the human rights commission in BC and create a new, smaller council. This decision led to the summary dismissal of Mary Woo Sims through a very public process that was symptomatic of a lack of concern or respect for these appointments.[134]

Another idiosyncratic[135] removal took place when Judy Parrack, the BC Tribunal member who had decided the *Datt* v. *McDonald's Restaurants* case in 2009, was not renewed – effectively ending her decade-long career as a human rights adjudicator – with less than three weeks' notice. Ron Ellis has written about the case and observes that there was no official explanation for the removal. Parrack's involvement in another difficult case involving the recognition of foreign credentials, coupled with the controversy surrounding the *Datt* complaint, suggested to members of the adjudicator community that the unpopularity of her decisions, at least in some circles, was connected to her abrupt termination.[136]

Concerns about deficient or arbitrary appointments, renewals, and removals are not exclusive to Canada's human rights system: they are shared across the entire administrative justice system. As Ellis observes, "the arbitrary denial of reappointment of meritorious members of judicial tribunals and the exclusion of chairs from the appointment and reappointment process ... are inherently incompatible with the concept of an independent and impartial administrative justice system."[137] All of these factors conspire to encourage patronage and discourage meaningful independence. In Quebec, there is some case law on the meaning of the legislative requirement for independence and impartiality in section 23 of the Charter of Human Rights and Freedoms. A Quebec Court of Appeal decision in 2001 said that independence and impartiality apply not only to the appointments process but also to the reappointment process, which implies security against interference by the executive in a discretionary or arbitrary manner.[138] But there are few comparable cases anywhere else.

Lack of independence, or at least its appearance, is aggravated when tribunals are appointed by or connected to human rights commissions. As noted earlier, the members of Nova Scotia's board of inquiry are appointed by the commission itself. Although there is a legal condition that board of inquiry members cannot be drawn from commission members, direct connections between commissions and tribunals raises concerns about conflict of interest and apprehension of bias for the obvious reason that the same organization that investigated a complaint should have no connection to the decision on that complaint. Prince Edward Island has a similar arrangement.

Alberta's situation is more extreme. Although the commission and the tribunal are distinct in law, the tribunal draws its members from the commissioners.[139] Commissioners are named as adjudicators (tribunal members) once the chief commissioner renders a decision to refer a case for a hearing. Under the Alberta Human Rights Act the chief commissioner is head of both the commission and the tribunal. Some may argue that there is no real bias in such arrangements, which have the advantage of being practical and inexpensive. The Alberta Court of Appeal has held that the Alberta statute and its operationalization do not raise an apprehension of bias and that internal safeguards and operational firewalls protect independent decision-making.[140]

There may be practical and economic reasons for such arrangements, but the increasing pressure to ensure judicial independence militates against a commission appointing a tribunal. Tribunals should have structures and appointment processes that are as independent as possible within the strictures of executive authority.

There is another factor at work in Canada that affects independence, and that is the political climate in which independent agencies and watchdogs work. The current environment is unsupportive at best and hostile at worst, at least at the federal level. Parliamentary officers have alleged that the federal government withholds key information, ranging from budget information, to responses to access to information requests.[141] Others have expressed concern about lack of proper scrutiny and oversight in relation to appointments, a recurring theme. The heads of these organizations say that their recommendations to government are simply ignored.[142]

There are, however, worse things than being ignored – the federal government has interfered with supposedly independent public service organizations on a number of occasions.[143] Several heads of institutions have been removed from their positions or been subject to political interference, defunding, or public censure just for doing their jobs. Linda Keen, former head of the Canadian Nuclear Safety Commission, was fired in 2008 for shutting down a nuclear reactor for safety reasons; Paul Kennedy was removed as head of the Commission for Public Complaints against the RCMP in 2009 after advocating for a more independent commission; Marty Cheliak, chief superintendent of the Canadian Firearms program, was removed from his functions in 2010, one year into his mandate, for supporting the long gun registry; Munir Sheikh, a respected and long-serving economist, resigned from his position as the head of StatsCan in 2010 following the misrepresentation of his position about the abolition of the mandatory Long-Form Census; and Pat Stogran, the first Veterans Ombudsperson, was fired in 2010 for being a strong advocate for veterans and criticizing government treatment of veterans. Similar stories of interference and unwarranted attacks on independent agents of Parliament, regulators, and watchdogs have been reported for Elections Canada, the Parliamentary Budget Officer, the Information Commissioner of Canada, the Wheat Board of Canada, and others whose messages became controversial or inconvenient.[144] Rémy Beauregard, former head of Rights and Democracy, had to resort to an access to information request to discover attacks on his reputation contained in a secret performance appraisal orchestrated by a group of government appointees shortly after his real (and positive) performance appraisal had been completed by the board. The allegations against him turned out to be unfounded, but too late: after his death in 2010, the government quietly awarded Beauregard posthumous merit-based increases in pay.

It is the brave and exceptional head of an agency or tribunal who will speak out against a government in circumstances in which patronage or the risk of arbitrary removal may be the least of one's worries.

Financial Independence

All of the public sector is subject to financial constraints and each part of government must submit budgets and secure adequate financing. Beyond that, using financial levers to control the substantive human rights work of a commission, directly or indirectly, is unacceptable. Heads of human rights institutions should have the ability to independently develop and then defend their own budgets, and then to decide the allocation of funding within the budget envelope.

By international standards, Canadian commissions and tribunals do well financially. The Paris Principles require that governments provide commissions with adequate funds, but there is little detail beyond that. Many Canadian institutions have faced steady pressure from economic constraints over the years, along with growing mandates, increased levels of responsibility, and rapidly changing legal environments.[145]

Sometimes these pressures operate in ways that, while undramatic, are still telling. Max Yalden, former chief commissioner of the Canadian Human Rights Commission, describes an incident that took place in 1990 after the commission had issued a series of critical comments about the federal government's treatment of Aboriginal peoples. Prime Minister Mulroney made his displeasure known by denying Yalden the normal pay raise for officials at his level: "Yet another argument, it seems to me," he said, "for ensuring the absolute independence of commissioners of this sort from the government of the day, including the matter of setting salaries."[146] Salaries should be set by an independent agency or established in a manner that removes any taint of interference.

Operational Independence

For commissions that report to ministers and have a degree of operational integration with their host ministries, there is ample room to exercise influence through the normal chain of command. Informal channels are available to exert pressure on members and senior staff. Careers, pensions, and reputations depend on loyalty to the public service and not to the institutions or the chief commissioner or president. This affects effective management and collegiality within the organizations.[147]

Rémy Beauregard, executive director of the Ontario Commission between 1994 and 2001, reported directly to the deputy minister of the Ministry of Citizenship, Culture and Recreation. Beauregard recalled instances in which senior ministry officials tried to direct the commission towards "different approaches" to complaints management.[148] "This was not direct interference," Beauregard was careful to say, "The ministry was scrupulous about not interfering with particular cases or even policy directions." There were clear lines that could not be crossed: Beauregard recalled an incident in the late 1990s when a member of the legislature had asked a political assistant to "find out" about a case under investigation following a human rights complaint against a constituent. This was not an intentional attempt to influence a decision-maker, in his view, but rather an example of an inexperienced aide who blundered into the bailiwick of an independent decision-maker. Whatever the motivation, Beauregard recalled that this incident was taken seriously and did not help the political aide's career.[149] He acknowledged, however, that the ministry was "worried" about the case backlog. This was a legitimate concern, in his view, raising questions about "administrative efficiency" and concern about the ministry's "loss of control."[150] The ministry in Ontario had considerable indirect influence on the selection of strategic priorities, which then served as performance measures, using the tool of ministerial business planning to reinforce the government's own priorities.[151] It is a reasonably good bet that the priorities established through business planning processes negotiated with the responsible ministry (in jurisdictions that report to a ministry, of course) will be the same priorities that a commission will end up focusing on. This can occur at the expense of other issues that the commission may have identified as important. For example, at the Ontario Commission in the late 1990s, ministry business plans targeted improvements in processing times for complaints as the main performance measure. Little attention was paid at the level of the ministry to setting targets and rewarding performance in relation to other aspects of the mandate, some of which tended to result in criticism of government actions, including its litigation and policies.

Daily operational demands, especially in jurisdictions where the chief commissioner reports to a minister and where the executive director has a reporting relationship to the deputy minister instead of solely to the chief commissioner, can raise significant concerns about the commission's ability to control its own work. What may seem like minor issues, such as commission staff having to produce briefing notes for ministers on demand, can raise important questions about the appropriateness of such requests and the relationship between a human rights commission and the ministry. Requests for information, especially on substantive human rights issues, may imply a subordinate or direct report relationship that is inconsistent with institutional independence. Certainly, this was an ongoing issue during my time at the Ontario Human Rights Commission, when commission staff were regularly asked to prepare or coordinate briefing notes, information notes, and updates on a wide range of issues for the ministry.

An egregious example of direct control and interference in substantive human rights decision-making occurred when politicians instructed Alberta's commission not to intervene in the *Vriend* case. The case eventually went before the Supreme Court on the ground of equality for gays and lesbians in Canada.[152] Charlach Mackintosh recalled that he had received specific instructions not to take up the *Vriend* case or intervene before the courts,[153] which is why the Canadian Association of Statutory Human Rights Agencies ended up intervening before the Supreme Court of Canada and not the Alberta Commission.

The example of Kathleen Ruff in British Columbia, where politicians tried to shut down a complaint by women seeking the ability to go curling in the evenings because the time spot that previously have been reserved for men, was also a blatant case of interference.

Shelagh Day recalled her time at the fledgling Saskatchewan Human Rights Commission in 1980 and an episode that led directly to her firing. In 1983, the commission was getting reports that "the police had been using dogs to go after Aboriginal kids, who were coming in with dog bites."[154] Ken Norman said that the commission had begun investigating the matter. In June 1983, in a public letter, the commission had urged the City of Regina to stop using dogs on suspects, the vast majority of whom were Aboriginal.[155] Day recalled that one of the investigators working at the commission was a young man who had previously been on the staff of the Regina Civil Liberties Association and had been prominent in bringing the use of dogs by the Regina Police to light. Norman's time as chief commissioner ended in October 1983 as his term was not renewed. Meanwhile, Day learned that the new chief commissioner, appointed by the Grant Devine government, intended to get rid of the young investigator and she believes the instructions to do so came directly from government. "I made sure that all contractual and union issues were being properly addressed and that protected our investigator and saved his job. I was fired for that because I stood in the way," Day said.[156] She was fired in July 1984.

Other channels of influence can operate to apply pressure, directly or indirectly, for instance, in the case of a troublesome report or initiative of a commission. This happened in 2001 when the Ontario Human Rights Commission released a discussion paper on the accessibility of public transit. The paper revealed that only a third of Ontario municipalities at that time were committed to fully accessible and integrated transit systems or had even developed funded plans to achieve that objective. In the early days of the project the report became a source of friction between the commission and the Ministry of Culture and Citizenship in the early days of the project.[157] (The Ontario minister of Citizenship, Culture and Recreation of the day was Helen Johns.) The deputy minister's office was concerned about the discussion paper.[158] The paper contained the results of a survey of twenty-five municipalities and transit service providers on the accessibility of their transit systems. The results were not encouraging and were a potential source of embarassment to the government as they showed wide variations in the level of available transit for people with disabilities and a low level of commitment from many municipalities to even consider providing such services.

Public service protocol would normally require that the executive director of the commission meet with the deputy, who at the time would have been Rémy Beauregard. However, both Beauregard and the chief commissioner were absent, and so I was called in. The initial questions suggested that the document had been released without the knowledge of the commissioners. However, the public release of documents of this kind always required prior review and approval, which took place at a full meeting of the commissioners. It then became clear that there was a good deal of unhappiness because of the perception that the discussion document had not been circulated to the ministry before being released. It is noteworthy that this discussion document did not yet reflect a proposal with regard to policy. Nor were any of the facts presented in the paper contested, at least not in my presence. Nonetheless, a warning was issued that the minister was never to be "embarrassed." Johns was demoted in a cabinet shuffle on 8 February 2001 and was named associate minister of Health and Long-term Care.

The meeting and its message were the topic of discussions with Norton and Beauregard. Beauregard told me at the time that he was concerned about an unjustified intrusion into the commission's independence. At the same time, the deputy was "doing what she had to do." Norton shared concerns about the commission's independence. At the same time, he wanted to make sure that the human rights commission stayed effective and relevant, and to do this he needed the government's support, or at least its ear. As a former minister, Norton was sensitive to the need to keep ministers aware of issues in their bailiwick. The incident also raised questions about the interaction between independence and the judgement call as to how much, if any, advance notice a commission is obliged to give when it speaks out on any issue.

CONCLUSION

Several arguments have been brought to bear against human rights systems in terms of the way they function and the implications for fairness. Most of the criticisms are based on myths and misunderstandings about the way that human rights systems work and have had the effect of distracting us from the pressing and serious issues facing commissions.

Canada's human rights system suffers from legal and procedural deficiencies in terms of independence, impartiality, and competence at the institutional level. All three standards are connected to the rule of law and equality before the law and are grounded in inadequate legislative guarantees of independence. An excessively close reporting relationship and operational integration with ministries or between commissions and tribunals is a genuine concern in Canada. The lack of an adequate breadth of mandate for commissions, as well as abundant opportunities for patronage, lack of procedural protections for tribunal chairs, and inadequate criteria for appointment and reappointment all fall far short of the international standard for human rights adjudication for tribunals and of the Paris Principles for human rights commissions. The answer to these concerns is to create structural guarantees of independence, impartiality, and competence for both commissions and tribunals that are appropriate for their regulatory and adjudicative functions, respectively.

The issues discussed in this chapter concern detailed points of criticism against the human rights system in Canada in terms of its administrative and procedural fairness. There is, however, another layer of criticism about the types of cases human rights system should be addressing and, more fundamentally, the extent to which equality rights claims can and should engage with other types of rights and freedoms. This is the topic of chapter 5.

5

Signal Cases, Rights Conflicts, and Building a Human Rights Culture

Justice without equality is no justice at all.
Madam Justice L'Heureux-Dubé[1]

The legal orientation of the Charter differs from human rights legislation in that the Charter is a constitutional document that applies to government action, whereas human rights legislation is quasi-constitutional law aimed at protecting victims from discrimination, regardless of who is responsible. The Supreme Court of Canada has affirmed that both human rights systems and the Charter are aimed at preventing the same general wrong.[2] The central principle of equality anchored in the Charter is the same general principle that underpins human rights legislation and the work of human rights commissions and tribunals. Humans rights protections exist not only for established, recognized groups, but also for those who are new to Canada or whose rights have been more recently recognized.

Human rights commissions and tribunals are creatures of statute and can only do what their statutes say that they can do. One of the first arguments one hears about the appropriate role of human rights systems is that they should be limited to handling "ordinary" discrimination cases and should not handle cases that involve other types of rights and freedoms. In earlier chapters, it was pointed out that most commissions already have a broader mandate to engage with human rights in general on the promotional side of their mandate. But when it comes to human rights complaints, there is a concern that commissions, by engaging with other types of social values, or even other rights, especially fundamental freedoms, are straying from their appointed paths and exceeding their legal remits. The difficulty is that human rights are interdependent and equality complaints almost inevitably engage with other rights and freedoms. At the same time, other rights and freedoms – including language rights, religious freedoms, free speech, freedom of political opinion, and a range of social and economic rights, such as the right to housing and education – are frequently built into human rights laws. What might at first glance appear to be a "routine" case of discrimination often involves other values, rights, and freedoms. The BC case of *SELI Canada,* discussed in earlier chapters, is a good example, pitting human rights against negotiated contracts.[3]

Human rights legislation's quasi-constitutional status reflects a fundamental social choice, one that elevates human rights over other legislative areas like contract law, property law and family law, except in cases where other statutes say that their provisions apply notwithstanding human rights legislation.[4] The rule of law, with its attendant principles of constitutionalism, equality before the law, and respect for minority rights, supports the view that quasi-constitutional legislation should also prevail over social values, cultural norms, and business practices that are incompatible with human rights. In its Policy on Competing Human Rights, the Ontario Human Rights Commission asserts that when human rights laws compete with other types of values and interests, including commercial interests, human rights should prevail as a matter of law.[5] The Ontario policy is not revolutionary: it does not say much that is new in theory but it does reflect and remind us of these legal principles and of what the law actually says about situations when rights collide with other rights and freedoms or with social values.

There are qualifications to this principle, notably where application of a human rights standard would impose undue hardship on the respondent or interfere with public safety and security. At the constitutional level, another qualification is that all rights are subject to reasonable limits that can be justified in a free and democratic society.

Rights conflicts are common in human rights complaints. Issues that may appear mundane or not especially serious can cause considerable controversy and dispute. Heather MacNaughton, the former chair of the BC Human Rights Tribunal, offered the following examples from her years at the BC Tribunal:

- A Jewish patient asked a doctor to see him ahead of other patients so that he could go home early on Friday afternoon for the Sabbath.

- A Muslim woman refused to see a male doctor for religious and modesty-related reasons.
- A female prisoner was prevented for security and safety reasons from engaging in religious observances that required her to light candles in her cell.
- An emergency nurse was prohibited by a health authority from wearing a hijab due to perceived safety risks.[6]

Each of these cases involves rights conflicts or social and cultural practices that come into collision with rights. Resolving them involved careful analysis of the rights and interests on both sides, rather than general rules.

It is rare that analysis of a discrimination claim solely on the basis of equality rights will suffice. What might seem to be a routine discrimination case can camouflage the presence of other rights, which may not be immediately obvious or discernible because they have been submerged by a standardized legal approach that has been adopted for certain types of cases. Such cases reflect an established but unspoken assumption that some rights and interests should recede in order to ensure equality rights. Examples include the rule that parties cannot use collective agreements to contract out of the members' human rights (a fact pattern that engages freedom of expression, contract law principles of consent, and labour law, as well as equality rights), and the prohibition against sexual harassment, which can constrain the respondent's freedom of expression or opinion (as in the Lisa McIntosh case, discussed below).

In other cases, the rights are present and explicit, and require the tribunal or court to sort out which one will prevail. In one case that came while I was at the Ontario Commission, a nursing assistant refused to provide services to a lesbian couple's child: the nurse's right to freedom of religion was pitted against the child's right to equal health services, as well as the parents' rights not to be discriminated against because of sexual orientation and family status. These rights are, or appear to be, in conflict and have to be reconciled. Heather MacNaughton said that in her experience such rights conflicts are among the most important and contentious cases facing the human rights system today.[7] They may not be novel, but the heightened sensitivities to religion, free speech, and reasonable accommodation in Canada mean that they draw more attention.

Richard Moon takes a nuanced approach to such cases in the context of freedom of expression, one of his areas of research focus and expertise. Parties to complaints often end up arguing about whether or not people have the right to say something. Moon believes that human rights commissions should not deal with rights conflicts at all, at least not where speech is engaged:

> When you are looking at whether to censor speech, we look at the risk of harmful consequences. But this is not enough. You also need to look at whether the individual being targeted [who is hearing the speech] is capable of making an independent decision or not. You look at context, the availability of alternative views, and [the] issue of power imbalances ... You also need to look at whether institutions are capable of dealing with these issues. I think that this is what is wrong with the Canadian Human Rights Commission's jurisdiction over hate speech: it is too broad in its sweep. It imposes such a high burden on complainants. There is something very different about human rights complaints and speech issues. Human rights are too broad, and speech is too narrow an issue to be dealt [with]. It is not the kind of thing human rights commissions are about.[8]

There is another way of looking at the interaction between rights and at what "human rights commissions are about." The Supreme Court of Canada's pivotal 2013 decision in the *Whatcott* case held that when the exercise of a right (in the *Whatcott* case, it was a free speech right) has discriminatory effects, the right may be legitimately restricted. The court also made it clear that human rights systems have a legitimate role to play in mediating conflicts between equality rights and the effects of free speech rights.[9] But these rights conflicts have engendered vociferous criticisms that equality rights – and human rights – systems are a danger to "individual" rights and to liberty.

WHEN RIGHTS AND FREEDOMS COLLIDE[10]

The idea that human rights commissions and tribunals are the enemies of civil rights and freedoms has a long and toxic pedigree. Terry O'Neill, writing for the defunct right-wing newsmagazine B C *Report*, said in 1999: "While many Canadians think of human rights and civil liberties as essentially the same thing, a growing number of observers say it is increasingly apparent that federal and provincial human rights initiatives are at war with individual rights and civil liberties."[11] Bundled in this statement is the assumption that equality rights are about "groups" whereas individual rights are about, well, individuals and that the latter are superior.

This section considers these arguments in the context of cases where equality rights appear to bump up against other types of rights and freedoms, notably freedom of religion and expression. First, it is worth confronting the idea that rights are either individual or collective and therefore more or less suspect, depending on one's ideological leanings. Although they are claimed by individuals, many fundamental freedoms make sense only in the context of groups. Freedom of assembly can only occur if you actually assemble with someone else. Freedom of association presupposes the rights of groups to come together and act together. Freedom of religion generally requires some form of collective faith and collective action. Aboriginal rights and language rights can, of course, be claimed by individuals but their existence, expression, and legitimacy depend on the history and legacy of communities, cultures, and nations. The fact that most rights and freedoms can be articulated in the context of individual rights as well as the interests and identities of groups does not diminish the rights in any of their forms, but it does change the way in which rights claims are understood and negotiated.

The three examples discussed in this section are based on high profile cases that have taken place in Canada in recent years. They engage with different categories of rights, including fundamental freedoms. The first two engage with free speech. In the third case of religious freedoms, the Christian Horizons case, the respondent's counterclaim was grounded in the assertion of its identity and its rights as a religious organization. The three cases show the progression from complaints that were analyzed completely within an equality rights framework (despite the presence of competing rights and values which were not mentioned or only weakly articulated) to an analytical framework that explicitly balances equality rights and other types of rights and freedoms.

Lisa McIntosh brought a sex discrimination claim against her boss, Zbigniew Augustynowicz, under BC's Human Rights Code.[12] McIntosh had been in a consensual sexual relationship with Augustynowicz. After they broke up, he repeatedly "sexted" her at work. His text messages contained lewd insinuations about needing "a nooner," as well as sexual invitations to McIntosh and her daughter. Although McIntosh had made it clear that his messages were completely unwelcome, he continued to send them. McIntosh testified that she went on stress leave because the situation "was making her physically and mentally ill." Although she was not fired or demoted, the harassment eventually forced her to leave her job.[13]

The BC Human Rights Tribunal found that Augustynowicz's conduct constituted sexual harassment, a form of sex discrimination. In addition to damages for lost wages and expenses, the tribunal ordered $12,500 in damages for injury to McIntosh's dignity, feelings, and self-respect. (Although British Columbia's human rights law does not provide for punitive damages, the aggressive and provocative nature of the "sext" messages appeared to be a factor in the damages award.)

Augustynowicz's only discriminatory "act" was expressive behaviour, namely texting. One could argue, as critics have in other cases, that McIntosh was merely offended and that this should not have given rise to a human rights complaint. While she may have been offended, the case was a textbook example of sexual harassment: the incidents took place squarely in the employment setting and, as an employee, it was difficult for Lisa McIntosh to walk away from the situation without losing her job. Reading the case as a standard discrimination and sexual harassment complaint, most readers would accept the tribunal's decision easily, without considering the other rights potentially at play. The harassment aspect is so well recognized that it masks the other rights and interests. The tribunal did not mention free speech at all, even though speech was clearly the major component of the harassment. The McIntosh case was a classic discrimination analysis in the relational context or area of employment.

The second example is Lorna Pardy's claim against stand-up comic Guy Earle. The case made the news after Pardy became a target of verbal abuse during a night out with friends at a restaurant.[14] Pardy, a lesbian, filed a human rights complaint against Earle for his vulgar and aggressive comments during his open-mic show in 2007. She also filed a complaint against the restaurant.

According to the evidence before the BC Human Rights Tribunal, the restaurant staff had asked Pardy and her partner to move from the patio to a table inside the restaurant. The commotion of settling into the new table and ordering drinks disturbed Earle's performance. Earle saw Pardy receive a kiss on the cheek from her partner, and he said to the audience: "Don't mind that inconsiderate dyke table over there. You know lesbians are always ruining it for everybody." An audience member booed in response. Looking at Pardy, Earle said: "Do you have a strap-on? You can take your girlfriend home and fuck her in the ass." Pardy was shocked and embarrassed. She booed Earle. He continued: "Are you on the rag[?] [I]s that why you're being such a fucking cunt?"

Pardy's friend told Earle he was being ignorant. Pardy threw two glasses of water at Earle, and he broke her sunglasses.

A complaint was filed on the grounds of discrimination because of sex and sexual orientation, contrary to section 8 of BC's Human Rights Code.[15] Since Earle had harassed Pardy and her partner in a restaurant where they had paid for a meal, the tribunal decided the case under the BC Human Rights Code's provision prohibiting discrimination in services. The tribunal found in favour of Pardy and ordered $22,500 in damages. It rejected the claim that "free speech" can be used to justify discrimination and harassment.

Like *McIntosh,* the main issue was whether speech-based conduct could underpin a human rights complaint. Unlike *McIntosh,* Earle specifically invoked free speech as a defence and as a freestanding Charter right. In response, the tribunal said: "'Discriminatory statements' may arise in the context of other areas in which discrimination is prohibited, including services (s. 8), tenancy (s. 10), and employment (s. 13) of the Code. There is nothing about the structure of the Code, or the cases decided under it, to support the view that complaints about expression can only be brought under s. 7 (the section dealing with hate speech). *Indeed, it is difficult to imagine a case in which discrimination would not necessarily involve at least some form of "expression" by words or conduct* (emphasis added)."[16]

Verbal harassment is a common component in the context of employment and services, such as those in *McIntosh* and *Pardy.* In *Pardy,* however, the speech aspect came through explicitly because the "service" involved the work of an entertainer. The tribunal ruled that Earle's discriminatory comments had had the effect of humiliating and injuring Pardy in order to "shut her up."[17] Sexual orientation was the instrument Earle used to attack Pardy. Because of the free-speech angle, the media was predictably unhappy with the case.[18] The tribunal decisions in *McIntosh* and *Pardy* were both in favour of the complainants. Both based their decisions on the discriminatory behaviour that was expressive or speech-based.

Human rights commissions work at precisely this intersection of equality rights and other types of rights, freedoms, and values. Jane Bailey, a law professor at the University of Ottawa, asked why it is that some rights advocates argue fundamental freedoms should automatically trump equality rights in any circumstance, whereas equality arguments need a powerful and compelling reason to limit fundamental freedoms: "[W]hy do we have to justify an incursion into certain freedoms but not into equality rights? This seems like a radical question, but it isn't. History has taught us that sometimes the state needs to intervene between groups ... [T]he most vulnerable groups are those who are worried about survival. And there are people who get threatened, beaten and killed for being who they are or for taking up unpopular causes."[19]

Implicit in Bailey's observation is the assumption that fundamental freedoms such as speech are always more important than equality rights. This is not true, for the reasons that Bailey notes. The reverse proposition is not true either. Both Canadian courts and international law repudiated the notion of a hierarchy of rights decades ago. Very few rights can be articulated or implemented, let alone enforced, in isolation from each other.

At the World Conference on Human Rights in 1993, the world's nations came together to reject hierarchies of rights through the Vienna Declaration and Programme of Action. "All human rights are universal, indivisible and interdependent and interrelated. The international community must treat human rights globally in a fair and equal manner, on the same footing, and with the same emphasis." [20]

Canadian courts have also rejected the idea that human rights exist in a hierarchy of importance.[21] Equality does not trump other rights. Other rights do not trump equality.

The trick is to recognize that no right is absolute. Competing rights need to be balanced with (and sometimes against) each other. There are always legal limits to rights in free and democratic societies. This balancing act is already enshrined in our Canadian Charter. The assertion that any right or freedom automatically has precedence over any other ignores these basic principles.[22]

The third rights conflict case is *Heintz v. Christian Horizons,* which juxtaposes a different set of rights, namely religious rights and the rights of gays and lesbians.[23] Connie Heintz was an employee of Christian Horizons, an evangelical organization that operates approximately 200 group homes for people with developmental disabilities in Ontario. At the time of the case, Christian Horizons received $75 million annually in public funding and its residential programs were 100 percent funded through the provincial government. It had over 2,500 employees and provided care and support to about 1,400 individuals.

As a support worker, Connie Heintz's duties included cooking, cleaning, doing laundry, and helping residents to eat, wash, and toilet. Like all employees at Christian Horizons, her contract included a "Lifestyle and Morality Statement" prohibiting homosexuality. When Heintz's co-workers confronted her about her sexual orientation, she admitted to being in a lesbian relationship. Her supervisors told her to undergo "Christian counseling" to "cure her of her sexuality." Heintz refused.[24] She resigned after her employers made it clear that she would be fired. A human rights complaint was filed, alleging harassment. Heintz won her case before the Human Rights Tribunal of Ontario.[25] She also won on appeal to the Ontario Divisional Court, although certain aspects of the tribunal's ruling were modified to give proper consideration to Christian Horizons' claim regarding its religious beliefs and principles.[26]

Critics alleged that the tribunal's decision infringed Christian Horizons' religious freedom.[27] In fact, section 24(1)(a) of the Ontario Human Rights Code allows organizations with a religious mission to discriminate in favour of their own religion under certain conditions.[28] Balancing freedom of religion and equality rights is integral to the legislation. The Divisional Court explained: "Subsection 24(1)(a) seeks to balance the rights of certain groups against equality rights. An approach to s. 24(1)(a) that takes into account, in the determination of the primary activity of a religious organization, the perspective and purpose of the organization is consistent with the guarantee of freedom of religion. At the same time, the [bona fide occupational requirement] found in s. 24(1)(a) upholds the important *Charter* protection for equality rights."[29] The court explicitly recognized Christian Horizons as a religious organization even though it served people from other religious groups. However, since Connie Heintz's sexual orientation could not be rationally connected to the duties in her job description, the court found that there was no justification for imposing the terms of the Lifestyle and Morality Statement.

Contrary to what was portrayed in some of the reports on the case, the court was highly sensitive and deferential to Christian Horizons' religious mission when considering the legitimacy of its "Lifestyle and Morality Statement." At the same time, the court noted:

[N]otwithstanding some of the Christian practices engaged in by the support workers with the residents ... the Tribunal found that [Heintz] was not engaged in actively promoting an Evangelical Christian way of life and that services were provided to the people with developmental disabilities of all faiths and those without any faith. There is nothing about the performance of the tasks (cooking, cleaning, doing laundry, helping residents to eat, wash and use the bathroom, and taking them on outings and to appointments) that

requires an adherence by the support workers to a lifestyle that precludes same sex relationships. In fact, Ms. Heintz, herself, remains
an Evangelical Christian, a follower of Christian Horizons' ethos in
every other way, and is committed and quite capable of performing
the job functions of a support worker with the love and care that has
typically characterized Christian Horizons' service to people with
developmental disabilities and with respect for the Christian activities in the homes.[30]

The Divisional Court did not presume that the organization's religious
claims trumped Heintz's rights. Nor did it take the starting position that
Heintz's equality rights should prevail. This balanced approach would
have applied whether the organization was Christian, Jewish, or Muslim.
It might be compared with testimony from a representative of Christian
Horizons. Reverend Stan Cox, the vice chair of the organization's Board
of Directors, said that Christian Horizons sincerely believes that homosexuality is a sin and that homosexuals cannot be part of "the community," and went on to say:

> [Homosexuality] might reflect the fact that *they're not really commit-
> ted to our vision and what it means to be human and what it means
> to be a flourishing human being.* So if they're not committed in that
> area, in what other areas might they also not be committed to
> expressing in practical ways this strong Christian conviction about
> God's creation of us in his image? *So sexual behaviour then becomes
> really almost a touchstone among other behaviours of their commit-
> ment to our vision of what it means to be a human being in a faith.*
> ... If they don't want to follow what we're committed to as God's
> way in that area, who knows what other areas they may also not
> follow.[31]

Read that again. "They're not really committed to our vision and what it
means to be human and what it means to be a flourishing human being."

Clearly, Heintz was not committed to their vision, at least inasmuch as
that vision excluded her from her own religious community. But the
second half of the sentence is troublesome. There is no possibility of
reaching a civilized resolution to a human rights complaint, or any other
type of dispute for that matter, when one party claims that the other
party is not fully human because of protected characteristics that are
deeply connected to that person's identity. The *Christian Horizons* case
did not mean that human rights laws can impose secular views on

religious organizations. It meant that rights are exercised in context and that none are absolute. For example, the Human Rights Tribunal of Ontario dismissed a discrimination claim against a priest who had made anti-homosexual comments during a religious service. The tribunal affirmed that the "actions of a clergyperson performing purely religious functions are not covered by the social area of 'services' in the Code."[32]

Nor did the *Christian Horizons* case mean that Christian (or other religious) organizations can no longer structure themselves around their belief systems. What it did say was that when religious organizations impose rules, they must do so in a manner that is consistent with human rights law. Human rights laws apply to everyone in society, with narrowly circumscribed exceptions, and some of those exceptions have been carved out for religious organizations. Equality principles operate to moderate and shape both religious freedom and the right to be free from discrimination. It is worth noting that the collective rights of the organization as a Christian evangelical mission were specifically recognized under the Ontario Human Rights Code. After the Divisional Court decision, Christian Horizons and the Ontario Human Rights Commission announced a partnership initiative in 2013 that would allow certain job applicants to apply for employment regardless of the applicant's creed.

> Christian Horizons is committed to serving people living with developmental disabilities with respect and dignity, recognizing and supporting their talents, gifts and diversity. It works to encourage open and accepting communities by modeling healthy and positive relationships. The Commission and Christian Horizons recognize the importance of Christian Horizons' foundation as a faith-based organization. At the same time, the Commission and Christian Horizons believe that employing support workers and program managers who hold a variety of views on matters of faith will strengthen its capacity to support people from diverse communities.[33]

In all three cases, we were dealing with standard discrimination and harassment complaints. The difference, though, from *McIntosh* through to *Christian Horizons* was the prominence of the competing right or freedom, not its existence. In all three cases, the human rights systems had legislative authority to deal with the rights at play. Resolving these conflicts requires an assessment of how human beings and the public interest are affected, as well as a decision to put the interests of people over dogma and ideologies. A climate where people are vilified and deemed less than human is a poisoned society where individuals cannot go about their daily lives without fear of being singled out, harassed, racially profiled, or denied the basic goods of life, from education and employment to government services and housing. The ability to identify these situations and to distinguish them from incidents that do not merit legal attention is a litmus test for the effectiveness of human rights systems. One of these tests is the "hallmarks of hate,"[34] a non-exhaustive list of features that are likely to expose members of the targeted group to hatred or contempt.[35] The hallmarks are an important contribution by the Canadian Human Rights Tribunal to the legal landscape on hate speech and what constitutes discrimination and have been cited with approval by the Supreme Court of Canada.[36] They include:

1   The "Powerful Menace" Hallmark: The targeted group is portrayed as a powerful menace that is taking control of the major institutions in society and depriving others of their livelihoods, safety, freedom of speech, and general well-being;

2   The "True Story" Hallmark: The messages use true stories, news reports, pictures, and reference from purportedly reputable sources to make negative generalizations about [the] targeted group";

3   The "Predator" Hallmark: The targeted group is portrayed as preying upon children, the aged, the vulnerable, etc.;

4   The "Cause of Society's Problems" Hallmark: The targeted group is blamed for the current problems in society and the world;

5   The "Dangerous or Violent by Nature" Hallmark: The targeted group is portrayed as [being] dangerous or violent by nature;

6   The "No Redeeming Qualities" Hallmark: The messages convey the idea that members of the targeted group are devoid of any redeeming qualities and are innately evil;

7   The "Banishment" Hallmark: The messages communicate the idea that nothing but the banishment, segregation, or eradication of this group of people will save others from the harm being done by this group;

8   The "Sub-human" Hallmark: The targeted group is de-humanized through comparisons to and associations with animals, vermin, excrement, and other noxious substances;

9   The "Inflammatory Language" Hallmark: Highly inflammatory and derogatory language is used in the messages to create a tone of extreme hatred and contempt;

10   The "Trivializing or Celebration of Past Tragedy" Hallmark: The messages trivialize or celebrate past persecution or tragedy involving members of the targeted group;

11   The "Call to Violent Action" Hallmark: [The messages include] calls to take violent action against the targeted group.[37]

Some or all of these hallmarks have been used in the context of hate speech cases in Canada to combat discriminatory practices that poison society and render it progressively less accepting and tolerant. The cases discussed in the following section examine the type of rights conflicts that ensue when liberty is put into the service of efforts to exclude entire groups of people from participation in human society

POISONING THE PUBLIC WELL

You have to make a distinction between hate promoters and free speech absolutists. Hate promoters are not worth debating or confronting directly. Where their incitement is grave enough, legal remedies should be invoked. Free speech absolutists are different: they should be debated. They hold on to their simple idea of free speech *über alles* with almost religious fervour and are unlikely to be persuaded [otherwise]. But the public needs to know the other side. Free speech absolutists would presumably even appreciate that.

David Matas[38]

A common argument in favour of free speech is that it leads to truth and therefore to a better functioning democracy. This proposition is most often associated with John Stuart Mill's famous essay *On Liberty*. Richard Moon has another take on the issue, arguing that free speech is important not only, or even primarily, because of the familiar arguments about democracy and the market place of ideas but because of its deep connection to who we are as people and our ability to influence the world around us: "Free speech is less an individual right, in fact, than it is a deeply social right bound up with personal and social identity. When you look at it this way, you can make more sense of the claim for speech that it is about protecting democracy. And when thought about this way, the idea that free speech is either instrumental to democracy or intrinsic to it, is not helpful."[39]

Moon's argument is based on the important idea that speech is essential to our sense of self, our ability to function in a community, and our ability to communicate, formulate, convey, and receive ideas. The argument is attractive not only because of its foundation in freedom but also because of its egalitarianism. The arguments in favour of personal agency only make sense if freedoms are available to everyone without discrimination, allowing us to be who we are, within the bounds set by law.

Hate speech, on the other hand, has precisely the opposite effect: it diminishes free speech by silencing people through vilification and stigma, portraying them as less deserving of human dignity. According to Mark Freiman, "Hate speech results in the dehumanization of its target[s] and makes them deserving of whatever they get."[40]

Human rights laws in Canada contain protections against hate speech that has the effect of generating detestation and involves vilification of the targeted group. Freiman foreshadowed the Supreme Court of Canada's unanimous decision in *Whatcott* when he saw the prohibitions against hate speech as being "entirely within the paradigm of section 15 [the equality provision of the Charter]. And as for the Moon Report, Dick Moon consulted me and I think that he got it exactly wrong by trying to criminalize speech behaviour."[41]

The decision of the Supreme Court of Canada in *Whatcott* marks an important milestone for human rights commissions' role in regulating hate speech. It was a long battle for many equality-seeking groups. This section takes a closer look at the case that started it all and that marks the departure point for the colliding trajectories of equality, freedom of expression, and freedom of religion.

It is 1965. A German shepherd barks in the snowy front yard of an Ontario farmhouse as an electrician installs a new circuit for a printing press. The farm belongs to John Ross Taylor, a self-described leader of "Natural Order." According to a voiceover, Taylor is converting his farm into a "Hate Headquarters" where he will print hate literature and train recruits. An anti-communist, anti-Semitic fascist, Taylor describes himself as being "as far right as you can go." He believes in "the Bible's call to a holy war against communists and Jews."

Taylor has been distributing his "truth literature" for over thirty years. He boasts of a 5,000 percent increase in his production over the past year. Taylor advocates for the mass deportation of Canadian Jews to Madagascar as an act of "love." He complains bitterly about the "abominable thing that the Canadian government did to destroy the free speech of the Canadian people," referring to the government's decision to ban the *Thunderbolt,* a fascist publication.

When asked to describe hate literature, Taylor picks up a copy of the Talmud and says: "This is hate literature." Taylor asserts that civilization is in danger due to the invasion of foreign elements, especially Jews and communists. He refers to these groups as less than human and as inherently decadent or degraded. Canadian law would later classify such views as hallmarks of hate.[42]

This portrait of John Ross Taylor and his mission appeared in 1965 in the "Opinions Fly" episode of the CBC news show *This Hour Has Seven Days*.[43] Taylor's statements are an incitement to violence, hostility, and discrimination. The episode is described by the CBC as taking us "from the sublime to the ridiculous," juxtaposing advice maven Anne Landers with "merchants of hate." A psychologist depicts group hate as a power neurosis whereby people who accuse others of plotting world domination, committing heinous crimes, being deviant and the like, based on the targeted groups' race, religion, etc., are described as projecting their own fantasies onto others. The episode also includes an interview with then-minister of justice Guy Favreau. In the clip, Favreau discusses the need to strike a proper balance between protecting free speech and preventing what he calls "despicable" attacks on the dignity of citizens. He announces the appointment of a panel of experts headed by Dean Max Cohen of McGill University to provide an opinion on what should be done about extremist and hateful views.

In 1966, the Special Committee on Hate Propaganda in Canada issued the Cohen Report.[44] In 1970, the Criminal Code was amended to prohibit promotion and incitement to genocide and hatred, as well as the distribution of hate propaganda. The Canadian Human Rights Act (CHRA) came into force a decade later. Section 13 of the CHRA deals with hate-inciting speech outside the criminal context. This provision first went before the courts in a case involving the aforementioned John Ross Taylor. In 1979, the Canadian Human Rights Commission brought complaints against Taylor and the Western Guard Party about hate messages transmitted via telephone. On appeal to the Supreme Court of Canada in 1990, four out of seven judges upheld the constitutionality of section 13 of the CHRA.[45]

Section 13 originally only dealt with hate messages distributed via telephone. In the aftermath of 9/11, it was extended to include the Internet. This was not a substantive change in the sense that it was only enacted for "greater certainty." In determining whether a message incites hate, the focus should be on the message's content, not on its platform or publisher. According to sources at the Canadian Human Rights Commission, catching mainstream newspapers and magazines in the tangle of the Internet was an unintended consequence of the amendment, although it would have been a foreseeable consequence had anyone been able to predict the vast expansion of telecommunications in the years that followed.

The Supreme Court's decision in *Taylor* remained the law of the land for more than two decades. In it, Chief Justice Dickson highlighted the founding values of Canadian society and the connection between liberty, equality, and dignity in a multicultural society: "Since the release of the *Report of the Special Committee on Hate Propaganda in Canada*, numerous other study groups have echoed [its] conclusion that hate propaganda presents a serious threat to society. ... It can thus be concluded that messages of hate propaganda undermine the dignity and self-worth of target group members and, more generally, contribute to disharmonious relations among various racial, cultural and religious groups, as a result eroding the tolerance and open-mindedness that must flourish in a multicultural society which is committed to the idea of equality."[46]

Between 2007 and 2013, Chief Justice Dickson's ringing words seemed to have lost their resonance. Indeed, those who opposed hate speech were branded as anti-civil liberties censors. Irwin Cotler described such efforts as "an attempt to win the debate by labeling. That's an attempt to decide the debate without having to debate [and] an attempt to use labels to predetermine outcomes ... it is a cowardly approach to the discussion and the argument." He added that freedom of expression is not simply a philosophical inquiry that operates in isolation; it is part of an exercise that engages with several core values.[47]

Today's legal context is very different from anything that John Stuart Mill could possibly have envisaged 150 years ago. There are now constitutional and international norms for rights, and the Internet is both an information thruway and a "superhighway of hate."[48] According to Cotler, "there is, in Canada, a dialectical encounter between the rise in hate speech on the one hand and a comprehensive legal regime to combat it on the other hand. We probably have one of the most comprehensive legal regimes, including those of a civil and criminal character, as well as of an international character, to buttress it. I happen to think that's a good thing."[49]

Human rights legislation and the Criminal Code are not the only mechanisms that prohibit hateful messages or content in Canada. Radio and television regulations under the Broadcasting Act prohibit broadcasts that expose people to hatred or contempt.[50] As well, the Canadian Broadcast Standards Council (CBSC), an independent, non-governmental organization, can receive complaints about material that is abusive or discriminatory under its Equitable Portrayal Code.[51] For example, in 2010, the CBSC decided that the television program *Word TV* (formerly known as Word.ca) had violated both the Code of Ethics and the Equitable Portrayal Code of the Canadian Association of Broadcasters when the program's televangelist, Charles McVety, portrayed gays and lesbians as sinful and suggested that gay adults have a predilection towards criminal activity.[52] The Customs Tariff[53] and the Canada Post Corporation Act[54] also control the importation and transmission of prohibited material.

Cotler argues that these regulatory schemes and rules create a broad framework to combat hate.[55] According to Cotler, this framework "is ignored or excluded from the discourse. [It] was put in there for a reason, in order to prohibit hate speech: it is even framed in equality terms."[56]

The nuanced range of options under Canadian law means that Canada is an international model in terms of its approach to hate speech, according to Jane Bailey: "We are the envy of the world. When I go and give presentations, for example in Washington for the International Network against Cyberhate, a collective of anti-hate organizations, Canada is viewed with admiration, as compared with the US. The US is a haven for hate speech and [it] protects hate speech. If you are regulating speech, the view is that you are China. The recent hate speech debates and the media treatment of them is not what Canada is about. Our reputation was built on being halfway between the US and the European approaches, and we should be proud of this."[57]

The Canadian legal framework described by Cotler is buttressed by international human rights law.[58] Cotler notes: "We are a state party to international treaties that exclude hate speech from the ambit of protected speech. The free speech debate has been carried on in utter unawareness, ignorance or willful blindness of the international law configurations. It's fine to quote Article 19 [of the International Covenant on Civil and Political Rights], but you also have to quote Article 20."[59] Article 19 of the International Covenant on Civil and Political Rights (ICCPR) provides broad rights for holding an opinion without interference and for freedom of expression in all of its forms. Article 20 prohibits any propaganda for war and says that "Any advocacy of national, racial or religious hatred that constitutes incitement to discrimination, hostility or violence shall be prohibited by law."[60]

Canada acceded to the ICCPR on 19 May 1976 without making any reservations. Article 20(2) of the ICCPR is important. Cotler said:

I don't see people joining issue with this. [International law] has just been read out of the discussion, and that, to me, is ahistorical and simply lacks seriousness. In fact, it goes [against] a clear and conclusive determination of the applicability of those treaties to freedom of expression and removing hate speech from the ambit of freedom of expression and its application to Canada. We are obliged to excise hate speech from protected speech either on speech grounds or discrimination grounds. This is the chief justice of Canada saying this, not me. But none of this has been referred to in the current debate.[61]

The unconstitutionality of hate speech had been upheld by a narrow majority in the Supreme Court of Canada's 1990 decision in *Taylor*.[62] A quarter century later, it came under renewed challenge.

   Naseem Mithoowani is a lawyer at one of Canada's leading immigration and human rights law firms. In 2007, she and three other Muslim students noticed more than twenty *Maclean's* magazine articles that appeared to target Muslims.[63] Barbara Amiel wrote: "Normally, a people don't willingly acquiesce in the demise of their own culture, especially one as agreeable as Western democracy, but you can see how it happens. Massive Muslim immigration takes place[.]"[64] Mark Steyn whose previously cited article, "The Future Belongs to Islam," an excerpt from his book *America Alone,* predicted a global Muslim takeover with the only remaining question being "how bloody the transfer of real estate will be."[65] In "Celebrate Tolerance, or You're Dead," Steyn clarified his views on Muslims, stating that he was *not* trying to say that "the cities of the Western world will be filling up with sheep-shaggers." And channelling the polemicist Oriana Falacci, Steyn cites "livelier examples" of "contemporary Islam" such as sex with nine-year-old girls and with sheep, the propriety of of roasting one's sexual partner, and a more generic reference to "hitting on the livestock."[66] Aside from the over-involvement with farm animals, Steyn's articles are recognizably part of the sub-genre of writing that has sought to demonize Muslims as depraved, bestial, and prone to pedophilia. Neither Amiel nor Steyn fit the "hate merchant" profile of John Ross Taylor. Steyn's depiction of "contemporary Islam" may be uncomplimentary, but it is less problematic than outright incitement to murder, mayhem, and mass deportation.

   Still, the law students felt the articles and others like them elicited hostility towards Muslims. The articles certainly caused consternation in their community.[67] The students attended local community meetings and saw that while many of their co-religionists were deeply disturbed by the public portrayal of Muslims, no one quite knew what to do. The repercussions extended beyond hurt feelings and dismay. According to Mithoowani, many Muslims wanted to ignore what was happening and assumed a "head in the sand approach." This gave permission through silence, she felt, to writers who "felt they could get up and say what they did. No one stood up to say that this is unacceptable."[68] Mithoowani attributed the passivity of such individuals to what she called the "collective guilt that Muslims feel about what is happening worldwide."[69]

Writers like Steyn and Levant were being portrayed as free speech heroes.[70] Online and anonymous comments that were previously limited to extremist web sites began appearing more widely. Online comments, allegedly in response to writings by Steyn and from the *Western Standard*, submitted by the complainants as evidence before the BC Human Rights Tribunal in *Elmasry*, speak for themselves.

From "Free Republic," under a re-published version of Steyn's "The Future Belongs to Islam." "where the number of Muslims is expanding like mosquitoes.
What is the Muslim-eradicating DDT equivalent?"
Comment
Well-aimed, precisely-delivered neutron bombs. Several dozen of them. Let the world howl. Get rid of the population; keep the oil production systems in place ... throughout the Middle East. At some point, it may very well be them or us.
From a blog discussion: published by the *Western Standard*.
It makes me think that [right-wing commentator] Ann Coulter was right – Muslims have to be converted to Christianity or killed if we are to survive.
Comment
There is no such thing as INNOCENT muslims. They are all islamic-fascists whether they know it or not. They must all be KILLED. ALL OF THEM.

· "They must all be KILLED. ALL OF THEM." I'd start with deportation from Western countries. If they don't behave back there – and threaten us with missiles and nuclear weapons – then I'd be in favour of their eradication

"The number of Muslims is expanding like mosquitoes." ... and what do we do with disease-laden mosquitoes?"[71]

Collectively, those posts meet most, if not all, of the "hallmarks of hate."

The law students argued that this type of speech intimidates and stifles minorities, Muslim minorities in particular. Jameel Jaffer, a staunch supporter of free expression in the robust tradition of the First Amendment, is the litigation director with the American Civil Liberties Union. He is unimpressed by the argument that hate speech stifles speech. Jaffer observed that "attempts to suppress speech are used by all sides as a critique and are not the exclusive property of any particular agenda. They are used by interest groups against speech they do not like, and this includes free speech activists." Nonetheless, Jaffer observed that claims about Muslims seeking to take over the world were "paranoid and delusional."[72]

The students were fed up with being perceived as terrorists-in-waiting or as demographic time bombs about to explode and engulf Canadian society in a tide of Islamic extremism. They requested a meeting with the *Maclean's* editors, planning to ask the magazine to print a "counter article." The students were flabbergasted at their hostile reception at the March 2007 meeting: "It was an extremely condescending meeting. Ten or fifteen minutes only. They had already dismissed our position and said we could never "interfere" with the creative direction of their editors. We thought we were going to have a conversation ... [W]e had faith that they would try to resolve this. We thought that this would be a good way of attracting readership ... a good way to attract a strong response. I was shocked at the complete shutting down of the idea of a response."[73] They were also astounded that Julian Porter, one of Canada's leading libel lawyers, had been invited to the meeting. Although they had hoped the meeting would be an opportunity to discuss balance in the media, they quickly decoded the unspoken message.

Porter later said that the students' demand to publish a 5,000-word rebuttal by an author of their choosing "went too far" by infringing on the rights of a privately owned publication.[74] According to Mithoowani, Porter asked the students what kind of legal research they had done. "He was very much asking us what avenues we had explored. We had not really discussed any legal avenues at that point." It had never occurred to us to do so, she said. "That is when we really started to think of legal avenues. We looked at each other and were at a loss. This is what really pushed us."[75]

Taking their cue to research potential "legal avenues," the students began examining their options. They assumed that Porter had been focusing on the criminal angle of hate speech, but the students discovered another angle: non-criminal remedies through human rights complaints. Before moving forward, they appealed to Brian Segal in his capacity as president and CEO of Rogers. Segal responded on 23 May 2007 by inviting them to make use of the magazine's "Letters to the Editor" section.

The students decided to use the human rights processes in Canada to launch a national campaign to protest what they saw as a national media assault on Muslims. They also sought the support of the labour and student movements. They filed a complaint with the Ontario Human Rights Commission in their own names but believed they could not take on a media giant and established writers or columnists by themselves. They enlisted the help of the Canadian Islamic Congress.

"We had never heard of the Canadian Islamic Congress [CIC] before," Mithoowani said. "The conditions of [the CIC fronting the complaint and acting as the complainant] were never made clear to all the parties. The CIC was supposed to be more of a silent partner. It was the name we needed to reach out in order to file the complaints at a national level." The CIC became the complainant at the federal level and the CIC's president, Dr Mohamed Elmasry, was a complainant in his personal capacity in the British Columbia case, alongside BC resident Dr Naiyer Habib.

The decision to involve the CIC had unintended consequences. Elmasry was a highly controversial figure because of alleged anti-Israeli statements he had made in another context that had been the subject of widespread commentary and criticism in the media. Muslims who spoke to me off the record and on condition of anonymity said that they deplored the statements and were deeply troubled by the way Elmasry's leadership reflected on the Muslim community. Most observers, including those who were sympathetic to the human rights complaints, agreed that asking the CIC to front the case was a mistake. His notoriety stole the show. A hostile press portrayed the students as "sock puppets" of a controversial sponsoring organization and its even more controversial president.[76] Instead of the story being about Canadian law students who spoke out against what they believed to be hate speech, the public debate was reframed as the takeover of Canadian legal institutions by extremists.

Mithoowani is hardly an extremist. She had grown up in the small southwestern town of Strathroy, Ontario. She had played hockey in her community. Even though she and her family were among the few Muslims around, she considered herself to be as Canadian as anyone else. "It simply never occurred to me that anyone would see me as one of 'them.' ... I was born and raised in Canada. I experienced the odd [anti-Muslim] comment growing up, but generally I never felt 'alien.' Filing a human rights claim totally changed things. The attacks on us personally ... made me afraid of applying for a job. I had never gone through anything like this before. We thought this was a multicultural society, but once you start speaking out, you feel like you are being attacked. It has made me question Canadian society."[77]

Mithoowani received threats and hate messages. Her family tracked the negative media and the anti-Muslim rhetoric. "They were afraid for me, especially when some of the Internet bloggers started their attacks. Some of the first blogs were vile – and this was frightening."[78] Muneeza Sheikh, one of the other students, recalled that her employer (a major cosmetics company) had received calls that were clearly designed to get her fired.[79] One student (there were initially four) dropped out because of the stress and pressure. None of the students had anticipated the ferocity or the antipathy of the reaction. Mithoowani said: "I think we were naïve. We simply assumed that *Maclean's* would want to clear this up. We did not expect the anti-Muslim rhetoric. And the hardest thing in the entire process was to hear the commentators talk about 'those Muslims' [who] are trying to take over Canadian legal processes."[80]

I asked Mithoowani whether anyone had ever asked the students about who they were as people or for the kind of biographic background information that normally provides the backdrop for an interview. She paused and said that not many had. She felt that such information would have forced readers to see her and her fellow students as people who believed in justice, and as Muslims who were as Canadian as anyone else. It was easier, perhaps, to portray them as "sock puppets" of Islamists.

Jane Bailey had been watching the deterioration of the public debate with growing dismay: "Calling hate propaganda what it is – a practice of discrimination that has played an integral role in the dehumaniza-tion of whole groups of people – is essential at this juncture in human history as economic, political, and social turmoil leave many search-ing for scapegoats. In this climate of fear and upheaval, it is perhaps more important than ever to name hate propagation as a practice of discrimination."[81]

Ultimately, the complaints failed in all three jurisdictions. The reasons differ because, as discussed in chapter 1, each jurisdiction in Canada has different rules. In Ontario, the commission dismissed the complaint in April 2008 because the complaint did not engage an area over which the commission had jurisdiction. The magazines themselves could not be considered a service and the Human Rights Code does not confer the ability to receive complaints about publications and statements. In June 2008, the Canadian Human Rights Commission dismissed the case as well. It did have jurisdiction over hate speech on the Internet, but was of the view that the evidence was insufficient to make the claim. The CHRC therefore declined to send the matter to a hearing. In British Columbia, where there is jurisdiction over hate speech in publications and statements, the case went to a hearing at the tribunal, but was dismissed as well, also for evidentiary reasons.

Section 7(1)(b) of the BC Human Rights Code requires that the complainant produce objective evidence and not subjective perceptions about hatred and contempt.[82] In the 1990 *Taylor* case, the Supreme Court of Canada had made it clear that human rights laws governing speech should only be used in extreme cases.[83] The tribunal in *Elmasry* applied this principle, which still stands as a bulwark against the erosion of free speech. Although it found Steyn's writings to contain "numerous factual, historical, and religious inaccuracies about Islam and Muslims" and even to have provoked fear of Muslims,[84] this was not enough to demonstrate hate.

> We think that Dr. Rippin put it best when he said that the [Mark Steyn] Article is a rallying cry to the "West". The Article may attempt to rally public opinion by exaggeration and causing the reader to fear Muslims, but fear is not synonymous with hatred and contempt.
>
> We accept that it may be possible to link feelings of fear with hatred and contempt but in the absence of any expert evidence which makes that link in the context of the Article, we cannot find that it was done so in this case.[85]

Despite the defeat, none of the students felt defeated or regretful about having initiated the claims. They saw their fight as important not only for Muslim communities but also for a more accepting Canada. "It was a testament to the strength of support of our community, and especially the community in London, Ontario. They have been so supportive. Instead of standing up when people treated us unfairly, we [Muslims] just took it. We internalized the criticism. But once we took a stand, we have been treated as heroes [in our community]. I don't think we did anything so extraordinary, but the Muslim community's feelings of isolation and neglect meant that we did stand out."[86]

One of the unfortunate effects of the hate-speech debates was the coarsening of anti-Muslim rhetoric and the increased public acceptance of blatant intolerance, which would extend to other groups as well. The marketplace of ideas was transformed into a bully pulpit. Paul Champ, a civil liberties lawyer, observed: "There is a racist element to this, and the current paradigm is making it okay to judge [Muslims] based on their ethnic backgrounds. Stereotypes are being used to shape policy, and this is something that we have not seen in decades."[87] This was precisely what the students in the *Maclean's* cases were trying to combat. The characterization of hate speech as a censorship issue, without any other redeeming and important rights at stake, had a profound impact on the public perception of human rights systems. The interaction between equality rights and other rights and freedoms was downplayed by the media and other free speech advocates who saw only free speech interests.

The next prominent case began with a letter written by Reverend Stephen Boissoin. It was entitled "Homosexual Agenda Wicked" and was published in Alberta's *Red Deer Advocate* on 17 June 2002. Boissoin began the letter by offering sympathy, love, and fellowship to those "suffering from an unwanted sexual identity crisis." The letter then changed tack:

My banner has now been raised and war has been declared so as to defend the precious sanctity of our innocent children and youth, that you so eagerly toil, day and night, to consume. ... The masses have dug in and continue to excuse their failure to stand against horrendous atrocities such as the aggressive propagation of Homo-and bisexuality... From kindergarten class on, our children, your grand-children are being strategically targeted, psychologically abused, and brainwashed by homosexual and pro-homosexual educators.

Our children are being victimized by repugnant and premeditated strategies, aimed at desensitizing and eventually recruiting our young into their camps. Think about it, children as young as five and six years of age are being subjected to psychologically and physiologically damaging pro-homosexual literature and guidance in the public school system; all under the fraudulent guise of equal rights. ... Your teenagers are being instructed on how to perform so-called safe same gender oral and anal sex and at the same time being told that it is normal, natural and even productive. Will your child be the next victim that tests homosexuality positive?

...Where homosexuality flourishes, all manner of wickedness abounds. ... These activists ... are perverse, self-centered and morally deprived individuals who are spreading their psychological disease

into every area of our lives. Homosexual rights activists and those
that defend them, are just as immoral as the pedophiles, drug dealers
and pimps that plague our communities.[88]

The letter goes on to exhort readers to take "whatever steps are necessary," and to start "taking back what the enemy took from you."[89]
Professor Darren Lund, a married heterosexual father of two, read
Boissoin's letter and recalled "thinking how awful it was that this person
was able to make links between homosexuals, pedophilia, and drug use.
I thought someone should file a complaint."[90] On 4 July 2002, the
Advocate reported that a teenager had been beaten in an apparent gay-
bashing incident in downtown Red Deer. Although the article did not
mention the Boissoin letter, Lund saw a broader connection: "I heard
that the young man – the victim – had said that he did not feel safe. I
thought, 'You are not safe if a letter can be published like that.'"

On 18 July 2002, Lund filed two complaints under Alberta's human
rights statute[91] – one against Boissoin and one against the *Red Deer
Advocate*. The *Advocate* called Lund to ask him why he had filed the
complaints. The newspaper offered to settle the matter by changing its
letter publishing policy. The *Advocate* agreed that it would "not publish statements that indicate unlawful discrimination or intent to discriminate against a person or class of persons, or are likely to expose
people to hatred or contempt because of ... sexual orientation."[92] Lund
explained: "That is why I dropped the complaint against them. I thought
this was a positive outcome. And I thought this was the end of it."[93]

He was wrong. During the interview with the *Advocate*, Lund made
reference to earlier hate speech cases against known fascists and extremists. Lund said he then received a phone call from Ezra Levant, who said
he was representing Boissoin and that "things are about to get bad for
you – you are about to be sued." Levant's name then materialized on the
letterhead of a Calgary law firm called Chipeur Advocates. In the letter,
dated 12 December 2002, Levant confirmed the earlier telephone conversation, namely that the firm had been retained to represent Boissoin
in a defamation suit against Lund. The letter warns Lund about the
unwisdom of using the court of public opinion and advises Lund not to
speak out about the case. The letter offers helpful tips about the complexities of defamation law, encouraging Lund to get a lawyer and settle
the case, threatening to sue if not.

On 22 December 2002 Boissoin sued Lund for defamation, claiming
$400,000. Lund claims that he was told that he could settle and "make

the whole thing go away for $20,000."[94] The phone call and settlement offer were confirmed in a letter sent to Lund and signed by Levant (the letter offering to settle the case in exchange for a payment is also discussed in chapter 4).

Lund refused to settle. Eventually, Boissoin consented to have the matter dismissed in 2005. Although Lund considered it a "nuisance suit," it absorbed considerable time and money.

> All the name-calling is designed to prevent citizens from being more democratically engaged. It should be about finding a healthy balance between protection against hate speech and protection of speech. I did not think about suing Boissoin myself because I was seeking to rise above their behaviour ... My concern was that a pastor had published a letter against a vulnerable group, and whether these guys were behaving in a defamatory manner was not my primary goal.
>
> The frustrating part was that while the nuisance suits were going on, there was a clear attempt to intimidate me through blog posts and comments [like]: "Let's swamp this guy. Let's teach him a lesson." I received numerous emails, including one about my daughter.
>
> I got emails attacking me as an f-ing sodomite, and worse. I had two young kids at the time. This was intended to teach me a lesson. I don't claim to speak for others. To me, it just seemed like human rights defenders should be able to do the kind of work that I am doing.[95]

Lund won before the human rights panel of Alberta.[96] The decision was then reversed by the Court of Queen's Bench in 2009.[97] By that time, the onslaught against human rights systems because of the hate speech issue was in full swing. The court's main reason for overturning the panel's decision was that the language in Boissoin's letter did not show the level of contempt or hatred required to trigger the relevant provisions of the human rights legislation. The Alberta Court of Appeal upheld the decision of the Court of Queen's Bench: "while the language of the letter "may be jarring, offensive, bewildering, puerile, nonsensical and insulting," it was not likely to expose homosexuals to hatred or contempt within the meaning of the Alberta statute. It therefore constituted an expression of opinion that did not infringe the statute."[98]

Darren Lund paid a high price for his advocacy. He received death threats and alleges that there were attempts to have him dismissed from his teaching position at the University of Calgary. Fortunately, "although the University did not take sides in terms of the stand that I took, my academic freedom was respected and protected."[99] Protective measures were put in place to ensure his safety. Lund said that for a considerable period of time he had difficulty finding a lawyer to represent him in the hate speech case. The Court of Appeal finished the matter by ordering costs against Lund. The decision came down a year before the Supreme Court of Canada rendered a very different ruling in the *Whatcott* case from Saskatchewan.

Hate speech and human rights systems' role in prohibiting them were once again under the microscope in *Saskatchewan (Human Rights Commission) v. Whatcott*.[100] As in the *Boissoin* case, the facts stood at the intersection of equality rights, free speech, and religious rights.

In 2001 and 2002, William Whatcott distributed a series of anti-gay pamphlets on behalf of a group called the Christian Truth Activists. The flyers objected to school teachings about same-sex relationships. Whatcott claimed that these teachings degenerated into "a filthy session where gay and lesbian teachers used dirty language to describe lesbian sex and sodomy to their teenage audience." He asserted that "sodomites and lesbians" are "sex addicts." His flyer entitled "Sodomites in Our Public Schools" claimed that "Sodomites are 430 times more likely to acquire AIDs and 3 times more likely to sexually abuse children." Another flyer said that the law should discriminate against "sodomites and lesbians." Whatcott wrote: "In 1968 it was illegal to engage in homosexual acts[;] now it is almost becoming illegal to question any of their sick desires. Our children will pay the price in disease, death, abuse, and ultimately eternal judgment[.]"[101] He actively encouraged readers to discriminate against gays and lesbians.

Four complaints were filed about the flyers by Guy Taylor, James Komar, Brendan Wallace, and Kathy Hamre. The complainants claimed that the material violated section 14 of the Saskatchewan Human Rights Code which prohibits both hate speech and speech inciting discrimination.[102] The Human Rights Tribunal ruled in their favour as did the Court of Queen's Bench.[103] The latter decision was issued in 2007, the year in which the *Maclean's* hate speech debate took off and the public discourse about speech began changing rapidly under sustained negative media commentary. Although most public commentators disliked Whatcott's controversial views, the statements were seen as harmless or even legitimate expressions of political speech in defence of religious views.

The parallels to the *Boissoin* case were obvious. Both Boissoin and Whatcott associated homosexuals with pedophilia and other forms of criminality. Both indicated that homosexuals are diseased, predatory, and engaged in proselytizing children.

The Saskatchewan's Court of Appeal overturned the lower decisions in 2010. There was now a trilogy of cases where hate speech had been upheld, with the *Whatcott* Court of Appeal decision joining the Canadian Human Rights Tribunal's decision in *Warman v. Lemire* and the Court of Appeal's decision in *Boissoin*.[104] The Court of Appeal in *Whatcott* relied on three main arguments: first, that the material was not so offensive when read in context; second, that Whatcott was targeting homosexual behaviour and not homosexuals themselves; and third, that inciting hate against people based on grounds such as race, ethnicity, and religion is different than hate based on sexual orientation. The court ruled that the latter is somehow more permissible since it is part of a broader public debate.[105] The Court of Appeal said: ""[W]here, on an objective interpretation, the impugned expression is essentially directed to disapprobation of same-sex sexual conduct in a context of comment on issues of public policy or sexual morality, its limitation is not justifiable in a free and democratic society."[106]

This reasoning, in particular the third element, was greeted with shock by human rights lawyers. As discussed in chapter 3, human rights have evolved over the years, with new rights coming to the fore. However, the reasoning of the Court of Appeal appeared to have looked at the historical sequencing of rights movements and attached legal significance to it. According to Dominique Clément, "I do not understand how people who engage in that kind of homophobic speech ever get away with it. There is something about [attitudes toward] gays and lesbians today. They are facing the challenges Jews did in the 1930s. Maybe it is evolutionary. We secured the right of recognition that anti-Semitism is wrong. Hopefully the courts will be able to draw on the inner logic of human rights in the same way."[107]

That is exactly what happened when the *Whatcott* case was appealed to the Supreme Court of Canada. Whatcott had positioned his statements squarely within the realm of political speech that was designed to express his sincerely held religious views. This approach had succeeded before the Saskatchewan Court of Appeal. Like Boissoin, Whatcott was advocating for a social and/or political community that excludes homosexuals, especially from the education sector. This speech was indirect or direct incitement to hostility and discrimination. But it was also political speech based on a particular religious view.

Numerous groups intervened before the Supreme Court on both sides of the argument. Civil liberties, free speech, Catholic, and evangelical groups lined up in support of Mr Whatcott's views or his right to express them. Among them was the Canadian Constitution Foundation, which had also opposed Jeffrey Moore's bid to access public education in the 2012 *Moore* case discussed in chapter 3. On the other side were two attorneys general, five human rights commissions, the United and Unitarian churches, Egale Canada, LEAF, the African Canadian Legal Clinic, Aboriginal groups, Jewish groups, and the Canadian Bar Association.[108]

The Supreme Court issued its much-anticipated decision on 27 February 2013.[109] In a unanimous ruling, the court upheld the constitutionality of human rights legislation that prohibits hate speech but also imposed certain limits. To the relief of human rights advocates, the Supreme Court rejected the Saskatchewan Court of Appeal's distinction between discrimination against "behaviour" and against gays and lesbians as individuals, noting that in the circumstances of the case no reasonable distinction can be made between the two. Attacks on people that expose them to detestation and vilification on an objective basis do in fact constitute hate speech. Such speech does not merely target behaviour; it targets people.[110]

In its decision in *Whatcott*, the court set a very high standard for something to be considered hate speech. The speech must seek to marginalize people, subject them to vilification and detestation, and affect their social status and acceptance in the eyes of the majority. The court affirmed: "Hate speech legislation is not aimed at discouraging repugnant or offensive ideas. ... It does not target ... ideas, but [rather] their mode of expression in public and the effect that this mode of expression may have."[111] Hate speech that incites hostility or discrimination constructs a narrative about people that portrays them as less than human. The targets are accused of attacking and degrading all that is good in civilized society, and especially children. Such portrayals marginalize the targeted group and minimize its freedom to function in an open society.

The Supreme Court also directly addressed the argument that people were being found liable for hate speech because they had "offended" others, ruling that rather than looking at whether a person is affronted or offended, one must look at the objectively verifiable effects of the speech. Any controls on speech (short of prohibitions on inciting violence) still violate freedom of expression under the Charter, but all rights in Canada, even free-speech rights, are subject to reasonable limits. The court did pare back section 14 of the Saskatchewan Human Rights Code by removing the possibility that a hate speech complaint could succeed merely for belittling or ridiculing someone. It held that speech that only "ridicules, belittles or otherwise affronts dignity" does not provoke vilification and detestation to the extent that justifies limitations on freedom of expression. The balance of the section survived.

In upholding the constitutionality of civil (i.e., non-criminal) prohibitions on hate speech in human rights laws, the court maintained a key element in Canada's toolbox of policy instruments designed to address public vilification and group hate. The court's unanimity put to rest questions about the validity of the *Taylor* case (which had been decided on the thinnest of majorities) and the uncertainty about the law on hate speech that had been circulating ever since the *Maclean's* hate speech cases.[112] The Supreme Court of Canada also validated the role of human rights commissions and tribunals as offering a viable, conciliatory, and non-criminal recourse.

Andrew Coyne expressed a view that was very prevalent among supporters of the right to hate speech when he said that the *Whatcott* outcome was "calamitous." Many people who agreed with him, particularly after the earlier Court of Appeal decisions in *Boissoin* and *Whatcott* and having been exposed to the overwhelmingly one-sided position in the mainstream media, had felt victory was inevitable.[113] Indeed, at the federal level, legislation repealing section 13 of the CHRA has since been passed, but the Saskatchewan, Alberta, Northwest Territories, Manitoba, and BC laws remain in place and have been considerably strengthened by the *Whatcott* decision.

The easiest way to dehumanize people and ensure that they are seen and perceived as threats is to paint them as having characters, cultures, or practices that are so debased, barbaric, and disgusting that they do not merit tolerance, let alone human rights. This process is often jump-started by stirring up fears of invasion and by unfavourably comparing "others" to one's own culture and country. These tactics are particularly powerful as part of a nationalistic and patriotic rhetoric that looks on immigrants and foreigners with deep suspicion. There is a long and insidious tradition of placing entire civilizations at loggerheads. This sort of writing relies on several standard tropes that conjure up images of patriots and heroes, unflinching and alone, facing dangerous, imminent, and/or bloody invasions. Mark Steyn's *America Alone* did not invent the genre. US anti-immigration and eugenics enthusiast Lothrop Stoddard's 1932 polemic, *Lonely America*, opens with a portrait of America personified as an isolated and troubled defender of civilized values: "On the summit of the nation's watchtower stands a solitary figure. Silent and inscrutable, his gaze sweeps the wide expanses of the outer world. And, as he gazes, his eyes grow troubled; his brow knits in lines of introspective thought. What does he see, this symbolic personification of our country?"[114] Well, he sees many bad things. Each is worse than the last: menacing Russian communists, the "swarming races" of the "Orient" and other assorted dangers. And then there are the hostile and ungrateful Europeans who fail to appreciate America's intervention in the First World War: Stoddart argued that in European eyes, "Uncle Sam has turned out to be a very despicable and dangerous "Uncle Shylock."[115] *Lonely America* exhorts the defenders of America to stand firm against foreigners, feminists, and those menacing "others" by waking up and grasping the dangers that surround them.

Such depictions of "others" as threats to national security and nationhood are depressingly familiar. Bernie Farber was for many years the CEO of the Canadian Jewish Congress (CJC). Farber recounted the experiences that he had within the Jewish community in Canada and the way Jews had been characterized as threats: "Our community has a history of dealing with this kind of vilification. Saul Hayes was one of the people who was concerned about this issue and managed to convince the legislature that something had to be done. Working with Sydney Harris and others, they helped to create the momentum to get the Cohen Commission going. We believe that education is the most important tool, but human rights complaints should be available as the last means ... I was called all sorts of names: a book burner, etc. And the CJC was accused of bankrolling the Canadian Nazi party. These people just make it up."[116] Farber says that he was identified as a target of right-wing elements by a Canadian Security Intelligence Service report in 1996. "But you have to live your life," he said. "I was careful, but you can't get too carried away." Like Clément, Farber is concerned about the current impact of hate speech on other communities. "In some respects, Muslims today must feel as Jews did in the 1950s and 1960s. There is still anti-Semitism out there, but the environment today, where people are being attacked simply for being Muslims, must be very disturbing."[117]

Jane Bailey also saw discrepancies between the ways in which the two communities have been treated by the legal system. "Muslims have looked at the hate speech cases and their outcomes, and how they were themselves treated in the public sphere compared to other communities, and they perceive that the law in Canada is not for them."[118] This reasoning also applies to people who are claiming newer categories of rights, such as gay and lesbian rights. It is an important part of the reason why it was so important to have Jewish organizations like B'nai

B'rith and the Canadian Jewish Congress standing in solidarity as inter-
veners in the *Whatcott* case. It is also why the presence of organizations
like the African Canadian Legal Clinic, with its history in the civil rights
movement, was important as an interlocutor to rebut the Saskatchewan
Court of Appeal's argument that newer categories of rights, and the people who claim them, are less deserving of equality, liberty, and dignity.

Portraying people with whom we are uncomfortable as foreign and
dangerous makes the targets doubly vulnerable because they cannot
readily speak for themselves or rise above the stereotypes applied to
their communities. The Supreme Court has said that "hate speech can
also distort or limit the robust and free exchange of ideas by its tendency
to silence the voice of its target group. It can achieve the self-fulfillment
of the publisher, but often at the expense of that of the victim."[119] Seen
in this light, hate speech is another form of discrimination, albeit an
extreme form. It seeks to shut its targets out of public discourse, which
makes it much easier to exclude them from everything else as well.

Muslim women are among the targets of stereotypes and of campaigns
to silence them. Pascale Fournier is an associate professor of law at the
University of Ottawa. Religious Muslim women have borne the brunt of
stereotyping and racism.[120] Fournier argues that the law itself is com-
plicit in maintaining prejudices against women because the courts almost
always look to men for religious authority. Disputes about religious
observances often shut out women as sources of authority or alternative
discourses about their religion. They are trapped between patriarchy and
their faith. "A woman with an unorthodox [religious] viewpoint will
necessarily be shut out of the legal process when the viewpoint of conservative orthodoxies is at issue. Feminists who are working within their
own communities cannot bring forward their own perspectives
easily."[121]

Alia Hogben, executive director of the Canadian Council of Muslim
Women, has struggled to make visible the moderate Muslim perspective in
Canada. Although the organization has been active since 1982, it only got
really involved in the media after 9/11: "We are constantly caught in the
middle between conservative interpretations of Islam and moderate
Muslim women who are committed to their faith and also to women's
equality within their faith. But there are many different kinds of Muslims
and many different Muslim communities. When we began the Canadian
Council of Muslim women, we developed guidelines saying that we do not
speak for all Muslim women. We had no idea how true that would be."[122]

Fournier saw no small irony in the fact that the hostility faced by devout women has been exacerbated by other Muslim women.[123] She pointed to Somalian-born Ayaan Hirsi Ali, a self-described ex-Muslim, who has been highly critical not only of Islamist repression of women but also of Muslims in general. She also points to Canadian Irshad Manji, who works in the context of her own faith to critique her religion. Fournier points out that both women have written best-selling works highlighting the appalling discrimination that many Muslim women face.[124] At the same time, however, as one scholar has observed, a key factor in the success of their books was the political and media push in the United States to frame the war in Afghanistan as a "righteous war by virtue of our concern to save the women."[125] Fournier thinks that is why Hirsi Ali and Manji have been embraced by the American conservative right. In the case of Hirsi Ali, scholar Leila Ahmed observes that it is especially problematic when public statements are used to stereotype Muslim women as ignorant and oppressed.[126] Fournier added that "I have great difficulty with secular, pro-Western, and uncritical voices of women who have been making money off the hatred of fellow Muslim women."[127] It is possible, Fournier argued, to oppose the widespread discrimination against women in many Muslim countries without attacking all Muslims or all Muslim women. At the same time, attempts by radical Muslims to shut down and physically threaten writers like Hirsi Ali are completely unacceptable in any democratic society.

While the latter issue has garnered considerable public attention and support, getting the media to pay attention to the first issue, the effects of anti-Muslim sentiment on moderate communities, has been difficult. Fournier thought this difficulty has occurred in part because anti-Muslim writers have a high media profile, whereas progressive and moderate Muslims working within their traditions receive little or no attention. Alia Hogben cited a number of Muslims who are working within the Islamic tradition to promote reform and women's rights, such as Pakistani academic Asma Barlas, former diplomat, prominent author, public figure, South African scholar, and political activist Farid Esack, and Laleh Bakhtiar, a US-raised student of Islam. Bakhtiar has translated the Quran in a way that places women and men in a complementary rather than subservient relationship. Her translations are highly controversial – Mohammad Ashraf, the Canadian president of the Islamic Society of North America, reportedly said that his organization's bookstore would not carry Bakhtiar's work.[128] Hogben explained that for writers like Bakhtiar, the situation is frustrating because it tends to reinforce the popular view that there is no such thing as Muslim women writers who are both moderate and observant and who care about women's rights. Citing Bakhtiar as one of the most prominent examples, Hogben says that: "There are actually a lot of these reform writers who are almost completely unknown ... These writers are blacklisted by the petrodollar countries and they do not stand a chance."[129] Meanwhile, people who stereotype Muslims as violent and inherently extreme are given free reign and access to public space to air their views and prejudices. Hogben said, "This makes me despondent. It allows them to be racist and discriminatory."

Hogben sees the climate facing young Muslims, both men and women, as distressing and dangerous. Immediately after the events of 9/11, American researchers and academics documented a 1,600 percent rise in attacks on Arab Americans and Muslims, including women and girls wearing hijabs.[130] In 2013, the Quebec government released its proposal for a "charter of values," a hyper-secularist policy aimed at barring anyone working in the public or the para-public sectors from wearing conspicuous religious symbols. Even though the proposal also prohibited large crucifixes, turbans, and kippas, Muslim women were quickly seen and understood to be the real targets of this initiative. Within weeks, an Ontario hospital began recruiting healthcare workers using an ad featuring a woman wearing a Muslim headscarf and a caption saying "We don't care what's on your head. We care what's in it." In October, a group of twenty-one women calling themselves the "Jeanettes" released an open letter criticizing Muslim women who choose to wear the headscarf. In the letter and in interviews, they described women who wear the headscarf as manipulated, deluded, and crazy.[131] Media reports began to surface about physical and verbal attacks on Muslim women wearing the headscarf in Quebec malls, streets, and in the metro. A a new civil liberties organization – Quebec Muslims for Rights and Freedoms – was created to respond to these developments.[132]

The phenomenon of seeing entire groups of people as foreign and dangerous is at the heart of what the Canadian human rights system is designed to address. Human rights commissions and tribunals have been working together collaboratively, alongside civil society actors, to support the progressive interpretation of human rights law in a way that is capable of meaningfully protecting people. The intersection of different rights and its impact on discrimination law is fundamental, not peripheral, to what human rights systems do. When the Ontario Human Rights

Commission spoke out against Steyn's anti-Muslim writing and encouraged a more responsible approach to public commentary, it was not doing indirectly what it could not do directly. The broad authority vested in the commission to address issues of social tension provided a legislative framework within which this type of social conflict can be responsibly addressed.

The collision between equality rights and other rights was also front and centre in *R. v. N.S.* before the Supreme Court of Canada. The complainant said that she had been sexually assaulted by two family members when she was a young girl.[133] She wanted to wear a niqab when she testified at the preliminary inquiry in 2008, but she was ordered to remove it so that the accused could see their accuser, thus protecting the common law right to face one's accuser in open court and test her credibility without a veil that might shield facial expressions.

The Court of Appeal held in 2010 that the preliminary inquiry judge had not adequately assessed the complainant's right to religious freedom. The accused's fundamental common-law right to a fair trial must be balanced against the complainant's religious rights. Although the Court of Appeal did not engage in the process of weighing the competing claims itself, it did decide that the complaint's religious claim should not have been dismissed out of hand.

The majority of the Supreme Court of Canada ruled that a witness who, for sincere religious reasons, wishes to wear the niqab while testifying should be accommodated where possible. However, she will be required to remove the niqab if two conditions are met. The first occurs when there is a serious risk to the fairness of the trial (the risk of an accused being convicted on the strength of testimony from a witness whose face is covered and whose credibility cannot be tested as easily), because reasonably available alternative measures will not prevent the risk. The second condition is that the salutary or positive effects of requiring the victim to remove the niqab outweigh the deleterious effects of doing so, including the effects on freedom of religion.[134] The court developed a four-part test that essentially required a case-by-case analysis. Abella J. wrote a dissenting opinion in the case, noted that forcing someone to remove the niqab could actually infringe gender equality by preventing rape victims or witnesses from Muslim communities from coming forward.[135] The Ontario Human Rights Commission decided to intervene in the case in order to uphold religious rights as an important consideration in the mediation of potentially conflicting rights and the justice system. The majority of the Court decided to remit the matter back to the preliminary inquiry judge to be decided in accordance with the Court's ruling. Once that happened, the preliminary judge promptly ruled that he had considered the religious aspects of the case and ordered the victim to remove her face covering. Her lawyer announced that he would be appealing. Nonetheless, the Supreme Court of Canada's decision reinforced once again the importance of not assuming that some rights, be they religious rights, free speech rights, or equality rights, automatically trump other rights, or that certain people, professions, or interest groups can exempt themselves from human rights law.

In June 2008, I was asked to speak at a conference of the Canadian Association of Statutory Human Rights Agencies (CASHRA). On the panel with me was Mel Sufrin, at the time executive secretary of the Ontario Press Council. He stated that media should be exempt from all speech limits in human rights laws. Although this may have been a slip of the tongue, it is essentially what most free speech absolutists believe. In 2013, the Supreme Court of Canada in *Whatcott* reminded us that no one should be able to claim an exemption from human rights law or the rule of law. Free speech absolutists and those who assume that equality rights must always cede to other rights (or those who believe the reverse proposition) have ignored the balanced nature of our laws and the built-in limits on the worst types of excesses. It has taken years to redress the balance. The *Whatcott* decision has been encouraging in another way. Although there are many people who continue to express legitimate concerns about the decision and its implications for freedom, most of the vicious rhetoric, threats, and verbal assaults that had been so prevalent and visible between 2007 and 2013 appear to have subsided after the ruling, leaving only the usual cranks to foment hate in their dark corners. There is a great deal to be said for the role of the Supreme Court of Canada in this country.

CONCLUSION

Human rights commissions have made important contributions not only by intervening in many of the cases discussed in this book but also by encouraging public education and developing policies on how to balance competing rights, freedoms, and social values.[136] They have a legitimate role to play in mediating different, and multiple, rights. Indeed, as discussed in the *Christian Horizons* case, such provisions can serve to protect freedoms. Removing the ability to consider other rights and freedoms from the ambit of human rights cases would restrict tribunals' ability to understand the broader context. If an equality rights claim infringes on other rights and freedoms, defences of those rights and freedoms must be considered. According to the Hon. Frank Iacobucci, a former justice of the Supreme Court of Canada, "The key to rights reconciliation, in my view, lies in a fundamental appreciation for *context*. Charter rights are not defined in the abstraction, but rather in the particular factual matrix in which they arise."[137] Preventing equality rights from engaging with other rights, liberties, and freedoms essentially removes a key to the puzzle by stripping out part of the factual matrix along with the legal issues that accompany it. It also makes it more difficult to help those who are more vulnerable to the unbalanced or distorted approach to human rights that characterizes so many rights conflicts.

A broad and progressive approach to human rights is a cornerstone of building a culture of human rights. Doing so effectively depends on substantive changes to the way our human rights system is structured and how it operates. Ideas for the way forward are addressed in the next and closing chapter.

6

Ideas for the Way Forward

Human rights lawyer Shelagh Day has said that the cumulative effect of the campaign against human rights institutions has been an inhospitable environment for human rights and a fertile ground for the dismantling of human rights protections. While there have always been critiques of the human rights system, Day observed, "there is something qualitatively different happening in its intensity in Canada. What I see is a shift. The values that human rights institutions embody are antithetical to the views of people who see attacks on commissions as a way of attacking a value system that they are seeking to discredit."[1]

Although some might argue that the supposed demise of the "pan-Canadian consensus" on tolerance and human rights is behind this shift, the survey data discussed in the introduction suggests that the Charter and multiculturalism continue to be highly valued by Canadians. All those I interviewed felt that there is a remarkable consensus in Canada that discrimination is wrong and should be illegal. I see no support for the thesis that Canadians today are less committed to human rights or tolerance, or to a vision of Canada that is less accepting of equality. Nonetheless, the criticisms have found their mark at the institutional and personal levels. Many of the criticisms, as well as the responses to them, have been the subject of this book. It is easy to criticize these institutions because so much of the public's impression of them has been fostered and fomented by those who are openly hostile to the human rights system and everything it stands for. It is also possible to assume that criticisms are biased and reject calls for change. Neither approach is very helpful, in my view. While those interviewed expressed concern about the future of the human rights system, most acknowledged that the status quo is not entirely acceptable either.

Governments should think long and hard before making fundamental changes to human rights laws. There are inevitable trade-offs in any major reform, as the highly divisive debate in Ontario about Bill 107 demonstrated. That said, this is a good time to consider our system as a whole and to engage in a national dialogue about reform. There is heightened awareness about human rights institutions and we now have the benefit of considerable experience with different configurations of first-generation human rights systems and reasonably good data on how well direct access is working in second-generation systems. The rapid evolution that has taken place in administrative law means that there are strong advocates in the practitioner community for more stringent application of the principles of independence, impartiality, and competence for human rights tribunals. Human rights commissions, for their part, are subject to their own standards of independence, impartiality, and competence. Human rights systems as a whole should be leading the push towards improved respect for these standards, not trailing in its wake. A serious attempt to develop uniform human rights laws across Canada is long overdue. According to the Uniform Law Conference of Canada, there has been no consideration of any initiative with regard to the harmonization of human rights statutes in Canada since 1961.[2]

The following sections offer ten ideas and twenty-two recommendations for improving human rights systems in Canada and their governance, while maintaining what is best in these unique Canadian institutions. Addressing shortcomings does not require diminishing the human rights involved or the institutions that protect them. These steps should assist in gaining (or regaining) the trust of Canadians. I do not pretend that the ideas that follow are original or comprehensive solutions. Indeed, they may be accused of what Alan Borovoy calls "disjointed incrementalism."[3] In my defence, I offer Borovoy's words: "I [have come] to view 'disjointed incrementalism' as a largely sensible approach to human affairs. When we adopt solutions incrementally or piecemeal, we are able to see and address more effectively the countervailing considerations. When we move disjointedly, we increase the likelihood that our priorities will respond to the needs of real people. Conversely, the more attached we are to theories and doctrines, the less sensitive we are likely to be to the needs of the people who will be affected by them."[4]

Given that we have fourteen distinct systems in Canada that evolved quite differently and over different periods of time, it seems that we have been moving disjointedly and incrementally in any event. Moreover, we will likely continue to do so. The most obvious and coherent solution – harmonizing our entire human rights system by creating a single national human rights law and institution – requires a big change that is unlikely to take place. It would require a constitutional amendment, or at least a full-scale and full-hearted attempt at cooperative federalism in which Quebec is unlikely to be an enthusiastic participant. As well, the diversity of our human rights systems suggests that a one-size-fits-all proposal is unlikely to work. While I am pessimistic about a grand scale solution, we should at least be focused on creating a governance environment that is more hospitable to human rights institutions and conducive to their effective functioning, independence, and accountability. Creating this environment is mainly the job of governments.

1 IMPROVING THE GOVERNANCE ENVIRONMENT

Human rights systems will never be in a position to do their work properly if governments do not step up and do theirs. The circle of responsibility for human rights systems starts with the state as the first line of protection for human rights under international law: the state is obliged to respect, protect, and fulfill human rights. Human rights laws and institutions help the state meet its responsibilities in this regard, but they cannot do their jobs alone.

All-Government Approach to Human Rights

Building a human rights culture does not happen solely or even mainly because there is a human rights system. A cursory glance at the long list of struggling human rights institutions in the world shows that the task of building a rights culture is made much more difficult, if not impossible, when governments delegate the job of protecting human rights to an independent agency and then consider themselves more or less absolved of further responsibility.

At the risk of stating the obvious, human rights-based approaches to governance should be the concern of all parts of government. Governments must make sure their own houses are in order and work to create an environment conducive to the development and protection of such rights. A healthy human rights culture is a shared enterprise, and governments cannot leave commissions and tribunals to deal with the task alone.

The allegations raised in the lawsuit brought by Department of Justice official Edgar Schmidt that the federal government has become much less concerned with respecting the Charter, and is now willing to put forward bills that do not clearly comply with it, hoping they will make it through a court challenge, have yet to be proved. However, my own experience with a federal government department in the early 1990s and with a central agency of the federal government a decade later suggests that there is something to the allegations. In some of the areas of government in which I have worked, public servants often see human rights and the Charter as constraints or obstacles to be circumvented, not as legal tools that empower citizens, let alone as legal tools that should be encouraged and developed. The result has been that medium-term policy development is rarely driven or even informed by human rights considerations.[5] The "5 percent solution" that Schmidt has alleged, whereby potential Charter violations are ignored by the federal government if there is even a 5 percent chance of winning in court, is completely unacceptable. When governments fail to uphold the rights they are legally bound to protect, the burden falls on others, including NGOs, legal associations, human rights defenders, and human rights commissions. Private citizens, non-profit organizations, and human rights systems end up having to challenge unfair or discriminatory laws and practices because the government has failed to do its job. More worrying, the funds for litigation to challenge discriminatory laws and other rights violations have been drying up at exactly the time that lack of respect for human rights and for the independence of watchdog institutions appears to have reached its peak, as discussed in chapter 4. The Court Challenges Program was cut in 2006 and civil society organizations dealing with immigration and refugee rights, Aboriginal rights, gender equality, pay equity, and HIV/AIDS have also seen their funding cut.

Tracking these developments and their impact is itself a challenge. Most people probably have little idea of whether a government's track record is good or not. Public and transparent reporting by government would help make such information more easily available. For instance, government departments and institutions should provide human rights impact reports. Disaggregated data (disaggregated by race, disability, ethnic origin, and other grounds) can be collected in a manner that is consistent with human rights law. Human rights treaty bodies have been requesting combined, disaggregated national data from Canada for years.

There are resources to help in the development of data in Canada, including a useful guide developed by the Ontario Human Rights Commission on how to collect data for human rights purposes.[6] In the area of law enforcement, the settlement with the Ottawa police in the *Aiken* racial profiling case discussed in chapter 4 is a good model that could be used by law enforcement officials elsewhere. There is no reason why similar efforts cannot be undertaken more systematically. National security and policing organizations, as well as their oversight bodies, should provide systematic and regular reports to the public about their compliance with human rights standards. These services are precisely the ones where human rights issues, especially those involving discrimination and racial profiling, can have the most serious consequences. In the introduction, I noted that few law enforcement and security organizations have any sort of systems to ensure accountability for their own human rights records. Most are not obliged to report to the public on human rights impacts.[7]

Human rights commissions can fulfill their roles by speaking out and ensuring that governments are living up to their legal responsibilities and preparing their own reports on government compliance and on effective ways of tracking human rights progress. In 2010, the Canadian Human Rights Commission developed a *Framework for Documenting Equality Rights* that provides information about how to report on equality rights using available policy-relevant data in Canada. Recently, the *Framework* has been used to generate a report on the equality rights of Aboriginal peoples.[8]

Recommendation 1: Government departments, agencies, and watchdog bodies should issue regular reports that allow Canadians to evaluate the extent to which Parliament and legislatures are building human rights objectives into their medium-term planning and are complying with the Charter and with international human rights obligations.

Recommendation 2: Human rights systems should track and report on the extent to which governments and independent agencies are complying with international and national human rights standards and reporting on their own human rights records.

Chapter 1 provided an overview of human rights systems and of the extent to which Canadians are not equal before the law in the areas of human rights protections, access to justice, and remedies. The uneven application of the law is not the fault of human rights systems. It is the direct responsibility of government. Assuring the consistency and coherence of laws and their application in human rights policy and practice is fundamental. In the absence of a national human rights commission, however, there is no obvious platform for such discussions. One obvious choice at the governmental level would be to make use of the federal Continuing Committee of Officials on Human Rights (CCOHR), which operates under the auspices of the Department of Canadian Heritage. Broader dialogue and interaction among jurisdictions and public officials would improve human rights systems in Canada. The CCOHR already brings together officials from federal, provincial, and territorial governments. At the moment, however, its activities are limited to international human rights issues and the implementation of human rights treaties in Canada. As well, its meetings are in camera and confidential – members of civil society organizations are not entitled to attend. Human rights commissions are not mentioned on the Canadian Heritage website and a Canadian Heritage staff member confirmed to me that there are currently no plans to include commissions as members of the CCOHR.[9] It is odd that this important exercise is located in the Department of Heritage and not Justice, given that the issues at stake are legal norms.

Human rights commissions should be involved in discussions about the domestic implementation of human rights instruments and about international reporting to treaty bodies. As well, the work of the CCOHR should extend to human rights and human rights systems in Canada, and should also address disparities in terms of human rights and access to justice. Human rights commission officials should have some permanent status at these meetings. The Department of Justice should be closely engaged in the process.

It is entirely appropriate that policy makers and public servants would want to meet in camera without the presence of arms-length institutions or members of civil society. However, this does not preclude the addition of separate sessions where human rights commissions could have a place at the table to provide input on compliance with international human rights obligations, as well as on the development of human rights systems at the domestic level across the country.

Recommendation 3: Heritage Canada should expand the Continuing Committee of Officials on Human Rights to include additional sessions where human rights commissions can attend as regular and active participants.

Recommendation 4: Heritage Canada should expand the mandate of the Continuing Committee of Officials on Human Rights to include work towards harmonizing and improving human rights legislation across Canada.

Professor Lucie Lamarche argues that the overwhelming focus on the Charter and on human rights litigation may have placed too heavy a burden on human rights systems and as a result, responsibility for human rights issues is not always seen as part of the mandate of other organizations: "There are other spaces where social mediation in its broad sense can take place, but these spaces are largely empty in Canada. I come from the perspective that sees law as a broader social phenomenon and not simply a set of individual disputes. If we look at things this way, people can work together to reach solutions outside the adversarial process of human rights commissions and tribunals. Section 15 [of the Charter] is not all there is."[10]

Even within the realm of individual disputes, there is more we can do to be creative and flexible. In Ontario, for instance, Bill 107 introduced an interesting reform that partially removed the human rights system's monopoly on human rights adjudication. Following the 2008 amendments to the Ontario system, section 46.1 of the Human Rights Code now allows Ontario courts to hear cases about human rights complaints under the Code if the plaintiff also pleads another recognized civil cause of action such as wrongful dismissal. Even though section 46.1 of the Code does not permit a lawsuit *solely* on human rights grounds, it opens the doors more widely, at least as far as the courts are concerned.[11]

While human rights systems are usually best placed to adjudicate matters dealing exclusively with equality rights complaints, not all human rights violations come in neat categories. Complex cases with multiple legal aspects can lead to considerable unfairness to litigants, who find themselves facing procedural motions to shift a dispute from one forum to another, resulting in a lack of certainty and predictability. The ability to file civil lawsuits about matters containing a human rights element would create an additional choice for litigants and allow the courts to deal with matters like unjust dismissal that are squarely within their bailiwick.

Recommendation 5: Canadian governments at all levels should consider permitting litigants to bring claims that contain a human rights element to the courts, provided that there is another civil cause of action. This should not detract from the ability to bring a human rights complaint to a human rights system.

When creating alternative avenues, it is important to avoid undermining the human rights system. One of the most significant areas of interaction between human rights systems and other parts of the justice system is labour relations and in this area, the pendulum may have swung too far, at least in Quebec. In Ontario, as in most other Canadian jurisdictions, there has been a push to ensure that labour relations systems are able to deal with human rights claims. However, according to the 2012 Pinto Report, unionized employees and employees in organizations with internal discrimination policies still have access to Ontario's Tribunal.[12] In Quebec, on the other hand, unionized employees have virtually no access to the human rights system at all. Human rights in Quebec have also been undermined by a steady stream of cases severely restricting access to the tribunal.

Recommendation 6: Unionized employees should have access to human rights systems and should be able to file complaints before these systems if their unions prove unable or unwilling to represent their members.

It is critical that we have empirical evidence about the extent to which – and how adequately – other decision-makers in Canada are actually addressing human rights issues. We do not have national research networks or institutes that focus on the work of human rights institutions, nor is Canada part of a regional network of commissions like those that exist in Africa, Europe, or Asia. Given the fact that Canada is a federation, it makes sense to have a more formal structure that can engage in standard-setting, international liaison, and advocacy on behalf of commissions. The Canadian Association of Statutory Human Rights Agencies (CASHRA) is an umbrella organization that fosters collaboration among its member commissions and provides a national voice on human rights on matters of common concern. There was a near-consensus among those interviewed that CASHRA does little beyond its annual conference and maintaining a website. Its annual business meeting, which is generally restricted to commission officials, was viewed with less than complete enthusiasm as an effective vehicle for future development.

None of this is surprising. CASHRA is an association of human rights commissions and has no significant institutional base or funding of its own, although there have been attempts in the past to establish a standing secretariat and make its funding base more stable, with a more formal operating structure.[13] It has intervened in legal cases from time to time, but this has been a relatively rare occurrence.[14]

Funding and support are the obvious problems. One possibility is that human rights commissions could provide funding to CASHRA based on a proportion of their budgets, although no one will greet this suggestion with joy. Provincial and national bar associations are another potential source of financial or in-kind support. Part of the funding should come from governments – federal, provincial, and territorial – in the interest of ensuring a more unified, coherent, and national approach to human rights and anti-discrimination law. This recommendation is not new and takes up ideas proposed by the Senate of Canada in 2001. It deserves more serious consideration in the future.[15] The main difference between the 2001 recommendation and this one flows from the fact that such an organization is not the responsibility of the federal government because it is an association of commissions and, ultimately, commissions should shoulder a portion of the responsibility. A renewed national organization would need resources for a secretariat to coordinate its work and to support research initiatives such as the harmonization of legislation, discussion of national policy issues, and a national strategic litigation capacity.[16] These initiatives would include spearheading specialized training and professional development programs for human rights officials and staff.

Recommendation 7: Commissions should initiate discussions to strengthen the institutional base of a national rights organization that would provide a Canada-wide national learning and research platform on human rights and human rights systems.

Recommendation 8: Commissions should initiate discussions with federal, provincial, and territorial governments, as well as bar associations, to develop and institute ways of better using and supporting the work of a national organization.

All of these ideas – better engagement with and by government, requiring governments to be accountable for and to report on human rights impacts, and creating national platforms for dialogue and reform – would widen the circle of engagement with human rights systems and alternatives to them, creating more avenues for social mediation of human rights. In the long term, such ideas can only serve to strengthen the human rights system by improving the governance environment.

2 IMPROVE ACCESS TO JUSTICE: PERMIT FULL OR PARTIAL DIRECT ACCESS TO TRIBUNALS

Human rights remedies must be accessible in order to be effective. The systems in Ontario and, to a lesser degree, in British Columbia show that direct access to a tribunal offers superior results in terms of access to justice (at least with respect to access to a neutral decision-maker) and reducing delays. The success of direct access to tribunals has also served to highlight how inaccessible many first-generation systems have become: as mentioned earlier, while about 80 percent of cases get through preliminary screening in Ontario's second-generation system to reach its tribunal, only about 5 percent ever make it past the Quebec Commission to get to the Quebec Human Rights Tribunal. Such disparities are troubling and do not meet international standards in terms of access to a tribunal. The right to a hearing, even if it is a summary hearing, is clear in Ontario. It barely exists in Quebec. The rest of the country is scattered in between these two extremes.

Delays are closely connected to access to justice. Delays in first-generation systems are a serious problem. I was involved in a case at the time of writing this book that illustrates the point. In late 2011, a complaint was filed against a client before one of the larger human rights commissions. The client received notice of the complaint more than four months later. The client worked around the clock to provide the commission with a formal and detailed response within eight weeks. A *year* later, the investigator had not interviewed a single representative or witness on the respondent's side. No one from the commission had contacted the respondent at all, except to reply to a letter inquiring about the status of the matter. Statistics discussed elsewhere in this book show that delays of two or more years are common for full investigations and this does not count the two years or more it takes to get a decision from a tribunal. This story is typical of the cases I saw at the Ontario Commission in the pre-Bill 107 years and many that I have seen in Quebec. If the commission does refer the matter to a tribunal, the whole process, such as it was, starts all over again. Complainants are often afraid to raise concerns about basic service standards for fear their file will be put on the back burner, and respondents are afraid that an otherwise dormant file will be activated. Both sides worry that the investigating officer will become antagonistic if concerns are raised about bias, delay, or lack of professionalism in the handling of files.

The Supreme Court of Canada in *Blencoe* held that delays alone are not enough to render a process unconstitutional for lack of administrative fairness,[17] but even delays that fall short of unconstitutionality can wreak havoc. These delays and the access to justice considerations discussed elsewhere make it difficult to argue for first-generation human rights commissions in their present form. As noted in chapter 4, regulators and legislatures should be very concerned about systems where it routinely takes more than two and up to five years or more for cases to be resolved before a tribunal. Almost every interviewee for this book, even the most pro-commission, was deeply concerned about delays and backlogs in first generation systems.

Many who work in first-generation commissions will no doubt feel that some of these comments are unfair and unwarranted. However, delays, backlogs, and bottlenecks have become intractable problems and have eroded trust in commissions and tribunals.

The federal report *Promoting Equality: A New Vision*, published by the Canadian Human Rights Act Review Panel in 2000, and discussed in chapter 2, contained more than 160 recommendations on virtually every aspect of the Canadian Human Rights Act. While certain of its recommendations may now be somewhat dated, and others have been implemented, most of its central recommendations have not been put in place. One of them was direct access to a tribunal. The report recommended: "*Claims would be filed directly with the Tribunal.* This process would have a pre-hearing process to ensure that cases without merit would not proceed to a full hearing before the Tribunal. The Tribunal would ensure through its rules and orders that the parties to the case were fully informed of the issues and the evidence of the other side before proceeding to a full hearing. Legal assistance would be provided to ensure that claimants and impecunious respondents had the help needed to present their case."[18] Eliminating or moderating first-generation system commissions' "monopoly" over screening human rights cases would lighten commission caseloads and offer litigants more options. This would affect eleven of the twelve commissions in Canada (recalling that the Ontario Commission no longer receives complaints).

It is not necessary to completely remove the gatekeeping function from commissions in order to achieve better results. A more moderate proposal was implemented in Yukon in 2010. The Yukon Human Rights Commission describes it in the following terms:

[The Yukon human rights] Commission has the ability to refer some complaints directly to a hearing before a Board of Adjudication without an investigation in certain cases. Examples of cases where the Commission may do this are:

- where a speedy resolution is needed because of urgent circumstances; or
- where there is agreement on the facts but not on how the law applies to the facts; or
- where there are no witnesses to the alleged discrimination other than the complainant and respondent who do not agree on what happened.[19]

A third option is a modified version of what happens, or should be happening, in Quebec, where parties can go to the tribunal on their own if the commission declines to represent them. This procedure has been severely restricted by case law,[20] but widening the gateway to the tribunal would allow a complainant to proceed in cases where the commission decides not to. Complainants and respondents should not have to go through the type of procedural wrangling that occurred in the *Gallardo* case (discussed in chapter 3), where the complainant ended up spending years and resources to fight a school board and a government that were arguing for a very limited interpretation of the tribunal's jurisdiction.[21] Implicit in this recommendation is the idea that human rights commissions should have some ability to determine where they are going to invest their advocacy resources.

The Canadian Human Rights Commission's decision to allow complainants to go forward alone before the tribunal were constrained by the Supreme Court of Canada's *Mowat* decision.[22] The case nonetheless demonstrated that commissions are looking for ways to invest resources in strategic and important cases and to withdraw from others. The requirement that commissions appear in all cases before a tribunal is becoming increasingly untenable.

At the same time, it is important to provide legal assistance to complainants. In Quebec, legislation specifically prohibits people from getting legal aid in human rights cases because the commission, as a public body, is supposed to assume this role in the case if it goes to tribunal. In other words, Quebec sees the commission as representing the complainant and providing support and assistance, thus obviating the need for additional legal support and resources.[23] The Quebec policy position compares unfavourably to that in Ontario, both before and after the reforms, where claimants have some access to community clinics and legal aid.²⁴ Even in British Columbia, where there is no commission, legal clinic services are available to provide support to claimants.

Since the Ontario reform, the Human Rights Legal Support Centre in Ontario has provided legal support for claimants (not respondents or the public interest) at all stages. The services are unbundled so that different levels of support are available at different stages. For example, a person may ask for legal information about how to file a complaint, or may require assistance only for the mediation part of the process. In other cases, the HRLSC will offer a full range of services, up to and including representation before the tribunal. The second-generation system in Ontario appears to offer an acceptable or at least improved way of ensuring screening, while maximizing the right to a hearing.

All of these arrangements envisage some degree of direct access to a specialized tribunal. Tribunals offer important advantages over courts and, while there have been valid criticisms of tribunals for reasons set out in this book, guarantees of judicial independence as well as measures to ensure impartiality and competence of appointments would address most if not all of these legitimate concerns. Tribunals offer expertise and faster decision-making in a forum that is less formal, less expensive, and more accessible than the courts. As noted in chapter 4, tribunals also have the advantage of developing the substantive law faster than the courts. For these reasons, I believe the complete elimination of specialized tribunals would be a mistake. The Canadian judicial system has spent almost thirty years trying to divert cases out of courts and into alternative dispute resolution. The executive branch has been creating administrative tribunals to deal with specialized legal issues for much longer than that. Eliminating these resources would mean an additional 7,000 cases a year would have to be shunted to crowded court systems and it is difficult to believe that this would – or should be – tried. Anecdotal evidence from interviewees suggests that second-generation systems have an additional benefit, namely the rapid development of a more sophisticated, engaged, and knowledgeable group of human rights lawyers who act for both claimants and respondents, which has raised the quality of the overall tribunal process.

Arguments by critics who favour courts over human rights systems have been buttressed by claims that respondents in human rights systems end up having to pay for lawyers whereas claimants do not. This argument leads to the conclusion that the system as it is now structured is heavily stacked against respondents and that a move into the courts would improve matters. Claimants would at least be forced to pay for their own lawyers.

These arguments are misleading and the reality is far more complex. Litigation before the courts is prohibitively expensive, more so than before administrative tribunals, for both parties. The impression that all claimants end up getting support from commissions is untrue. Only a small number of cases are actually heard on their merits before a tribunal, and an even smaller number receives formal legal support at the tribunal. As discussed in chapter 4, only 11 percent of claimants are represented by counsel provided by the Human Rights Legal Support Centre. The rest pay for their own lawyers or have no representation at the tribunal. As the Pinto Report noted, the 11 percent figure number is too low, not too high.

The courts do not perform better than the human rights system and certainly no better than second-generation systems. Timing varies across the country, but in Toronto, one of the busiest judicial districts in the country, one study showed that two-year targets, from the time a case is scheduled for trial to the hearing, are considered realistic for civil courts.[25] Since the process of getting a case set down for trial can take several months, this would mean a total (average) delay, from filing a claim to a decision, of two-and-a-half to three years. It is here that the direct access system has scored its most decisive victory: second-generation jurisdictions like Ontario and BC have delays of only about one year for the entire process. High costs and long delays are important arguments against a full-scale transfer of human rights claims to the courts, especially in second-generation systems with no commission to screen cases out.

Recommendation 9: Governments that have first-generation systems should amend human rights laws to introduce some measure of direct access to tribunals. Direct access should be accompanied by public support for complainants.

3 KEEP COMMISSIONS: HUMAN RIGHTS SYSTEMS SHOULD INCLUDE AT LEAST A COMMISSION AND A TRIBUNAL

Since Saskatchewan only recently abolished its specialized tribunal, its system is too new to allow any assessment of the effectiveness of a system with no tribunal. However, according to Ken Norman, the current structure raises concerns about how the legislative changes will affect claimants, respondents, and access to justice:

> Legislative amendments give the Chief Commissioner the last word as to who would get their "day in court" and make his discretion complete. He need only declare, "having regard to all the circumstances of the complaint, a hearing of the complaint is not warranted." Complainants whose cases are dismissed by the Chief Commissioner have no avenue of redress except to apply for judicial review by the courts at their own expense. Those 25 static years under the *Saskatchewan Bill of Rights* tell us how that will go!
>   This seems to signal that leadership in human rights enforcement seems to have moved from the Commission, a deliberative body, to the office of the Chief Commissioner alone.[26]

The reasons behind Saskatchewan's decision to centralize decision-making and increase the chief commissioner's discretion are clear: the already crowded and expensive courts now receive cases directly from the commission, which must have a strong "screen" with few avenues for appeal to make sure that the courts are not overwhelmed. As argued in chapter 4, human rights tribunals in Canada have inadequate structural guarantees of independence, impartiality, and competence. In this respect, the concerns of David Arnot and the government about the previous tribunal were fair. If adequate guarantees of structural and judicial independence, impartiality, and competence were put in place, however, the need to push cases into the courts would disappear.

Specialized administrative decision-makers have an advantage over courts, which approach remedies in a way that does not always lend itself to the systemic solutions that human rights tribunals have used for years. The attempt by the Supreme Court of Canada to restrict the scope of systemic remedies in the *Moore* case appears to have been at least in part an effort to keep complainants at the centre of claims.[27] The courts tend to bring a traditional litigation lens to human rights cases. It is natural that those trained in the courtroom will see remedies as centering on the dispute between the parties, rather than on eradicating discrimination or dealing with broader systemic or social issues. It is important to remember, though, that human rights systems are required not only to compensate claimants but also to eradicate discrimination.[28] Courts do not take it upon themselves to assume the broader responsibility for addressing underlying systemic causes. Given the specific legislative mandates of tribunals and commissions, and their position as part of the executive branch, they have, or should have, more room to work with parties to move towards more systemic solutions. Tribunals have a long history of providing a mixed compensatory and public-interest approach to human rights adjudication. In many respects, systemic approaches offered by human rights systems are more efficient. That is because most tribunals can make a wide range of orders to remedy almost any aspect of a human rights complaint. All these factors point towards rather than away from specialized human rights tribunals.

Recommendation 10: The Saskatchewan government should undertake a study of the Saskatchewan human rights system to determine the impact of the loss of a specialized human rights tribunal on the level of access to justice, the types of remedies offered, and the length of delays as compared to other systems in Canada.

Human rights commissions are also critical components of the human rights system and have unique responsibilities and expertise. As statutory bodies with a wide range of regulatory functions, they assist the state in fulfilling its obligations under international human rights law. They develop policy, speak out on human rights issues, and can initiate or intervene in systemic and strategic cases. Commissions offer a legal framework that promotes a culture of human rights through all these functions. Their independent status and social mission are different from but complementary to the role of tribunals.

From a programmatic and regulatory perspective, tribunals lack the mandate to promote (as distinct from protecting) human rights. Because of their neutrality as decision-makers, tribunals are limited in their ability to take proactive public steps to craft or put forward new policy positions on legislative change or initiate litigation. NGOs cannot replace commissions because they are not legally accountable to the state for the state's human rights responsibilities. Nor should governments assume these functions directly: the importance of what commissions do is underpinned by their institutional independence. When British Columbia decided to take the educational and promotional responsibilities that had been the responsibility of the commission and fold them into a government department, the capacity to speak out independently of government disappeared.

British Columbia and Nunavut have no commission. As such, neither jurisdiction has a public institution with a statutory mandate to both promote and protect rights. There has been a recent recommendation to establish a commission in Nunavut, partly because of evidence showing the difficulty of building a human rights culture in a jurisdiction where only a tribunal exists.[29] In British Columbia, calls for the reestablishment of a commission have gone unheeded to date.

Recommendation 11: The legislatures of British Columbia and Nunavut should establish independent human rights commissions that can undertake research, public education, and systemic litigation.

4 THE COURAGE AND CAPACITY TO SPEAK OUT: ADDRESSING THE FULL RANGE OF HUMAN RIGHTS

Commissions should have a broad mandate to protect *and* promote human rights. The Paris Principles say that a human rights institution should have the general authority to take up "any situation of violation of human rights," as well as to consider "any questions falling within its competence."[30] In Canada, commissions do not have a wide mandate on the protection side of their work: they do not have the general authority to "take up any situation of violation of human rights" because they are restricted to dealing mainly with one type of rights, namely equality rights in the context of discrimination complaints.

However, on the promotional side of their work, human rights systems should have a clear, broad, and unrestricted mandate. They should be able to speak, write, and report on the full range of human rights. They should be able to provide advice and information to government with regard to any aspect of policy or the legislative agenda. On the promotional side of their work, therefore, human rights commissions should not be restricted, or see themselves as being restricted, to equality rights.

Some readers might see this as a major expansion of mandate. It isn't. The Canadian Human Rights Act and Ontario's Human Rights Code both contain language that allows their respective commissions to address or inquire into human rights issues generally.[31] Commissions that have this power already should use it.

Recommendation 12: Governments should modify human rights statutes, as appropriate, to widen their promotional mandates and to confer or clarify the role of commissions to speak out about any human rights issue across the full range of human rights.

5 STRENGTHEN THE INTERNATIONAL CONNECTION: RECOGNIZE AND ENCOURAGE THE ROLE PLAYED BY HUMAN RIGHTS COMMISSIONS IN THE INTERNATIONAL HUMAN RIGHTS SYSTEM

The basic mandate of human rights systems is domestic and is carried out within each system's borders. Human rights and the systems that implement them, however, are matters of both national and international concern. The executive branch of government is responsible for ratifying international human rights treaties in Canada. The CCOHR brings together federal officials and their provincial and territorial counterparts to discuss the implementation of international human rights obligations but, because these meetings take place behind closed doors, very few people are aware of how international human rights standards are incorporated into Canadian law, let alone the implications for Canadian human rights systems. A more open process would foster improved awareness of human rights and of the work that human rights commissions do.

Human rights commissions today play a role in the international human rights system that they did not have even a decade ago. The Canadian Human Rights Commission (CHRC) is the only human rights institution in the country with national reach and it is therefore designated by the International Coordinating Committee of National Institutions for the Promotion and Protection of Human Rights (ICC) as Canada's "national human rights institution." The CHRC has developed considerable expertise and experience in the international human rights system. Human rights commissions across Canada have also contributed to the development of national and regional systems in countries as diverse as India, Indonesia, Rwanda, Mauritania, Uganda, Tajikistan, Nepal, and many others, by accepting staff from other countries in international exchanges and internships, and by sending Canadians to help establish and develop institutions in other countries.[32]

National human rights institutions that have "A" status (that is, that are fully compliant with the Paris Principles) have certain prerogatives: they are entitled to make oral statements, submit documents, and have separate seating in all sessions of the UN Human Rights Council.[33] They can also participate in the Universal Periodic Review process and other international forums, treaty bodies, and mechanisms to provide alternative or complementary information to that contained in reports submitted to the UN by their countries.[34] Canada, as an A status country, should take advantage of these opportunities on a regular basis and these interventions should be recognized as a standard part of its work.

At home, human rights commissions should actively advocate for the ratification of international human rights treaties. The ICC has observed that advocacy for the implementation of international standards is fundamental to the work of human rights institutions.[35] The federal commission was actively involved in developing international standards under the Paris Principles, and supports the ICC in Geneva. The Quebec and Ontario Commissions also work with human rights officials from other countries and use international standards in the development of their policy positions.

CASHRA has undertaken positive and forward-looking initiatives with regard to public policy issues of national concern that have international dimensions. One recent example is the motion passed by CASHRA members in March 2013 urging the government of Canada to work with Aboriginal peoples' organizations to develop a national action plan, especially in light of the international calls to establish a commission on missing and murdered women: "The plan would focus urgent attention on addressing and preventing the root causes of violence against Aboriginal women and girls, including poverty and systemic discrimination. It further calls on the Government to establish an independent and inclusive inquiry into missing and murdered Aboriginal women and girls in Canada."[36]

In recent years, various UN human rights instruments have included a provision that calls on ratifying countries to designate "national mechanisms" that are given the responsibility to support and implement the rights contained in the instrument. Human rights commissions are natural candidates to take up these functions and responsibilities, for example under the Convention on the Rights of Persons with Disabilities.[37] Given the significant amount of work that has to be done to implement this convention in Canada, making clear that commissions should be involved is a priority.

A national human rights organization could serve as a voice for commissions on these and other matters of national importance. It could co-ordinate reports from human rights commissions to international treaty bodies and to the Universal Periodic Review process. It could also see that responsibility for international liaison is shared among all commissions in Canada, instead of the current practice, where most of the international activity takes place mainly in the Canadian Commission and, to a lesser extent, the Ontario and Quebec Commissions.

International work is not and should not be the focus of what commissions in Canada do – their main focus is national and domestic. Most of the work involved in implementing international human rights norms in the domestic sphere can take place in Canada and does not have to involve extensive travel outside the country. The work of human rights commissions is, however, intimately connected to the international human rights system. Commissions are part of a global human rights community. By contributing to that community, they enrich their work at home and support human rights in other countries. International liaison helps to develop the law, provide solidarity between institutions, and promote good practices. It also helps the Canadian public better understand the close connection between the international human rights system and domestic protection of rights. Canadian support for the international human rights system and for the international community of human rights institutions should be acknowledged and encouraged.

Recommendation 13: Human rights commissions in Canada should work together to support international human rights processes, including the ICC and the Universal Periodic Review process.

Recommendation 14: Governments should amend human rights legislation to include specific authority to work with international human rights networks and the international human rights system.

6 HARMONIZE HUMAN RIGHTS: DEVELOP A UNIFORM HUMAN RIGHTS CODE IN CANADA

Section 15 of the Canadian Charter of Rights and Freedoms guarantees equality before the law, but equality are not uniform across Canada, either on paper or in application. Examples discussed earlier include different levels of protection for family status and caregiving responsibilities, social condition and social origin, political views and opinion, religious freedoms, gender expression and gender identity, and language rights, to name a few. As well, people have disparate levels of access to decision-makers and are entitled to very different remedies that have varying financial implications for both claimants and respondents. New and emerging rights receive inconsistent protections, and the intersection between equality, hate speech, and religion remains contentious.

As well, several jurisdictions, including the federal human rights system, have limited or no ability to award costs (tribunals or courts can order the payment of legal costs incurred by one or another party, based on a fixed tariff, usually to the winning party). Manitoba, Nova Scotia, Nunavut, and Saskatchewan, however, allow certain costs to be awarded as a disincentive to improper behaviour.[38] In both Alberta and Newfoundland and Labrador, decision-makers have full authority to award costs. The issue of costs is connected to access to justice and to the nature and extent of awards for damages. The prospect that significant costs may be awarded operates as a disincentive to file complaints because of the financial risk. Costs awards that penalize bad behaviour have similar policy objectives as punitive and exemplary damages. We have no national research study on the comparative role and effectiveness of costs and damages in Canada in human rights systems, and this topic would be an important part of a national effort to harmonize the law and improve consistency and predictability.

The law also needs to be much clearer about SLAPP suits and the relationship between human rights systems and the civil justice system in matters of retaliatory lawsuits. The protections provided by Quebec's system are a good model, not only for the victims of such lawsuits but also to protect free expression and encourage participation in public debates. Since activists and human rights defenders can use human rights complaints to highlight social issues and address injustice, complainants are especially vulnerable to retaliatory lawsuits of this type. At the same time, respondents who have legitimate concerns about libel and defamation need a clear legislative signal that their rights will be preserved and they will be protected from reprisal complaints.

At present there is no effective national mechanism to harmonize the substantive, remedial, or procedural aspects of the fourteen human rights systems in Canada. This is not an ideal state of affairs. The problem is how to proceed. There is little appetite for constitutional amendment on any issue in Canada, let alone on human rights systems. The difficulty, as has been amply demonstrated in the past, is that individual jurisdictions tend to hold onto their particularities and specificities. Provinces with more progressive human rights laws would be understandably concerned that attempts at harmonization would lead to rights rollbacks. Ontario is an example of a reform that happened for the right reasons, but changes to the BC, Saskatchewan, and federal systems appear to point the other way. Provinces with less progressive laws may be reluctant to enact legislation for which they feel their populations are not yet ready. In addition, Quebec's participation in national conversations about uniform legislation is not likely to involve a full and constructive engagement. However, nothing prevents governments from working with commissions in Canada to develop common approaches, and a research-based initiative would provide the groundwork. Most Canadian human rights law requires a refresh if not a reset. A national project would be a good start.

Recommendation 15: Human rights commissions, law reform bodies, academics, and the Uniform Law Conference of Canada should work cooperatively towards the development of a uniform model of human rights law that:

- reflects the Canadian Charter of Rights and Freedoms and our international commitments;
- ensures that Canadians are equal before the law;
- guarantees human rights protections based on the highest standards of protection, access to justice, and fair and appropriate remedies;
- incorporates good practices and recommendations from prior reports on human rights systems in Canada;
- ensures that commissions and tribunals have statutory guarantees of institutional independence, impartiality, and competence that are consistent with international standards, including the Paris Principles (for commissions) and the ICCPR (for tribunals), as well as with stringent standards of judicial independence for tribunals.

7 PROVIDE INFORMATION AND SUPPORT FOR RESPONDENTS

Although it is a myth that commissions always represent complainants, there is a popular perception to that effect.[39] Second-generation systems like Ontario's are more claimant-oriented because the state provides specific, albeit limited, resources for claimants. Both Shelagh Day and Michael Gottheil acknowledged that the issue of fairness to respondents is more acute in these direct-access jurisdictions. Prior to the adoption of Bill 107 in 2006, the Ontario Human Rights Commission provided advice and information to the public at large, which, of course, included respondents. During the period I was at the commission, we published a specialized and detailed guide for respondents on navigating the human rights process and dedicated another publication to human rights at work, recognizing the critical importance of employment in the human rights context in Canada from the perspective of both complainants and respondents. The call centre fielded requests from respondents inquiring about their rights. Respondents also routinely sought support and advice from the policy branch where I worked, asking for direction and advice about the commission's position on specific parts of the Ontario Human Rights Code.

Although the Ontario Commission continues to have a public education and awareness function, it no longer provides advice tailored to individual respondents. Its call centre has been closed. The practical result is that respondents have fewer information sources than they did before. Not only is Ontario's Human Rights Legal Support Centre solely for claimants, its legal mandate precludes it from advising respondents.

There are affordable options available to address this issue. One option is to create dedicated advisory services similar to those offered by the Office of the Employer Advisor in Ontario, which deals with workplace safety and provides confidential and free services for employers. If human rights compliance is a public policy priority, then a public investment in respondents should be a worthwhile expenditure.

Another possibility in the case of direct access jurisdictions, according to the Pinto Report in its 2012 review of the Ontario system, is to re-establish a call centre in commissions. Such a call centre could be smaller than its first-generation counterpart, mainly because it would not be dealing with calls from claimants about filing complaints.[40] A public information line would have the added benefit of allowing commissions to keep their finger on the pulse of what is happening on a day-to-day basis even though they are not receiving complaints directly.

Recommendation 16: All human rights systems in Canada should provide state-funded information and advisory services for respondents as well as complainants.

8 ENSURE COMPETENT, INDEPENDENT, AND IMPARTIAL TRIBUNALS: ADOPT STANDARDS OF JUDICIAL INDEPENDENCE THAT REFLECT THE INTERNATIONAL STANDARD FOR COMPETENT, INDEPENDENT, AND IMPARTIAL TRIBUNALS

International human rights law guarantees a "competent, independent and impartial" tribunal under Article 14 of the ICCPR.[41] In practical terms, this means that tribunals must be free from bias or the appearance of bias, as well as from internal collusion and external manipulation.[42]

In 2007, the UN Human Rights Committee issued a General Comment that the standard of a "competent, independent and impartial tribunal" apples to administrative proceedings, meaning that the standard applies to administrative tribunals as well as courts.[43] Similar standards have been upheld in the European context.[44]

In comparison to the ICCPR, Canada's administrative law standard for independence is less rigorous, conferring only a "sort-of-quasi-right to institutional independence."[45] Canadian courts have decided that the independence of adjudicative decision-makers is based in the common law, meaning that governments can override independence simply by legislation.[46] As I argue in chapter 4, human rights laws should be consistent with the higher standard of competence, independence, and impartiality in international law. Emerging standards of judicial independence for administrative tribunals are being advocated by experts in Canadian administrative law and there are powerful reasons to move towards these higher standards.

The argument for the importance of ensuring that Canadian administrative law measures up to international standards is explained in a legal article by Gerald Heckman and Lorne Sossin:

> [O]ur claim regarding the dissonance between international norms and Canadian administrative law is important for at least three reasons. First, insofar as the federal executive, by ratifying international human conventions, has made an international commitment on behalf of the Canadian state that decision-making in Canada would respect the procedural standards expressed in these conventions, concern is appropriate where Canada is failing to honor its commitment ... if the government of Canada has undertaken such a commitment, it should be seen as a legal obligation[.]
>
> Second, international human rights norms, because they are forged from a broad consensus among disparate nations (including, of course, Canada in some instances), provide an important measuring rod with which to assess the scope and content of procedural safeguards in Canadian administrative law[.]
>
> Third and finally ... as the Supreme Court observed in *Suresh v. Canada (Minister of Citizenship and Immigration)*, both the common law of procedural fairness rules and international human rights

norms form part of the principles of fundamental justice for the purposes of the *Charter*.[47]

Human rights tribunals make decisions about important rights and interests. In light of this and the increasingly functional approach taken by the courts concerning the degree of deference to which human rights tribunals are entitled, the legal context demands a high degree of independence. Again, this is consistent with Article 14 of the ICCPR. I am not aware of any court decisions in Canada that have applied this international standard to human rights tribunals. However, the Quebec Charter and the 1960 Canadian Bill of Rights do provide procedural guarantees: for example, section 2(e) of the Canadian Bill of Rights provides that no law of Canada shall be construed or applied to "deprive a person of the right to a fair hearing in accordance with the principles of fundamental justice for the determination of his rights and obligations." This right exists for any type of hearing, whether before a tribunal or a court. Similar provisions should be adopted in other jurisdictions.

Recommendation 17: Where such a right is lacking, governments in Canada should enact the right to a human rights tribunal that is independent, impartial, and competent, in accordance with the principles of fundamental justice.

9 HUMAN RIGHTS COMMISSIONS: INDEPENDENCE AND ACCOUNTABILITY

Human rights commissions are not adjudicative decision-makers like tribunals. While the criteria for their independence bear some similarity to those discussed in relation to tribunals, there are differences that are related to their regulatory nature, principles of administrative law, and the Paris Principles.

Structural Independence

Human rights statutes should state clearly that commissions are autonomous and independent, while subject to government accountability standards for public administration such as those found in treasury board or management board guidelines. If human rights commissions are integrated into government ministries or departments or have to report to such ministries or departments about anything other than administrative and financial matters, they are not independent, at least not in the sense of the Paris Principles. National Human Rights Institutions (NHRIS) should be free to undertake work on any human rights issue that is within their area of competence.

Commission staff should report and be accountable to the chief commissioner, although day-to-day responsibilities may be delegated to an executive director or equivalent position. There should be no avenue to appoint or dismiss senior staff except through a decision of the chief commissioner or his/her delegate. The Alberta Human Rights Commission, for example, has only limited control over the hiring of its own director and its employees. Its internal bylaws have no effect unless the minister has approved them.[48] On the other side of the ledger is the Manitoba Human Rights Code, which provides that the Manitoba Human Rights Commission is an "independent agency" with full authority to exercise its responsibilities. Quebec's commission also has a high degree of independence: its president is named by the legislature and its staff are not part of the public service. These are excellent practices, but they are also exceptional.

One obvious way to ensure structural independence is to have commissions report directly to legislatures. This ensures public accountability. At the same time, a minister (usually the minister of Justice or the attorney general, depending on the jurisdiction) retains overall responsibility for human rights legislation and serves as an advocate for the institution within government.[49] According to the Sheldon Chumir Foundation, "to best protect the independence of a human rights commission and minimize the possibility of political interference in its work, a human rights commission should report directly to the legislative assembly, as do the following commissions: the Canadian Human Rights Commission (reporting to Parliament) and the Yukon and Nunavut territorial human rights commissions (reporting to their respective territorial assemblies)."[50] In the same report, the foundation recommended that the Alberta Human Rights Commission report through the chief commissioner directly to the Legislative Assembly and that the chief commissioner be treated as an officer of the Legislative Assembly.

Recommendation 18: Governments should amend human rights legislation to include a statement that human rights commissions are independent institutions, and to provide that human rights commissions report directly to the legislature in jurisdictions where the statutes are silent or inconsistent with these recommendations.

Administrative Independence and Accountability

Formal, structural independence is important but, as discussed in chapters 1 and 4, there are many ways to exert pressure on institutions. Excessive focus on formal processes can obscure the "behind closed doors" operational issues: "[Many] Canadians will have their rights and interests adjudicated without the guarantee that the adjudicating body is independent and impartial. Additionally, even where procedural protections are in force, the analysis tends to focus on judiciary-oriented concerns of financial independence and security of tenure rather than more executive-oriented concerns about political interference from supervising ministries and the partisan political staff of the government of the day."[51]

Recommendation 19: Internal reporting arrangements, commission bylaws, memoranda of understanding, and other tools used to structure the day-to-day workings of commissions and their relationship to government must be predicated on the principles of institutional independence in terms of commissions' human rights work.

Appointment, Renewal, and Dismissal of Commissioners

The Paris Principles require that human rights institutions respect the principles of pluralism. Commissioners should reflect the diversity of the society that they represent. Men and women should be equitably represented and efforts should be made to reach out to underrepresented communities. As well, legislatures and not the executive branch should name heads of commissions.

The ICC sets out criteria to ensure a transparent process of appointments that support pluralism. The criteria include:

• Wide consultation throughout the selection and appointment process.
• Advertising vacancies broadly.
• Maximizing the number of potential candidates from a wide range of societal groups.[52]

More open and transparent processes take nominations outside the sole purview of the executive branch and engage the legislature and the public as part of the democratic process.[53]

Criteria for experience, qualifications, and personal integrity are as important for appointees to human rights commissions as they are for tribunals, but they involve some different considerations since appointees are not adjudicators. Both Keith Norton and Mark Freiman expressed concerns about lack of qualifications and the partisan nature of appointments to commissions. According to Freiman, "the consequences can be severe and I think this is actually quite a cynical game where governments want to be seen to be putting community leaders into place. This has been a problem."[54] Norton agreed. He was careful to say that most commissioners with whom he has worked were competent and capable people, but this was despite the process and not because of it. The process, Norton said, does not "lend itself to competent or qualified appointments or to appointments that inspire public confidence."[55]

The responsibility for these problems does not lie with commissions or tribunals. It lies with legislatures that have not brought their laws up to date with contemporary demands and expectations for positions of this nature or stature. Even laws that do contain criteria could be improved: the Ontario Human Rights Code states that commissioners must have "knowledge, experience or training." Surely these should not be alternative requirements.

There have been public concerns about which qualifications are necessary, as well as the extent or need for legal training. These issues can be addressed in part by looking at the history of commissions and what commissioners are supposed to do. Commissioners are not judges. As has been pointed out several times in this book, they do not engage in judicial decision-making. They are supposed to be independent from the public service and serve as community peers or representatives. They approve policies, make public statements, and speak out on matters of concern. None of this requires legal training. I would make an exception for those commissioners who make decisions that effectively put an end to the rights of parties in the context of first-generation commissions. I have always thought it problematic that non-lawyers can or should make decisions to dismiss cases, not because of professional chauvinism but rather because community representatives who do not have a legal background lack the requisite training to analyse and weigh evidence and work with constitutional, administrative, or human rights law. Non-lawyers will of course argue that commission meetings are attended by staff lawyers who advise commissioners on the best course of action.

Having seen the process in action over many years, I have to say I am not comforted by this fact, for the simple reason that the staff lawyers end up running the show unless the commissioners are exceptionally astute and experienced or are themselves lawyers. Second-generation systems with full or modified direct access can avoid some or all of these problems. For first generation systems, it should be a matter of law for a prescribed sub-set of commissioners to have legal training.

Most jurisdictions in Canada have a statutory term for chief commissioners and/or the heads of tribunals that is in the range of three to five years. Canadian and Quebec laws permit the appointment of a chief commissioner or president for up to seven years and ten years, respectively. The Quebec legislation provides that the term of the initial appointment cannot be reduced afterwards, a good control that offers better tenure for an incumbent. In my view, anything under three years, but preferably five years, strains the appointee's independence and autonomy.[56]

Because commissions are frequently involved in policy decisions and public statements or human rights complaints that involve government, they should be shielded from retaliation. Human rights laws should specify, in detail, the circumstances under which a member may be dismissed and should be limited to wrongdoing of a serious nature or a member's proven incapacity. The general observations of the ICC set out principles in this regard:

- Dismissal or forced resignation of any member may result in a special review of the accreditation status of the national human rights institution.
- Dismissal should be made in strict conformity with all the substantive and procedural requirements as prescribed by law.
- Dismissal should not be based solely on the discretion of appointing authorities.[57]

Appointments and dismissals that are at pleasure, meaning that they can be revoked at any time for no reason, leave human rights institutions vulnerable and their leadership weak and susceptible to government preferences and the vagaries of public sentiment. International standards require that only Parliament or legislatures should have the power to convene, appoint, and dismiss chief commissioners and other members.

Finally, idiosyncratic or arbitrary removals or non-renewals should be constrained by provisions in law that require governments to provide at least six months' notice to incumbents, failing which the person's term should be automatically renewed for a further term. This would minimize last-minute decisions to dump incumbent commissioners for reasons that are often unrelated to their performance on the job.

Recommendation 20: Human rights legislation should be amended to set out clear, appropriate, and transparent criteria and processes for naming commissioners by legislatures. Procedures and criteria should exist for renewing commissioners and dismissing them in accordance with the Paris Principles. The duration of appointments should be benchmarked against current practices in other regulatory agencies and protected by law.

Improve Training and Development

When human rights commissions were first set up in the 1960s and 1970s, there were few human rights courses available anywhere, let alone those that could address the kind of applied work investigators, mediators, policy analysts, and other human rights professionals undertake. Now, there is a large array of courses, seminars, international internships, online training, and other educational opportunities. There is no excuse for human rights staff not to have the necessary qualifications, not only in human rights but also in constitutional law, evidence, administrative law, and international human rights.

Mark Freiman contended that training is essential and must take place across all levels of the organization. He cited an example from the judiciary where non-lawyers receive extensive and appropriately modified training. "This does not mean that you legalize the system," he added, "because not everything needs to be litigated. But it needs to be done and you can only do that if there is political will – right now there is no political capital to be gained in improving the system."[58]

Commissions should provide ongoing professional training and continuing legal education for both commissioners and staff. The same should apply to tribunals. Lawyers are already subject to mandatory professional development (continuing legal education) requirements in order to maintain their professional membership in their law society and thus retain the right to practice law. For those who are not lawyers, however, ongoing training is at least as critical. This is an area where CASHRA or a national organization could take a stronger role in standardizing training requirements for incoming staff and providing continuing education for human rights professionals across Canada, potentially in partnership with a university or college that has a strong human rights teaching record or a law faculty that emphasizes human rights in its curriculum. There is no standardized curriculum in Canada at the moment for human rights professionals in NHRIS, and Canada could serve as a leader in this regard, drawing on the extensive training materials that are available worldwide. We already have a successful model for the judiciary in Canada, and if we take the idea of judicial independence seriously, a similar body would be a constructive part of professional development.

Recommendation 21: Commissions should work with academics and training centres, in partnership with CASHRA or other national associations, to develop a standard curriculum for human rights professionals that focuses on the work of national human rights institutions.

10 PROTECT HUMAN RIGHTS DEFENDERS

The hate speech debates helped to create a highly critical public discourse about commissions and tribunals, in which their competence and role came under question. Public officials handling sensitive and contentious issues like human rights understand that criticism is part of the rough-and-tumble attached to this type of work. However, in the period between 2007 and 2013, the public had become sufficiently inured to vitriolic rhetoric about commissions that little of the excessive, mendacious, or ad hominem commentary was even questioned.

People who work in or with human rights institutions, as well as human rights lawyers and activists, are all human rights defenders. The United Nations has developed broad criteria under the Declaration on Human Rights Defenders to protect people who work either on a volunteer or professional basis. The UN has observed that what is most important "is not the person's title or the name of the organization he or she works for, but rather the human rights character of the work undertaken. It is not necessary for a person to be known as a 'human rights activist' or to work for an organization that includes 'human rights' in its name in order to be a human rights defender."[59]

Human rights defenders in Canada do not confront the same types of issues as those in developing countries, totalitarian regimes, or countries where human rights work involves daily risk to life and limb. But these defenders still deserve protection. Richard Warman, Darren Lund, and the students who spearheaded the *Maclean's* hate speech cases are all human rights activists and human rights defenders. So are commission staff. When those working in human rights take up unpopular or controversial causes or associate themselves with others who are doing so, they should be protected from actions that go beyond criticism and rise to the level of threats, intimidation, public vilification, and reprisal. Shared responsibility for human rights and the important role activists play in advocating for the rights of others are now central features of international human rights principles under the UN Declaration on Human Rights Defenders.

Two types of provisions in Canadian human rights laws already exist to protect human rights defenders and activists. The first is the right to be free from discrimination on the ground of association. Ontario is one of several jurisdictions in Canada that protects people based on their association with individuals or groups who experience discrimination based on any of the grounds listed in their laws. Other jurisdictions, however, including British Columbia, Quebec, and Saskatchewan, do not offer explicit protection for people based on association. This is an area that should be addressed in a uniform code or other harmonization measure.

The second provision is the protection against reprisal. Prohibitions against reprisal exist in most jurisdictions, either in the form of human rights complaints based on reprisal, criminal sanctions, or both. Criminal sanctions are rarely used. The problem with human rights complaints based on reprisal is that they tend to be as slow and ponderous as the original human rights complaints themselves. These types of complaints do not lend themselves to the type of rapid response that is often required for genuine reprisal.

The human rights complaint of Aboriginal rights activist Cindy Blackstock, whose organization spearheaded the *First Nations Child and Family Caring Society* case discussed earlier in the book, is a case in point. The original human rights complaint was filed with the Canadian Human Rights Commission in 2007, alleging that First Nations children on reserve receive funding that is inferior when compared to that received for children off-reserve. The complaint alleged that this discrepancy is discriminatory. After several procedural motions, Blackstock alleged that the federal government had placed her under surveillance as a direct result of her having filed the original human rights complaint. When she attempted to amend her complaint to include retaliation, the federal government strenuously opposed the motion. The tribunal took two years to reach a decision. The hearing on the merits and the particulars of the amended complaint were before Canadian Human Rights Tribunal at the time of writing. Such cases illustrate the difficulties that reprisal complainants face. Such problems are particularly likely to occur in first generation systems.

In 2000, the Canadian Human Rights Act Review Panel recommended that reprisal provisions be expanded and clarified: individuals who participate in inquiries conducted by a commission or who otherwise attempt to enforce human rights laws by bringing or supporting complaints should be protected from harassment and retaliation. A person who is fired, demoted, or personally harassed for having filed a human rights complaint or supported a complainant as a witness has few practical or short-term recourses. Criminal sanctions for reprisal are almost never used, probably because they are seen as being very heavy-handed. Human rights tribunals or the courts should be given the authority to issue interim or provisional injunctive relief to order the cessation of reprisals or discrimination on the grounds of association.

Recommendation 22: Governments should review human rights legislation to ensure that there are effective, rapid recourses available through injunctive relief or comparable remedies to protect human rights defenders, complainants, and witnesses.

CONCLUSION

Human rights occupy not only the rarefied air of international human rights law and the Charter but are also integral to the places and spaces where people live, work, and play. Human rights laws must be not only legally sound but also effective and accessible. This is a difficult balance.

Human rights systems are an intrinsic part of our democratic system of government, providing a check on majority-ruled legislatures and safeguarding a wide diversity of voices in a multicultural society. These objectives deserve to be respected. Canadian human rights systems are unique in their roots, their diversity, and their development. Their failures and successes have left traces that can help us to better understand how these systems might be designed in future.

The idea of a functional approach to human rights is given expression through the political will of legislatures that have created both regulatory agencies and specialized administrative tribunals. Human rights systems offer justice in a venue that is more approachable and accessible than the courts and express the aspirations and ideals of human rights. They represent an unequivocal expression of the public policy position that discrimination is unacceptable. It is in that expression that the rights revolution in Canada has been most successful.

There is a genuine concern – one that is shared by most of those interviewed for this book – that we are in danger of losing sight of these positive contributions. From the abolition or threat of abolition of commissions and tribunals to the vituperative attacks on human rights systems and their personnel, there is ample evidence of attempts to roll back human rights systems and undermine our ability to address discrimination.

And yet, there are positive signs as well. Commissions are being asked to play roles that were unforeseen and even unimagined when they were first introduced. Migrant workers, Aboriginal peoples, trans people, and many others are standing up – not as victims but to assert their full citizenship as well as their specificity, with all of the rights and responsibilities that this entails. Economic and social rights are better understood and are gradually receiving stronger, albeit piecemeal, protection across the country. We are getting better at managing rights conflicts.

The ideas offered in this chapter, while incremental and modest, are offered in the spirit of re-establishing trust in human rights systems in Canada to allow them to do their work more effectively and to link their public work more visibly to the full range of human rights. Central agencies of government need to pay more attention to what is happening in human rights commissions and tribunals, making sure that the best possible appointments are made based on merit and through transparent, competitive processes, not based on political opportunism or partisan choices. The people of Canada need to be more aware and involved in these important choices and their implications.

All of this presupposes an approach that gives pride of place to the Canadian Charter of Rights and Freedoms and to human rights laws at the federal, provincial, and territorial levels. Together, these are what bind Canada's human rights protection system to the Charter, other human rights systems around the world, and the majestic principles of the Universal Declaration of Human Rights.

APPENDICES

Interviews

Name	Affiliation	Date and Location
Anand, Raj	Partner, WeirFoulds Chair, Human Rights Legal Support Centre	14 September 2009 Toronto
Arnot, David	Chief commissioner, Saskatchewan Human Rights Commission	16 June 2009 Montreal
Awan, Khurrum	Lawyer	25 June 2009 Telephone
Bailey, Jane	Associate professor, Faculty of Law (Common Law Section), University of Ottawa	6 May 2009 Ottawa
Baker, David	Principal, Baker Law	30 July 2009 Toronto
Beauregard, Rémy	President, Rights and Democracy	15 September 2009 Montreal
Bernhardt, Kim	Human rights and labour lawyer	14 September 2009 Toronto
Blight, Margo	Partner, Borden Ladner Gervais LLP (BLG)	16 September 2009 Telephone
Borovoy, Alan	Former general counsel, Canadian Civil Liberties Association (CCLA)	14 September 2009 Toronto
Bosset, Pierre	Professor, Department of Legal Sciences, Political Science Department, Université du Québec à Montréal	16 September 2009 Montreal
Champ, Paul	Principal, Champ & Associates Counsel, British Columbia Civil Liberties Association	29 June 2010 Telephone
Clément, Dominique	Assistant professor, Department of Sociology, University of Alberta	7 December 2011 Telephone
Cotler, Irwin	Member of Parliament for Mont-Royal (Liberal) and Liberal critic for human rights	25 June 2009 Montreal

Name	Affiliation	Date and Location
Cousineau, Gaétan	President, Commission des droits de la personne et des droits de la jeunesse (CDPDJ)	21 April 2010 Montreal
Daley, Krista	Director and CEO, Nova Scotia Human Rights Commission	13 May 2009 Telephone
Day, Shelagh	Lawyer	9 March 2011 Telephone
	President and senior editor of *Canadian Human Rights Reporter.*	
Dean, Audrey	Senior legal counsel, Alberta Human Rights Commission	28 April 2009 Telephone
Dufresne, Philippe	Director and senior counsel, Canadian Human Rights Commission	4 May 2009
	Part-time professor, Faculty of Law (Common Law Section), University of Ottawa	13 May 2009 Telephone
Eberts, Mary	Ariel Sallows chair in Human Rights, College of Law, University of Saskatchewan	24 April 2009 Toronto
Farber, Bernie	CEO, Canadian Jewish Congress	22 April 2009 Toronto
Farha, Leilani	Executive director, Centre for Equality Rights in Accommodation	2 October 2009 Telephone
Fournier, Pascale	Assistant professor, Faculty of Law (Civil Law Section), University of Ottawa	6 April 2009 Ottawa
Freiman, Mark	Lead commission Counsel for the Commission of Inquiry into the Investigation of the Bombing of Air India Flight 182.	1 May 2009 Toronto
Gottheil, Michael	Chair, Human Rights Tribunal of Ontario	22 April 2009 Toronto
	Executive chair of Social Justice Tribunals Ontario	24 August 2011 Telephone
Hall, Barbara	Chief commissioner, Ontario Human Rights Commission	22 April 2009 Toronto
Hogben, Alia	Executive director, Canadian Council of Muslim Women	16 September 2009 Telephone
Jackman, Martha	Professor, Faculty of Law (Common Law Section), University of Ottawa	9 September 2009 Telephone
Jaffer, Jameel	Counsel, American Civil Liberties Union	15 May 2009 Telephone
	Director of the National Security Project and the Center for Democracy	
Knipe, Patricia	Communications director, Manitoba Human Rights Commission	5 February 2010 Telephone
Laird, Kathy	Executive director, Human Rights Legal Support Centre	2 October 2011 Telephone

Name	Affiliation	Date and Location
Lamarche, Lucie	Professor, Faculty of Law (Common Law Section), University Ottawa (Gordon F. Henderson Human Rights Chair)	24 April 2009 Telephone
Larsen, François	Director of research, education, cooperation, and communications, Commission des droits de la personne et des droits de la jeunesse (CDPDJ)	10 September 2010 Montreal
Lund, Darren	Professor, Faculty of Education, University of Calgary	18 August 2011 Telephone
Lynch, Jennifer	Chief commissioner, Canadian Human Rights Commission	6 April 2009 Ottawa
Macdonald, Roderick	F.R. Scott Professor of Constitutional and Public Law, Faculty of Law, McGill University	1 September 2009 Montreal
Mackintosh, Charlach	Former chief commissioner, Alberta Human Rights and Citizenship Commission[1]	20 May 2009 Telephone
MacNaughton, Heather	Former chair, British Columbia Human Rights Tribunal	2 February 2010 Telephone
Malhotra, Ravi	Associate professor, Faculty of Law (Common Law Section), University of Ottawa	13 May 2009 Telephone
Matas, David	Human rights lawyer Senior legal counsel, B'Nai Brith Canada	22 April 2009 Toronto
McKinnon, Gordon A.	Partner, Thompson Dorfman Sweatman LLP	5 March 2010 Telephone
Miller, John	Professor Emeritus, School of Journalism, Ryerson University	15 May 2009 Telephone
Mithoowani, Naseem	Lawyer, Lerners LLP	7 May 2009 Telephone
Moon, Richard	Professor, Faculty of Law, University of Windsor	21 April 2009 Telephone
Niemi, Fo	Executive director, Center for Research-Action on Race Relations (CRARR)	11 January 2011 Montreal
Norman, Ken	Professor, College of Law, University of Saskatchewan	16 November 2010 Telephone
Norton, Keith	Former president, Canadian Human Rights Tribunal; Former chief commissioner, Ontario Human Rights Commission	21 April 2009 Toronto
Pace, John	Associate, Sydney Centre for International Law, University of Sydney	19 December 2012 Telephone
Parsons, Margaret	Executive director, African Canadian Legal Clinic	10 June 2009 Telephone
Rivet, Michèle	President, Quebec Human Rights Tribunal	23 June 2009 Montreal

Name	Affiliation	Date and Location
Sampson, Fiona	Executive director, the equality effect Commissioner, Ontario Human Rights Commission	11 May 2009 Telephone
Scarth, Dianna	Executive director, Manitoba Human Rights Commission	2 February 2010 Telephone
Sheikh, Muneeza	Lawyer	25 June 2009 Telephone
Sheppard, Colleen	Professor, McGill University (Faculty of Law) Director, Centre for Human Rights and Legal Pluralism (CHRLP)	30 April 2009 Montreal
Sims, Mary-Woo	Former chief commissioner, BC Human Rights Commission	18 September 2012 Telephone
Vizkelety, Béatrice	Director, Secretariat and Legal Department, Commission des droits de la personne et droits de la jeunesse (CDPDJ)	29 January 2010 Montreal
Warman, Richard	Public servant	4 May 2009 Telephone
		20 September 2009 Telephone
Williams, Byron	Director, Public Interest Law Centre (PILC)	9 February 2010 Telephone

Note: Affiliations are listed as of the interview dates

The Paris Principles

NOTE: In October 1991, the UN Centre for Human Rights convened an international workshop to review and update information on existing national human rights institutions. Participants included representatives of national institutions, states, the United Nations and its specialized agencies, and intergovernmental and non-governmental organizations.

In addition to exchanging views on existing arrangements, the workshop participants drew up a comprehensive series of recommendations on the role, composition, status and functions of national human rights institutions.

The Paris Principles were adopted by the General Assembly of the United Nations in its Resolution 48/134 of 20 December 1993.

PRINCIPLES RELATING TO THE STATUS OF NATIONAL INSTITUTIONS

Competence and responsibilities

1 A national institution shall be vested with competence to promote and protect human rights.
2 A national institution shall be given as broad a mandate as possible, which shall be clearly set forth in a constitutional or legislative text, specifying its composition and its sphere of competence.
3 A national institution shall, inter alia, have the following responsibilities:
   (a) To submit to the Government, Parliament and any other competent body, on an advisory basis either at the request of the authorities concerned or through the exercise of its power to hear a matter without higher referral, opinions, recommendations,

proposals and reports on any matters concerning the promotion and protection of human rights; the national institution may decide to publicize them; these opinions, recommendations, proposals and reports, as well as any prerogative of the national institution, shall relate to the following areas:

(i)   Any legislative or administrative provisions, as well as provisions relating to judicial organizations, intended to preserve and extend the protection of human rights; in that connection, the national institution shall examine the legislation and administrative provisions in force, as well as bills and proposals, and shall make such recommendations as it deems appropriate in order to ensure that these provisions conform to the fundamental principles of human rights; it shall, if necessary, recommend the adoption of new legislation, the amendment of legislation in force and the adoption or amendment of administrative measures;

(ii) Any situation of violation of human rights which it decides to take up;

(iii) The preparation of reports on the national situation with regard to human rights in general, and on more specific matters;

(iv) Drawing the attention of the Government to situations in any part of the country where human rights are violated and making proposals to it for initiatives to put an end to such situations and, where necessary, expressing an opinion on the positions and reactions of the Government;

(b) To promote and ensure the harmonization of national legislation, regulations and practices with the international human rights instruments to which the State is a party, and their effective implementation;

(c) To encourage ratification of the above-mentioned instruments or accession to those instruments, and to ensure their implementation;

(d) To contribute to the reports which States are required to submit to United Nations bodies and committees, and to regional institutions, pursuant to their treaty obligations and, where necessary, to express an opinion on the subject, with due respect for their independence;

(e) To cooperate with the United Nations and any other organization in the United Nations system, the regional institutions and the national institutions of other countries that are competent in the areas of the promotion and protection of human rights;

(f) To assist in the formulation of programmes for the teaching of, and research into, human rights and to take part in their execution in schools, universities and professional circles;

(g) To publicize human rights and efforts to combat all forms of discrimination, in particular racial discrimination, by increasing public awareness, especially through information and education and by making use of all press organs.

Composition and guarantees of independence and pluralism

1 The composition of the national institution and the appointment of its members, whether by means of an election or otherwise, shall be established in accordance with a procedure which affords all necessary guarantees to ensure the pluralist representation of the social forces (of civilian society) involved in the promotion and protection of human rights, particularly by powers which will enable effective cooperation to be established with, or through the presence of, representatives of:

(a) Non-governmental organizations responsible for human rights and efforts to combat racial discrimination, trade unions, concerned social and professional organizations, for example, associations of lawyers, doctors, journalists and eminent scientists;

(b) Trends in philosophical or religious thought;

(c) Universities and qualified experts;

(d) Parliament;

(e) Government departments (if these are included, their representatives should participate in the deliberations only in an advisory capacity).

2 The national institution shall have an infrastructure which is suited to the smooth conduct of its activities, in particular adequate funding. The purpose of this funding should be to enable it to have its own staff and premises, in order to be independent of the Government and not be subject to financial control which might affect its independence.

3 In order to ensure a stable mandate for the members of the national institution, without which there can be no real independence, their appointment shall be effected by an official act which shall establish the specific duration of the mandate. This mandate may be

renewable, provided that the pluralism of the institution's membership is ensured.

Methods of operation

Within the framework of its operation, the national institution shall:

(a) Freely consider any questions falling within its competence, whether they are submitted by the Government or taken up by it without referral to a higher authority, on the proposal of its members or of any petitioner;

(b) Hear any person and obtain any information and any documents necessary for assessing situations falling within its competence;

(c) Address public opinion directly or through any press organ, particularly in order to publicize its opinions and recommendations;

(d) Meet on a regular basis and whenever necessary in the presence of all its members after they have been duly convened;

(e) Establish working groups from among its members as necessary, and set up local or regional sections to assist it in discharging its functions;

(f) Maintain consultation with the other bodies, whether jurisdictional or otherwise, responsible for the promotion and protection of human rights (in particular ombudsmen, mediators and similar institutions);

(g) In view of the fundamental role played by the non-governmental organizations in expanding the work of the national institutions, develop relations with the non-governmental organizations devoted to promoting and protecting human rights, to economic and social development, to combating racism, to protecting particularly vulnerable groups (especially children, migrant workers, refugees, physically and mentally disabled persons) or to specialized areas.

Additional principles concerning the status of commissions
with quasi-jurisdictional competence

A national institution may be authorized to hear and consider complaints and petitions concerning individual situations. Cases may be brought before it by individuals, their representatives, third parties, non-governmental organizations, associations of trade unions or any other representative organizations. In such circumstances, and without prejudice to the principles stated above concerning the other powers of the commissions, the functions entrusted to them may be based on the following principles:

(a) Seeking an amicable settlement through conciliation or, within the limits prescribed by the law, through binding decisions or, where necessary, on the basis of confidentiality;

(b) Informing the party who filed the petition of his rights, in particular the remedies available to him, and promoting his access to them;

(c) Hearing any complaints or petitions or transmitting them to any other competent authority within the limits prescribed by the law;

(d) Making recommendations to the competent authorities, especially by proposing amendments or reforms of the laws, regulations and administrative practices, especially if they have created the difficulties encountered by the persons filing the petitions in order to assert their rights.

NOTE:

1. A/36/440 (1981), A/38/416 (1983), E/CN.4/1987/37 (1987), E/CN.4/1989/47 and Add. 1(1989), E/CN.4/1991/23 and Add. 1(1991).

Overview of Human Rights Systems in Canada

NOTES: This appendix provides an overview "at a glance" of features and functions of human rights systems in each of the fourteen jurisdictions in Canada. The emphasis is on issues highlighted in the book. It does not purport to be exhaustive and the reader should verify information by checking with official versions of legislation.

FIRST-GENERATION SYSTEMS have "gatekeeping" commissions that promote and protect human rights. One of their main functions is to screen and investigate complaints. Specialized hearing bodies such as boards of inquiry and tribunals render decisions and orders. Most jurisdictions in Canada have first-generation systems; Quebec and Saskatchewan have modified first-generation systems.

SECOND-GENERATION SYSTEMS provide complainants with direct access to a hearing body without having to go through a commission. Ontario, British Columbia, and Nunavut have second-generation systems. Ontario is the only jurisdiction with three distinct human rights institutions: a tribunal, a commission (which focuses on promotional activities), and a legal support centre to assist complainants.

"Minister": Reference to "minister" refers to the designated member of cabinet or council who is responsible by law for human rights systems as described pursuant to each human rights law.

Section references are to the human rights law for each jurisdiction unless otherwise specified.

ABBREVIATIONS

BOI	Board of Inquiry
CC	Chief Commissioner
GIC	Governor in Council
HRLSC	Human Rights Legal Support Centre
LEB	Labour and Employment Board
LGC	Lieutenant Governor in Council

System/ Human rights grounds	Institutional Independence[1]	Qualifications/ Appointments/ Dismissals	Damages/ Remedies	Costs	Criminal Sanctions	Additional information and features
ALBERTA *Alberta Human Rights Act*, RSA 2000, c A-25.5 First generation • Alberta Human Rights Commission • Human Rights Tribunal Age Ancestry Colour Disability[2] Family status Gender Marital status Place of origin Race Religious beliefs, including native spirituality Sexual orientation Source of income (ss 3–9, 44)	*Reporting:* Annual report to minister; "any other information that the minister may require." (s 19) *By-laws:* By-laws must be approved by minister (s 17 (3)) *Staffing:* LGC appoints director (s 18(1)); Minister may appoint employees to administer the act (s 18(2)) Tribunal drawn from commission members (s 27(2))	*Qualifications:* N/A *Appointments:* Commission members (s 15(1)) and director (s 18(1)) are appointed by LGC No criteria specified for either commissioners or tribunal members Tribunal consists of commission members (s 27(2)) *Dismissal* N/A	*Pecuniary:* Tribunal may order compensation for lost wages or income, or expenses incurred (s 32(1)(b)(iv)) *Other Remedies:* Cease behaviour; refrain from committing same or similar contravention; make available rights, opportunities or privileges that were denied; "any other action" that would make the complainant whole (s 32(1)(b))	Tribunal may make "any" award of costs (s 32(2))	Obstruction: offence with a fine of up to $10,000 (s 42)	*Mandate:* In addition to protection activities, commission has jurisdiction over pay equity (s 6(1)). Promotional activities include educational programs on discrimination (s 16(1)(e)), awareness of multiculturalism 16(1)(b); public and private human rights programs (s 16(1)(g)) *Discriminatory/hate speech:* Prohibited s 3(1) *Exemptions* : Nonprofit organizations composed of persons with same religious, political beliefs, or of same ancestry/place of origin (s 3(3)(b)) *Intent:* Relevant re discriminatory/hate speech (s 3(1)(a)) Other: *Education:* Parents may withdraw their children from school teachings dealing with religion, human sexuality, or sexual orientation (s 11.1)

System/Human rights grounds	Institutional Independence[1]	Qualifications/Appointments/Dismissals	Damages/Remedies	Costs	Criminal Sanctions	Additional information and features
BRITISH COLUMBIA *Human Rights Code*, RSBC 1996, c 210 Second generation • British Columbia Human Rights Tribunal Age, Ancestry Colour Criminal offences (area of employment (s 13); unions and associations (s 14) only) Disability Family status Marital status Place of origin	*Reporting:* Annual report to minister (s 39 .1) *Staffing:* Appointments pursuant to the *Public Service Act*, RSBC c 385; See s 33(1) *Human Rights Code*	*Qualifications:* "merit based" (s 31(1); no further details provided. *Appointments:* Tribunal members appointed by LGC through merit based process (s 31(1) Term: 5 years (s 31(2)) Renewable for further 5 years *Dismissal:* For cause (s 8, *Administrative Tribunals Act*)	Tribunal may order: *Pecuniary damages:* Compensation for lost wages or salary, or expenses incurred (s 37(2)(d)(ii) *Non-pecuniary:* Compensation for injury to dignity, feelings, and self-respect (s 37(2)(d)(iii)) *Other:* Make available the lost right, opportunity or privilege 37(2)(d)(i)	Tribunal may award costs due to improper conduct or for contravention of certain rules (s 37(4))	N/A	*Mandate:* No commission in BC. Educational, research mandates conducted by minister (ss 5-6) *Intent:* Discrimination does not require intent (s 2) *Discriminatory/hate speech:* Prohibited (s 7(1)) *Exemptions:* Certain non-profits are exempt from Code if they grant preferences to the people they serve (e.g. charitable, philanthropic, (s 41 Tribunal may allow any person or group to intervene in a complaint (s 22.1) Preliminary dismissal of complaints can occur on 7 grounds, with or without a hearing (s 27(1))

System / Human rights grounds	Institutional Independence[1]	Qualifications / Appointments / Dismissals	Damages / Remedies	Costs	Criminal Sanctions	Additional information and features
Political belief area of employment (ss 11, 13); area of membership in unions and associations (s 14) Race Religion Sex[3] Sexual orientation Source of income (lawful tenancy only – s 10) (Ss 7-14)			Order to cease contravention (s 37(2)(a)) Declaratory Order (37(2)(b)) Take steps to ameliorate effects / adopt special program or employment equity program 37(2)(c)			
CANADA *Canadian Human Rights Act*, RSC 1985, c H-6 First generation • Canadian Human Rights Commission • Canadian Human Rights Tribunal	*Reporting:* Commission and tribunal report annually directly to Parliament *Internal governance:* CC has supervision and direction over commission (s 31(1)).	*Qualifications:* Commissioners: No criteria specified Tribunal members must have "experience, expertise and interest in, and sensitivity to, human rights"	*Pecuniary:* Compensation for lost wages and expenses incurred (s 53(2)(c)) Compensation for additional costs of obtaining alternative goods, services, etc. (s 53(2)(d))	N/A	Obstruction, reprisals and reducing wages to eliminate discriminatory practices, are an offence with a fine of up to $50,000	*Mandate:* In addition to protection activities, commission is responsible for public information and education regarding discrimination; may review regs and other instruments if inconsistent with principles of equality and non-discrimination and liaison with other commissions in Canada. Can consider, inquire into, or report on human rights

System/Human rights grounds	Institutional Independence[1]	Qualifications/Appointments/Dismissals	Damages/Remedies	Costs	Criminal Sanctions	Additional information and features
Age Colour Conviction for a pardoned offence or a suspended record Disability Family status Marital status National or ethnic origin Race Religion Sex Sexual orientation (s 3)	Commission's internal by-laws must be approved by Treasury Board (s 37) *Staffing:* CC and president of tribunal have direction over staff in their respective organizations	Regional representation required Tribunal chair and vice-chair must be members in good standing of a provincial bar or of Chambre des notaires du Québec for at least ten years At least two other members must be members in good standing of a provincial bar or of Chambre des notaires (s 48.1)	Compensation to victims specifically identified by hate speech (s 54(1)(b)) Special penalty (s 54(1)(c)) *Non-Pecuniary:* Compensation up to $20,000 for pain and suffering (s 53(2)(e)) *Punitive:* Up to $20,000 for wilful or reckless conduct (s 53(3)) *Other:* Make available the lost right, opportunity or privilege 53(2)(b)		Prosecution for obstruction, etc., requires consent of attorney general (s 60)	issues generally, undertake studies on human rights and freedoms, provide advice to government with respect to legislation (s 27) The commission has jurisdiction over pay equity (ss 7, 10, 11). *Intent:* Relevant to penalty for hate speech under s 54(1)(c): see s 54(1.1)(b) *Hate speech:* Prohibited (s 13(1)); special penalty in s 54(1)(c), subject to repeal in 2014 Minister can direct how complaints that raise issues of national security are dealt with (s 45) *Aboriginal issues:* the repeal of Section 67 of the Canadian Human Rights Act took effect in 2011. Commission now has jurisdiction over human rights complaints related to decisions taken respecting the *Indian Act*

System/Human rights grounds	Institutional Independence[1]	Qualifications/Appointments/Dismissals	Damages/Remedies	Costs	Criminal Sanctions	Additional information and features
		Appointments: Commissioners and tribunal members appointed by GIC (ss 26, 48.1). Commissioners' terms up to 7 years (full-time) or 3 years (s 26(3)) *Dismissal:* Commissioners: "good behaviour" or removal by GIC (s 26(4)) Tribunal members: hold office during "good behaviour"; Chair can be removed for cause (s 48.2(1))	Cessation of contravening behaviour, take steps to prevent recurrence (s 53(2)) Declaratory order Set up special program or plan (s 53(2)(a))			

System / Human rights grounds	Institutional Independence[1]	Qualifications/ Appointments/ Dismissals	Damages/ Remedies	Costs	Criminal Sanctions	Additional information and features
MANITOBA *Human Rights Code,* CCSM c H175 First generation • Manitoba Human Rights Commission • Adjudication panel Age Ancestry, including colour and perceived race Disability Ethnic background or origin Gender identity Marital or family status Nationality or national origin Political belief, association or activity	*Reporting:* Commission is responsible to minister (s 6(1)) Commission provides annual report to minister for both commission and adjudication panel (s 6(2)) *Internal governance:* Commission may determine own practice and procedures (s 3.1) Commission is designated as "independent agency" (s 2(1))	*Qualifications:* Commissioners: N/A Tribunal members: Cannot be commission members (s 8(2)) No other criteria specified *Appointments:* Commissioners appointed by LGC (s 2(2)) for three year term (possibility of less than three years in certain circumstances (s 2(3))	Adjudicator may order: *Pecuniary:* Compensation for financial losses, expenses incurred, or lost benefits (s 43(2)(b)) *Non-pecuniary:* Damages for injury to dignity, feelings, or self-respect (s 43(2)(c)) *Punitive:* Penal or exemplary damages for malice or recklessness (ss 43(2) (d) and 43(3)) *Other:* An order to do or refrain from doing anything (s 43(2)(a))	Adjudicator may award costs due to frivolous or vexatious conduct (s 45(2))	Contraventions of the Code can be prosecuted by way of summary conviction offence Obstruction and failure to comply with an order are an offence with a fine of up to $5,000 for individuals or $25,000 for organizations (s 51(1))	*Mandate:* In addition to protection activities, the commission promotes the principle that people are free and equal in their rights, equality of opportunity, exercise of civil and legal rights; educational programs designed to eliminate discrimination (s 4). Code defines discrimination (s 9 (1)) *Intent:* Relevant re discriminatory signs, statements (s 18(a)) Commission uses "board-directed mediation" if there is evidence of a contravention. The process is voluntary

System/ Human rights grounds	Institutional Independence[1]	Qualifications/ Appointments/ Dismissals	Damages/ Remedies	Costs	Criminal Sanctions	Additional information and features
Religion or creed, or religious belief, association, or activity Sex Sexual orientation Source of income Social disadvantage (s 9(2)) Association with people based on any of these grounds (s 9(1)(c))		Members of adjudication panel appointed by LGC (s 8(1)) for three-year term. Dismissal: For cause Commission: s 2(5) Tribunal: s 8(4)	Adopt, implement an affirmative action or other special program (s 43(2)(e))		Prosecution requires consent of minister (s 51(3))	
NEW BRUNSWICK Human rights Act, RSNB 2011, c 171 Labour Board and Employment Act SNB 2011, c 182 First generation • New Brunswick Human Rights Commission	Reporting: Commission is responsible to minister (s 30) Staffing: Commission staff appointed by LGC (s 15)	Qualifications: Commission: No criteria specified No criteria for human rights knowledge or experience in Act for LEB members	Pecuniary: Expenditures, financial losses, or lost benefits (s 23(7)(e)) Non-pecuniary: Emotional suffering, including injury to dignity, feelings, or self-respect (s 23(7)(f))	Reasonable costs associated with filing, etc., of LEB order recoverable s 24 (5)	Certain discriminatory practices, reprisals, failure to comply with an order are an offence (s 25)	Mandate: In addition to protection functions, commission also promotes the principle that each person is equal in dignity and rights, without discrimination, and develops educational programs in relation to discrimination. Intent: Limited to discriminatory notices, signs, symbols (s 7 (1))

System/Human rights grounds	Institutional Independence[1]	Qualifications/Appointments/Dismissals	Damages/Remedies	Costs	Criminal Sanctions	Additional information and features
• Labour and Employment Board Age Ancestry Colour Disability Marital status National origin Place of origin Political belief or activity Race Religion Sex Sexual orientation Social condition (Ss 4-8)		*Appointments:* Commission: By LGC (s 12(3)) No term specified LEB members: Five (Chair) and three-year terms (LEB Act) *Dismissal:* Commissioners: N/A Appointment of board members may be revoked for cause	*Other:* Do or refrain from doing any act, rectify any harm, restore a party to the position the party would have been in but for the violation, reinstate a person in employment (s 23(7) (a) (b) (c)(d))		Prosecution requires consent of minister (s 26)	Human rights complaints, regardless of whether they occur in the employment context or not, are referred to LEB for hearing.
NEWFOUNDLAND AND LABRADOR *Human Rights Act, 2010,* SNL 2010, c H-13.1	*Reporting:* "Commission shall report on business and activities "as required" by minister (s 23(g))	*Qualifications:* Commission: members must "collectively possess experience with human rights	BOI may award compensation, *Pecuniary:* "including compensation for lost wages or income, or expenses	BOI may award costs (s 39(2))	Contravention of act is summary conviction offence (fines up to $500	*Mandate:* : In addition to protection functions, has both discrimination and more general human rights promotional functions (s 23) Jurisdiction over equal pay for same or similar work (s 16)

System/ Human rights grounds	Institutional Independence[1]	Qualifications/ Appointments/ Dismissals	Damages/ Remedies	Costs	Criminal Sanctions	Additional information and features
First generation • Newfoundland and Labrador Human Rights Commission • Boards of Inquiry (BOI) Age Colour Conviction for offence (employment only) (s 14(1)) Disability, including perceived and predisposition Disfigurement Ethnic origin Family status Marital status Nationality Political opinion Race Religion		issues and an interest in and sensitivity to human rights" (s 22(3)) BOI Members: Must "possess experience, knowledge or training with respect to human rights law and issues" (s 36(3)) Cannot be commission members (s 36(4)) Appointments: Commission members appointed by LGC (s 22(2)) Fixed term of 5 years	incurred" (s 39(1)(b)(iv)) Other: Cease present and refrain from future contraventions; make available to the person rights, opportunities, or privileges; take whatever other action is appropriate (s 39(1)(b)(i)(ii)(iii) (v))		for individuals, and $1,000 for organizations (s 45(1)) Obstruction or failure to comply with an order: summary conviction offences (fine up to $500 for individuals, $1,000 for organizations) (s 45(1))	*Intent:* Discrimination does not require intent (s 10), except re discriminatory notices, signs, etc. indicating intent to discriminate (s 19(1)) *Exemptions:* Religious, philanthropic, etc. organizations are partially exempted from act (s 11(3)(d)) *Aboriginal rights:* Protection of impacts and benefits agreements for Labrador Inuit and Innu (s 4)

System/Human rights grounds	Institutional Independence[1]	Qualifications/Appointments/Dismissals	Damages/Remedies	Costs	Criminal Sanctions	Additional information and features
Religious creed Sex Sexual orientation Social origin Source of income Association with people based on any of these grounds (s 9)		Members of BOI appointed by LGC (s 36(1)) For three years. *Dismissal:* Commission: "A member ... shall hold office until he or she is reappointed or his or her successor is appointed" (s 22(5)) BOI: May be terminated for cause (s 36(6))				
NORTHWEST TERRITORIES *Human Rights Act,* SNWT 2002, c 18	Commission is responsible to Legislative Assembly (s 19)	*Qualifications:* Commission members: "experience and an interest in, sensitivity to human rights" (s 16(3)	Adjudicator may order: *Pecuniary:* Compensation for lost wages or income, or expenses incurred (s 62(3)(a)(iv))	Adjudicator may award costs against complainant due to frivolous or vexatious	Contraventions of act: an offence with a fine of up to $2,000 for individuals	*Mandate:* In addition to protection mandate, it is the function of the commission to promote understanding and mutual respect in all areas of rights, as well as research to promote human rights. Public education

System/ Human rights grounds	Institutional Independence[1]	Qualifications/ Appointments/ Dismissals	Damages/ Remedies	Costs	Criminal Sanctions	Additional information and features
First generation • Northwest Territories Human Rights Commission • Adjudication panel	*Reporting:* Annual report submitted to speaker (s 21(1)) *Internal governance:* Commission may establish its own rules and procedures (s 18.2). Public may attend meetings s 18(2). *Staffing:* Commissioner of NWT appoints Director on recommendation of Legislative Assembly (s 23(1))	Adjudication panel members: "experience and an interest in, as well as sensitivity to human rights" Must be members of at least five years in good standing of law society, or have five years' experience with an administrative tribunal or a court. Cannot be commission members (s 48)	*Non-pecuniary:* Compensation for injury to dignity, feelings, and self-respect (s 62(3)(a)(v)) *Punitive:* Exemplary or punitive damages of up to $10,000 for wilful or malicious conduct or repeated contraventions (s 62(3)(a)(vii)) *Other:* Cease present and refrain from future contraventions; make available any rights, opportunities, or privileges; reinstate in employment; other action as proper (s 62(3)(a)(i)(ii)(iii)(vi)(vii))	conduct or for extra-ordinary reasons (s 63)	and $10,000 for organizations (s 72(1)) Retaliation, obstruction, or failure to comply with an order are an offence with a fine of up to: $5,000 for individuals and $25,000 for organizations (s 72(2)) Prosecutions require consent of attorney general (s 73)	and information are linked to discriminatory practices (s 20) *Intent:* Discrimination does not require intent (s 6), except with respect to intention to discriminate in a statement, notice, or sign, etc. (s 13(1)) *Exemptions:* for non-profit charitable, educational, fraternal, religious, social, or cultural organizations (s 7(5)) *Aboriginal rights:* Act does not derogate from Aboriginal rights (s 2) Act does not derogate from denominational schools (s 3)
Age Ancestry Colour Conviction subject to a pardon or record suspension Creed Disability, including perceived or predisposition Ethnic origin Family affiliation Family status Gender identity Marital status Nationality Place of origin Political association Political belief Race						

System / Human rights grounds	Institutional Independence[1]	Qualifications/ Appointments/ Dismissals	Damages/ Remedies	Costs	Criminal Sanctions	Additional information and features
Religion Sex Sexual orientation Social condition Association with people based on any of these grounds (s 5)		*Appointments:* Commissioner of NWT appoints commissioners "during good behaviour for a term of four years" Adjudication panel members appointed by commissioner of NWT on recommendation of Legislative Assembly (s 48(2)) *Dismissal:* Commissioners: for cause (s 17(9)) Members of adjudication panel: holds position "during good behaviour" (s 49(1))	Declaratory order (s 62 (3) (b))			

System/ Human rights grounds	Institutional Independence[1]	Qualifications/ Appointments/ Dismissals	Damages/ Remedies	Costs	Criminal Sanctions	Additional information and features
NOVA SCOTIA *Human Rights Act, RSNS 1989, c 214* First generation • Nova Scotia Human Rights Commission – Race Relations, Equity and Inclusion Division • Board of Inquiry (BOI) Age Colour Creed Disability Ethnic, national, or Aboriginal origin Family status Gender expression Gender identity Irrational fear of illness or disease Marital status	*Reporting:* Commission reports to minister through its annual report (s 24(2)) *Staffing:* GIC appoints director of human rights, who is also CEO (s 26(1)) Officers, employees are appointed pursuant to *Civil Service Act* (s 27)	*Qualifications:* Commissioners: No criteria specified in act BOI: No criteria specified in act. *Appointments:* Commission members appointed by GIC (s 22(2)) No minimum term in Act BOI appointed by commission on ad hoc basis Cannot include commission members (s 32A) *Dismissal:* N/A	BOI may order compensation for any injury (s 34(8))	BOI may award costs, but not against complainant (s 34(8))	Contraventions of the act or failure to comply with an order constitutes an offence with a fine of up to $500 for individuals and $1,000 for organizations (s 38) Prosecution requires consent of minister (s 39(1))	*Mandate:* In addition to protection activities, Commission shall undertake education, research, and public information on "human rights" in general, cooperate with other individuals and bodies inside or outside the province, advise and assist the government on human rights matters (s 24 (1)) *Intent:* Discrimination does not require intent (s 4), except with respect to intention to discriminate in a statement, notice, or sign, etc. (s 7 (1) *Exemptions:* non-profit religious or ethnic organizations (ss 6(c), (d))

System / Human rights grounds	Institutional Independence[1]	Qualifications / Appointments / Dismissals	Damages / Remedies	Costs	Criminal Sanctions	Additional information and features
Political belief, affiliation, or activity Race Religion Sex Sexual orientation Source of income Association based on any of these grounds (s 5)						
NUNAVUT *Human rights Act,* SNu 2003, c 12 Second generation • Human Rights Tribunal Age Ancestry Citizenship Colour	*Reporting:* Annual report submitted to minister and then laid before legislative assembly (s 20(1)) *Staffing:* Employees appointed pursuant to *Public Service Act* (s 17(3))	*Qualifications:* Must have "interest in and a sensitivity to human rights and to Inuit culture and values" (s 16(2))	*Pecuniary:* Compensation for lost wages or income, or expenses incurred (s 34(3)(a)(iv)) *Non-pecuniary:* Compensation for injury to dignity, feelings, or self-respect (s 34(3)(a)(v))	Tribunal may award costs for knowingly making a false claim (s 35(a)) or for frivolous or vexatious conduct (s 36)	Retaliation or failure to comply with an order are an offence with a fine of up to $25,000 (s 45) Prosecution requires consent of attorney general (s 46)	*Mandate:* Receives complaints, has powers pursuant to *Public Inquiries Act* *Intent:* Discrimination does not require intent (s 8) except with respect to intention to discriminate in a notice, sign, etc. (s 14) *Aboriginal rights:* Recognizes Nunavut Land Claims Agreement (s 3), ; Act does not derogate from Aboriginal rights (s 4)

System / Human rights grounds	Institutional Independence[1]	Qualifications/ Appointments/ Dismissals	Damages/ Remedies	Costs	Criminal Sanctions	Additional information and features
Conviction for which a pardon has been granted Creed Disability Ethnic origin Family status Marital status Place of origin Pregnancy and adoption Race Religion Sex Sexual orientation Source of income (lawful) Association with people based on any of these grounds (S 7)		*Appointments:* Members appointed by Commissioner of Nunavut in Executive Council (s 16(1)) Term: Four years, or two to four years (s 16(3)) *Dismissal:* For cause only (s 16(6))	*Punitive:* c) Compensation for malice or recklessness (s 34(3)(a) (vii) d) Damages for injury to respondent's reputation for knowingly making a false claim (s 35(b)) *Other:* Cease contraventions; make available to the person rights, opportunities, or privileges; ameliorative programs/affirmative action; apology; any other action having regard to Inuit values, culture. (s 34(3)(a)(i), (ii), (iii),(vi), (viii), (ix), (x))			Employment exemption for non-profit charitable, educational, fraternal, religious, athletic, social, or cultural organizations (s 9(6)) Tribunal remains seized of matter until order is fully implemented (s 34(5)) (if an order is not respected, the tribunal retains authority until the order is fully implemented).

System / Human rights grounds	Institutional Independence[1]	Qualifications/ Appointments/ Dismissals	Damages/ Remedies	Costs	Criminal Sanctions	Additional information and features
ONTARIO *Human Rights Code,* RSO 1990, c H19 Second generation[4] • Ontario Human Rights Commission • Anti-Racism Secretariat (s 31.3) • Disability Rights Secretariat (s 31.4) • Human Rights Tribunal of Ontario • Human Rights Legal Support Centre (HRLSC)	*Reporting:* Commission: Annual report submitted to speaker of assembly (copy to be given to minister 30 days prior) (s 31.6) Tribunal: Annual report to minister (s 45.10) HRLSC: Annual report to minister (s 45.17(1)) Centre is independent from but accountable to government (s 45.11(5)) Not a Crown agent (s 45.11(3))	*Qualifications:* Commissioners must have knowledge, experience, or training with respect to human rights law and issues (s 27(3)) Membership must reflect diversity of population (s 27(4))	*Pecuniary/Non-pecuniary:* Tribunal may order compensation for loss, including injury to dignity, feelings, and self-respect (s 45.2(1)(1)) *Other:* Restitution to party whose right was infringed, including restitution for injury to dignity, feelings, and self-respect (s 45.2(1)(2)) Anything the party ought to do to promote compliance with this Act (45.2(1)3); (s 45.3)	N/A	Contraventions of the code, obstruction or failure to comply with an order are an offence Fine of up to $25,000 Prosecution requires consent of attorney general (s 46.2)	*Mandate:* Commission no longer has the power to receive and investigate complaints. May initiate reviews and inquiries into any incidents of tension or conflict; policy development; can intervene in legal proceedings, etc. (s 29) Commission may apply to tribunal (s 35) or intervene in an application (s 37) *Intent:* Intention to discriminate applies to discrimination in notice or sign, etc. (s 13(1)) *Exemptions:* For services, facilities, and employment for religious, philanthropic, educational, fraternal, or social institutions (ss 18 and 24(1)(a)); solemnization of marriage by religious officials (s 18.1)

System/ Human rights grounds	Institutional Independence[1]	Qualifications/ Appointments/ Dismissals	Damages/ Remedies	Costs	Criminal Sanctions	Additional information and features
Note: Parties to make human rights claims before the civil courts, provided that there is another independent cause of action (s 46.1) Age Ancestry Citizenship Colour Creed Disability Ethnic origin Family status Gender identity Gender expression Marital status Place of origin Race Receipt of public assistance (accommodation only – s 2)	*Staffing:* Commission appoints own employees (s 27(9)) Tribunal appoints own employees (s 32(9))	Tribunal members: Must undergo competitive process to establish experience, knowledge, or training with respect to human rights law and issues; aptitude for impartial adjudication; aptitude for applying alternative adjudicative practices and procedures (s 32(3))				

System / Human rights grounds	Institutional Independence[1]	Qualifications/ Appointments/ Dismissals	Damages/ Remedies	Costs	Criminal Sanctions	Additional information and features
Record of offences (employment only – s 5)		*Appointments:* Commissioners appointed by LGC (s 27(7)) for "such term as may be specified"				
Sex		Tribunal members appointed by LGC (s 32(2)) in a competitive selection process for "such term as may be specified"				
Sexual orientation						
Source of income – see receipt of public assistance (Ss 1-7)		HRLSC: Centre's Board of Directors appointed by LGC (s 45.14 (2))				
Association with people based on any of these grounds (s 12)		Term of appointment and reappointment fixed by regulation (s 48(2))				

System/Human rights grounds	Institutional Independence[1]	Qualifications/Appointments/Dismissals	Damages/Remedies	Costs	Criminal Sanctions	Additional information and features
PRINCE EDWARD ISLAND *Human Rights Act, RSPEI 1988, c H-12* First generation • Prince Edward Island Human Rights Commission • Human Rights Panels Age Colour Creed Criminal or summary conviction (employment only (s 6(1)(b)) Disability Ethnic or national origin Family status Gender expression Gender identity Marital status Political belief	*Reporting:* Annual report to minister (s 22.1); reports "as required by the minister" (s 18(d)) Commission responsible to minister (s 17) *Staffing:* May appoint staff who are not subject to Civil Service Act. (s 19) Note: Panels consist of commission members (s 26(2))	*Qualifications:* N/A *Appointments:* Commission: Appointed by Legislative Assembly on recommendation of Standing Committee on Social Development (s 16 (2)) Term not exceeding three years (s 16(3))	*Pecuniary:* Panel may order compensation for lost wages or income, or expenses incurred (s 28.4(1)(b)(iv)) *Other:* Cease contraventions; make available to the person rights, opportunities, or privileges; take other action as considered proper (s 28.4(1)(b)(i),(ii),(iii), (v))	Panel may award costs (s 28.4(6))	Contraventions of the act, failure to comply with an order are an offence with a fine of $100-$500 for individuals and $200-$2,000 for organizations (s 29) Conviction requires reasonable preponderance of evidence supporting the charge (s 30(2))	*Mandate:* In addition to protection activities, Commission shall undertake education in "human rights," advise government (s 18) *Intent:* Intention to discriminate applies to notice, sign, etc. (s 12(1)) *Exemptions:* Employment and volunteer exemptions for non-profit religious or ethnic organizations (ss 6(4)(c) and 10(2)) *Initiating complaints:* Third-party complaints permitted; commission and commission employees cannot initiate own complaint (s 22 (1))

System/Human rights grounds	Institutional Independence[1]	Qualifications/Appointments/Dismissals	Damages/Remedies	Costs	Criminal Sanctions	Additional information and features
Race Religion Sex[5] Sexual orientation Source of income (s 1(1)(d)) Association with people based on any of these grounds (s 13)		Human rights panel members: Chairperson appoints commission members to Human Rights Panels (unless special circumstances warrant additional members (s 26)				
QUEBEC *Charter of human rights and freedoms*, RSQ, c C-12 First generation* • Commission des droits de la personne et des droits de la jeunesse[6] • Human Rights Tribunal	*Reporting:* Commission submits annual reports to president of National Assembly (s 73) *Staffing:* Commission appoints its own staff (s 62)	*Qualifications:* Five of 13 commission members must be "persons capable of making a notable contribution" respecting human rights and freedoms" (s 58.1)	*Pecuniary/ Non-Pecuniary:* Compensation for moral or material prejudice (s 49) *Punitive:* Punitive damages for unlawful and intentional interference (s 49) *Other:* cessation of behaviour (s 49)	Tribunal may award costs, disbursements (s 126)	Failure to comply with a tribunal decision constitutes contempt of court and may result in imprisonment for up to one year and/or a fine of up to $50,000,	*Mandate:* In addition to protection activities, commission undertakes broad range of research, education, and information activities on all human rights and fundamental freedoms (s 71); youth protection; also addresses exploitation of older persons (s 48) Discrimination defined (s. 10)

System/ Human rights grounds	Institutional Independence[1]	Qualifications/ Appointments/ Dismissals	Damages/ Remedies	Costs	Criminal Sanctions	Additional information and features
*Note: Complaints may be filed with commission or courts. Complainants may also apply to the tribunal themselves if the commission chooses not to do so on their behalf, in very limited circumstances (s 84) Age Civil status Colour Criminal or penal conviction (employment only – s 18.2) Disability (handicap) Ethnic or national origin Language Political convictions Pregnancy	Internal governance: Commission makes its own internal by-laws (s 70) Tribunal is administratively integrated into the Quebec court system	Tribunal president: Judge with "notable experience and expertise in, sensitivity to and interest for matters of human rights and freedoms" (s 101) Appointments: Commission members: appointed by 2/3 of National Assembly (s 58) Term of office may not exceed ten years; cannot be reduced once set (s 58.3)			without prejudice to any suit for damages (s 131) Contraventions of the act, obstruction, and reprisals are an offence (s 134) Commission may institute penal proceedings (s 136)	Contains a bill of rights protecting: • Right to life, personal security (ss 1,2) • Fundamental freedoms (s 4) • Property and privacy rights (s 6- 9) • Political, democratic rights (s 22) • Judicial rights (ss 23-38) • Children's rights (s 39-42, 57) • Economic and social rights: rights related to education, employment, ethnic minority rights/ cultural rights, environmental rights (ss 43-46, 46.1)) *Note:* Commission can receive complaints only in discrimination matters. *Exemption:* For non-profit charitable, philanthropic, religious, political, or educational non-profit institutions in employment (s 20)

System/ Human rights grounds	Institutional Independence[1]	Qualifications/ Appointments/ Dismissals	Damages/ Remedies	Costs	Criminal Sanctions	Additional information and features
Race Religion Sex Sexual orientation Social condition (See s 10)		Commission members remain in office until replaced, except in the case of resignation. (s 60) Tribunal members appointed by government for 5 years President of tribunal chosen in consultation with chief judge of Court of Québec (s 101) *Dismissal:* See above				*Initiating investigations:* Commission may undertake investigations on its own initiative (s 71(1)) *Interventions:* Any person or organization with sufficient interest may intervene before tribunal (s 116)

System / Human rights grounds	Institutional Independence[1]	Qualifications / Appointments / Dismissals	Damages / Remedies	Costs	Criminal Sanctions	Additional information and features
SASKATCHEWAN *Saskatchewan Human Rights Code,* SS 1979, c S-24.1 Saskatchewan Human Rights Commission (Human rights tribunal abolished) Complaints referred to Court of Queen's Bench Age Ancestry Colour Creed Disability Family status Marital status Nationality Place of origin Race or perceived race	*Reporting:* Commission is responsible to minister (s 26) Commission reports to minister (s 49) *Staffing:* May appoint its own staff (s 23)	*Qualifications:* No criteria specified for commissioners (Judges of Queen's Bench subject to judicial processes and criteria for appointment) *Appointments:* Commission members appointed by LGC (s 21(3)) Three, four or five year terms (s 21(5))	Court may award compensation for *Pecuniary:* Lost wages and benefits, and expenses incurred (s 31.3(1)(c)) Additional costs of obtaining alternative goods, services, facilities, or accommodations s 31.3(1)(d) *Non-pecuniary,* *Punitive:* Up to $10,000 for wilful or reckless conduct, or injury to feeling, dignity, or self-respect (s 31.4)	Court may award costs only if vexatious, frivolous, or abusive conduct (s 29.8)	Failure to comply with an order is an offence with a fine of up to $500 for an individual's first offence and up to $2,000 for subsequent offences, or up to $2,000 for an organization's first offence and up to $3,000 for subsequent offences (s 35)	*Mandate:* Protection activities; commission also undertakes education on discrimination issues, promotional activities with respect to legal rights and cultural rights, research on human rights, and measures to prevent and address systemic issues (s 25) *Intent:* Relevant for discriminatory employment advertisements (s 19(1)) *Discriminatory/hate speech:* Prohibited for notices, signs, etc., and also for articles and statements (s 14(1)) *Exemptions:* Code creates exemptions for educational facilities (s 16(5)) and non-profit charitable, philanthropic, fraternal, religious, racial, or social organizations (s 16(10))

System/ Human rights grounds	Institutional Independence[1]	Qualifications/ Appointments/ Dismissals	Damages/ Remedies	Costs	Criminal Sanctions	Additional information and features
Receipt of public assistance Religion Sex Sexual orientation Source of income – see Receipt of public assistance (S 2(1)(m.01))			*Other:* Cease contraventions; adopt program; make available to the person rights, opportunities, or privileges; ensure accessibility of premises (s 31.3 (1))			Contains a bill of rights protecting fundamental freedoms; legal rights; e.g., freedom from arbitrary imprisonment; democratic rights
YUKON *Human Rights Act, RSY 2002, c 116* First generation • Yukon Human Rights Commission • Panel of adjudicators Age Ancestry, including colour and race Criminal charges or records	*Reporting:* Commission is accountable to Legislature (s 16(1)) Annual report submitted to speaker of Legislature (s 18) Panel of adjudicators accountable to Legislature, chief adjudicator (s 22(8))	*Qualifications:* Commission: No criteria specified *Appointments:* Commission members appointed by Legislature for three-year term (s 17(1))	*Pecuniary:* Any financial loss (s 24(1)(c)) *Non-pecuniary:* For injury to dignity, feelings, or self-respect (s 24(1)(d)) Exemplary damages for malicious conduct (s 24(1)(e))	Panel may award costs (s 24(1)(f)) Costs can be awarded for frivolous or vexatious proceedings (s 25(a)) or providing false information (26(a))	Obstruction, retaliation, and providing false information are summary conviction offences; fine up to $2,000 (ss 29-32)	*Mandate:* In addition to protection activities, commission "shall" promote principles of equality and cultural diversity, promote education and research related to discrimination, and undertake education research on pay equity (s 16) Contains a bill of rights that protects fundamental freedoms; property rights Commission may refer matter directly to adjudication without investigation (s 20(1)(d))

System/ Human rights grounds	Institutional Independence[1]	Qualifications/ Appointments/ Dismissals	Damages/ Remedies	Costs	Criminal Sanctions	Additional information and features
Disability	*Internal governance/staffing:* After consultation with commission, commissioner in Executive Council may make regulations regarding procedures of commission and panel, and hiring of commission's staff (s 36)	Chief adjudicator appointed by Legislature for three-year term (s 22(2))	Damages for injury to respondent's reputation if complaint was frivolous or vexatious (s 25(b)) or was based on false information (s 26(b))			*Exemption:* For services, employment offered by religious, charitable, educational, social, cultural, or athletic organizations (s 11(1), (3 (a))
Ethnic or linguistic background or origin						
Marital or family status		Adjudicators appointed by legislator				*Aboriginal issues:* Act does not affect Aboriginal rights (s 1(2))
National origin		*Dismissal:* Commissioners may be removed by resolution of legislature (s 17(2))				
Political belief, association, or activity						
Religion or creed, or religious belief, association, or activity						
Sex						
Sexual orientation						
Source of income						
Association with people based on any of these grounds (s 7)						

Recommendations for Changes to Human Rights Systems

1 Government departments, agencies, and watchdog bodies should issue regular reports that allow Canadians to evaluate the extent to which Parliament and legislatures are building human rights objectives into their medium-term planning and are complying with the Charter and with international human rights obligations.

2 Human rights systems should work to track and report on the extent to which governments and independent agencies are complying with international and national human rights standards and reporting on their own human rights records.

3 Heritage Canada should expand the Continuing Committee of Officials on Human Rights to include additional sessions where human rights commissions can attend as active participants.

4 Heritage Canada should expand the mandate of the Continuing Committee of Officials on Human Right's to include work towards harmonizing and improving human rights legislation across Canada.

5 Canadian governments at all levels should consider permitting litigants to bring claims that contain a human rights element to the courts, provided that there is another civil cause of action. This should not detract from the ability to bring a human rights complaint to a human rights system.

6 Unionized employees should have access to human rights systems and should be able to file complaints before these systems if their unions prove unable or unwilling to represent their members.

7 Commissions should initiate discussions to strengthen the institutional base of a national rights organization that would provide a Canada-wide national learning and research platform on human rights and human rights systems.

8 Commissions should initiate discussions with federal, provincial, and territorial governments, as well as bar associations, to develop and institute ways of better using and supporting the work of a national organization.

9 Governments that have first-generation systems should amend human rights laws to introduce some measure of direct access to tribunals. Direct access should be accompanied by public support for complainants.

10 The government should undertake a study of the Saskatchewan human rights system to determine the impact of the loss of a specialized human rights tribunal on the level of access to justice, the types of remedies offered, and the length of delays as compared to other systems in Canada.

11 The legislatures of British Columbia and Nunavut should establish independent human rights commissions that can undertake research, public education, and initiate systemic litigation.

12 Governments should modify human rights statutes, as appropriate, to widen their promotional mandates and to confer or clarify the role of commissions to speak out about any human rights issue across the full range of human rights.

13 Human rights commissions in Canada should work together to support international human rights processes, including the ICC and the Universal Periodic Review process.

14 Governments should amend human rights legislation to include specific authority to work with international human rights networks and the international human rights system.

15 Human rights commissions, law reform bodies, academics, and the Uniform Law Conference of Canada should work cooperatively towards the development of a uniform model of human rights law that:
   • reflects the Canadian Charter of Rights and Freedoms and our international commitments;
   • ensures that Canadians are equal before the law;
   • guarantees human rights protections based on the highest standards of protection, access to justice, and fair and appropriate remedies;
   • incorporates good practices and recommendations from prior reports on human rights systems in Canada;

- ensures that commissions and tribunals have statutory guarantees of institutional independence, impartiality, and competence that are consistent with international standards, including the Paris Principles (for commissions) and the ICCPR (for tribunals), as well as with stringent standards of judicial independence for tribunals.

16 All human rights systems in Canada should provide state-funded information and advisory services for respondents as well as complainants.

17 Where such a right is lacking, governments in Canada should enact the right to a human rights tribunal that is independent, impartial, and competent, in accordance with the principles of fundamental justice.

18 Governments should amend human rights legislation to include a statement that human rights commissions are independent institutions, and to provide that human rights commissions report directly to the legislature in jurisdictions where the statutes are silent or inconsistent with these recommendations.

19 Internal reporting arrangements, commission bylaws, memoranda of understanding, and other tools used to structure the day-to-day workings of commissions and their relationship to government must be predicated on the principles of institutional independence in terms of commissions' human rights work.

20 Human rights legislation should be amended to set out clear, appropriate, and transparent criteria and processes for naming commissioners by legislatures. Procedures and criteria should exist for renewing commissioners and dismissing them in accordance with the Paris Principles. The duration of appointments should be benchmarked against current practices in other regulatory agencies and protected by law.

21 Commissions should work with academics and training centres, in partnership with CASHRA or other national associations, to develop a standard curriculum for human rights professionals that focuses on the work of national human rights institutions.

22 Governments should review human rights legislation to ensure that there are effective, rapid recourses available through injunctive relief or comparable remedies to protect human rights defenders, complainants, and witnesses.

Notes

ACKNOWLEDGMENTS

1 Appendix 1 contains a list of interviewees, their affiliations, and interview dates. References to interview dates appear in the notes.

ABOUT THIS BOOK

1 Part I of the *Constitution Act, 1982*, Schedule B to the *Canada Act 1982* (UK), 1982, c 11 [Charter].
2 The citation of legal material is based on the *Canadian Guide to Uniform Legal Citation* (Toronto: Carswell, 2010, 7th ed), with some minor adaptations.
3 Some additional issues are updated to 31 August 2013.

PREFACE

1 The full name in French is Commission des droits de la personne et droits de la jeunesse. There is no official English equivalent.
2 Interview of Raj Anand (14 September 2009) [Anand].
3 William Walker, "Rights Commission Hiring Was Flawed, Report States," *Toronto Star* (3 June 1989) A8.
4 Anand, *supra* note 2. Anand has since received awards and distinctions for his contributions to human rights and to the rights of minority communities in Ontario. A senior partner in a major Toronto law firm, he became the first chair of Ontario's Human Rights Legal Support Centre in 2008.
5 Interview of Rémy Beauregard (15 September 2009).
6 Interview of Keith Norton (21 April 2009).

7 Interview of Dianna Scarth (2 February, 2010).

8 RSO 1990, c H-19.

9 Ontario Human Rights Commission, *Policy and Guidelines on Disability and the Duty to Accommodate* (Toronto: Ontario Human Rights Commission, 2000), online: OHRC <http://www.ohrc.on.ca/en/policy-and-guidelines-disability-and-duty-accommodate>.

10 See *Eagleson Co-Operative Homes, Inc. v. Théberge* (2006), 274 DLR (4th) 359, 218 OAC 321 (Sup.Ct. (Div.Ct.)) at para 16.

11 The Commission did not work in isolation on these issues. Organizations such as the Human Resources Professionals Association of Ontario, the Canadian Association of Retired Persons, the Canadian Civil Liberties Association, ARCH Disability Law Centre, the Centre for Equality Rights in Accommodation, the African Canadian Legal Clinic, and many others were crucial players.

12 See, e.g., "Former Ont. Minister Dies at 69," *The Globe and Mail* (1 February 2010), online: The Globe and Mail <http://www.theglobeandmail.com>; see also the discussion of the Commission's role in addressing age-based discrimination in *Assn. of Justices of the Peace of Ontario v. Ontario (Attorney General)* (2008), 92 OR (3d) 16 at para 4.5

13 The UN uses the term "national human rights institution" to refer to commissions, public protectors, public advocates, and other institutions that are state-funded, independent, established by a constitution or legislation (or both), and are specifically mandated to protect and promote human rights.

14 I worked in Rwanda on several missions between 2000 and the end of 2003. I worked in Timor in 2008. Both missions were for the UN Office of the High Commissioner for Human Rights.

15 The International Bill of Human Rights refers to the following instruments: the *Universal Declaration of Human Rights*, GA Res 217 (III), UNGAOR, 3d Sess, Supp No 13, UN Doc A/810, (1948) 71; the *International Covenant on Civil and Political Rights*, 19 December 1966, 999 UNTS 171, Can TS 1976 No 47, 6 ILM 368 (entered into force 23 March 1976, accession by Canada 19 May 1976 its optional protocols and the 1966 *International Covenant on Economic, Social and Cultural Rights*, 16 December 1966, 993 UNTS 3, Can TS 1976 No 46 (entered into force 3 January 1976).

16 Interview of Irwin Cotler (25 June 2009). Cotler was minister of Justice from 2003 to 2006. He is currently the Liberal Member of Parliament for Mont-Royal.

17 Interview of Byron Williams (9 February 2010).

INTRODUCTION

1 The Supreme Court of Canada formulated the original dignity-based test for equality in *Law v. Canada (Minister of Employment and Immigration)*, [1999] 1 SCR 497. The test was abandoned a decade later in *R. v. Kapp*, [2008] 2 SCR 483.

2 The description of human rights is from Mary Robinson, "The Declaration of Human Rights" (Symposium on the Asia Pacific Region, delivered at UNU Headquarters, Tokyo, 27 January 1998). Thanks to Ken Norman for bringing this quote to my attention.

3 Article 2(1), *International Covenant on Civil and Political Rights*, 19 December 1966, 999 UNTS 171, Can TS 1976 No 47, 6 ILM 368 (entered into force 23 March 1976, accession by Canada 19 May 1976) [ICCPR].

4 Section 67 of the *Canadian Human Rights Act* had created this prohibition: RSC 1985, c H-6 [CHRA] and was repealed in 2008. See Bill C-21, *An Act to Amend the Canadian Human Rights Act*, 2nd Sess, 39th Parl, 2008 (assented to 18 June 2008), SC 2008, c 30. The repeal took effect in 2011 after a three-year transitional period.

5 See Mary Eberts, "Knowing and Unknowing: Settler Reflections on Missing and Murdered Indigenous Women" (2014) 77:1 Sask L Rev (forthcoming).

6 Evidence submitted by First Nationals Child and Family Caring Society shows that there is 22 percent less funding available on a per child basis for First Nations children living on reserves than for other children: *Canada (Human Rights Commission) v. Canada (Attorney General)*, 2012 FC 445 at para 21, aff'd (2013) FCA 75.

7 Canadian Centre for Policy Alternatives and Save the Children Canada, *Poverty or Prosperity: Indigenous Children in Canada* (Ottawa, June 2013), online: CCPA <http://www.policyalternatives.ca>.

8 An online archive of the legal documents from the trial and the execution, including an image of the confession obtained under torture, can be viewed online. See "Torture and the Truth: Angélique and the Burning of Montreal," online: Canadian Mysteries <http://www.canadianmysteries.ca/sites/angelique/proces/jugementetappel/indexen.html>. Slavery was abolished in 1833 in the United Kingdom.

9 Constance Backhouse, *Colour-Coded: A Legal History of Racism in Canada, 1900-1950* (Toronto: University of Toronto Press, 1999) [Backhouse, *Colour-Coded*]. R Brian Howe, "The Evolution of Human Rights Policy in Ontario" (1991) 24 Can J Pol Sci 783 at 788-789. See also Robin W Winks, *The Blacks in Canada: A History,* 2d ed (Montreal:

McGill-Queen's University Press, 1997); Donald H Oliver, "Our Shameful Legacy," op ed, *The [Montreal] Gazette* (27 February 2012) A21.

10 Desmond was prosecuted for cheating the government out of the one-cent tax revenue on the price difference between a balcony seat and a more expensive floor seat. Although Desmond had offered to pay the price difference, the theatre would not accept her payment. She was fined $20, plus $6 in costs. See Constance Backhouse, "Racial Segregation in Canadian Legal History: Viola Desmond's Challenge, Nova Scotia, 1946" (1994) 17:2 Dalhousie LJ 299 at 303, online: <http://www.constancebackhouse. ca> [Backhouse, "Racial Segregation"].

11 *His Majesty the King v. Viola Irene Desmond*, Halifax, Public Archives of Nova Scotia (RG 39, "C" Halifax, v. 937, Supreme Court of Nova Scotia, No 13347; *The King v. Desmond* (1947), 20 Maritime Provinces Reports 297 (Nova Scotia Supreme Court). Cited in Constance Backhouse, "The Historical Construction of Racial Identity and Implications for Reconciliation," report commissioned by the Department of Canadian Heritage for the Ethnocultural, Racial, Religious and Linguistic Diversity of Identity Seminar (2001) at p 17, online: Metropolis <http://canada. metropolis.net/events/ethnocultural/publications/historical.pdf>.

12 Backhouse, *ibid*. See also Backhouse, *Colour-Coded, supra* note 9.

13 Interview of Margaret Parsons (10 June 2009) [Parsons].

14 For an analysis of the public record regarding changing attitudes towards Asian immigrants, see Patricia E Roy, *A White Man's Province: British Columbia Politicians and Chinese and Japanese Immigrants, 1858–1914* (Vancouver: University of British Columbia Press, 1989). See also James W St G Walker, *"Race," Rights and the Law in the Supreme Court of Canada: Historical Case Studies* (Waterloo: Wilfrid Laurier University Press, 1997) at 254–55, and Peter S Li, *The Chinese in Canada*, 2d ed (Toronto: Oxford University Press, 1998).

15 See the *Chinese Immigration Act*, SC 1885, c 71 and the *Chinese Immigration Act*, SC 1923, c 38. Most Chinese immigrants were barred from Canada for twenty-four years after the head tax was abolished in 1923. See *Mack v. Canada* (Attorney General) (2002), 60 OR (3d) 737 (CA), leave to appeal refused, [2003] 1 SCR xiii. .

16 *Ibid*. Although the Court of Appeal in *Mack* acknowledged the historical reality of the head tax, the claim failed because the Charter did not exist when the head tax was in effect. The court held that the Charter could not be applied retroactively or retrospectively. It also refused to recognize international law that would have applied at the time and further rejected the claim based on unjust enrichment.

17 These and other chapters of Chinese Canadians' history are set out in an online documentation project. See Metro Toronto Chinese and Southeast Asian Legal Clinic, *Road to Justice: The Legal Struggle for Equal Rights of Chinese Canadians*, online: Road to Justice <http://www.roadtojustice.ca>.

18 In addition to the funds allocated to the Chinese community under the Community Historical Recognition Program, project funds were also provided for Indo-Canadian, Italian-Canadian, and Jewish-Canadian projects. An endowment fund was established for Eastern Europeans who were interned as enemy aliens in Canadian work camps during the First World War pursuant to the *War Measures Act, 1914*. The $10 million endowment, the "Canadian First World War Internment Recognition Fund" was established in 2008 to commemorate and educate Canadians about Canada's first national internment operations of 1914 to 1920.

19 Joe Friesen, "Head-tax Redress Funds Clawed Back," *Globe and Mail* (27 February 2013) A3.

20 In the First World War, thousands of Ukrainians were detained in camps in Canada as enemy aliens under the *War Measures Act, 1914*. As mentioned in note 18, in 2008, the federal government announced a $10 million grant for an endowment fund in recognition of the internment of Eastern European immigrants in Canadian work camps as part of the Community Historical Recognition Program.

21 Japanese Canadian Redress Agreement, PC 1988-9/2552, dated 31 October 1988. These measures were taken under the *War Measures Act*, the *National Emergency Transitional Powers Act 1945*, and other legislation. Many Canadian writers and historians have written about these events, including Ken Adachi, Addie Kobayashi, Muriel Kitagawa, Roy Miki, Robert Okazaki, and Mary Taylor.

22 See Michael Brown in in L Ruth Klein, ed., *Nazi Germany, Canadian Responses: Confronting Antisemitism in the Shadow of War* (Montreal: McGill-Queen's University Press, 2012) [Klein] 144 at 159; James Walker, "Claiming Equality for Canadian Jewry: The Struggle for Inclusion, 1932–1945" in Klein, at 218.

23 Irving Abella and Harold Troper, *None Is Too Many: Canada and the Jews of Europe 1933–1948* (Toronto: Lester and Orpen Dennys, 1982). See also David Matas with Ilana Simon, *Closing the Doors: The Failure of Refugee Protection* (Toronto: Summerhill Press, 1989).

24 Eugenics laws were enacted in Alberta and British Columbia. See *Sexual Sterilization Act*, SA 1928, c 37 and *Sexual Sterilization Act*, SBC 1933, c 59. See also, Doris L Bergen, "Social Death and International Isolation: Jews in Nazi Germany, 1933–1939" in Klein, *supra* note 22 at 9.

25 Leilani Muir was institutionalized as a child for being feeble-minded. She was sterilized without her knowledge and only discovered her sterilization as an adult. Her case against the Government of Alberta paved the way for many other victims to seek legal redress. See *Muir v. Alberta* (1996), 132 DLR (4th) 695 (Alta QB).

26 Interview of David Baker (30 July 2009).

27 *Canadian Multiculturalism Act*, RSC, 1985, c. 24.

28 This is not to say that multiculturalism is uncontested or universally admired. The classic critique of multiculturalism is Neil Bissoondath, *Selling Illusions: The Cult of Multiculturalism in Canada* (Toronto: Penguin Books, 1994). For a more recent analysis, see Phil Ryan, *Multicultiphobia* (Toronto: University of Toronto Press, 2010).

29 Focus Canada 2010, 2011, 2012 (Environics Institute: Toronto). Online: <http://www.environicsinstitute.org/institute-projects/current-projects/focus-canada>.

30 Ray Pennings and Michael Van Pelt, "Replacing the Pan-Canadian Consensus," *Policy Options* (March 2006) 52. At page 53, the authors refer to "an aggressive rights-based polity that identifies with tolerance over definition." Their description of the "new consensus" does not include multiculturalism, tolerance, or human rights. The article has been republished online on the web site of Cardus, a conservative Christian think tank. Online <http://www.cardus.ca/comment>.

31 See Thomas Walkom, "Harper's New, Grim Consensus," *Toronto Star* (3 February 2010), online: Toronto Star <http://www.thestar.com/opinion/article/759582--harper-s-new-grim-consensus#article>.

32 The CCP was created by the Trudeau Liberals in 1978 to support linguistic rights. It was expanded to cover equality rights when the Charter took effect in 1985. The program was axed in 2006, but its language rights component was revived in 2008.

33 The Canadian HIV/AIDS Legal Network is one of dozens of progressive organizations that the federal government has criticized, defunded, shut down, or threatened with a loss of charitable status since 2006 for "activism," "advocacy," and/or "human rights." See the Voices-Voix Documentation Project, online: Voices-Voix <www.voices-voix.ca>, and the submission of Voices-Voix, a Canadian coalition of civil society organizations, to the Universal Periodic Review Process, Submission to 16th session of the Universal Periodic Review Working Group of the Human Rights Council (22 April–3 May 2013). Online: Voices-Voix <http://voices-voix.ca/en/document/voices-voix-submission-un-universal-periodic-review>. I am on the editorial board of Democracy Dissent and The Law, a university research network that oversees the documentation project.

34 *Canada (Justice) v. Khadr*, [2008] 2 SCR 125; *Canada (Prime Minister) v. Khadr*, [2010] 1 SCR 44.

35 *Canada (Attorney General) v. PHS Community Services Society*, 2011 SCC 44.

36 See *Edgar Schmidt v. Canada (Attorney General)*, Statement of Claim, T-2225-12 (Federal Court). [Schmidt] Mr Schmidt was suspended without pay for whistle blowing. See Bill Curry, "Judge Raps Justice Officials for Treatment of Whistle-blower," *Globe and Mail* (16 January 2013) online: Globe and Mail <http://www.theglobeandmail.com/news/politics/judge-raps-justice-officials-for-treatment-of-whistle-blower/article7394559/?service=mobile>.

37 Bill C-10, the full title of which is *An Act to Enact the Justice for Victims of Terrorism Act and to Amend the State Immunity Act, the Criminal Code, the Controlled Drugs and Substances Act, the Corrections and Conditional Release Act, the Youth Criminal Justice Act, the Immigration and Refugee Protection Act and Other Acts*, 1st Sess, 41st Parl, 2012 (assented to 13 March 2012) SC 2012, c 1. Bill C-10 came into force in June 2012.

38 Editorial, "A Lesson for Canada as the U.S. Turns against Mandatory Minimums," *Globe and Mail* (14 August 2013) online: The Globe and Mail <http://www.theglobeandmail.com>.

39 See Eric Luna, "Mandatory Mandatory Minimum Sentencing Provisions under Federal Law" (Testimony to the United States Sentencing Commission, May 27 2010) online: Cato Institute <http://www.cato.org>.

40 *R v. Smickle*, 2012 ONSC 602. On appeal, the Court of Appeal upheld the finding of unconstitutionality: 2013 ONCA 678.

41 John Edwards, Willie Gibbs, and Ed McIsaac, "Jails Don't Keep People Out Of Jail," *Globe and Mail* (5 January 2012) A15, online: Globe and Mail <http://www.theglobeandmail.com/commentary/jails-dont-keep-people-out-of-jail/article1357501/>.

42 *The Act Protecting Canada's Immigration System Act*, SC 2012, c 17. See ss. 20.1, 57.1 of the *Immigration and Refugee Protection Act*, SC 2001, c 27

43 Cara Wilkie et al, *Human Rights Issues in National Security: An Inventory of Agency Considerations* (Ottawa: Canadian Human Rights Commission, 2008), online: CHRC <http://www.chrc-cdp.ca>.

44 *Schmidt, supra* note 36.

45 David Macdonald, "Attack on Evidence-based Public Policy." Delivered at Voices-Voix meeting on "The State and Health of Democracy in Canada," Ottawa, 11 May 2012

46 See Andrew Lui, *Why Canada Cares: Human Rights and Foreign-Policy in Theory and Practice* (Montreal and Kingston: McGill-Queen's University Press, 2011).

47 Kenneth Roth, "Reestablishing Canada's Leadership in Global Human
   Rights." Presentation to the Montreal Council on Foreign Relations,
   Montreal, 30 October 2009. Canada's ratification of the UN Convention
   on the Rights of Persons with Disabilities in 2010 was a welcome excep-
   tion. See GA Res 61/611, UNGAOR, 61st Sess, Supp No 49, UN Doc A/
   RES/61/106, (2007) 2 [*CRPD*].

48 Global Integrity, "Global Integrity Report: Canada – 2010," online: Global
   Integrity Report <http://www.globalintegrity.org/report/Canada/2010>.
   The Global Integrity Report assesses national government accountability,
   integrity, and democratic processes using more than 300 indicators. It measures the strength of countries' key laws and enforcement records.

49 Amnesty International, *Getting Back on the 'Rights' Track: A Human
   Rights Agenda for Canada* (Ottawa: Amnesty International, 2011.)>.

50 Amnesty International, News Release, "Canada – Time to Match
   International Commitments with National Action" (19 December 2012)
   online: Amnesty International <http://www.amnesty.ca/news/news-releases/
   canada-time-to-match-international-commitments-with-national-action>.

51 Excerpts from a 1999 interview with Terry O'Neil of *BC Report* newsmagazine, cited in *Maclean's*, "Harper Must Act Now to Protect Free
   Speech" (20 September 2009), online: *Maclean's* <http://www2.macleans.
   ca/2009/09/20/harper-must-act-now-to-protect-free-speech/>. The original
   interview appeared in the now-defunct conservative publication *BC
   Report:* "Happy-Faced Tyranny: Will Abortionists Be the Next "Protected
   Minority?" *British Columbia (BC) Report* (11 January 1999).

52 Kevin Libin, "Minister Warns of 'Illiberal' Attacks on Free Speech,"
   National Post (3 May 2008) A1.

53 *Canada (Human Rights Commission) v. Warman*, 2012 FC 1162.

54 R Brian Howe and David Johnson, *Restraining Equality: Human Rights
   Commissions in Canada* (Toronto: University of Toronto Press, 2000). See
   also Rosanna L. Langer, *Defining Rights and Wrongs: Bureaucracy, Human
   Rights and Public Accountability* (Vancouver: UBC Press, 2007).

55 Interview of Martha Jackman (9 September 2009).

56 Interview of Mark Freiman (1 May 2009).

57 Interview of Patricia Knipe (5 February 2010).

58 In 2005, the Danish newspaper *Jyllands-Posten* had published editorial
   cartoons featuring depictions of Mohammed in connection with terrorism.
   The newspaper said the cartoons aimed to contribute to debates about
   self-censorship and Islam. Muslims in Denmark and elsewhere saw the cartoons as racist and provocative. Worldwide protests ensued. Publications in
   several countries all over the world reprinted the cartoons in solidarity.

59 The post appeared in the *Western Standard's* Shotgun Blog on 2 December 2007.

60 The complaints, filed with the Alberta and Canadian Commissions, were withdrawn in December 2007, "Western Standard's Apology Averts Islamic Protest," *Calgary Herald* (21 December 2007) online: <http://www.canada. com>.

61 Naseem Mithoowani, Khurrum Awan, and Muneeza Sheikh, "Rights Complainants Want Only Reasonable Access to Media," *Gazette* [Montreal] (24 February 2008) at A15.

62 Mark Steyn, "The Future Belongs to Islam," *Maclean's* (20 October 2006), online: *Maclean's* <http://www.macleans.ca>.

63 The section is drawn in part from Pearl Eliadis, "The Controversy Entrepreneurs," *Maisonneuve* magazine (Fall 2008) at 38. A portion of the article is available online: <http://maisonneuve.org/pressroom/article/2009/ aug/20/controversy-entrepreneurs/> [Eliadis].

64 E.g., Lorne Gunter, "Alberta's Gauntlet of Bias," *National Post* (14 January 2008) online: <http://www.nationalpost.com>.

65 E.g., "Human Rights vs Human Ambitions," *National Post* (19 April, 2008) A16.

66 E.g., "A Disaster from Canada's Human Rights Commission," *National Post* (28 March 2008) A12; "How to Turn a Neo-Nazi into a Free-speech Martyr," *National Post* (25 March 2008) A8.

67 Interview of Alan Borovoy (14 September 2009).

68 See, in particular, Mark Steyn, "That Poor Woman Down the Street," *Maclean's* (2 April 2008) online: Macleans.ca <http://www.macleans.ca>.

69 See Office of the Privacy Commissioner of Canada, "Investigation Finds No Evidence that Canadian Human Rights Commission Accessed Individual's Internet Connection" (29 January 2009), online: Office of the Privacy Commissioner of Canada <http://www.priv.gc.ca/cf-dc/pa/2008-09/pa_2009 0127_e.asp>. See also Canadian Human Rights Commission, News Release, "RCMP Concludes that No Charges Will Be Laid against the Canadian Human Rights Commission" (27 November 2008), online: CHRC <http:// www.chrc-ccdp.ca/media_room/news_releases-eng.aspx?id=504>.

70 See e.g. Mark Steyn, "Kangaroo Court Is Now in Session," Opinion, *Maclean's* (26 March 2008); <http://www.macleans.ca/canada/opinions/arti-cle.jsp?content=20080326_105422_105422> [Steyn]; Ezra Levant, "A Travesty of a Mockery of a Sham," *Canadian Lawyer* (August 2008) 70; Editorial, "You Call This Human Rights?'" *National Post* (7 February 2011) A8.; Barry Cooper, "It's Time to Close Our Kangaroo Courts" [Montreal] *Gazette* (23 October 2009) A21 [Cooper, "Kangaroo courts"].

71 See e.g. Steyn, *supra* note 70, "metaphorically" referring to the Canadian
    Human Rights Commission as the Gestapo. Columnist George Jonas went
    on in a similar vein: "Like Canadian supporters of hate speech legislation,
    supporters of the Weimar Republic thought that their groups and causes
    would occupy all seats of authority and set all social and legal agendas for-
    ever." See George Jonas, "You Can't Outlaw Hateful Thoughts" [Montreal]
    Gazette (7 April 2008) A19. See also Ezra Levant, "The Free-Speech
    Debate (II)," Letter to the Editor, *National Post* (23 June 2009) A17: "[E]
    very single person who the CHRC has prosecuted has been convicted. Not
    even North Korea can boast a 100% conviction rate."

72 A *National Post* editorial stated that "the CHRC has a 100% conviction
    rate on hate speech" See "A Bit Late for Introspection," Editorial, *National
    Post* (19 June 2008) A20.

73 Mark Steyn, "I Prefer Living with Space Lizards," *Maclean's* (27 February
    2008) online: Macleans.ca <http://www.macleans.ca/article.jsp?cont
    ent=20080227_1488_1488>.

74 See e.g., Cooper, "Kangaroo Courts," *supra* note 70; "Stop the Rot to Our
    Right for Free Speech," Editorial, *Calgary Herald* (9 October 2009) A16;
    "Harper Must Act Now to Protect Free Speech," Editorial, *Maclean's* (20
    September 2009) online: Macleans.ca <http://www2.macleans.
    ca/2009/09/20/harper-must-act-now-to-protect-free-speech/>; David
    Warren, "Kafka Comes to Canada," *Ottawa Citizen* (5 September 2009)
    B6; "End the Witch Hunts for Good," Editorial, *National Post*
    (3 September 2009) A12.

75 There have been notable exceptions. For example, Irwin Cotler has been a
    staunch supporter of the hate speech prohibitions in the CHRA. Jack Layton,
    former leader of the New Democratic Party, sent Muneeza Sheikh and
    Khurrum Awan a letter of support after they filed the *Maclean's* complaints:
    Interviews of Khurrum Awan and Muneeza Sheikh, (25 June 2009).

76 Kevin Libin, "Minister Warns of 'Illiberal' Attacks on Free Speech,"
    National Post (3 May 2008) A1.

77 Keith Martin, "Freedom to Speak" (February 2008). (Copy on file). The
    material now appears on his personal web site, <www.keithmartin.org>.
    Martin was first elected as a member of the Reform Party. He later sat as
    an independent and subsequently ran and was re-elected as a federal
    Liberal. He is now retired.

78 See, e.g., "Keith Martin's Motion," *The Globe and Mail* (6 February 2008).
    Online: <www.theglobeandmail.com>.

79 *An Act to Amend the Canadian Human Rights Act (Protecting Freedom)*,
    S.C. 2013 c. 37.

80 Ken Norman, "Saskatchewan Marches to a Different, Distant Drummer," *Regina Leader Post* (11 December 2010); CUPE Saskatchewan, News Release, "CUPE SK Convention Calls for Independent Review of Human Rights Commission" (1 March 2012) online: CUPE Saskatchewan at <http://cupe.sk.ca/www/News/sk-convention-calls-independent-review>; Alex Neve and Ailsa Watkinson, "Saskatchewan Rights' Bill Is Regressive," *Regina Leader-Post* (18 March 2011) B8, online <http://www2.canada.com/reginaleaderpost/news/viewpoints/story.html?id=9cd9ce30-54b4-4f07-b68a-6ec88b7f2e94>.

81 See Wildrose Caucus, "Justice, Policing and Human Rights: Ensuring Safe Streets and an Effective Justice System for Albertans" (26 September 2011) at 11, online: Wildrose <http://www.wildrosecaucus.ca/media/2011/09/Justice.pdf>.

82 Interview of Philippe Dufresne (4 May 2009).

83 Richard Moon, "Report to the Canadian Human Rights Commission Concerning Section 13 of the *Canadian Human Rights Act* and the Regulation of Hate Speech on the Internet," (October 2008) online: CHRC <http://www.chrc-ccdp.ca>.

84 Interview of Richard Moon (26 January, 2010) [Moon].

85 *Ibid.*

86 Richard Moon, "The Attack on Human Rights Commissions and the Corruption of Public Discourse" (2010) 73 Sask L Rev 93 at 96.

87 Moon, *supra* note 84.

88 *Ibid.*

89 Jennifer Lynch, "The Federal Human Rights System: Modern Approaches, Modern Challenges." Opening remarks during a panel discussion at the Canadian Association of Statutory Human Rights Agencies 2009 Annual Conference in Montreal, 15 June 2009.

90 Canadian Bar Association, "Hate Speech under the Canadian Human Rights Act" (Ottawa: January 2010) at 2, online: CBA <http://www.cba.org>.

91 Interview of Paul Champ (29 June 2010) [Champ].

92 Interview of John Miller (15 May 2009) [Miller].

93 Haroon Siddiqui, "Free Speech Cannot Be an Excuse to Hate," *Toronto Star* (15 June 2008) Online: http://www.thestar.com/opinion/article/443340--free-speech-cannot-be-an-excuse-for-hate.

94 Rick Salutin "Free Speech If You Can Afford It," *The Globe and Mail* (25 April 2008) online <www.theglobeandmail.com>; Doug Saunders. "Canada's Public Sphere Just Got a Lot More Messy – and Free" *The Globe and Mail* (5 September 2009) F3.

95 Ontario Human Rights Commission, News Release, "Commission Issues Statement on Decision in *Maclean's* Cases" (9 April 2008) online: OHRC <http://www.ohrc.on.ca/en/news_centre/commission-issues-statement-decision-maclean-cases> [emphasis added].

96 See Eliadis, *supra* note 63.

97 *Ibid*. During an interview in 2008, *Maclean's* lawyer and co-counsel Julian Porter, one of Canada's leading libel specialists, said his client had declined to make a preliminary application out of "respect" for the Muslim community. I interviewed Porter on 25 July 2008 for the *Maisonneuve* magazine article.

98 *Elmasry and Habib v. Roger's Publishing and MacQueen* (No. 4), 2008 BCHRT 378.

99 Parsons, *supra* note 13.

100 *Saskatchewan (Human Rights Commission) v. Whatcott*, 2013 SCC 11 [*Whatcott*], at para 75.

101 "Muzzling the Human Rights Debate," Editorial, *National Post* (18 June 2009) A20.

102 *Vigna v. Levant*, 2010 ONSC 6308 at paras 132-133.

103 *Ibid* at paras 3-4.

104 Interview of Richard Warman (4 May 2009) [Warman]; Interview of Darren Lund (18 August 2011).

105 Interview of Charlach Mackintosh (20 May 2009) [Mackintosh]; Interview of Heather MacNaughton (2 February 2010).

106 Giacomo Vigna, a lawyer for the Canadian Human Rights Commission, claimed that he received personal threats and that he was aware that two security staff members had been followed home during a hearing before the Canadian Human Rights Tribunal. See *Vigna v. Levant*, 2010 ONSC 6308 at paras 13-14.

107 Warman, *supra* note 104. In 2008, I spoke with a member of the Ontario Provincial Police about threats to Warman. The officer would not confirm or deny that Warman had been the target of threats or received police protection. However, he said that the police take seriously threats uttered by members of known extreme right-wing groups pursuant to the Criminal Code.

108 See, e.g., *Zündel v. Canada (Human Rights Commission) (C.A.)*, [2000] 4 FC; *Whatcott, supra* note 100. See also B'nai Brith Canada, League for Human Rights, "Hate Jurisdictions of Human Rights Commissions: A System in Need of Reform." Report submitted to the Canadian Human Rights Commission, 2008, <http://www.bnaibrith.ca/league-for-human-rights/>.

109 See, for example, *Center for Research-Action on Race Relations v. www. bcwhitepride.com*, 2008 CHRT 1 (CanLII), <http://canlii.ca/t/1w5pp>.

110 Freiman interview, *supra* note 56. Warman was criticized for having allegedly posed as an extremist on two websites. The Canadian Human Rights Tribunal commented that it was possible that Warman's actions, if proven, could have precipitated further hate messages. See *Warman v. Northern Alliance*, 2009 CHRT 10 at para 63. There was, however, no evidence that this had actually occurred. Warman explained his use of this tactic: "When I started this ten years ago, there was no handy handbook [on how] to infiltrate the Nazi movement." See Warman, *supra* note 104.

111 See *Warman v. Grosvenor* (2008), 92 OR (3d) 663 (SCJ). See also *Warman v. Fromm*, [2007] OJ No 4754 (SCJ). Both cases contain details regarding the climate of threats and violence.

112 Meeting No 27, SDIR – Subcommittee on International Human Rights of the Standing Committee on Foreign Affairs and International Development (18 June 2009), online: ParlVU <http://parlvu.parl.gc.ca/Parlvu/ ContentEntityDetailView.aspx?ContentEntityId=4910>. The statement, which can be heard at time code 46:52, is protected by Parliamentary privilege. It has not been censured or withdrawn despite letters of protest to both the committee chair and the speaker of the House.

113 Eliadis, *supra* note 63.

114 Interview of Mary Eberts (24 April 2009) [Eberts].

115 See, e.g., Karen Selick, Opinion, "Accommodation in the Air," *National Post* (21 January 2008) A13.

116 Research led by Rob Whitley, assistant professor at the Douglas Mental Health University Institute at McGill University, analyzed close to 10,000 news stories from Canadian media over six years. The study indicated a "tendency for some of the news media to associate mental illness with violence, crime, and homelessness." The research was funded by the Mental Health Commission of Canada. See Mental Health Commission of Canada, Media Release, "Canadian News Media Regularly Stigmatize People with Mental Illness" (2 February 2012) online: MHCC <http:// www.mentalhealthcommission.ca/SiteCollectionDocuments/February_ 2012/OMpercent20_Ryerson_Symposium_Media_Release_ENG.pdf>.

117 See Jonathan Kay, "How to Turn a Neo-Nazi into a Free-Speech Martyr," *National Post* (25 March 2008) A12. Journalism professor John Miller recalled attending a debate in Halifax on free speech and hate speech. He was surprised at how hostile many people in the audience seemed to be. When he asked one of them why they were so angry, they answered: "I am sick of having my White heritage and my religion steamrolled by

people." Miller saw this as "White backlash." He added: "It surprised me how many of them there are. They have a powerful network." Miller, *supra* note 92.

118   The social conservative group REAL Women suggested that human rights protections for transgendered people would result in children being exposed to "child predators." See REAL Women, "The Transgendered Have Their Day," *REALity* 29:4 (July/August 2010) online: REAL Women <http://www.realwomenofcanada.ca/wp-content/uploads/2012/09/REALityJuly-Aug2010.pdf>. See also Margaret Wente, "Human Rights Commissions – A Day at the Theatre of the Absurd," *The Globe and Mail* (16 February 2008) A19, online: The Globe and Mail <http://www.theglobeandmail.com/news/national/a-day-at-the-theatre-of-the-absurd/article718263/>. See also Margaret Wente, "The Explosive Rethinking of Sex Reassignment," *The Globe and Mail* (24 August 2007) A19, online: Globe and Mail <http://www.theglobeandmail.com/incoming/the-explosive-rethinking-of-sex-reassignment/article1081150/>. For a response, see Barbara Hall, "Unpublished Letter to the *Globe and Mail* Regarding Coverage of Recent Human Rights Issues" (29 February 2008) online at: <http://health.groups.yahoo.com/group/TransHealthLobbyRHN/message/875>.

119   Interview of Shelagh Day (9 March 2011).

120   *Ontario Human Rights Commission v. Etobicoke*, [1982] 1 SCR 202. This case was brought by firemen who had been forced to retire at age sixty pursuant to a clause in their collective agreement. The court held that compulsory retirement was not a bona fide occupational qualification and requirement. The court disagreed that firefighting is "a young man's game." See *ibid* at 212.

121   *Insurance Corporation of British Columbia v. Heerspink*, [1982] 2 SCR 145.

122   *Janzen v. Platy Enterprises Ltd*, [1989] 1 SCR 1252. In this case, the respondents tried to deny liability by arguing that the harassing behaviour was not based on sex but on the person's attractiveness. The court held: "to argue that the sole factor underlying the discriminatory action was the sexual attractiveness of the appellants and to say that their gender was irrelevant strains credulity. Sexual attractiveness cannot be separated from gender." See *ibid* at 1290, per Dickson, CJ. This case also defined sexual harassment and set a standard for future cases.

123   *CN v. Canada (Canadian Human Rights Commission)*, [1987] 1 SCR 1114. This case is frequently referred to as "Action Travail des Femmes," the name of the plaintiff organization. The original complaint was about a

longstanding series of hiring and promotion policies that operated to exclude women from blue-collar jobs. The court upheld the employment equity program that the tribunal had imposed on CN. See also, *British Columbia (Public Service Employee Relations Commission) v. BCGSEU*, [1999] 3 SCR 3.

124 *Central Alberta Dairy Pool v. Alberta (Human Rights Commission)*, [1990] 2 SCR 489. The complainant's religion required that he not work on his Sabbath and holy days. The respondent employer had refused his request for leave without pay for Easter Monday because of the plant's particularly onerous operational requirements on Mondays. The court held that the employer had not met its burden of proving that it accommodated the complainant up to the point of undue hardship.

125 See *Moore v. British Columbia (Education)*, 2012 SCC 61.

126 Interview of Pierre Bosset (16 September 2009).

127 *Canada (Human Rights Commission) v. Taylor*, [1990] 3 SCR 892; *Whatcott, supra* note 100.

128 *Vriend v. Alberta*, [1998] 1 SCR 493. In this case, the Supreme Court of Canada accepted interventions from both the Canadian Human Rights Commission and the Canadian Association of Statutory Human Rights Agencies (CASHRA), which is the national association of Human Rights Commissions. The provincial government prohibited the Alberta Commission from intervening directly: Mackintosh, supra note 105.

129 Commission des droits de la personne du Québec, *Enquête sur les allégations de discrimination raciale dans l'industrie du taxi à Montréal: Rapport final* (Montréal : Commission des droits de la personne, 1984). In the 1970s and early 1980, Montreal's taxi industry excluded Black drivers (Haitians in particular). Quebec's commission helped to break this story and place the issue of racism and discrimination at the forefront of public awareness. The commission held a public inquiry, which found rampant discrimination among Montreal's leading taxi companies.

130 *Gwinner v. Alberta (Human Resources and Employment)*, 2002 ABQB 685, aff'd 2004 ABCA 210.

131 With the support of the Public Interest Law Centre, in 2006 Community Living Manitoba filed a complaint against the Government of Manitoba, the executive director of the Manitoba Development Centre, and the Public Trustee regarding the slow progress in moving institutionalized individuals into the community. The case was ultimately settled through mediation facilitated by the Manitoba Human Rights Commission in 2011. See Manitoba Human Rights Commission, News Release, "Human Rights Settlement Confirms the Right to Choose" (25 November 2011), online: Manitoba Human Rights Commission <http://www.manitobahumanrights.

ca/ publications/news_releases/2011_11_25.html>. See also Steve Lambert, "Manitoba Settles Human Rights Case on Intellectual Disabilities," *Canadian Press* (25 November 2011), online: *The Globe and Mail* online <http://www.theglobeandmail.com>.

132 See, e.g., Ontario Human Rights Commission, "Paying the Price: The Human Cost of Racial Profiling – Inquiry Report" (Toronto: Ontario Human Rights Commission, 2003) online: OHRC <http://www.ohrc. on.ca/en/resources/discussion_consultation/RacialProfileReportEN/pdf>; Commission des droits de la personne et des droits de la jeunesse, "Consultation Document on Racial Profiling" (March 2010), online: CDPDJ <http://www.cdpdj.qc.ca/publications/Documents/racial_ profiling_consultation.pdf>.

133 Eberts, *supra* note 114.

134 Champ, *supra* note 91.

CHAPTER ONE

1 Ron Ellis, *Unjust by Design: Canada's Administrative Justice System* (Vancouver: UBC Press, 2013) at 135 [Ellis].

2 Most provinces and municipalities in Canada have some sort of ombudsperson institution to deal with citizen complaints about government behaviour. In addition, there are several specialized institutions at the federal level, such as the Office of Commissioner of Official Languages Commission and the Privacy Commission.

3 Ellis, *supra* note 1 at 139.

4 *Ibid* at 137–138, referring to the application of the term "judicial tribunal" to administrative tribunals, citing Ontario, Royal Commission Inquiry into Civil Rights (James Chalmers McRuer, Chair) Report No. 1, Vol. 1 (Frank Fogg, Queen's Printer, 1968).

5 Ellis, *supra* note 1.

6 *Ibid* at 184–185.

7 See Principles Relating to the Status of National Institutions (The Paris Principles*)*, GA Res 48/134, UNGAOR (1993), online: OHCHR <http:// www2.ohchr.org/english/law/parisprinciples.htm> [Paris Principles]. The Principles are provided in Appendix 2 of this book.

8 The ICC is a non-profit corporation under Swiss law. The Office of the High Commissioner for Human Rights acts as secretariat for the ICC.

9 Information about the status of accredited NHRIs can be found on the website of the National Human Rights Institutions Forum. See NHRI

<http://www.nhri.net>. In February 2013, the ICC released its list of accredited institutions.

10 See, generally, International Council on Human Rights Policy, *Assessing the Effectiveness of National Human Rights Institutions* (Versoix, Switzerland: ICHRP, 2005), online: ICHRP <http://www.ichrp.org>; UN Office of the High Commissioner for Human Rights, *National Human Rights Institutions: History, Principles, Roles and Responsibilities,* Professional Training Series No 4 (Rev1), (New York: United Nations, 2010), online: OHCHR <http://www.ohchr.org>.

11 With a few exceptions, the ICC only accredits "national" institutions and not sub-national bodies such as provincial, territorial, and regional commissions. This has created an anomalous situation in Canada – the Canadian Human Rights Commission is designated as our "national" institution although it is national only in geographic terms and not in terms of its jurisdiction.

12 Office of the High Commissioner for Human Rights, *Survey on National Human Rights Institutions: Report on the Findings and Recommendations of a Questionnaire Addressed to NHRIs Worldwide* (Geneva: Office of the High Commissioner for Human Rights, 2009), online: OHCHR <http://nhri.ohchr.org> [NHRI Survey] at 9.

13 *Ibid.*

14 *Ibid* at 27.

15 *Ibid.*

16 *Ibid.* The survey uses the term "authorities."

17 *Ibid.*

18 Among surveyed countries, 39 percent had jurisdiction over the private sector. See *Handbook for National Human Rights Institutions on Women's Rights and Gender Equality* (Warsaw: OSCE/ODIHR, 2012), online: OSCE http://www.osce.org/odihr/97756 [OSCE/ODIHR].

19 For example, Articles 2(2), 2(3) and 27 of the *International Covenant on Civil and Political Rights,* 19 December 1966, 999 UNTS 171, Can TS 1976 No 47, 6 ILM 368 (entered into force 23 March 1976, accession by Canada 19 May 1976) [ICCPR] require that people have effective remedies for human rights violations and specific protection against discrimination.

20 OSCE/ODIHR, *supra* note 18 at 25.

21 Paris Principles, *supra* note 7.

22 Interview of John Pace (19 December 2012).

23 The ICC has designated the Canadian Human Rights Commission as the "national human rights institution" for Canada, even though it (a) has

only federal and not national jurisdiction over complaints and (b) represents only about 10 percent of human rights cases filed annually in Canada. The reasons seem to have more to with convenience than anything else, since the ICC appears unenthusiastic about the prospect of accrediting multiple institutions from a single country.

24 (UK), 30 & 31 Vict, c 3, reprinted in RSC 1985, App II, No. 5.

25 About a third of national human rights institutions around the world report that their countries' constitutions expressly provide for national human rights institutions. See *NHRI Survey, supra* note 12.

26 *Insurance Corporation of British Columbia v. Heerspink*, [1982] 2 SCR 145 at 158, Lamer J. This Supreme Court case determined that an insurance contract could not supersede British Columbia's *Human Rights Code*. The cited text is from three of the six majority judges, who also stated that "[s]hort of [the] legislature speaking to the contrary in express and unequivocal language in the *Code* or in some other enactment, it is intended that the *Code* supersede all other laws when conflict arises … Furthermore, as it is a public and fundamental law, no one, unless clearly authorized by law to do so, may contractually agree to suspend its operation, and thereby put oneself beyond the reach of its protection."

27 Section 9(1) of the *Human Rights Code*, CCSM, c H175 and *s 10* of Quebec's *Charter of Human Rights and Freedoms* do contain definitions.

28 *British Columbia (Public Service Employee Relations Commission) v. BCGSEU*, [1999] 3 SCR 3 at para 48.

29 ICCPR, *supra* note 19, Article 26.

30 See e.g. *Gosselin (Tutor of) v. Quebec (Attorney General)*, [2005] 1 SCR 238 at para 2.

31 Most NHRIs were established in the 1990s: NHRI Survey, *supra* note 12. Ontario preceded that by three decades when it consolidated its anti-discrimination statutes into a unified human rights code with a free-standing commission in 1962. Looking at other countries, the US Equal Employment Opportunity Commission was created in 1965 (although there were anti-discrimination commissions in the United States as early as the 1940s); the Equality and Human Rights Commission was established in Britain in 2007; the French Commission nationale consultative des droits de l'homme was established in 1947 (but does not handle individual complaints). The complaints-handling body in France is the Défenseur des droits, which was given legal status under the French constitution in 2008. In Australia, the Australian Human Rights Commission was established in 1981.

32 *Bell Canada v. Canadian Telephone Employees Association*, [2003] 1 SCR 884, 2003 SCC 36 at para 22–23.

33 Ellis, *supra* note 1 at 200.

34 *Blencoe v. British Columbia (Human Rights Commission)*, 2000 SCC 44 [*Blencoe*].

35 See, e.g. Ezra Levant, "Neo-Nazi Hate, Courtesy of the CHRC," *National Post* (15 July 2009) A10. Levant described the Canadian Human Rights Tribunal as "the kangaroo court that rubber-stamps CHRC censorship prosecutions."

36 Ellis, *supra* note 1 at 165 (quoting the dissent in *Committee for Justice and Liberty et al. v. National Energy Board et al.*, [1978] 1 SCR 369 at 401.)

37 See, generally, *Pushpanathan v. Canada (Minister of Citizenship and Immigration)*, [1998] 1 SCR 982 at para 36 [*Pushpanathan*] *and* the discussion in Ellis, supra note 1 at 162.

38 See, generally, Andrew Clapham, *Human Rights: A Very Short Introduction* (Oxford: Oxford University Press, 2007) at 2

39 Interview of Gaétan Cousineau (21 April 2010).

40 *Canadian Human Rights Act*, RSC 1985, c H-6, s 13 and *Human Rights Code*, RSBC 1996, c 210, s 7.

41 *Human Rights Code*, RSO 1990, c H.19. Section 13(1) prohibits the publication or display of "any notice, sign, symbol, emblem or other similar representation that indicates the intention ... to infringe a right ... or that is intended ... to incite the infringement of a right under Part I."

42 There was some discussion over whether the allegedly anti-Muslim articles transformed the magazines, or their sale, into a "service" within the meaning of human rights law, but such arguments had failed in the past and were unlikely to succeed here. See, e.g., *Findlay and McKay v. Four Star Variety* (22 October 1993), Toronto (Ont BOI). This case dealt with complaints about the display of "adult" magazines in corner stores in Ontario. For a brief discussion of the case, see Parliamentary Information and Research Service of the Library of Parliament, *The Evolution of Pornography Law in Canada,* (Ottawa: Library of Parliament, 2007) at 9, online: Parliament of Canada <http://www.parl.gc.ca/Content/LOP/Research Publications/843-e.pdf>.

43 Ontario Human Rights Commission, News Release, "Commission Issues Statement on Decision in *Maclean's* Cases" (9 April 2008) online: OHRC <http://www.ohrc.on.ca/en/news_centre/commission-issues-statement-decision-maclean-cases> [emphasis added].

44 Testimony of Mark Steyn before the House of Commons Standing Committee on Justice and Human Rights, *Evidence*, 40th Parl, 2nd Sess (5 October 2009) at 1635, online: Parliament of Canada <http://www.parl. gc.ca/HousePublications/Publication.aspx?DocId=4124876#Int-2877837>.

Cited in Canadian Bar Association, "Hate Speech under the *Canadian Human Rights Act*" (Ottawa: Canadian Bar Association, 2010) at 2, online: CBA <http://www.cba.org/CBA/submissions/pdf/10-03-eng.pdf>.

45 Section 29 the Ontario *Human Rights Code* allows the commission to inquire into incidents of tension or conflict, or conditions that lead or may lead to incidents of tension or conflict. The commission may also make recommendations, encourage and co-ordinate plans, programs, and activities to reduce or prevent such incidents or sources of tension or conflict, or report generally on the state of human rights.

46 Bill 107 abolished the Ontario Human Rights Commission's jurisdiction over complaints. See Bill 107, *An Act to Amend the Human Rights Code*, 2nd Sess, 38th Leg, Ontario, 2006 (assented to 20 December 2006), SO 2006, c 30 [Bill 107]. The majority of the Bill 107 reforms took effect in 2008.

47 Joseph Brean, "Free Speech's Friend or Foe?" *National Post* (19 April 2008) A10. Brean's pronouncement suggests that he was not aware of the promotional aspect of the commission's mandate, despite Chief Commissioner Barbara Hall's efforts to spell it out during in the interview.

48 Interview of Mark Freiman (1 May 2009).

49 *Ibid.*

50 Interview of Barbara Hall (22 April 2009).

51 Subsections 27(e) and (f) of the CHRA provide for powers to consider any recommendations, suggestions, and requests concerning human rights (not just equality rights) that the commission may receive from any source and to report on it; and to carry out studies on any human rights and freedoms referred by the minister of Justice.

52 See in particular the Canadian Human Rights Commission's Annual Reports from 1993–95. See also Maxwell Yalden, *Transforming Rights: Reflections from the Front Lines* (Toronto: University of Toronto Press, 2009) at 187–193 [Yalden].

53 Joe Friesen, "Angling for Justice." *The Globe and Mail* (3 October 2009) A17. Online: The Globe and Mail <http://www.theglobeandmail.com> [Friesen].

54 Interview of Barbara Hall, *supra* note 50.

55 Ontario Human Rights Commission, *Fishing without Fear: Report on the Inquiry into Assaults on Asian Canadian Anglers* (Toronto: Ontario Human Rights Commission, 2008) online: OHRC <http://www.ohrc.on.ca>. There were, however, controversial outcomes to the initiative, including the trial of a twelve-year-old child for allegedly knocking a Chinese Canadian into Canal Lake. See Friesen, *supra* note 53.

56 Bill 107, *supra* note 46.

57 Lorne Foster and Lesley Jacobs, "Shared Citizenship as the Context for Competing Human Rights Claims: Towards a Social Policy Framework" (2010) 8:3 Canadian Diversity 10 at 11.

58 Andrew Pinto, *Report of the Ontario Human Rights Review 2012* (Toronto: Queen's Printer for Ontario, 2012), at 189. [Pinto Report]

59 *Attorney General of Canada v. Johnstone*, 2013 FC 113 at para 62, citing the Canadian Human Rights Tribunal's lower decision in the case [*Johnstone*].

60 See *e.g.* Ontario Human Rights Commission, *Policy and Guidelines on Discrimination because of Family Status* (Toronto: Ontario Human Rights Commission, 2007), online: OHRC <http://www.ohrc.on.ca>; *Johnstone, supra* note 59.

61 *Alberta Human Rights Act*, RSA 2000, c. A-25.5 [Alberta HRA], s 44(1)(f).

62 Although the case law appears to be influx, civil status generally refers to the three basic elements of Quebec civil law, namely birth, marriage, and death. See, generally, *Brossard (Town) v. Quebec (Commission des droits de la personne)*, [1988] 2 SCR 279.

63 Matt Gurney, "A Fair Boss Is Nice, Not a Right," *National Post* (6 February 2013) A1.

64 Egale Canada reports that 78 percent of trans students in Canada feel unsafe at school and 37 percent have been physically harassed or assaulted. See Catherine Taylor and Tracey Peter, *Every Class in Every School: The First National Climate Survey on Homophobia, Biphobia, and Transphobia in Canadian Schools – Final Report* (Toronto: Egale Canada Human Rights Trust, 2011), online: Egale <http://egale.ca/every-class/>.

65 See, e.g., Bill 33, *An Act to Amend the Human Rights Code with Respect to Gender Identity and Gender Expression*, SO 2012, c 7. See Ontario Human Rights Commission, *Human Rights Policy in Ontario*, 1st ed (Toronto: CCH Canadian, 2001.

66 See Bill C-279, *An Act to Amend the Canadian Human Rights Act and the Criminal Code* (Gender Identity and Gender Expression), 1st Sess, 41st Parl, Canada 2011.

67 Ontario Human Rights Commission, *Policy on Discrimination and Harassment because of Gender Identity* (Toronto: OHRC, 2000), online <http://www.ohrc.on.ca/en/policy-discrimination-and-harassment-because-gender-identity>.

68 *Ontario Human Rights Commission v. Simpsons-Sears Ltd.*, [1985] 2 SCR 536 at para 12.

69 *An Act to Amend the Human Rights Code with respect to Gender Identity and Gender Expression* SO 2012 c 7.

70 ICCPR, *supra* note 19.

71 See, for example, *Gosselin v. Quebec (Attorney General)*, [2002] 4 SCR 429, 2002 SCC 84.

72 *Falkiner v. Ontario (Ministry of Community and Social Services)* (2002), 59 OR (3d) 481 (Ont CA). The government abandoned its appeal to the Supreme Court of Canada in 2004. Other more recent cases have declined to find that poverty-related grounds can be invoked as equality rights, albeit in the immigration context (ss. 7 or 15 of the Charter): see *Toussaint v. Canada (Minister of Citizenship and Immigration)*; *Ndungu v. Canada (Minister of Citizenship and Immigration)*, 2011 FCA 146, leave to appeal to the Supreme Court of Canada refused, 3 November 2011, 2011 Canlii 69660.

73 See also *Corbiere v. Canada (Minister of Indian and Northern Affairs)*, [1999] 2 SCR 203 at para 13.

74 See, e.g., *Chaoulli v. Quebec (Attorney General)*, [2005] 1 SCR 791.

75 Tribunal des droits de la personne, Communiqué, 29 July 2013, TDP online <www.tribunaux.qc.ca>. Details considering the threats were reported by *La Presse*: Philippe Teisceira-Lessard, "*Une mendiante recevra 8000$*" *La Presse* (5 August 2013) at A5. The tribunal had not released its full decision at the time of writing.

76 See s. 1, *Manitoba Human Rights Code*.

77 RSC 1985, c 31 (4th Supp).

78 The Canadian Charter says that that English and French are the official languages of New Brunswick. At the provincial level, the *Official Languages Act of New Brunswick* protects anglophone and francophone rights, and the ombudsman is the commissioner of official languages for New Brunswick. In Ontario, the ombudsman is the French language services commissioner of Ontario.

79 RSQ, c C-11.

80 See, e.g., Bill 14, *An Act to Amend the Charter of the French Language, the Charter of Human Rights and Freedoms and Other Legislative Provisions*, 1st Sess, 40th Leg. In August 2013, Pauline Marois announced that her government would likely have to let the bill die on the order paper.

81 Alberta, British Columbia, Canada, Nunavut, Ontario, and Saskatchewan lack this protection in their human rights statutes. See Appendix 3 for further details.

82 The *Saskatchewan Human Rights Code* contains a Bill of Rights in Part 1 that protects civil liberties, but it is separate from the section dealing with discrimination. The commission can only accept discrimination cases.

83 Section 13 of the CHRA prohibits communications that are "likely to expose a person or persons to hatred or contempt by reason of the fact that that person or those persons are identifiable on the basis of a prohibited ground of discrimination." At the time of writing, a bill to repeal section 13 of the CHRA had received Royal Assent: Bill C-304, *An Act to Amend the Canadian Human Rights Act (Protecting Freedom)*, S.C. 2013 c. 37.

84 Alberta HRA, *supra* note 61, s 3(1): "No person shall publish, issue or display or cause to be published, issued or displayed before the public any statement, publication, notice, sign, symbol, emblem or other representation that (a) indicates discrimination or an intention to discriminate against a person or a class of persons, or (b) is likely to expose a person or a class of persons to hatred or contempt."

85 See *Bou Malhab v. Diffusion Métromédia CMR inc,* [2011] 1 SCR 214.

86 *Ibid* at para 3.

87 Lorne Sossin, "Access to Administrative Justice and Other Worries." Paper delivered at the symposium "The Future of Administrative Justice" at the Faculty of Law, University of Toronto, 17–18 January 2008, online: University of Toronto <http://www.law.utoronto.ca/documents/conferences/adminjustice08_Sossin.pdf>. An updated version of the article appears in Lorne Sossin and Colleen Flood, eds, *Administrative Law in Context,* 2nd ed (Toronto: Edmond Montgomery Press, 2012), chapter 7.

88 Amendments to the *Saskatchewan Human Rights Code* in 2011 abolished the province's human rights tribunal. The commission still has a gatekeeping function but complaints are referred to the Court of Queen's Bench and not a tribunal. In Quebec, there is currently some debate about whether the Quebec Human Rights Tribunal is a judicial tribunal; a Quebec Court of Appeal decision decided that it is an administrative decision-maker, even though the president is a member of the judiciary and the tribunal is housed within the court system. See *Commission scolaire Marguerite-Bourgeoys c Gallardo*, 2012 QCCA 908.

89 See *Halifax (Regional Municipality) v. Nova Scotia (Human Rights Commission)*, 2012 SCC 10.

90 *Ibid*.

91 Interview of Paul Champ, (29 June 2010).

92 United Nations, *Consideration of Reports Submitted by States Parties under Articles 16 and 17 of the Covenant: Concluding observations of the Committee on Economic, Social and Cultural Rights: Canada,* UNCESR E/C.12/1/Add.31 (1998) at para 51.

93 United Nations, Human Rights Committee, *Consideration of Reports Submitted by States Parties Under Article 40 of the Covenant: Concluding Observations of the Human Rights Committee: Canada*, UNCCPR, 85th Sess, CCPR/C/CAN/CO/5, (2006) at para 11, online: UNHCHR <http://www.unhchr.ch/tbs/doc.nsf/898586b1dc7b4043c1256a450044f331/7616e3478238be01c12570ae00397f5d/$FILE/G0641362.pdf>.

94 See, e.g., Tribunal des droits de la personne and Barreau du Québec, eds, *La Charte des droits de libertés de la personne: Pour qui et jusqu'où?* (Cowansville, Que: Yvon Blais, 2005); Tribunal des droits de la personne and Barreau du Québec, *Access to a Specialized Human Rights Tribunal: An Urgent Need to Act in Quebec?* (Cowansville, Que: Yvon Blais, 2008). (The French title of the book is *L'accès direct à un tribunal spécialisé en matière de droit à l'égalité: L'urgence d'agir au Québec?*)

95 The Quebec Commission opened 761 cases in 2010–11 (after weeding out inadmissible cases) and 43 were sent to the tribunal. In 2011-12, the commission opened 1047 new files and 52 cases in total went to the tribunal. See Commission des droits de la personne et des droits de la jeunesse, *Rapport d'activités et de gestion: 2011-2012* (Montreal: CDPDJ, 2011) at 44, online : CDPDJ <http://www.cdpdj.qc.ca/publications/RA_2011_ 2012.pdf>. See also Tribunal des droits de la personne, *Bilan d'activités: 2010-2011* (Montreal: TDP, 2011), online: Tribunaux judiciaires du Québec http://www.tribunaux.qc.ca>; *Bilan d'activités: 2011-2012* (Montreal: TDP, 2012), online: Tribunaux judiciaires du Québec http://www.tribunaux.qc.ca> at 48.

96 Human Rights Tribunal of Ontario, *Annual Report 2009–10* (Toronto: HRTO, 2010), online: <HRTO http://www.hrto.ca>. (This is based on the number of cases that are dismissed on a preliminary basis, deferred, or withdrawn, which account for approximately 20 percent of the total new applications filed. The tribunal's 2010–11 Annual Report was not available as of January 2014.

97 *Tranchemontagne v. Ontario (Director, Disability Support Program)*, [2006] 1 SCR 513 at para 49.

98 See *Blencoe, supra* note 34.

99 Pinto *Report supra* note 58.

100 See Appendix 3.

101 *Ibid.*

102 The Supreme Court of Canada adopted a definition of systemic discrimination from the Abella Report as "practices or attitudes that have, whether by design or impact, the effect of limiting an individual's or a

group's right to the opportunities generally available because of attributed rather than actual characteristics." See *Canadian National Railway Co v. Canada (Canadian Human Rights Commission)*, [1987] 1 SCR 1114 [CN] at 1138.

103 CN *ibid*, *British Columbia (Superintendent of Motor Vehicles) v. British Columbia (Council of Human Rights)*, [1999] 3 SCR 868.

104 *Moore v. British Columbia (Education)*, 2012 SCC 61 [*Moore*].

105 *Ibid.*

106 *Ibid* at para 64.

107 For an overview of the types of powers that tribunals have, see Appendix 3.

108 *Pushpanathan supra* note 37 at para 36.

109 CBC, *The Current*, "Ottawa's Biggest Racial Profiling Study to Date in Canada" (26 March 2013) CBC Radio, online: CBC <http://www.cbc.ca/thecurrent/episode/2013/03/26/ottawas-biggest-racial-profiling-study-to-date-in-canada/> [CBC].

110 Interview of Virginia Nelder, counsel for Chad Aiken, in CBC, *ibid.*

111 *Moore, supra* note 104.

112 Keith Martin, "Freedom to Speak" (8 February 2008). His MP's web site has since gone offline, but the article reappeared dated February 15 2008, online at <www.keithmartin.org>. In a telephone conversation with me in April 2008, Martin said that he was unaware that the matters he put forward as fact were erroneous or at least potentially misleading. He promised to look into the matter. See also the discussion at note 77 in the Introduction.

113 *Blencoe, supra* note 34 at para 35.

114 J Sprague, "*Ocean Port Hotel v. British Columbia (General Manager, Liquor Control And Licencing Branch)*," Case Comment on, (1999) 12 Can J Admin L & Prac 349 at 356.

115 See *Blencoe, supra* note 34. "Bodies exercising statutory authority are bound by the Charter even though they may be independent of government." At para 35.

116 See e.g. Rex Murphy, "Mr. Harper: Tame These Commissions." *The Globe and Mail* (3 May 2008) A21.

117 *Baker v. Canada (Minister of Citizenship and Immigration)*, [1999] 2 SCR 817 para 70. [*Baker*].

118 *Reference Re Public Service Employee Relations Act (Alta)*, [1987] 1 SCR 313 at para 57. The chief justice stated: "The *Charter* conforms to the spirit of this contemporary international human rights movement, and it incorporates many of the policies and prescriptions of the various international documents pertaining to human rights. The various sources of

international human rights law – declarations, covenants, conventions, judicial and quasijudicial decisions of international tribunals, customary norms – must, in my opinion, be relevant and persuasive sources for interpretation of the *Charter's* provisions." The case involved the right to freedom of association in the labour context and more specifically the right to strike and compulsory arbitration. Dickson CJ and Wilson J dissented in this case, but this reasoning has been approved in other decisions. See e.g. *Health Services and Support – Facilities Subsector Bargaining Assn v. British Columbia*, [2007] 2 SCR 391 at paras 69-70. In 2013, the Supreme Court of Canada, in *Divito v. Canada (Public Safety and Emergency Preparedness)*, 2013 SCC 47, said that the rights protected in international instruments to which Canada is a signatory provide a "minimum level of protection" for rights that are guaranteed in the Charter (referring to mobility rights).

119 See *Slaight Communications Inc v. Davidson*, [1989] 1 SCR 1038; *Baker, supra* note 117. For an overview of Canadian courts' limitations in applying international standards, see Olivier Delas and Myriam Robichaud, "Les difficultés liées à la prise en compte du droit international des droits de la personne en droit canadien: Préoccupations légitimes ou alibis?" (2008) 21.1 RQDI 1.

120 Yalden, *supra* note 52 at 197.

121 For a discussion of the evolution of this practice, see Ontario Human Rights Commission, *Human Rights Policy in Ontario*, 1st ed (Toronto: CCH Canadian, 2001), preface at 10-12.

122 See e.g., UN Convention on the Rights of Persons with Disabilities GA Res 61/611, UNGAOR, 61st Sess, Supp No 49, UN Doc A/RES/61/106, (2007).

123 *Institution-Building of the United Nations Human Rights Council*, A/HRC/RES/5/1, adopted by the UN Human Rights Council (18 June 2007). This area of activity is, however, relatively undeveloped

124 NHRIs have the right to participate in the Universal Periodic Review process, as well as the UN Committee on the Rights of the Child, the Committee on Economic, Social and Cultural Rights, and the Committee on the Elimination of Racial Discrimination. See *Institution-Building of the United Nations Human Rights Council, supra* note 123.

CHAPTER TWO

1 Interview of Mary Eberts (24 April 2009) [Eberts].

2 Many scholars and practitioners have done important work on the evolution of human rights commissions as institutions and vehicles of public

policy in Canada: see *e.g.*, Arnold Bruner, "The Genesis of Ontario's Human Rights Legislation: A Study in Law Reform" (1979) 37 UT Fac L Rev 236; Dominique Clément, *Canada's Rights Revolution: Social Movements and Social Change, 1937-1982* (Vancouver: University of British Columbia Press, 2008) [Clément, *Rights Revolution*]; Dominique Clément, Will Silver, and Daniel Trottier, *The Evolution of Human Rights in Canada*, (Ottawa: Minister of Public Works and Government Services, 2012 [Clément, Silver. and Trottier]; William Pentney, *Discrimination and the Law* (Toronto: Carswell, 1990); R Brian Howe, "The Evolution of Human Rights Policy in Ontario" (1991) 24 Can J Pol Sci 783 [R Brian Howe]; R Brian Howe and David Johnson, *Restraining Equality: Human Rights Commissions in Canada* (Toronto: University of Toronto Press, 2000) at 3-36 [Howe and Johnson].

3 Interview of Roderick Macdonald (1 September 2009) [Macdonald].

4 *Christie v. The York Corporation*, [1940] SCR 139.

5 See, e.g., *Loew's Montreal Theatres Ltd v. Reynolds* (1919), 30 QR KB 459; *Franklin v. Evans* (1924), 55 OLR 349; *Rogers v. Clarence Hotel Co Ltd*, [1940] 2 WWR 545.

6 Macdonald, *supra* note 3.

7 See, e.g., *Re McDougall and Waddell*, [1945] OWN 272, [1945] 2 DLR 244. The deed in this case contained a covenant preventing the land from being sold to, let to, or occupied by "persons other than Gentiles (non-semetic [sic]) of European or British or Irish or Scottish racial origin."

8 *Re Drummond Wren*, [1945] OR 778 (HC). The presiding judge in that case, Justice Keiller Mackay, went on to become Ontario's lieutenant governor and the first president of the Canadian Civil Liberties Association. There were other cases in which courts upheld civil liberties by making appeals to public policy or to unwritten constitutional principles. However, most decisions were based on the constitutional division of powers rather than on a direct appeal to rights. See, e.g., *Switzman v. Elbing and AG of Quebec*, [1957] SCR 285; *Roncarelli v. Duplessis*, [1959] SCR 121.

9 SO 1944, c 51 [RDA].

10 *Noble et al v. Alley*, [1951] SCR 64.

11 Macdonald, *supra* note 3.

12 Clément, *Rights Revolution, supra* note 2.

13 Dominique Clément, *The Human Rights Movement: A History*, online: History of Rights <http://www.historyofrights.com/movement.html>. This website charts the evolution of human rights organizations and their roots in social movements from the 1930s to the 1970s.

14 Clément, Silver, and Trottier, *supra* note 2.

15 Interview of Alan Borovoy (14 September 2009) [Borovoy].

16 Interview of Margaret Parsons (10 June 2009) [Parsons]. Parsons described the unravelling of this relationship in later years, especially after the 2001 "World Conference against Racism, Racial Discrimination, Xenophobia and Related Intolerance" in Durban, South Africa. The conference, which was known as "Durban I," was widely criticized for providing a platform for virulent anti-Semitism and anti-Israeli sentiment. Parsons said the Jewish caucus refused to support the African caucus on the issue of reparations. "Many people in our African Canadian community felt betrayed," she said. "There is a sense of abandonment in our community." Parsons deplored the anti-Semitic elements among certain NGOs at Durban I. However, she argued that the final conference document contained no anti-Israeli or anti-Semitic elements. "I implore you, look at the [final] Durban document," she said. "There is nothing critical of Israel in there."

17 RDA, *supra* note 9.

18 *Saskatchewan Bill of Rights Act,* SS 1947 c 35. The practice of integrating liberties and civil right into equality rights statutes was carried over into the next generation of Saskatchewan human rights legislation in the late 1970s, *The Saskatchewan Human Rights Code,* SS 1979 c S-24.1. A bill of rights also features in the Quebec *Charter of human rights and freedoms,* RSQ, c C-12 [QC Charter].

19 Interview of Ken Norman (16 November 2010) [Norman].

20 Interview of Dominique Clément (7 December 2011) [Clément]. Although women may have been absent from the movement and its leadership, they were included in the early fair practices laws. See, e.g., *Female Employees' Fair Remuneration Act,* SO 1951, c 26

21 Clément, *ibid.*

22 Norman, *supra* note 19.

23 *Ontario Insurance Act,* SO 1932, c 24, s 4.

24 *Unemployment Relief Act,* SBC 1933, c 71.

25 Manitoba's *Libel Act,* SM 1934, c 23, s 13(a)). Group libel was defined as expression that was likely to expose people to "hatred, contempt or ridicule" that would "raise unrest or disorder."

26 Regarding employment, see, e.g., British Columbia's *Fair Employment Practices Act,* SBC 1956, c 16; Manitoba's *Fair Employment Practices Act,* SM 1953, c 18; New Brunswick's *Fair Employment Practices Act,* SNB 1956, c 9; Ontario's *Fair Employment Practices Act,* SO 1951, c 24; and Nova Scotia's *Fair Employment Practices Act,* SNS 1955, c 5. Regarding accommodation (i.e., housing), see, e.g., Ontario's *Fair Accommodation Practices Act,* SO 1954, c 28; New Brunswick's *Fair Accommodation Practices Act,* SNB 1959, c 6; Nova Scotia's *Fair Accommodation Practices*

Act, SNS 1959, c 4; Saskatchewan's *Fair Accommodation Practices Act*, SS 1956, c 68.

27 *Seneca College v. Bhadauria*, [1981] 2 SCR 181 at 184.

28 Borovoy, *supra* note 15. An account of this incident can also be found in A. Alan Borovoy, *Uncivil Obedience: The Tactics and Tales of a Democratic Agitator* (Toronto: Lester Publishing, 1991) at 73.

29 Borovoy, *supra* note 15. The *Ontario Anti-Discrimination Commission Act*, SO 1958, c 70 had appeared earlier, but was not a consolidated law.

30 See Francesco Capotorti, "Human Rights: The Hard Road towards Universality" in R St J Macdonald and D M Johnston, eds, *The Structure and Process of International Law: Essays in Legal Philosophy, Doctrine and Theory* (Dordrecht, Netherlands: Martinus Nijhoff, 1983) 977 at 978–982. See also Yves Fortier, "Human Rights: The View from the United Nations" in Irwin Cotler and Pearl Eliadis, eds, *International Human Rights Law: Theory and Practice* (Montreal: Canadian Human Rights Foundation, 1992) at 51.

31 Rod Macdonald argued that several other areas of law began as narrow remedies and evolved into broader legal concepts. The first example is the branch of law known as "judicial review," which emerged from historic writs such as mandamus and certiorari. These writs each had their own legal trajectories and distinct technical requirements. Over time, however, a more global and unified concept of judicial review emerged, allowing litigants to invoke the supervisory jurisdiction of the courts without having to meet the requirements of a particular writ. Similarly, secured transactions began as distinct property rights. Over time, they became associated with a more generic concept that permitted creditors to secure their interests. Macdonald, *supra* note 3.

32 Macdonald, *supra* note 3.

33 See the discussion in Ian Ward, *Introduction to Critical Legal Theory*, 2d (New York: Routledge-Cavendish, 2004) at 105 ff.

34 Macdonald, *supra* note 3.

35 Ch 118, § 1, [1945] NY Laws 457.

36 Elmer A Carter, "Fighting Prejudice with Law" (1946) 19:5 J of Ed Psych 299.

37 See also R. Brian Howe, *supra* note 2, at 790. Howe refers to Kalmen Kaplansky (director of the Jewish Labour Committee and the Labour Committee for Human Rights), Benjamin Kayfetz (executive director of the Canadian Jewish Congress), Irving Himel (executive secretary of the Association for Civil Liberties), and Alan Borovoy (executive secretary of the Ontario Labour Committee for Human Rights) as the main forces behind the Ontario legislation. *Ibid* at 791.

38 Norman, *supra* note 19.

39 The *Ontario Human Rights Code,* 1961-62, SO 1961-62, c 93

40 QC Charter, *supra* note 18.

41 Ken Norman, written communication to the author dated 12 November 2010. On file.

42 Norman, *supra* note 19.

43 See Ken Norman and John Whyte, "Rough Justice: Saskatchewan Human Rights Bill," *Leader-Post* (Regina) (11 December 2010) C10.

44 Universal Declaration of Human Rights, GA Res 217 (III), UNGAOR, 3d Sess, Supp No 13, UN Doc A/810, (1948) 71 [UDHR].

45 Norman, *supra* note 19.

46 UDHR, *supra* note 44.

47 For example, the preamble of the Ontario *Human Rights Code,* RSO 1990, c H-19 states: "Whereas recognition of the inherent dignity and the equal and inalienable rights of all members of the human family is the foundation of freedom, justice and peace in the world and is in accord with the Universal Declaration of Human Rights as proclaimed by the United Nations."

48 19 December 1966, 999 UNTS 171, Can TS 1976 No 47, 6 ILM 368 (entered into force 23 March 1976, accession by Canada 19 May 1976) [ICCPR].

49 RSC 1985, c H-6 [CHRA].

50 ICCPR, *supra* note 48; 16 December 1966, 993 UNTS 3, Can TS 1976 No 46 (entered into force 3 January 1976)

51 Federal-Provincial Ministerial Conference on Human Rights, *Final Communiqué* (Ottawa: 11–12 December 1975).

52 Neither respondents nor claimants need lawyers to appear before human rights commissions, administrative tribunals, or panels. However, some interviewees indicated that unrepresented parties are at a distinct disadvantage.

53 Colleen Sheppard, *Inclusive Equality: The Relational Dimensions of Systemic Discrimination in Canada* (Montreal: McGill-Queen's University Press, 2010) at 48–49 [Sheppard] at 4.

54 Interview of Kim Bernhardt (14 September 2009), [Bernhardt].

55 Borovoy, *supra* note 15.

56 SS 1979, c S-24.1.

57 Mary Eberts, Alex Neve, and Ken Norman, Wrong Moves for Saskatchewan Human Rights, *Leader Post* (Regina), (30 March 2012). See also Norman and White, *supra* note 43.

58 SBC 1969, c 10.

59 SBC 1973, c 119.

60 Clément, *supra* note 20.

61 Clément saw this incident as symptomatic of a broader malaise with BC's progressive Human Rights Code. Clément, *supra* note 20. The incident was described to Clément by Ruff in an interview dated 14 April 2010 and is described in greater detail in Dominique Clément, *The Rise and Fall of British Columbia's Human Rights State, 1953-1984* (UBC Press, forthcoming).

62 The Code was replaced by the Human Rights Act, BCS 1984, c 22. See William W Black, *B.C. Human Rights Review: Report on Human Rights in British Columbia* (Victoria: Government of British Columbia, 1994) [Black]. The new minimalist Human Rights Council was bitterly contested in BC and subject to criticism across Canada. The 1984 Human Rights Act was viewed as a throwback to the ineffective 1969 *Human Rights Act.*

63 See Ontario Human Rights Commission, *Life Together: A Report on Human Rights in Ontario* (Toronto: OHRC, 1977).

64 Bernhardt, *supra* note 54.

65 This section is based in part on previously published material. See Pearl Eliadis, "Power Asymmetries and Performance Audits: The Canadian Human Rights Commission and the Auditor General of Canada" in Pearl Eliadis, Jan-Eric Furubo, and Steve Jacob, eds, *Evaluation: Seeking Truth or Power?* Comparative Policy Evaluation, vol 17 (New Brunswick, NJ: Transaction, 2011) [Eliadis et al.] at 199.

66 Office of the Auditor General of Canada, *Report of the Auditor General of Canada, Chapter 11 – Canadian Human Rights Commission* (Ottawa: OAG, 1985), online: OAG <http://www.oag-bvg.gc.ca/internet/English/parl_oag_198511_11_e_4186.html#0.2.L39QK2.SWM8GB.FG5R1F.H6> [*OAG Report -1985*].

67 *Ibid* at para 11.4.

68 See the discussion in Jeremy Lonsdale, "Using Their Discretion: How State Audit Institutions Determine Which Performance Audits to Undertake" in Eliadis et al, *supra* note 65 at 188.

69 Auditability means whether an area is amenable to audit based on the availability of adequately qualified internal and external resources, high political sensitivity, the complexity of the proposed area, and the experience of the audit team. See Office of the Auditor General of Canada, *Performance Audit Manual* (Ottawa: Minister of Public Works and Government Services Canada, 2004) at 20.

70 The requirement that commissions both promote and protect human rights emerged from the 1993 Paris Principles, which are discussed in chapter 1.

See United Nations, *Principles Relating to the Status of National Institutions (The Paris Principles)*, GA Res 48/134, UNGAOR (1993), online: OHCHR <http://www2.ohchr.org/english/law/parisprinciples.htm> [Paris Principles].

71 To be fair, promotional activities such as education are often seen as "soft" and as difficult to evaluate. The OAG's decision to audit only case management may have reflected a bias towards activities that are easily quantifiable and easy to track over time. This is perfectly understandable from an auditor's perspective. Today, the evaluation of human rights education is much more developed: see, e.g., S Akermark, *Human Rights Education: Achievements and Challenges* (Turko/Abo, Finland: Institute for Human Rights, 1998); Equitas, *Evaluating Human Rights Training Activities: A Handbook for Human Rights Educators* (Montreal: Equitas and Office of the High Commissioner for Human Rights, 2011) Professional Training Series No. 18. Online <http://www.ohchr.org/en/publicationsresources/pages/trainingeducation.aspx>.

72 Office of the Auditor General of Canada, *Report of the Auditor General of Canada, Chapter 20 – Follow-Up of Recommendations in Previous Reports* (Ottawa: OAG, 1988), online: OAG <http://www.oag-bvg.gc.ca/internet/English/parl_oag_198811_20_e_4247.html> [OAG, *1988 Report*].

73 *Ibid* at 20.77.

74 *Ibid* at 20.72.

75 Sheppard, *supra* note 53 at 48–49.

76 Part I of the Constitution Act, 1982, being Schedule B to the Canada Act 1982 (UK), 1982, c 11.

77 Starting with *Mills v. The Queen*, [1986] 1 SCR 863.

78 *Slaight Communications Inc v. Davidson*, [1989] 1 SCR 1038.

79 *Douglas/Kwantlen Faculty Assn v. Douglas College*, [1990] 3 SCR 570; *Cuddy Chicks Ltd v. Ontario (Labour Relations Board)*, [1991] 2 SCR 5; and *TétreaultGadoury v. Canada (Employment and Immigration Commission)*, [1991] 2 SCR 22.

80 *R v. Conway*, [2010] 1 SCR 765.

81 *Ibid* at para 79.

82 Eberts, *supra* note 1.

83 In 1987, the definition of "spouse" was established in family law and family benefits legislation to apply to people who cohabited for three years.

84 *Falkiner v. Ontario (Ministry of Community and Social Services)* (2002), 59 OR (3d) 481 (CA). Government's appeal to the Supreme Court was abandoned.

85 *Canadian Odeon Theatres Ltd v. Huck* (1985), 6 CHRR D/2682 (Sask CA).

86 Interview of Shelagh Day (9 March 2011) [Day]. Tribunal and board decisions in one jurisdiction are not binding on other jurisdictions or even in future cases in the same jurisdiction.

87 I discuss the development of hate speech laws at greater length in chapters 4 and 5.

88 *Canada (Human Rights Commission) v. Taylor*, [1990] 3 SCR 892.

89 *Warman v. Lemire*, 2009 CHRT 26.

90 *Whatcott v. Saskatchewan (Human Rights Tribunal)*, 2010 SKCA 26; *Boissoin v. Lund*, 2009 ABQB 592. See also *Lund v. Boissoin*, 2012 ABCA 300.

91 *Canada (Human Rights Commission) v. Warman*, 2012 FC 1162.

92 The *Rules of the Supreme Court of Canada*, SOR/2002-156, permit people or organizations who are not parties to the original proceedings to intervene in the case and to present their particular interests and perspectives. The rules differ from those that apply to other courts and to administrative tribunals.

93 *Saskatchewan (Human Rights Commission) v. Whatcott*, 2013 SCC 11.

94 Bill C-304, *An Act to amend the Canadian Human Rights Act (protecting freedom)* S.C. 2013 c. 37. The Bill received Royal Assent on 26 June 2013.

95 See Howe and Johnson, *supra* note 2 at 78 (Table 3.3, Provincial Spending on Human Rights, per capita).

96 The approved year-end allocation for the 1993–94 fiscal year was $13,233,100. See Ontario Human Rights Commission, *Annual Report: 1993-94 and 1994-95* (Toronto: Ontario Human Rights Commission, 1996) at 25.

97 The OHRC's 2000–01 printed estimates were $11,165,900. See Ontario Human Rights Commission, *Annual Report: 2000-2001* (Toronto: Ontario Human Rights Commission, 2001) at 46, online: Legislative Assembly of Ontario <http://www.ontla.on.ca/library/repository/ser/3214/2000-2001.pdf>.

98 Ontario Human Rights Commission, *Annual Report: 2008-2009* (Toronto: Ontario Human Rights Commission, 2009), online: OHRC <http://www.ohrc.on.ca/en/resources/annualreports/ar0809/pdf>. An earlier study revealed that the trend toward diminished resources in relation to workload existed in the 1980s as well. Between 1982 and 1989, the Ontario Commission's workload increased by more than 200 percent, whereas its budget increased by only 24.5 percent. See R Brian Howe, *supra* note 2, at 801.

99 In Ontario, see Ontario Human Rights Code Review Task Force, *Achieving Equality: A Report on Human Rights Reform* (Toronto: Ministry of

Citizenship, 1992), (Chair: Mary Cornish) [Cornish Report]; and Office of the Ombudsman, *Ombudsman Special Report on the Ontario Human Rights Commission* (Toronto: Ombudsman of Ontario, 1993). In British Columbia, see Black, *supra* note 62. In Alberta, see Office of the Ombudsman, *Annual Report: 1995* (Edmonton: Alberta Ombudsman, 1995). The federal report came out in 2000: Canadian Human Rights Act Review Panel, *Promoting Equality: A New Vision* (Ottawa: Canadian Human Rights Act Review Panel, 2000), (Chair: Gérard La Forest), online: Government of Canada <http://publications.gc.ca/collections/ Collection/J2-168-2000E.pdf>.

100 Interview of Byron Williams (9 February 2010).

101 Cornish Report, *supra* note 99.

102 The commission was to continue under a new name and to retain "core" functions such as research, education, investigations, and interventions in systemic discrimination cases before the tribunal.

103 Interview of Rémy Beauregard (15 September 2009).

104 Ontario Human Rights Commission, *Annual Report: 1995-1996* (Toronto: Ontario Human Rights Commission, 1996) at 58. The section 34 policy caused bitter disagreement within the commission in the 1990s and by 2005 the number of cases had increased again, with the result that 150 cases had been referred to the tribunal.

105 In 1997, Keith Norton asked the commission's policy branch to develop an internal reform paper that put forward options to help alleviate the backlog of claims. One proposal put forward by my branch was to allow certain claims, especially those that were based primarily on evidentiary issues, to bypass investigations and go directly to a board of inquiry (as it was called then). The commission would keep cases that raised systemic issues or a new point of law. This would have resulted in a modified "direct access" system.

106 In 1985, 403 cases were filed and the commission's budget was $9.2M. In 1995, 1,010 cases were filed and the Commission's budget was $16.6M. Source: Canadian Human Rights Commission, *1985* and *Annual Report, 1995*.

107 Office of the Auditor General of Canada, *1998 September Report of the Auditor General of Canada – Chapter 10 – Canadian Human Rights Commission – Human Rights Tribunal Panel* (Ottawa: OAG, 1998) at 10.16, online: OAG http://www.oag-bvg.gc.ca/internet/English/parl_ oag_199809_10_e_9316.html#0.2.2Z141Z1.WAMWY8.LVY4ZE.A [*OAG 1998 Report*].

108 *Ibid* at 10.3.

109 *Ibid* at 10.73.

110 Sujit Choudry, "What Is a Canadian?" in Irvin Studin, ed, *What Is a Canadian?: Forty-Three Thought-Provoking Responses* (Toronto: McLelland & Stewart, 2006) 117 at 122–123. Multiculturalism had been a part of the "narrative" since the 1970s. However, the Charter and the rapidly increasing diversity of Canada's population have raised its profile.

111 Steve Jacob, "Sharing Power among Evaluation Players: Mission Possible?" in Eliadis et al, 2011, *supra* note 65, at 55. Jacob notes that the involvement of many societal actors creates a new dimension for evaluation. It confers another source of information and even a source of power for the evaluator, who is, of course, free to determine how and when to consider stakeholders' advice and its relative influence as compared to the institution itself.

112 *Ibid.*

113 *OAG 1998 Report, supra* note 107 at 10.58.

114 *Ibid* at 10.45–10.46 and 10.122. It also made policy-oriented recommendations, with a new emphasis on early mediation, which had had some success in Ontario.

115 Canadian Human Rights Act Review Panel, *Promoting Equality: A New Vision* (Ottawa: Canadian Human Rights Act Review Panel, 2000), (Chair: Gérard La Forest), online: Government of Canada <http://publications.gc.ca/collections/Collection/J2-168-2000E.pdf>.

116 *Canada (Canadian Human Rights Commission) v. Canada (Attorney General)*, [2011] 3 SCR 471 [*Mowat*] at para 63. To compensate successful claimants who had paid for their own lawyers, the Canadian commission asked the tribunal to award costs to claimants in order to permit them to recoup a portion of their legal fees. In *Mowat*, the Supreme Court of Canada held that the wording and legal history of the CHRA suggested that awarding costs was not part of the law's structure or history. This decision did not explicitly address the practice of leaving claimants to their own devices at the tribunal stage, but it did cast doubt on the legitimacy of the commission's approach to restricting its advocacy before tribunal under the CHRA. Unlike the CHRA, the human rights statutes in Alberta, New Brunswick, Newfoundland and Labrador, Nova Scotia, Prince Edward Island, Quebec, and Saskatchewan allow their tribunals to award costs, another example of the uneven application of human rights law in Canada. See Appendix 3 for a detailed description of each system.

117 See, e.g., Wanda Thomas Bernard, Viola Robinson, and Fred Wien, *Final Report on the Public Consultations: Organizational Review of the Nova Scotia Human Rights Commission* (Halifax: Praxis Research, 2001), online: Government of Nova Scotia <http://humanrights.gov.ns.ca/sites/default/files/files/reports/HRREVIEW.pdf>; *Après 25 ans : La Charte*

québécoise des droits et libertés – Vol 1: Bilan et recommendations (Montreal: CDPDJ, 2003), online: CDPDJ <http://www.cdpdj.qc.ca/Publications/documents/bilan_charte.pdf>; Ontario Human Rights Commission, *Consultation Report: Strengthening Ontario's Human Rights System – What We Heard* (Toronto: Ontario Human Rights Commission, 2005), online: Legislative Assembly of Ontario <http://www.ontla.on.ca/library/repository/mon/12000/256385.pdf> [OHRC, *2005 Consultation Report*]; Ontario Human Rights Commission, *Discussion Paper: Reviewing Ontario's Human Rights System* (Toronto: Ontario Human Rights Commission, 2005), online: Legislative Assembly of Ontario <http://www.ontla.on.ca/library/repository/mon/11000/255175.pdf>.

118 Bill 64, the *Human Rights Code Amendment Act, 2002,* passed third reading on 29 October 2002 and came into force on 31 March 2003. British Columbia had abolished its human rights agency for the first time in 1984. The events are described in the text accompanying notes 59–62.

119 Day, *supra* note 86. I found one other reference to someone who was effectively "fired" during question period, namely Ted Wetherill, former chair of the Canada Labour Relations Board. The incident took place during an exchange on the floor of the House of Commons: Ron Ellis, *Unjust by Design: Canada's Administrative Justice System* (Vancouver: UBC Press, 2013) at 95–98.

120 Interview of Mary Woo Sims (18 September 2012).

121 Bill 64, the *Human Rights Code Amendment Act,* 2002, 3rd Sess, 37th Parl, B.C., 2002 (assented to 31 October 2002), SB.C. 2002, c 62. Bill 64 came into force on 31 March 2003. For critiques of the Bill, see the policy brief by Shelagh Day, *Rolling Back Human Rights in B.C.: An Assessment of Bill 53 – the Government of British Columbia's Draft Human Rights Legislation* (Vancouver: Canadian Centre for Policy Alternatives, 2002), online: Policy Alternatives <http://www.policyalternatives.ca/documents/B.C._Office_Pubs/human_rights_code_brief.pdf>; International and Human Rights Law Association, University of Victoria, *Route 64– Another Detour on the Road to Equality: An Examination of the Current Human Rights System in British Columbia,* Devyn Cousineau, ed, (Victoria: IHRLA, 2006), online: <http://humanrights.apps01.yorku.ca/blog/wp-content/uploads/2009/08/another-detour-in-the-road-to-equality.pdf> [IHRLA Report].

122 British Columbia, Legislative Assembly, *Official Report of Debates of the Legislative Assembly (Hansard),* 37th Parl, 3rd Sess, Vol 9, No 5 (23 October 2002) at 3988-89 (Hon. G Plant), online: Legislative Assembly of British Columbia <http://www.leg.B.C..ca/Hansard/37th3rd/h21023p.htm>.

123 Any person or group of persons may file a complaint with the tribunal.
     Representative claims are allowed under certain conditions. The tribunal
     may permit both individuals and groups to intervene. See *Human Rights
     Code*, RSBC 1996, c 210, ss 21(1); 21(4) and (5); 22.1 [BC Code].
124 The services are offered by the BC Human Rights Coalition, a charitable
     community-based organization, in partnership with the Community Legal
     Assistance Society.
125 Day, *supra* note 86; Norman, *supra* note 19.
126 Interview of Heather MacNaughton (2 February 2010) [MacNaughton].
127 The ICC accredits national human rights institutions that comply with
     the Paris Principles. See International Coordinating Committee of
     National Institutions for the Promotion and Protection of Human rights
     (ICC), *Chart of the Status of National Institutions* (Geneva: ICC, 2012),
     online: NHRI http://nhri.ohchr.org/EN/Documents/Chart%20of%20
     the%20Status%20of%20NIs%20%2830%20May%202012%29.pdf.
     None of the institutions accredited by the ICC are purely adjudicative
     or protection-oriented.
128 Paris Principles, *supra* note 70. For a discussion of why a tribunal-only
     system is not a human rights institution, see the discussion in IHRLA
     Report, *supra* note 121 and Gwen Brodsky and Shelagh Day, *Strengthen-
     ing the Nunavut Human Rights System: A Report for the Government of
     Nunavut* (Iqaluit: Government of Nunavut, 2012), online: Legislative
     Assembly of Nunavut <http://assembly.nu.ca/library/GNedocs/2012/
     000707-e.pdf> [Brodsky and Day].
129 Brodsky and Day, *ibid.*
130 *CSWU Local 1611 v. SELI Canada Inc (No 8)(Seli)*, 2008 B.C. HRT 436.
131 A separate Labour Relations Board decision held that the terms of
     employment were not, in fact, discriminatory. The BC Supreme Court
     later ruled that there had been bias against the union and remitted the
     matter to the board for a new hearing. The BC Court of Appeal subse-
     quently overruled the BC Supreme Court's decision and dismissed the
     union's petition. See *Construction and Specialized Workers' Union,
     Local 1611 v. SELI Canada Inc*, 2010 BCCA 335.
132 *CSWU Local 1611 v. SELI Canada and others (No 8)*, 2008 BCHRT 436.
133 Shelagh Day, "Canada's Human Rights Institutions at Risk," *Rewriting
     Equality* (28 July 2010), online: Women's Court <http://womenscourt.
     ca/2010/07/canada%E2%80%99s-human-rights-institutions-at-risk/>.
134 British Columbia Law Institute, *Workplace Dispute Resolution Project:
     Report to the Ministry of Labour and the Ministry for the Attorney
     General* (Vancouver: B.C.LI, 2010) at 41, online: <http://www.B.C.li.org/
     B.C.lrg/publications/workplace-dispute-resolution-project>.

135 ICCPR, *supra* note 48.

136 See the discussion in the section "Access to Justice" in chapter 1. See also
     United Nations, Human Rights Committee, *Consideration of Reports
     Submitted by States Parties Under Article 40 of the Covenant: Concluding
     Observations of the Human Rights Committee: Canada*, UNCCPR, 85th
     Sess, CCPR/C/CAN/CO/5, (2006) at para 11, online: UNHCHR <http://
     www.unhchr.ch/tbs/doc.nsf/0/7616e3478238be01c12570ae00397f5d/
     $FILE/G0641362.pdf>. See also *Consideration of Reports Submitted
     by States Parties under Articles 16 and 17 of the Covenant: Concluding
     Observations of the Committee on Economic, Social and Cultural Rights:
     Canada*, UNSER, 36th Sess, E/C.12/CAN/CO/4 and E/C.12/CAN/CO/5,
     (2006) at para 40, online: UNHCHR <http://www.unhchr.ch/tbs/doc.nsf/
     0/87793634eae60c00c12571ca00371262/$FILE/G0642783.pdf>.

137 Bill 107, *An Act to amend the Human Rights Code*, 2nd Sess, 38th Leg,
     Ontario, 2006 (assented to 20 December 2006), SO 2006, c 30.

138 Interview of Keith Norton (21 April 2009). Norton's view was confirmed
     by an Ontario public servant who spoke on condition of anonymity who
     said that then-Minister Michael Bryant had told public servants during
     the public debates about Bill 107 that he had not been given the whole
     picture regarding the divisions within the human rights community at the
     time he had pitched the idea of reform to Cabinet. Bryant had been led to
     believe that there was consensus about the need for reform and about the
     broad outlines of Bill 107.

139 Murray Campbell, "Reforming Human-Rights System Turns into a
     Catch-22 for McGuinty," *The Globe and Mail* (11 November 2006) A9.
     François Larsen and Margaret Parsons both spoke about the highly
     adversarial nature of the debate about the reforms within the Ontario
     human rights community. See Parsons, *supra* note 16 and interview of
     François Larsen (10 September 2010) [Larsen].

140 Larsen, *ibid*.

141 Interview of Michael Gottheil (22 April 2009) [Gottheil 1].

142 Gottheil 1, *supra* note 141; Interview of Kathy Laird (2 October 2011)
     [Laird]; interview of Raj Anand (14 September 2009) [Anand].

143 Gottheil 1, *supra* note 141.

144 BC Code, *supra* note 123. Section 27(1) of the Code authorizes the tribu-
     nal to dismiss all or part of a complaint *with or without a hearing* if:
     "(a) the complaint or that part of the complaint is not within the jurisdic-
     tion of the tribunal; (b) the acts or omissions alleged in the complaint or
     that part of the complaint do not contravene [the] Code; (c) there is no
     reasonable prospect that the complaint will succeed; (d) proceeding with

the complaint or that part of the complaint would not (i) benefit the person, group or class alleged to have been discriminated against, or (ii) further the purposes of [the] Code; (e) the complaint or that part of the complaint was filed for improper motives or made in bad faith; (f) the substance of the complaint or that part of the complaint has been appropriately dealt with in another proceeding; (g) the contravention alleged in the complaint or that part of the complaint occurred more than 6 months before the complaint was filed unless the complaint or that part of the complaint was accepted under section 22(3)." (Emphasis added.)

145 Interview of Paul Champ (29 June 2010).

146 OHRC, *2005 Consultation Report, supra* note 117 at 36.

147 Andrew Pinto, *Report of the Ontario Human Rights Review 2012* (Toronto: Queen's Printer for Ontario, 2012) at 16, online: HRLSC <http://www.hrlsc.on.ca/docs/en/PintoReport.pdf> [Pinto Report] at 16.

148 *Ibid.*

149 *Ibid* at 42.

150 MacNaughton, *supra* note 126. The main reason for this difference is that the BC Tribunal has far more options available to dismiss cases on a preliminary basis. See B.C. Code, *supra* note 123, s 27(1). It is likely that this brings down the average age of cases considerably.

151 Gottheil 1, *supra* note 141.

152 *Ibid.*

153 The term used in Ontario to describe complainants.

154 According to Kathy Laird, the executive director of the Human Rights Legal Support Centre, all three branches of the Ontario human rights system are independent from one another. All three were particularly careful to ensure their independence throughout the process of implementing Bill 107. Nonetheless, all three institutions liaised regularly at the beginning of the new direct access system to ensure that operational issues were handled smoothly. Laird, *supra* note 142.

155 Anand, *supra* note 142. Inadequate levels of support for respondents under Ontario's new system were a concern for many interviewees. This issue is addressed in chapter 4.

156 HRTO Statistics, http://www.hrto.ca.

157 Laird, *supra* note 142.

158 Pinto Report, *supra* note 147, at 187.

159 Laird, *supra* note 142.

160 *Ibid.* See also HRLSC, 2011-2012 *Annual Report* (Toronto: HRLSC, 2012) online: <www.hrlsc.on.ca/en/AnnualRepHRLSCorts.aspx> at 5. Raj Anand pointed out that the HRLSC's multilingual website, the

development of self-help materials, and cooperation with legal clinics and other community resources had helped improve access to information about the Centre. See Anand, *supra* note 142.

161 The exact figure is 78 percent. Human Rights Tribunal of Ontario, "Fiscal Year 2012–2013," online: HRTO <http://www.hrto.ca>.

162 Gottheil 1, *supra* note 141.

163 Pinto Report, *supra* note 147, at 188.

164 Interview of David Baker (30 July 2009).

165 Gottheil 1, *supra* note 141.

166 Interview of Barbara Hall (22 April 2009).

167 Pinto Report, *supra* note 147, at 189.

168 Although commissions do not support respondents in the preparation of their proceedings, gatekeeping commissions offer respondents information and general advice about a range of procedural and substantive aspects of the human rights process.

169 *Human Rights Act*, SNu 2003, c 12.

170 "Nunavut Human Rights Tribunal Not Working, Says Minister," *CBC News* (8 March 2012), online: CBC. <http://www.cbc.ca/news/canada/north/story/2012/03/08/north-nunavut-rights-tribunal.html>.

171 Brodsky and Day, *supra* note 128.

172 *Ibid* at 4.

173 *Bill 160, An Act to amend The Saskatchewan Human Rights Code and to Make Consequential Amendments to The Labour Standards Act*, 4th Sess, 26th Leg, Saskatchewan, 2010 (assented to 18 May 2011), SS 2011, c 17. Bill 160 came into force in 2011.

174 Day, *supra* note 86. See also Ken Norman, "Saskatchewan Marches to a Different, Distant Drummer" (blog), online: Blogging Canadians <http://www.bloggingcanadians.ca/NonPartisan/government-fails-to-consult-on-changes-to-human-rights-code/>.

175 Norman, *ibid*.

176 This comment is no longer available on the commission's website. Screen shot on file.

177 Arnot, *ibid*. See also David Arnot, "Human Rights: We Can Be a Leader," *Leader-Post* (16 December 2010). Available online: SHRC Archives <www.shrc.gov.sk/pdfs/archives.html>.

178 Bill Rafoss, "Obligation to Defend Human Rights Applies to All Canadians," Opinion, *The StarPhoenix* (25 April 2012) A11, online: Canada.com <http://www2.canada.com>.

179 Section 84, Quebec *Charter of human rights and freedoms* RSQ c 12.

180 *Ménard c. Rivet et al*, [1997] RJQ 2108 (CA).

181 *Centre hospitalier St-Joseph de la Malbaie* c. *Lise Dufour et autres,* JE 98-2178 (CA); *La Procureure Générale du Québec c. La Commission des droits de la personne et des droits de la jeunesse.* C.A. 500-09-010164-002, 28 February 2002. Baudouin, Rousseau-Houle, Robert JJ; *Quebec (Commission des droits de la personne et des droits de la jeunesse) v. Quebec (Attorney General),* 2004 SCC 39 at para 14, and per Bastarache, diss, [2004] 2 SCR 185.

182 *Quebec (Commission des droits de la personne et des droits de la jeunesse) v. Quebec (Attorney General), ibid.*

183 Interview of Fo Niemi (11 January 2011) [Niemi]. See *Parry Sound (District) Social Services Administration Board v. OPSEU, Local 324,* [2003] 2 SCR 157. Although this case was from Ontario, Niemi said its interpretation in Quebec has been damaging.

184 Le Tribunal des droits de la personne, *Bilan d'activités: 2011-2012,* online: <http://www.tribunaux.qc.ca/TDP/BilanActivites/TDP-007_Bilan2011-12_E3.pdf> at 48. The total number of files received in each year is slightly higher, at 43, because as noted earlier, Quebec also permits claimants to proceed alone to the tribunal in limited circumstances.

185 Interview of Michèle Rivet (23 June 2009). There appears, however, to be little appetite for amendments. The Quebec Bar Association has taken the formal position that the Quebec Human Rights Commission should be maintained in its current form, even if changes are needed. See Barreau du Québec, *Position du Barreau du Québec concernant le Tribunal des droits de la personne,* (31 May 2010), online: Barreau du Québec <http://www.barreau.qc.ca/pdf/medias/positions/2010/20100531-droits-personne.pdf>.

186 Niemi, *supra* note 183.

187 Article 26, *ICCPR, supra* note 48.

CHAPTER THREE

1 Jonathan Kay, "Human Rights Commissions Have Had Their Day" (6 March 2013) *National Post,* online <http://fullcomment.nationalpost.com/2013/03/06/jonathan-kay-human-rights-commissions-have-had-their-day/> [Kay].

2 Interview of Fiona Sampson (11 May 2009).

3 Mark J Freiman, "Trial by Anecdote: A Controversial Polemicist Takes on Canada's Commitment to Human Rights." *Literary Review of Canada* (June 2009), online: LRC <http://reviewcanada.ca/reviews/2009/06/01/trial-by-anecdote/>.

4 Interview of Kim Bernhardt (14 September 2009).

5 Interview of Alan Borovoy (14 September 2009).

6 See also the discussion in chapter 1.

7 R Brian Howe and David Johnson, *Restraining Equality: Human Rights Commissions in Canada* (Toronto: University of Toronto Press, 2000), Table 3.1 at 73. The relationship between caseloads and the number of claims filed should be treated with some caution. Caseloads include the total number of active cases, regardless of when they were filed, and reflect commissions' effectiveness in dealing with claims as much as they reflect the number of incoming cases. Caseloads are thus indicative of both commissions' workload and their effectiveness.

8 The study looked at Alberta, British Columbia, Ontario, Nova Scotia, and Quebec. See John Samuel et al, *Identifying Human Rights Issues for the Next Decade: A Report Submitted to the Canadian Human Rights Commission* (Ottawa: John Samuel & Associates Inc, 1998) at 3, online: Samuel & Associates <http://www.samuelassociates.com>.

9 Editorial, "You Call This Human Rights?" *National Post* (7 February 2011) A8.

10 Ontario Human Rights Commission, *Annual Report 2007/2008* (Toronto: Ontario Human Rights Commission, 2008) at 48, 51.

11 Tribunal des droits de la personne and Barreau du Québec, *Access to a Specialized Human Rights Tribunal: An Urgent Need to Act in Quebec?* (Cowansville, Que: Yvon Blais, 2008).

12 Interview of Fo Niemi (11 January 2011) [Niemi].

13 Interview of David Baker (30 July 2009) [Baker].

14 Andrew MacKenzie, Matt Hurst, and Susan Crompton, "Living with Disabilities Series: Defining Disability in the Participation and Activity Limitation Survey" (2009) *Canadian Social Trends* 88, online: Statistics Canada <http://www.statcan.gc.ca/pub/11-008-x/2009002/article/11024-eng.htm> [MacKenzie et al]

15 Chantal Collin and Hilary Jensen, *A Statistical Profile of Poverty in Canada* (Ottawa: Library of Parliament, 2009), online: Parliament of Canada <http://www.parl.gc.ca/Content/LOP/ResearchPublications/prb0917-e.htm#a11>.

16 Human Resources and Skills Development Canada, "Canadians in Context – Aging Population" *Indicators of Well-being in Canada* website, online: HRSDC <http://www4.hrsdc.gc.ca/.3ndic.1t.4r@-eng.jsp?iid=33>.

17 Canadian Mental Health Association, *Integrating Needs for Mental Well-Being into Human Resource Planning*, Final Report. Project IN4M (Ottawa: CMHA, 2011). CMHA, online:<http://www.cmha.ca/public-policy/research-reports/> at ii, 8.

18 Andrew Solomon, *Far from the Tree: Parents, Children, and the Search for Identity* (New York: Scribner, 2012) at 221. Solomon's figures are based on American sources. In Canada, there is no government monitoring in place to provide accurate statistics, according to Autism Society Canada, online: <http://www.autismsocietycanada.ca/index.php?option=com_content&view=article&id=55&Itemid=85&lang=en>.

19 *Wynberg v. Ontario*, 213 OAC 48, 82 OR (3d)561 (Ont CA).

20 *Auton (Guardian ad litem of) v. British Columbia (Attorney General)*, [2004] 3 SCR 657.

21 Interview of Mary Eberts (24 April 2009).

22 See the text in the introduction accompanying notes 1–4.

23 See *Auton: Factum of the Intervener, Michelle Dawson*. Online, <http://www.sentex.net/~nexus23/naa_fac.html>, at paras 19 and 31. Thanks to Melanie Benard for bringing this aspect of the case to my attention.

24 Interview of Barbara Hall (22 April 2009) [Hall]. The Ontario Commission released its consultation paper on mental health in 2011. See Ontario Human Rights Commission, *Human Rights and Mental Health Research and Policy: Consultation Paper* (Toronto: OHRC, 2011), online: OHRC <http://www.ohrc.on.ca>.

25 Ontario Human Rights Commission, *Minds That Matter: Report on the Consultation on Human Rights, Mental Health and Addictions* (Toronto: OHRC, 2012), online: OHRC <http://www.ohrc.on.ca>.

26 *Ibid* at 3–4.

27 MacKenzie et al, *supra* note 14.

28 "Universal design" is the design of products, environments, programs, and services to be usable by all people, to the greatest extent possible, without the need for adaptation or specialized design. It does not, however, exclude assistive devices for particular groups of persons with disabilities, when needed.

29 Interview of Ravi Malhotra (13 May 2009) [Malhotra].

30 *Quebec (Commission des droits de la personne et des droits de la jeunesse) v. Montréal (City); Quebec (Commission des droits de la personne et des droits de la jeunesse) v. Boisbriand (City)*, [2000] 1 SCR 665 at paras 77–80.

31 Brian Doyle, *Disability, Discrimination and Equality Opportunities: A Comparative Study of the Employment Rights of Disabled Persons* (London and New York: Mansell Publishing Limited, 1995) at 5.

32 These observations are based on my own experiences as policy director during the period between 1995 and 2001. The concerns of commission staff have been documented independently in the literature with respect to

the commission's *Policy and Guidelines on Disability and the Duty to Accommodate*: "Many inquiry and intake staff cited the implementation of the 2001 (sic) OHRC policy on disability as the basis for increased inquiries and complaints; it also requires staff to familiarize themselves with the new area of enforcement, whose perimeters were not yet established"; Rosanna L Langer, *Defining Rights and Wrongs: Bureaucracy, Human Rights, and Public Accountability* (Vancouver: UBC Press, 2007) at 43. "Lawyers, for their part, complained that policy initiatives seemed to "come out of nowhere," *ibid* at 126. Such complaints are understandable, in the sense that the evolving legal and sociological realities of disability and discrimination required ongoing research and entailed new work. However, the notion that this work was not necessary, appropriate, or timely could not have been further from the mark. The reality is that all of the commission's major policy work, at least since the late 1990s, was initiated through internal proposals that were circulated to all staff, based on current case law, international legal developments, and changing legislative criteria. These were followed by major external consultations at the provincial level, resulting in reports that ultimately led to revised policy proposals. Proposals would then go forward to the entire commission for approval. New policies, the work preceding them, and the follow-up work that resulted would span a period of at least two to three years, followed by extensive staff training. Assertions that these developments "came out of nowhere," or that the staff were somehow left in the dark to manage the consequences are not only patently untrue but reflect a deep lack of understanding of the policy development process at the Ontario Human Rights Commission during this period. Langer's research was not informed by interviews with policy staff at the commission at the time, including me, nor was there any effort to determine what actually happened with respect to the policy development process during the period in question.

33 Malhotra, *supra* note 29. The *Americans with Disabilities Act* was passed in 1990 and was amended in 2008. See 42 USC § 12101.

34 *Council of Canadians with Disabilities v. VIA Rail Canada Inc*, [2007] 1 SCR 650. See also David Baker and Sarah Godwin, "All Aboard! The Supreme Court of Canada Confirms That Canadians with Disabilities Have Substantive Equality Rights" (2008) 39 Sask L Rev 41.

35 An example is the practice of announcing transit stops. The Ontario Commission filed complaints about the failure to announce stops in 2009. The cases were settled in 2011. Hall, *supra* note 24. See also Ontario Human Rights Commission, *Annual Report: 2009-2010 – Educate Empower Act*

(Toronto: OHRC, 2010) at 16, online: OHRC <http://www.ohrc.on.ca>; Ontario Human Rights Commission, Media Release Human Rights Cases Settled as Transit Providers Offer More Accessible Services" (29 September 2011), online: OHRC <http://www.ohrc.on.ca/en/news_centre/human-rights-cases-settled-transit-providers-offer-more-accessible-services>. These cases had a long history, dating from TTC cases on subway stop announcements brought by prominent disability activist and lawyer David Lepofsky: see *Ontario Human Rights Commission v. Lepofsky*, 2005 HRTO 36; Re: TTC bus and streetcar announcements, see *Lepofsky v. TTC*, 2007 HRTO 23 and *Lepofsky v. Toronto Transit Commission*, 2007 HRTO 41.

36 See, e.g., Ontario Human Rights Commission, *Discussion Paper on Accessible Transit Services In Ontario* (Toronto: OHRC, 2001), online: Legislative Assembly of Ontario <http://www.ontla.on.ca/library/repository/mon/1000/10293457.pdf>; Ontario Human Rights Commission, *Human Rights and Public Transit Services in Ontario: Consultation Report* (Toronto: OHRC, 2002), online: OHRC <http://www.ohrc.on.ca/>.

37 Online: <http://www.rapliq.org/2011/12/09/couverture-mediatique-en-anglais-english-press-coverage/>. See also "Montreal Transit Users with Disabilities File Human-Rights Complaint," *CBC News* (8 December 2011), online: CBC <http://www.cbc.ca/news/canada/montreal/story/2011/12/08/transit-users-with-disabilities-file-human-rights-complaints-metro-bus-access.html>. One of the community organizations involved in the complaint, the Committee for Research-Action on Race Relations (CRARR), observed that the applicants will be dead by the time Montreal's transit system reaches its 2085 accessibility targets.

38 Baker, *supra* note 13.

39 *Moore v. British Columbia (Education)*, 2012 SCC 61 [*Moore*].

40 *Moore v. B.C. (Ministry of Education) and School District No. 44*, 2005 BCHRT 580, at para 612.

41 *Moore, supra* note 39 at para 5.

42 Convention on the Rights of Persons with Disabilities (CRPD), 13 December 2006, 2515 UNTS 3. GA Res 61/106, (entered into force 3 May 2008, ratification by Canada 11 March 2010) [CRPD].

43 *Ibid*, Article 33.

44 Gus Reed, "Canada's Failing Grade on Disability Rights," *Globe and Mail* (2 August 2013) A 11.

45 *Janzen v. Platy Enterprises Ltd*, [1989] 1 SCR 1252 at 1290 per Dickson CJ. This case is also discussed in the introduction as one of the signal cases that was brought to the courts through human rights systems.

46 *Friedmann v. MacGarvie,* 2012 BCCA 445.

47 According to the Canadian Human Rights Commissions 2012 *Annual Report,* 86 percent of the sexual harassment complaints filed in the five-year period between 2007 and 2012 were filed by women. Canadian Human Rights Commission, *2012 Annual Report,* CHRC online <http://www.chrcreport.ca/index-eng.html> [CHRC 2012].

48 Interview of Rémy Beauregard (15 September 2009).

49 Natalie Stechyson and Bradley Bouzane, "Workplace Discrimination for Pregnancy on the Rise," *[Montreal] Gazette* (8 March 2012) A14.

50 *Maciel v. Fashion Coiffures,* 2009 HRTO 1804.

51 Stephen Smysnuik, "Woman Fired over Pregnancy Wins $35,000 in Rights Case," *The Toronto Star* (30 October 2009), online: The Star <http://www.thestar.com/iphone/GTA/article/718478>.

52 Inter-Parliamentary Union, "Women in National Parliaments," online: Inter-Parliamentary Union <http://www.ipu.org/wmn-e/classif.htm>. Women fared better in the Upper House, where in 2013 almost 38 percent of senators were women.

53 See, e.g., Council of Europe, *Parity Democracy: A Far Cry from Reality* (Strasbourg: Council of Europe, 2010), online: COE <http://www.coe.int/t/dghl/standardsetting/equality/03themes/women-decisionmaking/CDEG%20(2009)17_en_corrected.pdf>.

54 Equality and Human Rights Commission, *How Fair Is Britain? Equality, Human Rights and Good Relations in 2010: The First Triennial Review* (London, UK: EHRC, 2011), online: EHRC <http://www.equalityhumanrights.com>.

55 *Ibid* at 583.

56 The Supreme Court of Canada recognized pay equity as a human rights and discrimination issue in *Newfoundland (Treasury Board) v. NAPE,* [2004] 3 SCR 381. See also Pay Equity Task Force, *Pay Equity: A New Approach to a Fundamental Right – Federal Pay Equity Task Force Final Report, 2004* (Ottawa: Pay Equity Task Force, 2004), online: Government of Canada <http://publications.gc.ca/collections/Collection/J2-191-2003E.pdf>.

57 Interview of Shelagh Day (9 March 2011).

58 *Public Service Alliance of Canada v. Canada Post Corp,* [2011] 3 SCR 572.

59 CHRC 2012, *supra* note 47.

60 SC 2009, c 2, s 394.

61 The federal, Alberta, British Columbia, Manitoba, Newfoundland and Labrador, Northwest Territories, Prince Edward Island, Quebec and Yukon

commissions have specific or partial jurisdiction over pay equity or equality in wages beyond general discrimination prohibitions. As well, most jurisdictions now have specific pay equality laws.

62 Citizenship and Immigration Canada, *Facts and Figures 2012 – Immigration Overview: Permanent and Temporary Residents,* online: CIC <http://www.cic.gc.ca>. Once a person becomes a permanent resident, actual residence in Canada is required for several years before the person is eligible for citizenship.

63 In 2010, Citizenship and Immigration Canada had some of the highest levels of immigration in Canadian history (more than 280,000). *Ibid.*

64 *Singh v. Canada (Minister of Employment and Immigration),* [1985] 1 SCR 177.

65 *Ibid* at 202.

66 See, for example, *Suresh v. Canada (Minister of Citizenship and Immigration),* [2002] 1 SCR 3; *Charkaoui v. Canada (Citizenship and Immigration),* 2007, SCC 9.

67 Citizenship and Immigration Canada, Interim Federal Health Program Policy (June 30, 2012) online: CIC <http://www.cic.gc.ca/english/department/laws-policy/ifhp.asp>.

68 Columnist Jeffrey Simpson complains about the *Singh* case with some regularity because of the cost of our refugee determination system. See e.g. "Blame the Refugee System," *The Globe and Mail,* 14 July 2009, online: The Globe and Mail <http://www.theglobeandmail.com/news/opinions/blame-the-refugee-system/article1218134/>. Similar comments and concerns about Canada's supposed softness regarding potentially fraudulent refugees have been circulating for years. See, e.g., Anthony Wilson-Smith, "Debating the Numbers," *Maclean's* (7 November 1994) 22, online: HighBeam Business <http://business.highbeam.com/4341/article-1G1-15924197/debating-numbers>; Anthony Wilson-Smith, "Is Canada a Soft Touch?" *Maclean's* (7 November 1994) 28, online: HighBeam Business <http://business.highbeam.com/4341/article-1G1-15924199/canada-soft-touch-refugee-acceptance-rates-skyrocket>.

69 Statistics Canada, *The General Social Survey: An Overview* (Ottawa: Statistics Canada, 2006), online: Statistics Canada <http://www.statcan.gc.ca/pub/89f0115x/89f0115x2006001-eng.pdf>.

70 Regarding outcomes for ethnic and racial minorities, see Jeffrey G Reitz and Rupa Banerjee, "Racial Inequality, Social Cohesion and Policy Issues in Canada" in Keith Banting, Thomas J Courchene, and F Leslie Seidle, eds, *Belonging? Diversity, Recognition, and Shared Citizenship in Canada,*

The Art of the State, vol 3 (IRPP), (Montreal: McGill-Queen's University Press, 2007) 489, online: IRPP <http://www.irpp.org/books/archive/aots3/reitz.pdf>. See also Garnett Picot and Arthur Sweetman, *Making It in Canada: Immigration Outcomes and Policies*, IRPP Study No 29 (Montreal: IRPP 2012), online: IRPP <http://www.irpp.org/pubs/IRPPstudy/IRPP_Study_no29.pdf>.

71 Interview of Byron Williams (9 February 2010).

72 According to Citizenship and Immigration Canada statistics, there were 171,737 temporary workers in 1992. Twenty years later, there were 491,547, *supra* note 62. According to the United Food and Commercial Workers Union (UFCW)'s *Report on the Status of Migrant Workers in Canada 2011*, the Canadian government has significantly expanded its temporary migrant worker programs since 2006. While Ontario experienced a decline in permanent residents between 2005 and 2009, there was an increase in temporary migration; temporary residents totalled 64,741 in 2005 and reached 94,968 in 2009. British Columbia experienced similar trends; the number of permanent residents decreased between 2005 and 2009, while the number of temporary residents increased by 120 percent. See UFCW, *Report on the Status of Migrant Workers in Canada 2011* (Toronto: UFCW, 2011), online: UFCW <http://www.ufcw.ca/templates/ufcwcanada/images/Report-on-The-Status-of-Migrant-Workers-in-Canada-2011.pdf>.

73 *International Convention on the Protection of the Rights of All Migrant Workers and Members of their Families*, 18 December 1990, 2220 UNTS 3 (entered into force 1 July 2003).

74 *Quebec (Commission des droits de la personne et des droits de la jeunesse) v. Centre Maraîcher Eugène Guinois Jr Inc.*, [2005] RJQ 1315 (QC TDP).

75 Marie Carpentier with Carole Fiset, *Systemic Discrimination Towards Migrant Workers: Summary* (Montreal: CDPDJ, 2011), online: CDPDJ <http://www.cdpdj.qc.ca>.

76 Commission des droits de la personne et des droits de la jeunesse, Communiqué, "Québec doit modifier sa loi et ses programmes en matière d'immigration pour mettre fin à la discrimination systémique des travailleuses et travailleurs migrants, selon la Commission des droits de la personne et des droits de la jeunesse» (20 February 2012), online: CDPDJ <http://www.cdpdj.qc.ca/Comm_HTML/COMM_travailleurs_migrants_Fr_fev2012.html>

77 *Ibid*.

78 Interview of Heather MacNaughton (2 February 2010).

79 Ontario Human Rights Commission, *Annual Report 1993–94 and 1994–95* (Toronto: Ontario Human Rights Commission, 1996).

80 Ontario Human Rights Commission, *Annual Report 1993–94 and 1994–95* (Toronto: Ontario Human Rights Commission, 1996); HRTO, *Fiscal Year, 2011–12*, online: <www.hrto.ca>.

81 Human Rights Tribunal of Ontario, *Fiscal Year 2012–13* online: <http://www.hrto.ca/>.

82 *Brooks v. Canada Safeway Ltd*, [1989] 1 SCR 1219 at 1243–44. The Supreme Court of Canada ruled that the employer's disability plan discriminated against pregnant employees and therefore constituted discrimination based on sex.

83 *Hoyt v. Canadian National Railway*, 2006 CHRT 33.

84 *Attorney General of Canada v. Johnstone*, 2013 FC 113.

85 *Health Sciences Assoc. of BC v. Campbell River and North Island Transition Society*, 2004 BCCA 260. This case imposed a higher threshold for what constitutes discrimination on the ground of family status.

86 Joan C. Williams, Robin Devaux, Patricija Petrac, and Lynn Feinberg "Protecting Family Caregivers from Employment Discrimination" (AARP Public Policy Institute, August 2012), WorkLifeLaw, online: <http://worklifelaw.org/publications/>.

87 U.S. Equal Employment Opportunity Commission, Employer Best Practices for Workers with Caregiving Responsibilities (2011), online <http://www.eeoc.gov/policy/docs/caregiver-best-practices.html>.

88 Information obtained from the Equal Opportunities Ombudsman, 2011. On file.

89 Mary Eberts, "Knowing and Unknowing: Settler Reflections on Missing and Murdered Indigenous Women" (2014) 77 Sask L Rev (forthcoming). References have been omitted.

90 Native Women's Association of Canada, *What Their Stories Tell Us: Research Findings from the Sisters in Spirit Initiative* (Ottawa: NWAC, 2010) at 5.

91 *Human Rights Act*, RSNS 1989, c 214, s 5(1)(q), *Alberta Human Rights Act*, RSA 2000, c A-25.5, s 44(1)(m).

92 Section 4, *Human Rights Act, 2010*. SNL 2010 c. H-13.1

93 See *Human Rights Act*, SNu 2003, c 12. See also s. 2, *Human Rights Act*, SNWT 2002, c 18; s. 2(2) *Human Rights Act*, RSY 2002, c 116.

94 The Ontario Human Rights Commission did receive several human rights complaints from Aboriginal people who invoked race, or, more commonly, ancestry, but these tended to be isolated cases involving refusal of retail

services in hotels and restaurants, and sometimes employment, rather than broader systemic issues. In the late 1990s, the commission's Policy Branch started to work more closely with First Nations groups in Ontario. Preliminary meetings with elders at the reserve of the Six Nations of the Grand Territory, for instance, emphasized the low profile of human rights laws, including the Ontario Human Rights Code, among First Nations people in Ontario and the low levels of trust in government.

95 See Bill C-21, *An Act to amend the Canadian Human Rights Act*, 2nd Sess, 39th Parl, 2008 (assented to 18 June 2008), SC 2008, c 30. The repeal took effect in 2011 after a three-year transition period.

96 Canadian Human Rights Commission, *A Matter of Rights: Special Report of the Canadian Human Rights Commission on the Repeal of Section 67 of the* Canadian Human Rights Act (Ottawa: Canadian Human Rights Commission, 2005), online: CHRC <http://www.chrc-ccdp.ca/proactive_initiatives/section_67/toc_tdm-eng.aspx>.

97 Canadian Human Rights Commission, 2012 *Annual Report* CHRC online <http://www.chrcreport.ca/index-eng.html>.

98 *Daniels v. The Queen,* 2013 FC 6.

99 *Canada (Human Rights Commission) v. Canada (Attorney General),* 2012 FC 445.

100 *Canada (Attorney General) v. Canadian Human Rights Commission,* 2013 FCA 75.

101 GA Res 61/295, UNGAOR (2007).

102 All of the chief commissioners (past and present) who were interviewed for this book emphasized the importance of Aboriginal issues as institutional priorities.

103 Two good books on the general meaning of "human rights" are Andrew Clapham, *Human Rights: A Very Short Introduction* (Oxford: Oxford University Press, 2007), chapters 1 and 8, and Rhona KM Smith and Christien van den Anker, *The Essentials of Human Rights* (London: Hodder Arnold, 2005) at 353. I have drawn from both of these works in this section.

104 Thanks to Ken Norman for his take on this formulation. See also Dominique Clément, Will Silver, and Daniel Trottier, *The Evolution of Human Rights in Canada* (Ottawa: Canadian Human Rights Commission, 2012) at 1, online: CHRC <http://www.chrc-ccdp.ca/research_program_recherche/publications_publications-eng.aspx>.

105 *International Covenant on Civil and Political Rights*, 19 December 1966, 999 UNTS 171, Can TS 1976 No 47, 6 ILM 368 (entered into force 23 March 1976, accession by Canada 19 May 1976) [ICCPR].

106 *International Covenant on Economic, Social and Cultural Rights,*
16 December 1966, 993 UNTS 3, Can TS 1976 No 46 (entered into force
3 January 1976, accession by Canada 19 May 1976) [ICESCR].

107 *Convention on the Elimination of All Forms of Discrimination against
Women,* 18 December 1979, 1249 UNTS 13, Can TS 1982 No 31, 19
ILM 33 (entered into force 3 September 1981, ratification by Canada
10 December 1981); *Convention on the Rights of the Child,* 20 November 1989, 1577 UNTS 3, 28 ILM 1456 (entered into force 2 September
1990, ratification by Canada 13 December 1991); CRPD, *ibid,* note 42;
Convention relating to the Status of Refugees, 28 July 1951, 189 UNTS
137, Can TS No 6 (entered into force 22 April 1954, ratification by
Canada 4 June 1969).

108 *Whatcott v. Saskatchewan (Human Rights Tribunal),* 2010 SKCA 26.

109 *Libel Act,* SM 1934, c 23.

110 *Canadian Human Rights Act,* S.C. 1976-77, c. 33 (*CHRA*). Section 13 of
the CHRA was amended to include the Internet in 2001 after the events
of 9/11. Although the language of the statute was already clear, this
change made "for greater certainty." Internet-related telecommunications
did not exist when the CHRA was drafted in 1975.

111 ICCPR, *supra* note 105, Articles 19 and 20(2).

112 Richard Moon's objections to section 13 of the CHRA are based in part
on a related concern about the appropriateness of regulating freedoms in
an equality statute.

113 See, e.g., Marian Scott, "It's Time to Act on Racial Profiling, Commission
Says," *The [Montreal] Gazette* (12 March 2010); Center for Research-Action on Race Relations, "Racial Profiling in Public Transit: Montreal
Black Metro Rider Awarded $23,000 by Human Rights Commission"
(5 February 2012), online: CRARR <http://www.crarr.org/?q=node/
19401>. On national security issues and discrimination, see Pearl Eliadis,
National Security and Human Rights (Ottawa: Canadian Human Rights
Commission, 2011) online: CHRC <http://www.chrc-ccdp.ca> and
reports discussed there commissioned by the CHRC.

114 Ontario Human Rights Commission, *Paying the Price: The Human
Cost of Racial Profiling – Inquiry Report* (Toronto: OHRC, 2003),
online: OHRC <http://www.ohrc.on.ca>; Commission des droits de la
personne et des droits de la jeunesse, *Racial Profiling and Systemic
Discrimination of Racialized Youth: Report of the Consultation on
Racial Profiling and Its Consequences* (Montreal: CDPDJ, 2011),
online: CDPDJ <http://www.cdpdj.qc.ca/publications/Documents/
Profiling_final_EN.pdf>.

115 A discussion of the case and approximately ten other similar cases involving racial minorities and racial profiling in Montreal's transit system are discussed by the Center for Research-Action on Race Relations, "More Black Public Transit Riders Denounce Racial Profiling and Excessive Use of Force" (29 March 2012), online: CRARR <http://www.crarr.org>.

116 Interview of Ken Norman (16 November 2010). The U.S. has signed, but not ratified, the UN International Covenant on Economic, Social and Cultural Rights.

117 One writer for the Fraser Institute warned that the Supreme Court of Canada decision in an equality rights case coming from Quebec was a harbinger of a "right to welfare," even though the plaintiff lost; the article suggested that this trend was not a positive development. See Chris Schafer, "*Gosselin* Decision Forewarns of Right to Welfare," *Fraser Forum* (February 2003) at 22, online: Fraser Institute <http://www.fraserinstitute.org/research-news/research/display.aspx?id=13034>.

118 ICESCR, *supra* note 106, Art 9.

119 *Falkiner v. Ontario (Minister of Community and Social Services)*, (2002) 59 OR (3d) 481 [*Falkiner*]. This case addressed the withholding of benefits from cohabiting recipients of social assistance. Justice Laskin held that this disproportionately affected a vulnerable group (single women). Most importantly, it violated the recipients' equality rights by creating a demeaning rule that applied to them solely because they received social assistance. This case is also discussed in chapter 2.

120 General Comment No. 19, E/C.12/GC/19 (4 February 2008). See also the discussion in chapter 1.

121 ICESCR, *supra* note 106, Art 11.

122 (2000) CCT 11/00.

123 Susan Randolph, Sakiko Fukudo-Parr, and Terra Lawson-Remer, *Economic and Social Rights Fulfillment Index: Country Scores and Rankings*, Economic Rights Working Paper Series, Working Paper 11 (Connecticut: The Human Rights Institute, University of Connecticut, 2009) Table 5.

124 "This Is *Not* the Way Home," Editorial, *The Globe and Mail* (27 May 2010) A14. The editorial was a response to a Charter challenge to homelessness filed on 26 April 2010. See Social Rights Advocacy Centre, *Historic Charter Challenge to Homelessness and Violations of the Right to Adequate Housing in Canada*, online: SRAC <http://www.socialrights.ca/index.html#Historic>.

125 Sujit Choudhry and Claire E. Hunter, "Measuring Judicial Activism on the Supreme Court of Canada: A Comment on *Newfoundland (Treasury Board) v. NAPE*" (2003) 48 McGill LJ 525.

126 *Miron v. Trudel,* [1995] 2 SCR 418).

127 *Eldridge v. British Columbia (Attorney General),* [1997] 3 SCR 624).

128 *Gwinner v. Alberta (Human Resources and Employment,* 2004 ABCA 210.

129 *Moore, supra* note 39.

130 *Ontario (Human Rights Commission) v. Shelter Corp.,* [2001] OJ No. 297 (Ont Div Ct). This case relied on the evidence of experts, including Professor J David Hulchanski's social science data, which demonstrated the discriminatory impact of such practices. In 2009, the Government of Ontario acknowledged the connection between poverty and human rights, including a specific reference to housing, in the *Poverty Reduction Act,* SO 2009, c 10, s 2(3).

131 See also Ontario Human Rights Commission, *Policy on Human Rights and Rental Housing* (Toronto: OHRC, 2009), online: OHRC <http://www.ohrc.on.ca>.

132 Centre for Equality Rights in Accommodation, *Sorry, It's Rented: Measuring Discrimination in Toronto's Rental Housing Market* (Toronto: CERA, 2009), online: Equality Rights <http://www.equalityrights.org/CERA/docs/CERAFinalReport.pdf>.

133 Interview of Leilani Farha (2 October 2009).

134 See Gordon Laird, *Shelter – Homelessness in a Growth Economy: Canada's 21st Century Paradox* (Calgary: Sheldon Chumir Foundation for Ethics in Leadership, 2007) Sheldon Chumir, online: <http://www.chumirethicsfoundation.ca/files/pdf/SHELTER.pdf>; Stephen Gaetz, Jesse Donaldson, Tim Richter, and Tanya Gulliver, *The State of Homelessness in Canada 2013.* (Toronto: Canadian Homelessness Research Network Press, 2013).

135 Mary P Rowe, "Barriers to Equality: The Power of Subtle Discrimination to Maintain Unequal Opportunity" (1990) 3:2 Employee Responsibilities and Rights J 153 at 10, online: MIT <http://web.mit.edu/ombud/publications/barriers.pdf>.

136 See, e.g., Clayton P Alderfer et al, "Diagnosing Race Relations in Management" (1980) 16:2 J Applied Behavioural Science 135; Joyce K Fletcher, *Disappearing Acts: Gender, Power, and Relational Practice at Work* (Cambridge, MA: MIT Press, 1999); Albert J Mills and Peta Tancred, eds, *Gendering Organizational Analysis* (Newbury Park, CA: Sage, 1992); Karen L Proudford and Kenwyn K Smith, "Group Membership Salience and the Movement of Conflict: Reconceptualizing the Interaction among Race, Gender and Hierarchy" (2003) 28:1 Group and Organization Management 18; Ryan A Smith, "Race, Gender and Authority in the

Workplace: Theory and Research" (2002) 28 Annual Review of Sociology
509; Evangelina Holvino and Annette Kamp, "Diversity Management:
Are We Moving in the *Right* Direction? Reflections from Both Sides of
the North Atlantic" (2009) 25 Scandinavian J of Management 395.

137 Helena Kennedy, "Are Human Rights Universal?" in Helena Kennedy
et al, eds, *Do Human Rights Travel?* (London: British Council, 2004).

138 Colleen Sheppard, *Inclusive Equality: The Relational Dimensions of
Systemic Discrimination in Canada* (Montreal and Kingston: McGill-
Queen's University Press, 2010) at 67.

139 *Ibid.*

140 See, e.g., Kay, *supra* note 1; Margaret Wente, "Human Rights Commissions
– A Day at the Theatre of the Absurd," *Globe and Mail* (16 February
2008) A19, online: *Globe and Mail* <http://www.theglobeandmail.com/
news/national/a-day-at-the-theatre-of-the-absurd/article718263/>;
Margaret Wente, "The Explosive Rethinking of Sex Reassignment,"
Globe and Mail (24 August 2007), A19, online: The Globe and Mail
http://www.theglobeandmail.com/incoming/the-explosive-rethinking-of-
sex-reassignment/article1081150/;

141 See, e.g., Mark Steyn, "Human-rights Commissions Make Me Gag,"
[Montreal] Gazette (16 March 2008) A15; Ezra Levant, "Enough's Enough –
Exclusive Excerpt: How Mcdonald's Hand-Washing Policy Was Overruled,"
Maclean's (2 April 2009), online: Maclean's <http://www2.macleans.
ca/2009/04/02/enough%E2%80%99s-enough/> [Levant, "Enough"].

142 *Datt v. McDonald's Restaurants (No 3),* 2007 BCHRT 324.

143 See, e.g., Levant, "Enough," *supra* note 141.

144 Interview of Patricia Knipe (5 February 2010) [Knipe].

145 *Ibid.*

146 Levant, "Enough" *supra* note 141.

147 Mark J. Freiman, "Trial by Anecdote: A Controversial Polemicist Takes
on Canada's Commitment to Human Rights" Literary Review of Canada
(June 2009), online: LRC <http://reviewcanada.ca/magazine/2009/06/
trial-by-anecdote/>. See also Ron Ellis, *Unjust by Design: Canada's
Administrative Justice System* (Vancouver: UBC Press, 2013 at 82.

148 *Emergency Health Services Commission v. Cassidy,* 2011 BCSC 1003
(CanLII)

149 Knipe, *supra* note 144.

150 *Ibid.*

151 This was the same school board that had unsuccessfully challenged a student wearing a kirpan at school a few years earlier. See *Multani v.
Commission scolaire Marguerite-Bourgeoys,* [2006] 1 SCR 256.

152 *Charter of Human Rights and Freedoms*, RSQ, c C-12. Section 84 states: "Where, following the filing of a complaint, the commission exercises its discretionary power not to submit an application to a tribunal to pursue, for a person's benefit, a remedy ... it shall notify the complainant of its decision, stating the reasons on which it is based. Within 90 days after he receives such notification, the complainant may, at his own expense, submit an application to the Human Rights Tribunal to pursue such remedy and, in that case, he is, for the pursuit of the remedy, substituted by operation of law for the commission with the same effects as if the remedy had been pursued by the commission."

153 *Gallardo v. Bergeron*, 2010 QCTDP 5 at paras 120-126 (unofficial translation).

154 Niemi, *supra* note 12.

155 Conseil de presse du Québec, *Fo Niemi v. Louise Leduc et Éric Trottier*, D2008-10-026, online: Conseil de presse du Québec <http://conseilde presse.qc.ca/decisions/d2008-10-026/>.

156 Patrick Lagacé, "Fo Niemi a (encore) tout faux," *La Presse* (6 October 2008), online: La Presse <http://www.lapresse.ca/debats/chroniques/ patrick-lagace/200810/06/01-26693-fo-niemi-a-encore-tout-faux.php>.

157 Yves Boisvert, "Pourquoi un Tribunal des droits?," *La Presse* (6 May 2010), online: La Presse <http://www.lapresse.ca/debats/chroniques/yves-boisvert/201005/05/01-4277604-pourquoi-un-tribunal-des-droits.php>.

158 Barreau du Québec, *Position du Barreau du Québec concernant le Tribunal des droits de la personne*, (31 May 2010), online: Barreau du Québec <http://www.barreau.qc.ca/pdf/medias/positions/2010/20100531-droits-personne.pdf>.

159 *Commission scolaire Marguerite-Bourgeoys c Gallardo*, 2012 QCCA 908.

160 Interview of Pierre Bosset (16 September 2009).

161 See, *e.g.*, "Human Rights Commissions: Shake That Role of Policing Ideas," Editorial, *Globe and Mail* (4 February 2008).

162 Excerpts from a 1999 interview with Terry O'Neill of *BC Report* newsmagazine cited in *Maclean's*, "Harper Must Act Now to Protect Free Speech," (20 September 2009), online: Maclean's <http://www2.macleans. ca/2009/09/20/harper-must-act-now-to-protect-free-speech/>.

163 Interview of Charlach Mackintosh (20 May 2009).

164 Interview of Jennifer Lynch (6 April 2009).

165 *Human Rights Code*, RSO 1990, c H.19.

166 See *Findlay and McKay v. Four Star Variety*, (22 October 1993), Toronto (Ont BOI. See generally Ontario Human Rights Commission, *Annual Report 1995-1996* (Toronto: OHRC, 1996). See also Lyne Casavant and

James R Robertson, *The Evolution of Pornography Law in Canada,* (Ottawa: Library of Parliament, 2007) at 9, online: Parliament of Canada <http://www.parl.gc.ca>.

167 Interview of Roderick Macdonald (1 September 2009).

168 Tom Flanagan, "Time to Right Some Wrongs," *The Globe and Mail* (19 May 2009), online: Globe and Mail <http://www.theglobeandmail.com/commentary/time-to-right-some-wrongs/article4355596/>.

169 Elmer A Carter, "Fighting Prejudice with Law" (1946) 19:5 J of Educational Sociology 299.

170 Baker, *supra* note 13.

171 Peter W Hogg, *Constitutional Law of Canada,* 2010 Student Ed (Toronto: Carswell, 2010), chapter 34 at 34–37.

CHAPTER FOUR

1 Interview of Alan Borovoy (14 September 2009) [Borovoy].

2 *Vigna v. Levant,* 2010 ONSC 6308 at paras 3–4.

3 For media reports dealing with these criticisms, see the introduction at note 70 ff. See also Richard Moon, *Report to the Canadian Human Rights Commission Concerning Section 13 of the Canadian Human Rights Act and the Regulation of Hate Speech on the Internet* (Ottawa: CHRC, 2008), [Moon].

4 Borovoy, *supra* note 1.

5 *Canada (Canadian Human Rights Commission) v. Canada (Attorney General),* [2011] 3 SCR 471 at para 16.

6 See Albert Venn Dicey, *Lectures Introductory to the Study of Law of the Constitution,* 1st ed (London: Macmillan, 1885).

7 Interview of Gordon McKinnon (5 March 2010) [McKinnon].

8 Interview of David Baker (30 July 2009).

9 *Elmasry and Habib v. Roger's Publishing and MacQueen* (No 4), 2008 BCHRT 378 [*Elmasry*].

10 *Warman v. Lemire,* 2009 CHRT 26 [*Lemire*]; *Canada (Human Rights Commission) v. Warman,* 2012 FC 1162 [*Warman*]. Blight appeared in both the Tribunal and Federal Court of Canada proceedings.

11 *Citron and Toronto Mayor's Committee v. Zundel,* 2002 CanLII 23557 (CHRT).

12 Interview of Margot Blight (16 September 2009). Blight emphasized that she was speaking from her personal perspective and not for the commission.

13 *Ibid.*

14 *Warman, supra* note 10.

15 *Blencoe v. British Columbia (Human Rights Commission)*, 2000 SCC 44 [*Blencoe*].

16 *Lemire, supra* note 10.

17 *Ibid* at para 198.

18 *Ibid* at para 292.

19 *Vancouver (City) v. Ward*, 2010 SCC 27.

20 *Hill v. Church of Scientology of Toronto*, [1995] 2 SCR 1130 at para 196.

21 *Commission des droits de la personne et des droits de la jeunesse c Calego International Inc*, 2011 QCTDP 4 at para 478 (unofficial English translation), citing *Métromédia CMR Montréal Inc v. Johnson*, [2006] RJQ 395 (CA) at para 108. Article 49 of Quebec's Charter allows the human rights tribunal to award punitive damages for unlawful and intentional interference with a victim's Charter rights. See *Charter of Human Rights and Freedoms*, RSQ 1975, c C-12, Art 49 [Quebec Charter].

22 *Warman, supra* note 10.

23 *Canada (Human Rights Commission) v. Taylor*, [1990] 3 SCR 892 [*Taylor*].

24 RSC 1985, c H-6, s 54(1)(c) [*CHRA*]. See Bill C-304, *An Act to Amend the Canadian Human Rights Act (protecting freedom)*, SC 2013, c 37.

25 Canadian Human Rights Commission, *Special Report to Parliament: Freedom of Expression and Freedom from Hate in the Internet Age* (Ottawa: Minister of Public Works and Government, 2009) at 37 [CHRC, *Freedom of Expression*]. The Canadian Bar Association agreed with this recommendation.

26 McKinnon, *supra* note 7.

27 Interview of François Larsen (10 September 2010).

28 While more than three quarters of the human rights institutions in the Americas and Africa have the ability to provide remedies to victims, only 66 percent of the institutions in Asia and 38 percent of those in Europe have this ability. See Office of the High Commissioner for Human Rights, *Survey on National Human Rights Institutions: Report on the Findings and Recommendations of a Questionnaire Addressed to NHRIs Worldwide* (Geneva: Office of the High Commissioner for Human Rights, 2009) at 26, online: OHCHR <http://nhri.ohchr.org>.

29 Most human rights commissions seek some form of publicity for settlements that establish important principles or resolve longstanding disputes about high-profile issues.

30 *An Act to Amend the Human Rights Code*, 2nd Sess, 38th Leg, Ontario, 2006 (assented to 20 December 2006), SO 2006, c 30.

31 Ontario Human Rights Commission, *Mediation Services Participant Satisfaction Report for the Period May 8, 1998 to September 22, 1998* (Toronto: Queen's Printer for Ontario, 1999) [OHRC, *Mediation Services*]. Evaluation results for mediation services in British Columbia's human rights system can be found in Philip Bryden and William Black, "Mediation as a Tool for Resolving Human Rights Disputes: An Evaluation of the B.C. Human Rights Commission's Early Mediation Project" (2004) 37 UBC L Rev 73.

32 Interview of Keith Norton (21 April 2009) [Norton].

33 OHRC, *Mediation Services, supra* note 31.

34 Andrew Pinto, *Report of the Ontario Human Rights Review 2012* (Toronto: Queen's Printer for Ontario, 2012) at 28 [Pinto Report].

35 Owen M Fiss, "Against Settlement" (1984) 93:6 Yale LJ 1073.

36 Ezra Levant, *Shakedown: How Our Government Is Undermining Democracy in the Name of Human Rights* (Toronto: McClelland & Stewart, 2009).

37 Levant's remarks are from my written exchange with him in 2008. See "Ezra Levant Responds," *Maisonneuve* (Winter 2008) at 8–9.

38 Interview of Byron Williams (9 February 2010).

39 *Ibid.*

40 Manitoba Human Rights Commission, *Guide to Board-directed Mediation* online <http://www.manitobahumanrights.ca/guide_boarddirected_mediation.html>.

41 See Saskatchewan Human Rights Commission, *Mediation of Settlements – Pillar 2* (Saskatoon: SHRC, 2011), online: SHRC <http://www.shrc.gov.sk.ca/bill-160.html>.

42 Interview of Colleen Sheppard (30 April 2009).

43 Letter and offer to settle to Darren Lund per Ezra Levant, Action No. 0201-21407, dated 31 January 2003, copy on file.

44 Annual reports for the Human Rights Tribunal of Ontario, the British Columbia Human Rights Tribunal, and the Canadian Human Rights Commission do not provide consistent annual statistics on the breakdown of preliminary dismissals categorized by reason. However, in the years prior to Bill 107 reforms in Ontario, the Ontario Human Rights Commission's Annual Reports indicated that preliminary dismissals based on complaints that were found to be trivial, frivolous, and vexatious amounted to less than 2 percent of decisions.

45 *Doe v. A & W Canada*, 2013 HRTO 1259 (CanLII.).

46 RSY 2002, c 116, s 24(1)(e), 25(b) and 26(b); Quebec Charter, *supra* note 21.

47 See Vincent Pelletier, "Strategic Lawsuits Against Public Participation (SLAPPs) (and Other Abusive Lawsuits)" (Paper delivered at the Uniform Law Conference of Canada: Civil Section in Quebec City, August 2008) at para 4, online: ULCC <http://www.ulcc.ca/en/2008-quebec-city-qc/235-civil-section-documents/448-strategic-lawsuits-against-public-participation-slapps-report-2008>. A 2006 study noted that SLAPPs are increasingly common in Quebec. See Roderick A Macdonald, Pierre Noreau, and Daniel Jutras, *Les poursuites stratégiques contre la mobilisation publique – les poursuites-bâillons (SLAPP): Rapport du comité au ministre de la Justice* (Quebec: Ministère de la Justice, 2007) at 4, online: <http://www.justice.gouv.qc.ca/francais/publications/rapports/slapp.htm>.

48 The Quebec government introduced changes to its *Code of Civil Procedure* in 2009, *An Act to Amend the Code of Civil Procedure to Prevent Improper Use of the Courts and Promote Freedom of Expression and Citizen Participation in Public Debate*. Section 54.1 of the Code allows the court to dismiss "improper" proceedings at the preliminary stages if the lawsuit "restricts freedom of expression in public debate." The proceedings are aimed at unfounded, frivolous, or dilatory actions instituted in bad faith or to harm someone, as well as conduct that is vexatious or quarrelsome.

49 Interview of Philippe Dufresne (13 May 2009) [Dufresne]. Dufresne noted that such terms are commonly used in general-interest writing about human rights systems.

50 As noted in chapter 1, jurisdictions such as Ontario, Manitoba, and New Brunswick permit the possibility of criminal prosecution for discrimination complaints. These provisions are rarely, if ever, used and appear to be a throwback to earlier quasi-criminal legislation predating first-generation systems. As regards the types of enforcement-related sanctions that do result in criminal changes, these are not generally heard by commissions but by courts.

51 *Blencoe, supra* note 15 at para 94.

52 *Supra* note 50.

53 See Appendix 3.

54 *Ontario (Human Rights Commission) v. Simpsons-Sears,* [1985] 2 SCR 536 at para 14, [*Ontario v. Simpsons-Sears*]. In this decision, the court also distinguished between direct and indirect discrimination. This distinction was overturned in *British Columbia (Public Service Employee Relations Commission) v. BCGSEU* [1999] 3 SCR 3, but the focus on effects in discrimination law was reaffirmed. The Supreme Court reaffirmed that intent is not required to establish discrimination in *Andrews v. Law Society of British Columbia,* [1989] 1 SCR 143 at 175.

55 *Ontario v. Simpsons-Sears, supra* note 54 at para 14–16.

56 *CN v. Canada (Canadian Human Rights Commission)*, [1987] 1 SCR 1114.

57 *Taylor, supra* note 23 at 931.

58 RSBC 1996, c 210.

59 *Elmasry, supra* note 9 at para 147.

60 *Ibid* at para 145–146.

61 RSA 2000, c A-25.5 [emphasis added].

62 *Saskatchewan (Human Rights Commission) v. Whatcott*, 2013 SCC 11 [*Whatcott*] at para 127.

63 Dufresne interview, *supra* note 49.

64 *Taylor, supra* note 23; *Prescott-Russell Services for Children and Adults v. NG* (2006), 82 OR (3d) 686 (Ont CA) at para 27.

65 *Federal Courts Rules*, SOR/98-106, Rule 466.

66 *Taylor, supra* note 23. Section 13 makes it a discriminatory practice to communicate telephonically any matter likely to expose a person or group to hatred or contempt on the basis, inter alia, of race or religion. The provision was still in force at the time of writing.

67 *Ibid* at 934 (emphasis added).

68 *Warman v. Tremaine*, 2010 FC 1198.

69 *Ibid* at paras 1–4 (emphasis added).

70 *Ibid* at paras 9–11.

71 Section 11(f) of the Charter provides that a person finally acquitted of an offence is not to be tried for it again and, if finally found guilty and punished for the offence, is not to be tried or punished for it again.

72 A description of the *Maclean's* hate speech cases is provided in the introduction. All three cases were ultimately dismissed.

73 See, for example, the failed attempt to create a national securities commission in *Reference Re Securities Act*, [2011] 3 SCR 837. This effort, which is continuing through political means, is at least supported in the case of securities regulation by a strong federal trade and commerce power. There is no obvious equivalent for human rights laws. Under s 27(1)(c) of the CHRA, the Canadian commission is authorized to cooperate with other commissions to reduce the possibility of conflicts in handling complaints with overlapping jurisdictions, but the commission is still limited in is work to federal matters.

74 CHRC, *Freedom of Expression, supra* note 25 at 37.

75 *Taylor, supra* note 23 at 928. The original test referred to vilification, calumny, and detestation but the Supreme Court tightened the language to refer to "vilification and detestation" in *Whatcott, supra* note 62 at para 42.

76 *Ibid* at para 41.

77 Book review, Michael Plaxton, "Public Hostility: What Makes Hate Speech Wrong" (Review of Jeremy Waldron, *The Harm in Hate Speech)* 21 Literary Review of Canada (2013) 16 at 16.

78 Interview of John Ross Taylor by Tom Koch (17 January 1965) on *This Hour Has Seven Days*, CBC Television, Toronto, CBC Digital Archives at 47:05, online: CBC <http://www.cbc.ca/archives/discover/programs/t/this-hour-has-seven-days/this-hour-has-seven-days-january-17-1965.html>.

79 See *Payzant v. McAleer* (1994) 26 C.H.R.R. D/271, aff'd (1996), 26 C.H.R.R. D/280.

80 Moon, *Report to CHRC, supra* note 3 at 37.

81 *Criminal Code*, RSC 1985, c C-46, s 319(3)(a).

82 Mark Steyn, "The Future Belongs to Islam," *Maclean's* (20 October 2006), online: *Maclean's* <http://www.macleans.ca>; "Celebrate Tolerance, or You're Dead," *Maclean's* (28 April 2006), online: *Maclean's* <http://www.macleans.ca>.

83 The term "Eurabia" was popularized by Gisèle Littman, author of *Eurabia: The Euro-Arab Axis* (Madison, NJ: Fairleigh Dickinson University Press, 2005), writing under the pseudonym Bat Ye'or.

84 National Intelligence Council, *Mapping the Global Future: Report of the National Intelligence Council's 2020 Project Based on Consultations with Nongovernmental Experts Around the World* (Washington, DC: Government Printing Office, 2004).

85 *Ibid* at 83.

86 William Underhill, "Why Fears of a Muslim Takeover Are All Wrong," *Newsweek* (10 July 2009) 33. See also The Daily Beast <http://www.the-dailybeast.com/newsweek/2009/07/10/why-fears-of-a-muslim-takeover-are-all-wrong.html>.

87 Eric Kaufmann, *Shall the Religious Inherit the Earth? Demography and Politics in the Twenty-First Century* (London: Profile Books, 2010) at 118 ff. See also Doug Saunders, *The Myth of the Muslim Tide: Do Immigrants Threaten the West?* (Toronto: Alfred A. Knopf Canada, 2012).

88 *Elmasry, supra* note 9 at para 140. "*Maclean's* did not seriously challenge [the expert] evidence in cross-examination [.]" *Ibid* at para 129.

89 19 December 1966, 999 UNTS 171, arts 9-14, Can TS 1976 No 47, 6 ILM 368 (entered into force 23 March 1976, accession by Canada 19 May 1976) [ICCPR].

90 *Ibid*, Article 2(3).

91 Interview of Shelagh Day (9 March 2011), [Day].

92 Norton, *supra* note 32.

93 Interview of Kathy Laird, (2 October 2011).

94 *Ibid.*

95 McKinnon, *supra* note 7.

96 Pinto Report, *supra* note 34 at 10.

97 *Ibid* at 45.

98 *Ibid* at 144.

99 Interview of David Matas (22 April 2009).

100 Interview of Dianna Scarth (2 February 2010).

101 Ontario Human Rights Commission, *Annual Reports* from 1994-95 to 2000-2001. Recent reports are available online: OHRC <http://www.ohrc.on.ca/en/annual_reports>.

102 *Blencoe, supra* note 15.

103 See Ontario Human Rights Commission, Press Release, "Landmark Human Rights Case Settled" (27 August 2011), online: OHRC <http://www.ohrc.on.ca>; Ontario Human Rights Commission, Ministry of Community Safety and Correctional Services and Ministry of Government Services, *Human Rights Project Charter* (8 August 2011), online: OHRC <http://www.ohrc.on.ca/en/human-rights-project-charter-ohrc-mcscs-mgs>.

104 *Blencoe, supra* note 15.

105 *Ibid*, at para 116–131.

106 Interview of Heather MacNaughton (2 February 2010). Evidence before the Supreme Court of Canada in the *Blencoe* case quoted a report of the British Columbia Ministry where the average time to get to a hearing in British Columbia was three years; *Blencoe, supra* note 15 at para 129.

107 Pinto Report, *supra* note 34.

108 The principles of independence and impartiality as they apply to human rights tribunals and their relationship to commissions were applied in *Bell Canada v. Canadian Telephone Employees Association*, 2003 SCC 36, [2003] 1 SCR 884 at para 18 [*Bell* 2003].

109 *Valente v. The Queen*, [1985] 2 SCR 673 at para 27 (security of tenure), para 40 (financial security), and para 47 (administrative control), [*Valente*]. See the discussion in Ron Ellis, *Unjust by Design: Canada's Administrative Justice System* (Vancouver: UBC Press, 2013) [Ellis] at 69–71.

110 Article 14(1), ICCPR, *supra* note 89.

111 *Ocean Port Hotel Ltd. v. British Columbia (General Manager, Liquor Control and Licensing Branch)*, 2001 SCC 52, [2001], 2 SCR 781 [*Ocean Port*], but see, *Bell 2003, supra* note 108.

112 Readers can compare the types of appointments, the person responsible for making the appointment, and the criteria set out in the legislation of each human rights system in Appendix 3.

113 *Canadian Bill of Rights*, SC, 1960, c. 44; Quebec Charter, *supra* note 21.

114 Gerald Heckman and Lorne Sossin, "How Do Canadian Administrative Law Protections Measure Up to International Human Rights Standards? The Case of Independence" (2005) 50 McGill LJ 193 [Heckman and Sossin] at 196.

115 *Bell, supra* note 108.

116 *Ibid* at para 31.

117 *Ocean Port, supra* note 111.

118 Heckman and Sossin, *supra* note 114 at 196.

119 *Valente, supra* at note 109, at p 685 per Le Dain J.

120 Ellis, *supra* note 109.

121 Article 1, Principles Relating to the Status of National Institutions (The Paris Principles), GA Res 48/134, UNGAOR (1993), online: OHCHR <http://www.ohchr.org/EN/Countries/NHRI/Pages/NHRIMain.aspx>. The Principles are in Appendix 2 of this book.

122 Interview of Charlach Mackintosh (20 May 2009). [Mackintosh]

123 *Alberta Human Rights Act,* RSA 2000, c A-25.5 ss 17(3) and 18(2), [*Alberta HRA*]. Keeping a commission on such a tight administrative leash is more common in developing countries with a strong authoritarian head of government. In Sudan, for example, the government controls the commission's organizational structure and its by-laws dealing with staffing. See Republic of Sudan, *The National Human Rights Commission Act,* 2009 (8th Sess).

124 Norton, *supra* note 34, (15 September 2009).

125 In Nova Scotia, for example, the commission may appoint a board of inquiry. See *Human Rights Act*, RSNS 1989, c 214, s 32(a)(1). See Appendix 3.

126 Ed Ratushny, *Report of the Canadian Bar Association Task Force on the Independence of Federal Administrative Tribunals and Agencies in Canada* (Ottawa: Canadian Bar Association, 1990).

127 See, e.g., *Mckenzie. British Columbia (Minister of Public Safety and Solicitor General)* 2007 BCCA 507 and the discussion of the history of this case in Ellis, *supra* note 109 at 19–22.

128 Norton, *supra* note 34.

129 Ellis, *supra* note 109 at 117.

130 Norton, *supra* note 32.

131 Interview of Byron Williams (9 February 2010).

132 See Agency Reform Commission on Ontario's Regulatory and Adjudicative Agencies, *Everyday Justice,* (Gary Guzzo, Chair) (Toronto: Queen's Printer for Ontario, 1998).

133 Day, *supra* note 91.

134 *Ibid.* See also interview of Mary Woo Sims (18 September 2012).

135 The term "idiosyncratic removal" comes from the Hon. Roy McMurtry in 1997 at an annual conference where he stated that fear of "idiosyncratic removal" is integral to the independence of adjudicators. See Ellis, *supra* note 109 at 77.

136 Ellis, *supra* note 109 at 81–83.

137 *Ibid* at 15.

138 *Attorney General of Quebec v. Barreau de Montréal*, [2001] J.Q. 3882 (No 500-09-009146-002) (C.A.), leave to appeal to SCC refused 2002. A government representative was involved in the process of renewal of members of the Administrative Tribunal of Quebec (ATQ) which created an impression of dependence. As well, the presence of the ATQ president on the renewal committee was considered inappropriate because the role of the president in general administration.

139 *Alberta HRA, supra* note 123, ss 15; 25–27.

140 *Canada Safeway Limited v. Alberta Human Rights and Citizenship Commission*, 2000 ABQB 897. Commission officials continue to support this view: interview of Audrey Dean (28 April 2009); Mackintosh, *supra* note 122.

141 The difficulties experienced by Parliamentary Budget Officer Kevin Page in securing adequate information about the impacts of budgetary cuts are well documented. See, e.g., Leslie MacKinnon, "Budget Watchdog Gets Details on Savings, but Not on Cuts," *CBC* (1 November 2012), online: CBC <http://www.cbc.ca/news/politics/story/2012/11/01/pol-pbo-update-request-information.html>. Former information commissioner Robert Marleau stated that the Conservative government's "communications stranglehold" on the bureaucracy has led to even less information being released than before." Marleau resigned from his position after only two years. See "Information Watchdog Alarmed by Harper Government Clampdown," *Canadian Press* (22 January 2009) online: CBC <http://www.cbc.ca/news/canada/story/2009/01/22/access-harper.html>.

142 In December 2010, an unprecedented appeal from seven Parliamentary officers called for better scrutiny and oversight of appointments and of the actions of Parliamentary agents. Signatories included Lobbying Commissioner Karen Shepherd, Chief Electoral Officer Marc Mayrand, Information Commissioner Suzanne Legault, Privacy Commissioner Jennifer Stoddart, Official Languages Commissioner Graham Fraser, acting Public Sector Integrity Commissioner Mario Dion, and former auditor general of Canada, Sheila Fraser. See Kathryn May, "Agents of Parliament Working in the 'Wild West,' Expert Says" *Ottawa Citizen* (23 December

2011) A1. The head of the Canadian Human Rights Commission did
not sign.

143 Senior public servants are, of course, required to comply with political
direction. However, certain institutions are supposed to exercise independent judgment and decision-making. They should act as a check and balance to insulate important areas of decision-making or accountability measures from political interference. The Office of the Auditor General of Canada is one of many such institutions in Canada.

144 These and other case studies form part of the Voices-Voix documentation project. Online: <www.voices-voix.ca>. The project is now being managed through the national university research network Democracy, Dissent and the Law.

145 See generally, R Brian Howe and David Johnson, *Restraining Equality: Human Rights Commissions in Canada* (Toronto: University of Toronto Press: 2000).

146 Maxwell Yalden, *Transforming Rights: Reflections from the Front Lines* (Toronto: University of Toronto Press, 2009), at 22.

147 Norton, *supra* note 32. Similar observations have been made in the broader administrative law context by Ellis, *supra* note 109 at 10.

148 Interview of Rémy Beauregard (15 September 2009).

149 *Ibid.*

150 *Ibid.*

151 See, e.g., Ontario Government, Ministry of Citizenship, Culture and Recreation, *Business Plans*, online: Our Ontario <http://govdocs. ourontario.ca>.

152 See *Vriend v. Alberta*, [1998] 1 SCR 493.

153 Mackintosh, *supra* note 122.

154 Day, *supra* note 91.

155 Ken Norman, email communication with author, 7 October 2013. On file.

156 *Ibid*; Day, *supra* note 91.

157 Norton, *supra* note 32.

158 Ontario Human Rights Commission, *Discussion Paper: Accessible Transit Services in Ontario* (Toronto, OHRC, January 2001) online <http://www. ohrc.on.ca/en/discussion-paper-accessible-transit-services-ontario>.

CHAPTER FIVE

1 Remarks of Madam Justice L'Heureux-Dubé upon receiving an honourary LL.D. from the Law Society of Upper Canada in 2002. Cited in

Public Service Alliance of Canada v. Canada Post Corporation, 2005 CHRT 39 at para 51.

2 The Supreme Court of Canada held that human rights laws and section 15 of the Charter are aimed at the same general wrong in *British Columbia (Public Service Employee Relations Commission) v. BCGSEU,* [1999] 3 SCR 3, at para 48.

3 *CSWU Local 1611 v. SELI Canada and others (No 8),* 2008 BCHRT 436 at para 390, citing *Ontario (Human Rights Commission) v. Etobicoke (Borough),* [1982] 1 SCR 202.

4 See *Insurance Corporation of British Columbia v. Heerspink,* [1982] 2 SCR 145 at 157–158, Lamer J, concurring: "When the subject matter of a law is said to be the comprehensive statement of the 'human rights' of the people living in that jurisdiction, then there is no doubt in my mind that the people of that jurisdiction have through their legislature clearly indicated that they consider that law, and the values that it endeavors to buttress and protect, are, save their constitutional laws, more important than all others ... [I]t is intended that the [BC Human Rights] Code supersede all other laws when conflict arises."

5 Ontario Human Rights Commission, *Policy on Competing Human Rights* (Toronto: OHRC, 2012) at 4-5 [OHRC, *Policy on Competing Rights*].

6 Interview of Heather MacNaughton (2 February 2010).

7 *Ibid.*

8 Interview of Richard Moon (26 January 2010 [Moon].

9 *Saskatchewan (Human Rights Commission) v. Whatcott,* 2013 SCC 11 [*Whatcott* (2013)].

10 I hope Alan Borovoy will forgive me for this riff on the title of his book *When Freedoms Collide: The Case for Our Civil Liberties* (Toronto: Lester & Orpen Dennys, 1988).

11 "Happy-Faced Tyranny: Will Abortionists Be the Next 'Protected Minority?'" *British Columbia (BC) Report* (11 January, 1999).

12 *McIntosh v. Metro Aluminum Products and another,* 2011 BCHRT 34. McIntosh alleged discrimination in employment based on sex (i.e., sexual harassment), contrary to section 13 of the Human Rights Code, RSBC 1996, c 210.

13 *Ibid* at paras 74–75.

14 *Pardy v. Earle and others (No 4),* 2011 BCHRT 101 [*Pardy*].

15 *Ibid* at 307.

16 *Ibid* at para 459.

17 *Ibid* at para 451–452.

18 See, e.g., Tabatha Southey, "Canadian Ruling on 'Offensive' Comedy Is a Gag – But It's No Joke," *The Globe and Mail* (2 April 2010), online: The

Globe and Mail <http://www.theglobeandmail.com/news/politics/canadian-ruling-on-offensive-comedy-is-a-gag---but-its-no-joke/article1521532/>.

19 Interview of Jane Bailey (6 May 2009) [Bailey].

20 United Nations, *Vienna Declaration and Programme of Action*, GA Jun 1993, World Conference on Human Rights, A/CONF 157/23 (1003), online: UNHCHR <http://www.unhchr.ch/huridocda/huridoca.nsf/(symbol)/a.conf.157.23.en> (previously cited).

21 See, e.g., *Gosselin (Tutor of) v. Quebec (Attorney General)*, [2005] 1 SCR 238, at para 2.

22 Op Ed, Pearl Eliadis, "Quebec Status of Women's Position Is an Attack on Minority Rights" (4 October 2007) *[Montreal] Gazette*, online: Canada.com <http://www.canada.com>.

23 *Heintz v. Christian Horizons*, 2008 HRTO 22 [*Heintz*].

24 *Ibid* at paras 206–209.

25 *Ibid*.

26 *Ontario Human Rights Commission v. Christian Horizons*, 2010 ONSC 2105 [*Christian Horizons (2010)*].

27 See, e.g., Don Hutchinson, "You Can't Take the Mission Out of Christian Horizons," *National Post* (29 April 2008).

28 Although the tribunal had taken a narrower view of the defence available under section 24(1)(a) of the Code, the Divisional Court reaffirmed the full protection of this provision.

29 *Christian Horizons (2010)*, *supra* note 26 at para 71.

30 *Ibid* at para 104.

31 *Heintz*, *supra* note 23 at para 234 (emphasis added).

32 *Tesseris v. Greek Orthodox Church of Canada*, 2011 HRTO 775 at para 2.

33 Joint Statement, "The Ontario Human Rights Commission and Christian Horizons today released the following statement" (15 August 2013), online: OHRC <http://www.ohrc.on.ca/en/news_centre/ontario-human-rights-commission-and-christian-horizons-today-released-following-statement>.

34 *Warman v. Kouba*, 2006 CHRT 50 at paras 22–81 [*Kouba*].

35 *Ibid* at para 22.

36 The Supreme Court of Canada referenced the hallmarks with approval in its 2013 *Whatcott* decision. See *Whatcott* (2013), *supra* note 9 at para 44.

37 *Kouba*, *supra* note 34.

38 Email communication with the author (21 February 2008). On file.

39 Moon, *supra* note 8.

40 Interview of Mark Freiman (1 May 2009).

41 *Ibid*.

42 *Kouba*, *supra* note 34.

43 Interview of John Ross Taylor by Tom Koch (17 January 1965) on *This Hour Has Seven Days*, CBC Television, Toronto, CBC Digital Archives at timecode 47:05, online: CBC <http://www.cbc.ca/archives/discover/programs/t/this-hour-has-seven-days/this-hour-has-seven-days-january-17-1965.html>. I thank Dominique Clément for bringing this episode to my attention.

44 Canada, Special Committee on Hate Propaganda in Canada, *Report of the Special Committee on Hate Propaganda* (Ottawa: Queen's Printer, 1966).

45 *Canada (Human Rights Commission) v. Taylor*, [1990] 3 SCR 892 [*Taylor*].

46 *Ibid* at 919.

47 Interview of Irwin Cotler (25 June 2009) [Cotler].

48 *Ibid*. See also Irwin Cotler, "Hate Speech, Equality, and Harm under the Charter: Towards a Jurisprudence of Respect for a 'Free and Democratic Society'" (2005) 27 Sup Ct L Rev (2d) 105.

49 Cotler, *supra* note 47.

50 See, e.g., Radio Regulations, 1986, SOR/86-982, s 3(b); *Television Broadcasting Regulations, 1987*, SOR/87-49, s 5(1)(b); *Pay Television Regulations*, 1990 SOR/90-105. s. 3(b).

51 Canadian Broadcast Standards Council, Equitable Portrayal Code (17 March 2008), CBSC, online: <http://www.cbsc.ca>.

52 See *CITS-TV re Word.ca and Word TV* (22 June 2010) CBSC 08/09-2142 & 09/10-0383+, online: CBSC <http://www.cbsc.ca>.

53 The schedule to the Canadian Customs Tariff prohibits "Books, printed paper, drawings, paintings, prints, photographs or representations of any kind that ... (b) constitute hate propaganda within the meaning of subsection 320(8) of the *Criminal Code*." See Customs Tariff, SC 1997, c 36, Schedule, Item 9899.00.00.

54 *Canada Post Corporation Act*, RSC, 1985, c C-10.

55 Cotler, *supra* note 47.

56 *Ibid*.

57 Bailey, *supra* note 19.

58 Cotler, *supra* note 47.

59 *Ibid*.

60 Article 2(1), *International Covenant on Civil and Political Rights*, 19 December 1966, 999 UNTS 171, Can TS 1976 No 47, 6 ILM 368 (entered into force 23 March 1976, accession by Canada 19 May 1976) [ICCPR] (emphasis added).

61 Cotler, *supra* note 47.

62 *Taylor, supra* note 45.

63 One of the four students later dropped out of the efforts to counter the *Maclean's* articles.

64 Barbara Amiel, "Wake Up, Ostriches: Islam's in an Expansionary Phase. In Case You Hadn't Noticed," *Maclean's* (16 February 2006), online: *Maclean's* <http://www.macleans.ca/article.jsp?content=20060220_121867_121867&source=srch>.

65 Mark Steyn, "The Future Belongs to Islam," *Maclean's* (20 October 2006), online: *Maclean's* <http://www.macleans.ca>. See also, *America Alone: The End of The World as We Know It* (Washington, DC: Regnery Publishing 2006).

66 Mark Steyn, "Celebrate Tolerance, or You're Dead," *Maclean's* (28 April 2006), online: *Maclean's* <http://www.macleans.ca>.

67 Interviews of Khurrum Awan and Muneeza Sheikh (25 June 2009) [Awan and Sheikh]; Interview of Naseem Mithoowani (7 May 2009) [Mithoowani].

68 *Ibid.*

69 *Ibid.*

70 See, e.g., Rory Leishman, "Levant a Hero in the Fight against Unfair HRCs," *The London Free Press* 4 April 2009 at E5.

71 Submitted by complainants as evidence before the BC Human Rights Tribunal in *Elmasry*. Copy of pleadings on file. See also *Elmasry and Habib v. Roger's Publishing and MacQueen (No. 4)*, 2008 BCHRT 378 [*Elmasry*].

72 Interview of Jameel Jaffer (15 May 2009).

73 Mithoowani, *supra* note 67.

74 I interviewed Porter on 25 July 2008 for an article in *Maisonneuve* magazine. See Pearl Eliadis, "The Controversy Entrepreneurs," 29 *Maisonneuve* (Fall 2008) at 38. Parts of this section draw from the article.

75 Mithoowani, *supra* note 67.

76 Awan and Sheikh, *supra* note 67. "Sock puppets" are fake commentators who spread disinformation. See, e.g., Colby Cosh, "In BC, Sock Puppets Behaving Badly," Opinion, *National Post* (6 June 2008), online: National Post <http://www.nationalpost.com/opinion/columnists/story.html?id=78d0cbb4-f2f9-4b62-a1c1-84d0c94b59a0>. During an interview with *National Post* writer Joseph Brean in 2008, I referred to the students as "the *Maclean's* three." Brean told me that the media calls them sock puppets and that no one calls them "the *Maclean's* three."

He demanded to know where the term "the *Maclean's* three" came from. I told him I had heard Steve Paikin use it on his show on TVO.

77 Mithoowani, *supra* note 67.

78 *Ibid.*

79 Awan and Sheikh, *supra* note 67.

80 Mithoowani, *supra* note 67.

81 Jane Bailey, "Democracy Suffers When Equality Is Threatened," *Ottawa Citizen* (11 December 2008).

82 7(1). A person must not publish, issue or display, or cause to be published, issued or displayed, any statement, publication, notice, sign, symbol, emblem or other representation that

    ...

    (b) is likely to expose a person or a group or class of persons to hatred or contempt because of the race, colour, ancestry, place of origin, religion, marital status, family status, physical or mental disability, sex, sexual orientation or age of that person or that group or class of persons. Human Rights Code, RSBC 1996, c. 210.

83 *Taylor, supra* note 45.

84 *Elmasry, supra* note 71 at para 129.

85 *Ibid* at 157-158.

86 Mithoowani, *supra* note 67.

87 Interview of Paul Champ (29 June 2010).

88 *Lund v. Boissoin,* 2012 ABCA 300 at para 4. [*Lund*].

89 *Ibid.*

90 Interview of Darren Lund (18 August 2011) [Lund].

91 Alberta Human Rights, Citizenship and Multiculturalism Act, RSA 2000, c H-14, s 3(1)(b).

92 *Lund v. Boissoin* 2007, AHRC 11 at para 6.

93 Lund, *supra* note 90.

94 *Ibid.*

95 *Ibid.*

96 *Boissoin* 2007, *supra* note 92.

97 *Boissoin v. Lund,* 2009 ABQB 592.

98 *Lund supra* note 88.

99 Lund, *supra* note 90.

100 *Whatcott* (2013), *supra* note 9.

101 Whatcott's flyers are included in Appendix B of the Supreme Court of Canada's judgment. See *Whatcott* (2013), *supra* note 9.

102 This section states: "(1) No person shall publish or display ... any ... statement or other representation: ... (b) that exposes or tends to expose to hatred, ridicules, belittles or otherwise affronts the dignity of any person or class of persons on the basis of a prohibited ground. (2) Nothing in subsection (1) restricts the right to freedom of expression under the law upon any subject. See Saskatchewan Human Rights Code, SS 1979, c S-24.1.

103 *Wallace v. Whatcott* (2005), 52 CHRR D/264 (SHRT); *Whatcott v. Saskatchewan (Human Rights Tribunal)*, 2007 SKQB 450.

104 *Whatcott v. Saskatchewan (Human Rights Tribunal)*, 2010 SKCA 26 [*Whatcott* 2010].

105 Justice Hunter stated: "Dickson C.J. expressly limited his comments in *Taylor* to the context of hate propaganda directed at individuals on the basis of race and religion ... [I]t is open to this Court, in my view, to consider, on a reading of the judgment in *Taylor* as a whole, whether the restricted meaning given to the phrase 'promotes hatred or contempt', in terms of the emotive level of the expression, exhausts the considerations to be taken into account when determining whether and to what extent similar prohibitions may constitutionally be extended to speech on bases other than hate propaganda directed at individuals on the basis of race and religion. In short, it is my view that other considerations may come in to play in appropriate cases requiring limits to be placed on the interpretative scope of a statutory provision to insure that the section not be applied in a way that would remove it from the s. 1 justification advanced in *Taylor*." *Whatcott* 2010 at para 124.

106 *Ibid* at para 138.

107 Interview of Dominique Clément (7 December 2011).

108 I worked with the legal team supporting the preparation of the argument for the intervener, the African Canadian Legal Clinic.

109 *Whatcott* (2013), *supra* note 9.

110 *Ibid* at paras 121–125 and 176–177.

111 *Whatcott* (2013), *supra* note 9 at para 51.

112 See Pearl Eliadis, "Supreme Court Decision in *Whatcott* Case Is Fair and Balanced," Opinion, *[Montreal] Gazette* (27 February 2013) A17, online: The Gazette <http://www.montrealgazette.com>.

113 Andrew Coyne, "Hate Speech Ruling Intrudes," *[Montreal] Gazette* (27 February 2013), online: The Gazette <http://www.montrealgazette.com>.

114 Lothrop Stoddard, *Lonely America* (New York: Doubleday, Doran and Company, 1932) at v [Lonely America]. Stoddard devoted a separate volume to his views on Muslims. See Lothrop Stoddard, *The New World of Islam* (London: Chapman and Hall, 1922).

115 *Lonely America, supra* note 114 at 120.

116 Interview of Bernie Farber (22 April 2009) [Farber]. According to Farber, the allegation related to "bankrolling" the Nazi movement is a reference to an article published in 1966 by John Garrity, who went undercover with the Canadian Nazi Party on behalf of the Canadian Jewish Congress. The results of his assignment were published in *Maclean's* magazine; John Garrity "My 16 Months as a Nazi" *Maclean's* (1 October 1966).

117 Farber, *supra* note 116.

118 Bailey, *supra* note 19.

119 *Whatcott* (2013), *supra* note 9 at para 114.

120 Interview of Pascale Fournier (6 April 2009) [Fournier].

121 *Ibid.*

122 Interview of Alia Hogben (16 September 2009) [Hogben].

123 Fournier, *supra* note 120.

124 See e.g. Ayaan Hirsi Ali, *The Caged Virgin: An Emancipation Proclamation for Women and Islam* (New York: Free Press, 2006) and Irshad Manji, *The Trouble with Islam Today: A Muslim's Call for Reform in Her Faith* (New York: St. Martin's, 2004).

125 Leila Ahmed, *A Quiet Revolution: The Veil's Resurgence, from the Middle East to America* (New Haven, CT: Yale University Press, 2011) at 14 [Ahmed].

126 *Ibid.*; Fournier, *supra* note 120.

127 *Ibid.*

128 Ahmed, *supra* note 125 at 267–268.

129 Hogben, *supra* note 122.

130 Ahmed, *supra* note 125 at 200, citing Nadine Naber, "Look, Mohammed of the Terrorist Is Coming!" In *Race and Arab Americans Before and After 9/11: From Invisible Citizens to Invisible Subjects*, ed. Amany Jamal and Nadine Naber (Syracuse: Syracuse University Press, 2008), 289–290.

131 Katia Gagnon, "Elles sont manipulées," *La Presse* (16 October 2013) A2.

132 Quebec Muslims for Rights and Freedoms, online: <www.qmdl.org>.

133 *R v. NS*, 2012 SCC 72 [*NS* (2012)], [*R v. NS*].

134 *Ibid* at para 3.

135 *Ibid* at paras 92–96.

136 See e.g. OHRC, *Policy on Competing Rights, supra* note 5.

137 Honourable Justice Frank Iacobucci, "'Reconciling Rights': The Supreme Court of Canada's Approach to Competing Charter Rights" (2003) 20 Sup Ct L Rev (2d) 137, at 140.

CHAPTER SIX

1 Interview of Shelagh Day (9 March 2011)

2 Email communication with ULCC Project Coordinator (25 March 2013). On file.

3 See A. Alan Borovoy, *When Freedoms Collide: The Case for Our Civil Liberties* (Toronto: Lester & Orpen Dennys, 1988) at 310.

4 *Ibid* at 310–311.

5 Pearl Eliadis, "Inscribing Charter Values in Policy Processes" (2006) 33 Sup Ct L Rev 229.

6 Ontario Human Rights Commission, *Count Me In! Collecting Human Rights Data* (Toronto: OHRC, 2010), online: OHRC <http://www.ohrc.on.ca>.

7 Cara Wilkie et al., "Human Rights Issues in National Security: An Inventory of Agency Considerations" (Ottawa: Canadian Human Rights Commission, 2008), online: <http://www.chrc-cdp.ca>.

8 Canadian Human Rights Commission, *Report on Equality Rights of Aboriginal People* (Ottawa: Canadian Human Rights Commission, 2013). Online: CHRC <http://www.chrc-ccdp.gc.ca/eng/content/publications>.

9 Although this was confirmed by a Heritage Canada staff member, calls to the director responsible for the committee at Heritage Canada enquiring about the role and participation of human rights institutions as members of the CCOHR went unanswered.

10 Interview of Lucie Lamarche (24 April 2009).

11 Andrew Pinto, *Report of the Ontario Human Rights Review 2012* (Toronto: Queen's Printer for Ontario, 2012) at 28 [Pinto Report] at 72–73, online: Attorney General <http://www.attorneygeneral.jus.gov.on.ca/english/about/pubs/human_rights/Pinto_human_rights_report_2012-ENG.pdf> at 173.

12 *Ibid* at 195.

13 Interview of Rémy Beauregard (15 September 2009).

14 CASHRA intervened in *Vriend v. Alberta*, [1998] 1 SCR 493.

15 Senate of Canada, *Promises to Keep: Implementing Canada's Human Rights Obligations*, Report of the Standing Senate Committee on Human

16 *Ibid*.

Rights. Chair, The Honourable Raynell Andreychuk (December 2001), online: <http://www.parl.gc.ca>, Recommendation 7.

17 *Blencoe v. British Columbia (Human Rights Commission)*, 2000 SCC 44 [*Blencoe*].

18 Canadian Human Rights Act Review Panel, *Promoting Equality: A New Vision* (Ottawa: Canadian Human Rights Act Review Panel, 2000), (Chair: Gérard La Forest), online: Government of Canada http://publications. gc.ca/collections/Collection/J2-168-2000E.pdf (emphasis added).

19 Yukon Human Rights Commission, "What's New" YHRC online <http:// www.yhrc.yk.ca/11-whatsnew.htm>. The changes were the result of amendments to the *Human Rights Act:* Bill 71, *Act to Amend the Human Rights Act*, 32nd Legislative Assembly, 1st Sess. (2009).

20 *Ménard c. Rivet et al*, [1997] RJQ 2108 (CA); *Commission scolaire Marguerite-Bourgeoys c Gallardo*, 2012 QCCA 908. See the discussion in chapter 3.

21 *Ibid.*

22 *Canada (Canadian Human Rights Commission) v. Canada (Attorney General)*, [2011] 3 SCR 471. The Court did not deal directly with the issue of the CHRC's withdrawal of its services, since the issue in dispute was about costs. However, the role of costs had come to the fore specifically because of the CHRC's strategy of picking and choosing its cases and leaving complainants to proceed alone before the tribunal.

23 *An Act respecting legal aid and the provision of certain other legal services*, RSQ, c. A-14, section 4.11.

24 See chapter 1.

25 The Honourable Chief Justice Warren K. Winkler, *Evaluation of Civil Case Management in the Toronto Region: A Report on the Implementation of the Toronto Practice Direction and Rule 78 (2008) online:* <http://www. ontariocourts.on.ca/coa/en/ps/reports/rule78.pdf>.

26 Ken Norman, "The Wrong Moves for Saskatchewan Human Rights." Viewpoint, (2012) 13–4 Human Rights Digest (CHRR), online: <http:// www.cdn-hr-reporter.ca/new/viewpoints>.

27 *Moore v. British Columbia (Education)*, 2012 SCC 61.

28 *Blencoe, supra* note 17.

29 Gwen Brodsky and Shelagh Day, *Strengthening the Nunavut Human Rights System: A Report for the Government of Nunavut* (Iqaluit: Government of Nunavut, 2012), online: Legislative Assembly of Nunavut <http://assembly.nu.ca/library/GNedocs/2012/000707-e.pdf>.

30 Paris Principles, Section A, par. 3(a) (iii); Section C, par. 1. Appendix 2.

31 For example, s. 29 of the Ontario Human Rights Code permits the commission to issue reports on the state of human rights in the province, as well as to inquire into situations of tension and conflict. This authority is not limited to equality rights. Section 27(1)(e) of the *Canadian Human Rights Act* provides for broad authority to examine "such recommendations, suggestions and requests concerning *human rights and freedoms* as it receives from any source and, where deemed by the Commission to be appropriate[.]" Emphasis added.

32 Canadian Human Rights Commissions, notably the federal commission, the Ontario Human Rights Commission, and the Quebec Human Rights and Youth Rights Commission, have all been active in the international area, working with various UN bodies and regional human rights systems.

33 *Institution-Building of the United Nations Human Rights Council*, A/HRC/RES/5/1, UNHRC, 5th Sess. adopted by the UN Human Rights Council (18 June 2007) [*Institution-Building*].

34 NHRIs have the right to participate in the Universal Periodic Review process, as well as the UN Committee on the Rights of the Child, the Committee on Economic, Social and Cultural Rights, and the Committee on the Elimination of Racial Discrimination. See *Institution-Building, supra* note 33.

35 Sub Committee on Accreditation (SCA), "SCA General Observations" in *Compilation of the Rules and Working Methods of the SCA* (March 2009), [ICC-SCA], NHRI online,<http://nhri.ohchr.org/EN/AboutUs/ICC Accreditation/Pages/nextsession.aspx>.

36 Ontario Human Rights Commission, Press Release, "Canadian Human Rights Agencies Call for Action" (8 March, 2013), online: OHRC <http://www.ohrc.on.ca/en/news_centre/canadian-human-rights-agencies-call-action>.

37 See, e.g., UN Convention on the Rights of Persons with Disabilities GA Res 61/611, UNGAOR, 61st Sess, Supp No 49, UN Doc A/RES/61/106, (2007).

38 Nova Scotia has an unusual provision that permits the awarding of costs, except against the complainant (s. 34, *Nova Scotia Human Rights Act*).

39 Pinto Report, *supra* note 11 at fn 49. The obvious exception would be Quebec, where the commission essentially represents the claimant.

40 Pinto Report, *supra* note 11.

41 Article 14(1) of the International Covenant on Civil and Political Rights, 19 December 1966, 999 UNTS 171, Can TS 1976 No 47, 6 ILM 368 (entered into force 23 March 1976, accession by Canada 19 May 1976).

42 Gerald Heckman and Lorne Sossin, "How Do Canadian Administrative Law Protections Measure Up to International Human Rights Standards? The Case of Independence" (2005) 50 McGill LJ 193 [Heckman and Sossin] at 195.

43 UN Human Rights Committee, General Comment No. 32, *Article 14: Right to Equality Before Courts and Tribunals and to a Fair Trial,* CCPR/C/GC/32 (23 August 2007), UN OHCHR http://www2.ohchr.org/english/bodies/hrc/comments.htm at para 15.

44 Heckman and Sossin, *supra* note 42 at 202–203.

45 *Ibid* at 234.

46 See, generally, *Ocean Port Hotel Ltd v. British Columbia (General Manager, Liquor Control and Licensing Branch)*, 2001 SCC 52.

47 Heckman and Sossin, *supra* note 42 at 197–198. References omitted.

48 *Alberta Human Rights Act*, ss. 17, 18.

49 Interview of Remy Beauregard (15 September, 2009).

50 See Sheldon Chumir Foundation for Ethics in Leadership, *Toward Equal Opportunity for all Albertans: Recommendations for Improvement of the Alberta Human Rights Commission* (Calgary: Sheldon Chumir Foundation, 2008) at 19 (Recommendation 3), online: Sheldon Chumir Foundation <http://www.chumirethicsfoundation.ca/files/pdf/Toward-Equal-Opportunity_SCF.pdf> . The Quebec Commission also reports directly to the national assembly.

51 Heckman and Sossin, *supra* note 42.

52 ICC-SCA, *supra* note 35. For more detailed discussion of compliance with the Paris Principles and good practices in establishing Human Rights Commissions, see Office of the High Commissioner for Human Rights, *National Human Rights Institutions: History, Principles, Roles and Responsibilities* (Professional Training Series No. 4) (New York and Geneva: United Nations, 2010).

53 Paris Principles, *supra* note 30.

54 Interview of Mark Freiman (1 May 2009) [Freiman].

55 Interview of Ken Norton (21 April 2009).

56 A 2009 UN OHCHR survey showed that 78 percent of respondents indicated that their members were appointed for terms between three and five years, which is a reasonable period to ensure tenure of membership. See Office of the High Commissioner for Human Rights, *Survey of NHRIs: Report on the Findings* and *Recommendations of a Questionnaire Addressed to NHRIs Worldwide* (OHCHR: New York and Geneva, July 2009), online: <http://www.nhri.net/2009/Questionnaire%20-%20Complete%20Report%20FINAL-edited.pdf>.

57 ICC-SCA, *supra* note 35.

58 Freiman, *supra* note 54.

59 *Declaration on the Right and Responsibility of Individuals, Groups and Organs of Society to Promote and Protect Universally Recognized Human Rights and Fundamental Freedoms*, GA Res 53/144, UNGAOR, 53rd Sess., A/RES/53/144 (adopted 9 December 1998), online: OHCHR <http://www.ohchr.org>. See also, UN Office of the High Commissioner for Human Rights, "Who Is a Human Rights Defender?" Online <http://www.ohchr.org>.

APPENDIX ONE

1 Mr. Mackintosh retired in 2008. The commission's name was subsequently changed to the Alberta Human Rights Commission.

APPENDIX THREE

1 References to criteria for qualifications, appointments and dismissals in the second column are to the human rights statute in question, unless otherwise specified. For reasons of space, the table does not examine criteria from other laws that are of general application and may add additional generic requirements on administrative agencies.

2 Disability includes both physical and mental disabilities.

3 Statute does not mention pregnancy or harassment.

4 Commission has no gatekeeping function but it can initiate complaints and public inquiries.

5 Statute does not mention pregnancy.

6 There is no official English name for the commission. This reflects Quebec's legislative drafting policies regarding the names of institutions.

Index

Abella, Irving, 7

Abella, Rosalie, 67, 120, 237

Aboriginal peoples, 5, 135–138, 151; *Canadian Human Rights Act* and, 111, 135–138; child and family services, 5, 34, 135, 137, 271; child poverty, 5; cuts to organizations, 243; discrimination and, 78, 111, 135–136, 186, 271; employment equity and, 82; hate speech and, 176, 231; human rights laws and, 288–312; human rights systems and, 135–138, 198, 200, 244, 273, 389n8; increases in complaints from, 136; jurisdiction over, 34, 41, 89; language rights of, 47; Métis peoples, 134–136; national action plan, 258; prison population, 9; specificity of, 39, 135, 138. *See also* Assembly of First Nations; *Canadian Human Rights Act*; Canadian Human Rights Commission, Declaration on the Rights of Indigenous Peoples; First Nations Child and Family Caring Society of Canada; *McKinnon v. Ontario Ministry of Correctional Services. See also* individual human rights systems by jurisdiction

Aboriginal women, violence against, 5, 135, 258

abuse of process, 11, 151, 170–172, 177–178, 186. *See also* human rights complaints

access to justice, 22, 49–52, 249–253; access to lawyers and, 99; access to neutral decision-maker and, 50–51, 100; alternative dispute resolution and, 49; BC system and, 94–95; 99–102; Bill 107 (Ontario) and, 52, 94, 99; costs and, 260; cost of lawyers and, 49; delays and, 51, 90, 100, 107, 249–250; direct access and, 100–101; disparities in, 26, 29, 49, 245; equal protection of the law and, 49–52; first-generation systems and, 50–51, 68, 90, 107, 250; formality of legal proceedings and, 49; 49–52; neutral decision-maker and, 50–51; Ontario, 94–100; Ontario and BC compared, 95, 100, 187, 153; Ontario and Quebec compared, 52; quasi-criminal systems and, 68; reform and, 98, 249–253, 261, 314; remedies and, 52; Saskatchewan and, 253–254; second-generation systems and, 50–52, 102; United